MUSLIM LIVES IN EASTERN EUROPE

PRINCETON STUDIES IN MUSLIM POLITICS

Dale F. Eickelman and Augustus Richard Norton, Editors

Diane Singerman, *Avenues of Participation: Family, Politics, and Networks in Urban Quarters of Cairo*

Tone Bringa, *Being Muslim the Bosnian Way: Identity and Community in a Central Bosnian Village*

Dale F. Eickelman and James Piscatori, *Muslim Politics*

Bruce B. Lawrence, *Shattering the Myth: Islam beyond Violence*

Ziba Mir-Hosseini, *Islam and Gender: The Religious Debate in Contemporary Iran*

Robert W. Hefner, *Civil Islam: Muslims and Democratization in Indonesia*

Muhammad Qasim Zaman, *The 'Ulama in Contemporary Islam: Custodians of Change*

Michael G. Peletz, *Islamic Modern: Religious Courts and Cultural Politics in Malaysia*

Oskar Verkaaik, *Migrants and Militants: Fun and Urban Violence in Pakistan*

Laetitia Bucaille, *Growing up Palestinian: Israeli Occupation and the Intifada Generation*

Robert W. Hefner, editor, *Remaking Muslim Politics: Pluralism, Contestation, Democratization*

Lara Deeb, *An Enchanted Modern: Gender and Public Piety in Shi`i Lebanon*

Roxanne L. Euben, *Journeys to the Other Shore: Muslim and Western Travelers in Search of Knowledge*

Robert W. Hefner and Muhammad Qasim Zaman, eds., *Schooling Islam: The Culture and Politics of Modern Muslim Education*

Loren D. Lybarger, *Identity and Religion in Palestine: The Struggle between Islamism and Secularism in the Occupied Territories*

Bruce K. Rutherford, *Egypt after Mubarak: Liberalism, Islam, and Democracy in the Arab World*

Emile Nakhleh, *A Necessary Engagement: Reinventing America's Relations with the Muslim World*

Roxanne L. Euben and Muhammad Qasim Zaman, *Princeton Readings in Islamist Thought: Texts and Contexts from al-Banna to Bin Laden*

Irfan Ahmad, *Islamism and Democracy in India: The Transformation of Jamaat-e-Islami*

Kristen Ghodsee, *Muslim Lives in Eastern Europe: Gender, Ethnicity, and the Transformation of Islam in Postsocialist Bulgaria*

MUSLIM LIVES IN EASTERN EUROPE

GENDER, ETHNICITY, AND THE TRANSFORMATION OF ISLAM IN POSTSOCIALIST BULGARIA

Kristen Ghodsee

PRINCETON UNIVERSITY PRESS PRINCETON AND OXFORD

For Kristiana and Chris

Published by Princeton University Press, 41 William Street,
Princeton, New Jersey 08540

In the United Kingdom: Princeton University Press, 6 Oxford Street,
Woodstock, Oxfordshire OX20 1TW

Library of Congress Cataloging-in-Publication Data

Ghodsee, Kristen Rogheh, 1970–
  Muslim lives in Eastern Europe : gender, ethnicity, and the transformation of Islam in
postsocialist Bulgaria / Kristen Ghodsee.
      p. cm. — (Princeton studies in Muslim politics)
  Includes bibliographical references and index.
  ISBN 978-0-691-13954-8 (hardcover : alk. paper) — ISBN 978-0-691-13955-5
(pbk. : alk. paper) 1. Muslims—Bulgaria—Social conditions—Case studies.
2. Muslims—Bulgaria—Madan (Smolianski okrug)—Social conditions. 3. Islam—Social
aspects—Bulgaria—Case studies. 4. Islam and politics—Bulgaria—Case studies. 5. Sex
role—Bulgaria—Case studies. 6. Ethnicity—Political aspects—Bulgaria—Case studies.
7. Social change—Bulgaria—Case studies. 8. Communism—Social aspects—Bulgaria—
Case studies. 9. Bulgaria—History—1990– 10. Bulgaria—Religious life and customs—
Case studies. I. Title.
  DR64.2.M8G48 2009
  305.6'9709499—dc22
                                                                    2008056088

British Library Cataloging-in-Publication Data is available

This book has been composed in Sabon

Printed on acid-free paper.

press.princeton.edu

Printed in the United States of America

10 9 8 7 6 5 4 3 2 1

Contents

Illustrations   ix

A Note on Transliteration   xi

Acknowledgments   xiii

Introduction
The Changing Face of Islam in Bulgaria   1

Chapter One
Names to Be Buried With   34

Chapter Two
Men and Mines   56

Chapter Three
The Have-nots and the Have-nots   86

Chapter Four
Divide and Be Conquered   109

Chapter Five
Islamic Aid   130

Chapter Six
The Miniskirt and the Veil   159

Conclusion
Minarets after Marx   184

Appendix   205

Notes   207

Selected Bibliography   235

Index   243

Illustrations————————————————————

1 Girls dressed in the new "Arab" style 2
2 The center of Madan in winter 4
3 The GORUBSO Building 7
4 A building in Madan in 2005 8
5 The renovated façade of the Culture House, representing the ideal
  communist man and woman 9
6 The village of Madan in the 1950s 45
7 A Pomak girl in the 1950s 48
8 Madan developed as a communist city 53
9 The Central Department Store in Madan 54
10 A statue of a GORUBSO miner as a symbol of communist
   masculinity 58
11 Miners in Madan 60
12 One of the GORUBSO mines in 2005 68
13 An MRF campaign sign for the 2005 Parliamentary election 125
14 The Elhovets Mosque, built during the Ottoman era 146
15 The new mosque in Tŭrŭn 147
16 The new mosque in Rudozem 148
17 The new mosque in Chepintsi 149
18 The mosque in Madan 150
19 Girls leaving a summer Qur'an course 151
20 A woman dressed in the traditional style glaring at three girls
   dressed in the "Arab" style 162
21 Two Muslim women in miniskirts, Rudozem, 2005 164
22 Muslim women dressed in the new style in 2005 165
23 Three young Pomak women in 2005 168
24 A Muslim man and woman in 2005 174
25 A young Pomak girl in 2005 204

*A Note on Transliteration*_____

TRANSLITERATING THE Bulgarian Cyrillic alphabet into Latin letters presents particular challenges, as there are many different accepted traditions and much inconsistency regarding usage. Furthermore, some Bulgarians object to the Library of Congress transliteration system for their language because they feel that it looks "too Turkish." Thus, more than just a stylistic question, rendering Bulgarian into Latin letters is also a political one. I have tried my best to avoid these political questions by using the Latin letters that best represent the actual spoken sound of the more difficult Bulgarian characters. The most tricky characters are the Bulgarian в (which can be transliterated as *ff* or *v*), the ъ (which can be written as an *a* or *u*), the я (which can be transliterated as *ia* or *ya*) and the ц (which is either *tz* or *ts*). Throughout the book, when doing my own transliterations from the Bulgarian, I have chosen to use a *v* for в, a *ts* for ц, and the character *ŭ* for ъ. I have transliterated я as *ya* in most cases, although it also appears as *ia* in proper names and in the word *Bulgaria* when it is written in English. Also, in the case of previously published materials and names already transliterated into Latin letters by other authors, I have reproduced the words in their published transliterated form, and therefore there will inevitably be some inconsistencies in the text.

Acknowledgments

I AM INDEBTED TO the many people and institutions who have helped me create this book. Without the steadfast support of my friends and colleagues, the research and writing would have proven impossible. First and foremost, I would like to thank Joan Scott for bringing me to the Institute for Advanced Study at Princeton and giving me the time and intellectual encouragement I needed to finish the manuscript. Joan was a tireless advocate and helped me push through many theoretical dead ends and seemingly impenetrable walls of writer's block. Her critical questions and challenging insights were invaluable, and I feel incredibly fortunate to have had the opportunity to work with her. Also priceless was the scholarly camaraderie of the Institute and of the Schools of Social Science and Historical Studies at Princeton. Susanna Hecht was a thoughtful interlocutor on matters of all sorts, in addition to being a gourmet par excellence. She kept my mind, as well as my stomach, well fed at the Institute; her friendship, joie de vivre, and spontaneity made what otherwise could have been a very isolating experience into a year-long festival of scholarship. Special thanks to Rosalind Morris, who gave me thoughtful comments on several chapters and helped me work through various drafts of the conclusion. More importantly, she deserves the award for the best-timed offering of coq au vin in the history of humankind. Amy Borovoy, Jennifer Pitts, Patrick Chabal, Farzana Shaikh, and Lisa Ellis all deserve credit for reading very early drafts of the work and making helpful suggestions for improvement. I am also happy to have exchanged ideas with colleagues in historical studies: Karl Shoemaker, Ayten Kilic, Lisa Florman, Peter Arnade, Betsy Colwill, and Geoffrey Hoskins. My deepest gratitude to Linda Geraci, Linda Garat, Donne Petito, and Nancy Cotterman for making my stay at the Institute so delightful and to Peter Goddard, Hank Farber, Eric Maskin, Michael Walzer, and Freeman Dyson for our delightful lunchtime conversations. Special thanks also to my upstairs neighbors Attila Ambrus and Erica Field, who helped keep me sane and shared with equal passion my newly acquired BSG obsession, and to Ricarda and Conny Ameling for making sure I had Wednesday nights free to write.

While writing, I was blessed with help from several friendly readers who gave me detailed comments on the manuscript as a whole. Deepest appreciation goes out to Ali Eminov, Jim Clark, Irene Tinker, Genevieve Creedon, Ned Walker, Gail Kligman and the editors and anonymous readers at Princeton University Press. Special thanks to Fred Appel, Natalie

Baan, and Vicky Wilson-Schwartz. I am eternally indebted to my professors at Berkeley and other mentors: Pedro Noguera, Inderpal Grewal, Anton Allahar, Manuel Castells, Carol Stack, and Jean Lave. I am most especially grateful to Caren Kaplan for her ongoing support of my work despite the many different paths I have followed. She is the ideal academic role model, and without her example I surely would have veered away from many intellectual and personal challenges. Seven years out, the admiration I had for her in graduate school has not abated.

I was also fortunate to have had a fellowship at the Woodrow Wilson International Center for Scholars in 2005–6, where my closest colleagues were Melissa Bokovoy and Sonya Michel, especially Sonya, who gave me great feedback on early drafts. Thanks also to Marty Sletzinger at East European Studies as well as my colleagues at the Center: Marta Dyczok, Larry Rosen, Marwan Kraidy, and Karen Tranberg Hansen. The librarians, Janet Spikes, Dagne Gizaw, and Michelle Kamalich, were incredibly helpful and without them the historical research for this book would have been a thousand times harder. Joe Brinley was also a wonderful supporter and mentor. I am grateful to Angela Canon at the Library of Congress, who helped me navigate the Bulgarian collection as well as to the various librarians and archivists in the National Library of Bulgaria in Sofia. *Mnogo blagodareniya* to Christian Filipov, Krassimir Kanev, Maria Stoilkova, Dimo Bechev, Antonina Zhelyazkova, and Anelia Atanassova in Bulgaria, as well as to my many friends and coffee companions in Madan. Most importantly, I want to thank "Silvi" and "Iordan" for their immeasurable knowledge and their genuine friendship.

I want to express my appreciation to my wonderful colleagues at Bowdoin College: Rachel Connely, Jane Knox-Voina, Page Herrlinger, Arielle Saiber, Pamela Ballinger, and Virginia Hopcroft. Jane Lonergan was the travel agent extraordinaire who masterminded all of my complicated plane reservations. My greatest debt at Bowdoin is to Jennifer Scanlon, who has been a fantastic mentor and colleague. She also read and gave me comments on several early chapters, and more importantly, provided me with firm deadlines. Anne Clifford is the footnote and bibliography tsarina who helped me get my references in order. I also want to acknowledge the generosity of the Gender and Women's Studies program and the administration at Bowdoin for allowing me to take two years off to complete the research for this book and to write it. Finally, my colleague Scott Sehon forced me to puzzle through many a casual assertion. He was an ever-vigilant editor and a steadfast and ruthless annihilator of the "scare quote." My punctuation, as well as my "intellectual life" in Maine, were both much improved as a result of our "friendship."

Funding is always a beautiful thing to have, and I was very lucky to be supported by a variety of generous foundations. In addition to fellowships extended by the Institute for Advanced Study and the Wilson Center, I would like to acknowledge the grants I got from the National Council on Eurasian and East European Research (NCEEER), the International Research and Exchanges Board (IREX), the American Council of Learned Societies (ACLS), and the Fletcher Family Fund at Bowdoin College. Special thanks to Bob Huber at NCEEER for being such a great advocate for this research. Portions of chapter 6 were previously included in articles published in the journals *Social Politics* and *Historical Reflections*, and I would like to thank both journals for helping me develop and expand the material on the headscarf debate.

The majority of the images in the book are my own, save for one photograph and several postcards, which came from the personal collections of my informants and which I then photographed crudely with my digital camera. I want to thank the residents of Madan for sharing these with me, and would also like to thank the GORUBSO Mining Museum for allowing me to photograph its exhibits. All of the translations from Bulgarian to English are also my own, except where otherwise noted. Some of the Muslim literature and legal documents were translated by Bulgarian research assistants under my supervision. Rumyana Delcheva, Tanya Todorova, and Silviya Simeonova deserve great thanks for their hard work and patience, particularly Silviya, who proofread all of my transliterations.

And finally, I want to thank my family. My mother, Josephine Gussa, was always there for me: to listen, to cheerlead, and to proofread when the occasion demanded it. Cristina Lugo, Herman Gussa, Velichko Velichkov, and Vassilka Velichkova all provided essential moral support. My cousin, Roberto Fernandez, held my hand and guided me through the many minefields of my academic career. As the only other professor in my family, he was always generous with his time and advice and mentored me through one potential intellectual catastrophe after another. Thanks also to Carol Fernandez for always welcoming me into their home, for teaching me how to cook, and for joining me on emergency SWAT shopping excursions when they became existentially necessary. Most of all, I must express my most heartfelt appreciation to my daughter, Kristiana, who accompanied me in Madan and Sofia for all of my fieldwork when she was between the ages of three and six. I don't know how much she will remember being dragged around behind her loquacious and ever-inquisitive mother, but without her this research would have been impossible. She helped me see the world through different eyes and gave me plenty of reasons to loiter on playgrounds, where I could strike up conversations with other parents. Her constant companionship, boundless energy, and vibrant imagination also kept me entertained through the long Rhodope days and nights. Years from now, when she is old enough to read and understand this ethnography, I hope she will come to realize that Mommy's work was not really as boring as she thought it was at the time. It is to her and to her father, Christian Filipov, that I dedicate this book.

MUSLIM LIVES IN EASTERN EUROPE

Introduction

The Changing Face of Islam in Bulgaria

SILVI, A BULGARIAN MUSLIM and an Avon lady,[1] always worried about her roots. Not where she came from, nor who her great-grandparents were. Silvi obsessed about the roots of her hair—how many millimeters of white she could stand before she had to dye it again. When I met her in the small Bulgarian city of Madan in 2005, Silvi was in her late forties and had thick jet-black hair that hung all the way down her back. Over the years the gray had taken over, and it was only nine days after each dye that she could see the silvery sheen glistening at her temples once again. Silvi had been born with the name Aysel, which she was told means "moonlight" in Turkish. She did not care that the communists had made her change her name as she was a rather secular Muslim and really only cared about selling Avon products, which she had been doing for almost ten years. Silvi, short for Silvia, is a Western-sounding name whereas Aysel is Muslim. Since so many Bulgarians associated Muslims with rural life and tobacco growing, it was hard for someone with a Turkish name to project the aura of glamor needed to sell beauty products. "Women will buy more toiletries from 'Silvi' than they will from 'Aysel,'" she told me.

In recent months, there had been a growing trend that disturbed her: an increasing number of young women were dressing head to toe in a new Islamic style imported from abroad. Some of her best-selling Avon products were anticellulite and bust-firming creams, and Silvi wondered if the market for them would shrink as fewer and fewer young women wore the once ubiquitous combination of micro-miniskirts and ample décolletage. "If ugly old women wear a *kŭrpa* [kerchief], it does not matter. No one wants to see them anyway. But young girls?" She told me this as we walked to the center of town. She pointed to the big mosque. "Those *fanatitsi* [fanatics] will be bad for business." Silvi then began reciting a list of things that were changing in her home city of Madan: restaurants had stopped serving pork—once a staple of the local diet; some women were no longer allowed to leave their homes without their husbands' permission—something unheard of before 1989; men who went to the mosque were being given preference for local jobs; and old people who should be venerated were now being chastised as "bad" Muslims for carrying on local traditions practiced in the region since before the Second World War.

Figure 1 Girls dressed in the new "Arab" style

One of Silvi's Avon distributors was named Liliana (Lili for short), and she was the daughter of one of the oldest hodzhas (Muslim preachers) in the area. She was a tall, thin, clear-complexioned woman in her early thirties. Like Silvi, she had long, straight hair, but hers was a natural auburn while Silvi's was a chemical black. Lili preferred frosted lipsticks, nail polishes, and eye shadows, and the heavy dose of glitter in her makeup gave her a dated and almost otherworldly appearance. She lived in a village just outside of Madan with her aged mother and her chronically ill father, who even now still made *muski* (amulets) for those who took the trouble to come visit him. Lili had been married and was the mother of two school-aged children. Her husband had long since abandoned them, so she moved back in with her parents in the mid-1990s to help take care of her father.

The village where she lived was a thirty-minute walk from the center of Madan; Lili came into the city two or three times a week to look for work. Lili had only an eighth-grade education, and for women like her there were only three possible jobs: seamstress, shopkeeper, or waitress. Lili had taken a sewing course through the municipality and was hoping to find a position in one of the local garment factories. Since seamstresses were paid by the piece, she would earn as she produced, unlike the waitresses and shopkeepers, who might work twice as many hours for a tiny monthly wage. But most women in Madan were trying to find work in the garment factories; to land a job, you had to have the right connections or to be in the right place at the right time. So Lili ostensibly came into town to follow up on possible job leads, but she also wanted to take a break from the boredom of village life and the seemingly constant folding and unfolding of the prayer rugs.

Watching Lili come into Madan was always a curious affair. She would walk on the main road coming into the city wearing an ankle-length, long-sleeved, loose, patterned dress and a large square of cloth folded in half, draped over her head and tied beneath her chin. She always carried a large canvas bag slung over her shoulder on a long, yellow nylon strap. She dressed exactly as most women in the villages around Madan dressed, a style typical for the Bulgarian Muslims in this region. But each time she arrived, the first thing she would do was order an espresso at the pizzeria and then duck immediately into the bathroom to change. She would emerge moments later in skin-tight jeans and a low-cut blouse, her long hair spilling over her sometimes bare shoulders. I was accustomed to these costume changes because I had coffee in front of the pizzeria almost every morning.

"And do you change back into your other clothes when you go home?" I asked her one day.

"Of course," she said. "My father is very old. He believes in the old ways, and he is very proud that he is a hodzha. People respect him, because that was very difficult during communism. He is sick now. I do not want to make him angry."

Lili was fairly sure her father knew about the city clothes she changed into on her excursions away from the village, but he preferred not to see them. Lili believed that her parents, having lived most of their lives under communism, had limited understanding of the world after the coming of democracy in 1989 and none at all of the market economy, in which the state no longer guaranteed full employment. No matter how often she explained it to him, her father could not comprehend why there was not a job for Lili when she was willing to work. The last time that he had felt well enough to go into Madan for the Friday prayers, Lili's father had been perplexed by the many changes that had befallen his beloved city: the dirty streets, the abandoned buildings, the obviously drunken men stumbling into the mosque. Lili's father's heart had soared with joy when work began on a new mosque, so many years after the communists had

Figure 2 The center of Madan in winter

destroyed the old one. And so it was most upsetting of all when the new imam (congregational leader) and some young, local men who were studying in Saudi Arabia started saying that the old hodzhas were not true Muslims, that they were uneducated, and that they had deceived people into accepting practices which were un-Islamic.

"I am not sure which would kill him faster," Lili reflected one morning over coffee as two young girls dressed in the new *Arabski stil* (Arab-style) of Islamic dress passed us in front of the pizzeria. "To see me wearing a short skirt or to see me dressed like an *Arabka* [female Arab]. This is not the city he knew."

Madan, the small city that was home to women like Silvi and Lili, was named after the Arabic word for "mine." It is about a six-hour drive south and east from the Bulgarian capital of Sofia, most of it on secondary roads that wind precariously through the undulating peaks of the Rhodope Mountains. Bulgarians claim that this is the legendary land of Orpheus, the cradle of ancient Thrace. The mountains straddle the once impervious border between communist Bulgaria and capitalist Greece, and they are filled with small towns and villages tucked away into deep valleys or perched high atop remote peaks. Among these small towns, there are only a few cities, created through carefully planned projects of communist rural economic development. At a certain point in the drive down from Sofia, the crosses and bell towers of the small country churches found across most of Bulgaria are replaced by cone-tipped minarets—minarets recently rebuilt after having been systematically torn down by the communists. Cities like Madan, and nearby Smolyan and Rudozem, were clustered in the central part of the Rhodope Mountains and were home to the indigenous Bulgarian-speaking Muslim population: the Pomaks.[2] By 2005, the minarets in many Pomak settlements had sprouted anew, like resilient dandelions, in the fertile soil of newfound religious freedom.

Although Islam has a long history in Bulgaria, its local meanings and practices began changing after 1989 as the religion evolved and adapted to the exigencies of the global forces—social, political, and economic—unleashed by the end of socialism.[3] The contours of Bulgarian Islam were also being shaped by the contentious internal politics of its Muslim leaders as well as by the dynamic and increasingly controversial position of Islam in "old" Europe, where Muslim minorities began rejecting secularism and demanding that the Western nations make good on their promises of multiculturalism and tolerance. In this book, I examine the complex and ever-mutating trajectory of Islam through the lives of men and women living in one small corner of the European continent: the Rhodope Mountains. But rather than depicting Islam west of the Bosphorus as an undifferentiated totality, this case study of one Muslim city will demonstrate how the social meanings of Islam in former communist countries may be qualitatively different from its meanings on the other side of the now-phantom Iron Curtain.

Moreover, this case study shows that people embrace new forms of Islam for locally defined reasons, that is, in response to ground-level cultural, political, historical, and economic factors that do not easily fit into grand schematic models to explain the growing influence of Islam in Europe. Certainly, European Muslim communities share some common geopolitical circumstances, such as the ubiquity of globalization, the financial dominance of Saudi Arabia over the international Islamic charitable aid establishment, and growing worldwide Islamophobia. But these macro factors interact with particular local conditions to push or pull Muslim communities toward new beliefs and practices. This examination of Madan is just one glimpse into a change that seems to be occurring in Muslim communities around the world, namely, the eclipsing of "traditional" forms of Islam by "purified" ones imported from abroad. But as I will demonstrate, these changes are occurring in some Bulgarian Muslim communities while other, almost identical communities are relatively unaffected. The central questions are: Why here and not elsewhere? And why now?

Set within a shallow, narrow valley and bisected by the Madanska River, Madan hardly qualifies as a city; in 2005 there was only one road that led in and out. When I did my fieldwork there between 2005 and 2008, I had to drive south first to the regional capital of Smolyan, and then turn east and travel on a dilapidated two-lane road that led toward the Greek border and the twin Pomak cities of Madan and Rudozem. As I entered Madan, a small blue sign with white Cyrillic lettering informed me that I was 670 meters above sea level and that the city had a population of 9,000. I knew, however, that many people had left; Madan had dropped down to about 6,000 in the last few years. As I drove into town, one of the first things I passed on the right was an old communist garment factory, now owned by an Austrian company that produced luxury ski clothing. In the summer, the windows were always open, and I could see the women inside sewing and embroidering the individual jackets and pants that could cost as much as one year's worth of their wages. Yet the factory paid the highest piece rate in town, plus all of the required worker's insurances. On the left was a neighborhood called "25," full of ageing five- and six-storey apartment blocs and small local shops selling dry goods, vegetables, children's clothes from Turkey, and cheap, imported Chinese goods in the Bulgarian equivalent of a "dollar store."

Further up the road on the right there was a small cluster of businesses, including a gas station, a car wash, a restaurant, and a small hotel, all new and painted bright yellow. Although the signs read "Regal," the locals called the place "Saramov," the last name of the man who built and owned the businesses. Saramov was one of the 10 percent of Madan's residents, or Madanchani, who were Christian. Although his wife was a Bulgarian Muslim from a nearby village, a prominent banner of six naked blonde women advertised his car wash to those entering the city. Some of the locals interpreted the banner as a sign of disrespect for the more conservative religious values of Madan's increasingly devout Muslims. Some claimed that Saramov had links to the *mutri* (the Bulgarian Mafia). He drove a Mercedes jeep and had two large bodyguards, who hung around drinking coffee and glowering at the customers. Despite this, his restaurant was the most popular place in town, and his small hotel was always full.

The road curved slightly after I passed Saramov's complex, and it was from there that I caught first sight of the towering minaret of Madan's imposing new mosque. About a minute later, I would arrive in the center of town. Here, there were three important landmarks that could serve as architectural metaphors for the tempestuous postsocialist history of the city. The first was the old GORUBSO building, headquarters of the once all-important communist lead and zinc mining enterprise. The second was the Ivan Vazov Kulturen Dom (community center), and the third was the megamosque. If the Austrian-owned garment factory and Saramov's Regal

Figure 3 The GORUBSO building

complex represented the city's transitionary protocapitalist present, then the GORUBSO building stood as a symbol of Madan's once vibrant communist past. The community center, the façade of which was restored and repainted with funds from the European Union's "Beautiful Bulgaria" project,[4] represented one possible future for the Madanchani in the years leading up to their country's 2007 EU accession, while the mosque stood for another possible future that would draw them closer to the Middle East.

The GORUBSO building was the tallest structure in the city and sat at the top of the main intersection, where the single road took a sharp left turn and led drivers out of Madan and toward the city of Zlatograd. Although GORUBSO had divisions in five southern Bulgarian cities, Madan had been its administrative center. The nine-storey building held all of the administrative offices of the enterprise. This site had once supported Madan's old mosque, a picture of which can still be found in the GORUBSO mining museum. The low, humble, square structure with its telltale minaret had been the previous center of the city until it was bulldozed to make room for the lead-zinc enterprise headquarters. For over three decades, the GORUBSO building dominated the center of Madan, a shining beacon of communist modernity, just as the communist enterprise had once dominated the lives of all who lived in the city.

Figure 4 A building in Madan in 2005

GORUBSO brought immeasurable wealth to the city between 1945 and the early 1990s, when mining and metal processing were among the most respected and well remunerated professions in Bulgaria. Thousands of workers came from all over the country, and from as far away as China and Vietnam, to work for the thriving industry. Its success was based on the rich ore deposits in the Madan area, and GORUBSO invested heavily in the development of the city, building apartment blocs, recreation complexes, community centers, a soccer stadium, pools, schools, special hospital wards, etcetera. It supported the entire local community until Bulgaria was suddenly thrust into the global capitalist economy in the early 1990s, and a fatal combination of labor unrest, international market pressure, bungled privatization, and high-level corruption conspired to run the mines into bankruptcy.

The collapse of GORUBSO left thousands of men in Madan unemployed and destroyed the local economy, leaving the whole city to sink incrementally into a state of visible disrepair. Time and gravity swallowed up much of the infrastructure so proudly developed through the now-hackneyed communist ideals of progress and modernization. The coming of democracy had promised to make the lives of the miners even better, combining economic success with political and religious freedoms, but in Madan, as

Figure 5 The renovated façade of the Culture House, representing the ideal communist man and woman

elsewhere throughout the postsocialist world in Eastern Europe and Central Asia, democracy failed to live up to its promises and left thousands of deserted rural cities in its wake. Indeed, "living blocs" that once housed two families in each apartment were now empty and crumbling. In many places older buildings collapsed; the neighborhoods on the outskirts of Madan were pockmarked with the ruins of the failed enterprise, like an archeological site of the recent past. As in Russia, Eastern Germany, or Kyrgyzstan, where the closure of inefficient or highly polluting communist-era enterprises destroyed the local economies they once supported, Madan was decimated by the privatization of the lead-zinc mines. With few local reemployment opportunities, many men were forced to seek jobs as construction workers in Bulgaria's larger cities or in Western Europe. Those who stayed behind often turned to alcohol, drowning their despair in strong local *rakiya* (brandy).

As a pre-accession candidate to the European Union, however, Bulgaria was the beneficiary of many initiatives. The "Beautiful Bulgaria" project was one that tried to kill two proverbial birds with one stone. As a way to combat the high level of unemployment after the closure of the mines and to restore Madan's center to its former glory, the European Union invested in the restoration of the square and the buildings surrounding it: the Ivan

Vazov Kulturen Dom, the offices of the municipality, the fire station, along
with a few smaller projects. The main effort, however, was concentrated
on the roof, doors, windows, and plaster façade of the community center,
which all needed extensive repairs. The European Union measured the
success of the project by how many unemployed laborers were put to work
on it and for how many "man-months." The community center project employed twenty-four people for fifty-five man-months and left a beautifully
restored crimson building with white columns at the top of a wide plaza,
with a children's playground nearby. But when the work was finished, the
laborers were once again left without jobs. The community center was indeed a beautiful building, one of the few in a city in which almost every
other structure had fallen or was falling apart, and it stood regally as a
reminder of the promise of the European Union. But to many, it was also a
symbol of the shallowness of that promise. The Europeans might be happy
to repaint a few buildings, but there were those in Madan who questioned
whether the EU would ever substantially invest in the future of the city, or
if Madan, with its 90 percent Muslim population, would be a victim rather
than a beneficiary of the EU accession.

"The Europeans can do nothing for Bulgaria," said Hasan, a retired
miner who worked in the café of the new mosque. "The goods we have to
sell them, they already have. They only want to sell us their goods. Our
natural trading partners are in the Middle East and the [Soviet] Union, like
it was before democracy. We have goods that they need. Bulgaria should
establish closer ties with the Muslim world, and not with the Europeans.
The Europeans do not need us."

Hasan told me this while we shared tea in the café of the main mosque.
A thin blue curtain in the doorway billowed inward with the light breeze.
It was a sentiment that I had heard from others in Madan, particularly
from those frustrated in their attempts to penetrate the Bulgarian market
with the products of local industry. The owner of a small ice cream factory
complained incessantly that the aggressive Greeks had taken over Bulgaria
with their Delta ice cream, leaving him no choice but to seek markets in the
Middle East, where being a Muslim at least earned him some advantages.
On the walls of the café, there were three glossy posters of Mecca, and in
addition to the juices, hot drinks, snacks, and (Madan-made) ice cream,
Hasan sold an assortment of Islamic newspapers, magazines, books, and
compact discs for learning modern Arabic. Hasan told me that ordinary
laborers also looked to the Middle East for work when they could not find
it in Bulgaria and were unwilling to work illegally in Holland, Germany,
or Spain. The café we sat in was tucked on the ground floor of the three-
storey mosque, which included a huge windowed dome and a towering
minaret topped by a small silver crescent. The outside walls of the mosque
were a cool white, and the first three meters were tiled with large mosaic-

like pieces of smooth gray marble. The minaret was tall and white, with golden vertical stripes, two circular balconies, and four bullhorn speakers that delivered the call to prayer five times a day. It was an impressive structure.

The most impressive part of the Madan mosque, however, was the prayer hall. An elaborate five-tiered crystal chandelier hung in the center of the voluminous room, with twenty large arched windows streaming light in from the right and left sides. The main floor, where the men prayed, was carpeted with a luxurious indigo blue and gold rug. There was a U-shaped balcony supported by white columns that divided part of the hall into two floors; the upper level was the women's section, an architectural feature that most Bulgarian mosques did not have at the time. At the front of the hall, there were four more arched windows that dribbled light around an exquisitely decorated niche indicating the direction of Mecca and covered with blue mosaic tiles and Arabic script. The room evoked a sense of awe and grandeur that was quite out of place in the otherwise impoverished city.

The sheer size and opulence of the mosque led to many speculations about the origin of the funds responsible for its construction. Although no one could speak with certainty, many Madanchani thought the funds had come from abroad. They had first wanted to build the mosque in the early 1990s, and collections were taken up among the city's residents. Men volunteered their labor to help with its construction. But the project soon ran out of funds for materials as the future of GORUBSO became uncertain. The mosque languished unfinished through the middle part of the decade. Then, toward the end of the 1990s, the money suddenly appeared. Hasan claimed that the money had come from Madan residents who lived abroad. Silvi believed that the funds had come from Saudi Arabia, although some of her Avon clients whispered that it had come from Iran. In 2005, the mosque stood as a powerful reminder of the growing influence of the Muslim world on the small city. The mosque became a vibrant cultural and educational center, unlike the community center, the symbol of the EU's fleeting and superficial aid.

In the battle for hearts and minds in Madan, the promises of global Islamic solidarity challenged the still-remote allures of Western Europe. On Fridays, when the imam (congregational leader) gave his weekly sermon, the mosque was overrun with close to a thousand men, many of them former miners. The mosque had become the central distribution point for ritually sacrificed meats donated from abroad during the two big Islamic feasts: Ramazan Bayram and Kurban Bayram. During the month of Ramazan (Ramadan), at the end of each day's fast, the mosque distributed an almost endless supply of free cookies, pastries, and other sweets. The imam was also responsible for supporting the studies and ambitions of young people who hoped to get an Islamic education either in Bulgaria or, more importantly, abroad, in Turkey, Syria, Saudi Arabia, Jordan, or Kuwait. Most of the local businessmen and politicians congregated at the mosque, and in local affairs, the imam, who had also studied Islam abroad, was becoming more powerful with each passing year. In a community caught in a tempest of political and economic change, the mosque provided social and spiritual support for those desperately in need of a bulwark against the storm.

Why Bulgaria?

Of all of the EU countries, Bulgaria may seem the most obscure in which to examine the growing presence of Islam in Europe. But Bulgaria is a fascinating location to study the dynamism of Islam because it is a place where the "West" has historically met the "East." Although both NATO and the European Union have now embraced Bulgaria, it has been at the crossroads between the "Occident" and the "Orient" for over a millennium. It has been in turn part of the Roman, Byzantine, and Ottoman empires, and Roman Catholicism, Orthodox Christianity, and Islam have all left their legacies in the modern nation of fewer than eight million people. As a close Soviet ally, Bulgaria also experienced over four decades of the official state atheism of Marxist-Leninism and scientific socialism. During the 1990s, when internal conflicts tore apart neighboring Yugoslavia, Bulgaria remained stable and peaceful despite similar religious divides, severe economic hardships, and the massive social and political changes that followed the arrival of democracy and free markets. In 2008, Bulgaria had the largest Muslim population in the EU and was the only member state with a large, historically indigenous Muslim population. And unlike Muslim populations elsewhere in the EU, Bulgaria's Muslim Pomaks, Turks, and Roma have professed Islam for centuries. Finally, as the Americans moved their European military bases into the country to bolster strategic positions for future forays into the Middle East, the Middle East was strengthening its presence in Bulgaria through its religious aid to Muslims, the same aid that probably helped build the imposing new mosque in Madan. Bulgaria had become a meeting point once again.

Bulgaria has also had a long and tempestuous relationship with its eastern neighbor, Turkey, and its ethnic Turkish minority has been the subject of much international controversy. Bulgaria was part of the Ottoman Empire for the better part of five centuries before obtaining its independence in 1878. Although there were several emigration waves of ethnic Turks back to Turkey and large population exchanges after World War I, a sizeable Turkish minority remained in Bulgaria throughout the twentieth century. This was a particularly thorny issue for the Warsaw Pact Bulgarians, who feared that their own Turks were a "fifth column" for NATO-allied Turkey. Several attempts were made to assimilate the Turks of Bulgaria, including a massive name-changing campaign in the mid-1980s.[5] The situation came to a head when the Bulgarian communists unilaterally declared that there were "no Turks" in Bulgaria, precipitating a massive exodus to Turkey in May of 1989. By 2008, Turkey's desire to join the European Union found little support from those who believed that Europe should stop at the Bosphorus. This vexed geopolitical relationship with Turkey would be one important factor pushing Bulgaria's Pomaks to forge closer ties with the Gulf Arab states.

Although my analytical focus is on the micro level of human interaction, the questions that drive this book go beyond just one city on the edge of Europe; they apply to postsocialist populations from Budapest to Vladivostok. They shed light on how religious ideologies fare after decades of state-imposed atheism and Marxist critiques of capitalism. They also provide a window on the situation of Muslim minorities in the European Union, where a new passport-free travel regime means that Bulgarians will be more and more integrated into Western European Muslim networks and communities in Germany, France, England, and Spain, despite the fact that there may be significant differences in the reasons why Islam is embraced by different groups. The personal histories of individual men and women in a rural city like Madan give texture and detail to these questions and reveal the specificities of place within the transnational generalizations made possible by the persistence of communist material culture throughout the postsocialist world[6] and by the homogenizing effects of European legal harmonization.

Thus, one can explore pressing global issues by telling the stories of ordinary people: secular Muslims, atheist Muslims, Christianized Muslims, and the newly devout. In the pages that follow, you will encounter people like Iordan, an atheist Pomak and a laid-off miner, who agonized about his Christian name. His recollections of the period before 1989 will help to explain the situation of the Bulgarian-speaking Muslims during the communist period and the strident campaigns launched in order to assimilate them. A woman named Higyar explains how the "new" Islam differed from the "old ways," and Aisha will illuminate why so many Muslim youth felt that the Islam practiced by their parents was tainted by atheism and was in need of renewal. And Silvi, the former bank teller turned Avon lady who lived in Madan for almost five decades, will share her own perceptions and fears of the changes transforming her beloved city, changes she desperately wants to make sense of if only so that she can keep things from changing too quickly. As far as Silvi was concerned, one unexpected and world-shattering change, the almost instantaneous demise of communism, was enough for one lifetime.

The Problem of Terminology

Actually naming the new form of Islam that was making its way into Bulgaria during my fieldwork was a difficult task, and there are many scholarly debates on what it should be called.[7] After 1989, the increased contact with the Muslim world slowly began what has been termed the objectification of Islam in Bulgaria. This occurs when Muslim practices that had been observed without much critical reflection become the subject of intense public scrutiny and debate.[8] "Objectification is the process by which basic questions come to the fore in the consciousness of large numbers of believers: 'What is my religion?' 'Why is it important to my life?' and 'How do my beliefs guide my conduct?' "[9] Islam is extracted from its roots in local traditions and becomes a systematized body of ideas that is distinctly separable from nonreligious ones. In Central Asia, Adeeb Khalid has argued that the Soviet oppression of Islam prevented its objectification, leaving it fixed in the realm of tradition and custom throughout the socialist period.[10] Although Islam in Bulgaria was not subject to the extreme attempts at eradication that it was in the Soviet Union, and the Muslim clergy was left intact (albeit coopted by the communist government), it too remained part of the fabric of everyday cultures, rather than an objectified system of beliefs distinguishable from local custom. Bulgaria thus began the process of objectification after 1989.

But Islam in Bulgaria is very heterogeneous. This heterogeneity has made it difficult to have just one conversation about what Islam means in the Bulgarian context. Although 95 percent of the Muslims in Bulgaria are technically Hanafi Sunni, there is a very wide spectrum of beliefs subsumed in this category. Additionally, there is a small heterodox Shi'a population, called the Alevis, and a wide variety of Sufi brotherhoods such as the Bektashis, which have a long history in the country. In addition to this spectrum of beliefs, there are also three different ethnic groups that profess Islam: the Turks, the Roma, and the Pomaks, who are the focus of the present study. And even among the Pomaks, there are those that consider themselves to be Turks, those who consider themselves Bulgarians, and yet a third group which believes that "Pomak" is a separate ethnic identity altogether. This book hones in on the replacement of traditional practices of Islam with new forms of the religion imported from abroad among the latter two groups of Pomaks: why is this happening specifically among this population?

In the Bulgarian context, this new form of Islam seemed to come largely from Saudi Arabia and from the influence of the Jordanian Muslim Brothers. The Bulgarians who promoted it referred to this new interpretation of Islam as the "true Islam," because it supposedly came straight from the Arabian

Peninsula where the Prophet[11] had lived and died. Those who supported it positioned this "true" Islam in opposition to the Islam of Turkey, Iran, or the Balkans more generally. Because the resources that financed the publications and organizations that promoted this new form of objectified Islam were linked to Saudi-funded charities, members of the Bulgarian government and those in the leadership of the Bulgarian Muslim community who rejected it tended to refer to this Islam as "Wahhabism," specifically linking it to Saudi Arabia. Those ordinary Bulgarian Muslims who still clung to their own traditions referred to it as "Arab Islam," because they also saw it as originating with the Saudis, Jordanians, and Egyptians and contrasted it to their own Balkan or Turkish Islam, that is, Hanafi Sunnism. In Central Asia, Muslims also referred to "Arab Islam," because it was seen as distinctly foreign to local traditions.[12] Although "Arab Islam" was the term most commonly used by my informants in the field, it assumed a static and homogenous form of "Arab" Islam that did not actually exist in the Arab world, and also elided the ways in which Bulgarian religious leaders were actively recrafting foreign interpretations of Islam for their own purposes.

Recognizing that there were a variety of terms which meant different things to different people, I initially planned to use the terms most familiar to me in the discipline of anthropology and to refer to this form of Islam as "orthodox Islam," following the very influential work of Talal Asad,[13] even though it might be very confusing to use this terminology in a (big O) Orthodox Christian country. The term "orthodox Islam" seemed to work well in the Bulgarian context because of Asad's juxtaposition of "orthodox" Islam with traditional Islam and the ways in which proponents of the former use scriptural authority to claim a more "rightful" version of their religion. Asad describes (small o) "orthodox" Islam as the "scripturalist, puritanical faith of the towns"[14] and argues that it attempts "a (re)ordering of knowledge that governs the 'correct' form of Islamic practices."[15] For Asad, "orthodox" Islam has its historical roots in the "process by which *long-established indigenous practices* (such as the veneration of saints' tombs) were judged to be un-Islamic by the Wahhabi reformers of Arabia . . . and then forcibly eliminated" (emphasis in the original).[16] In her ethnographic study of women healers in Saudi Arabia, Eleanor Abdella Duomato also uses the term "orthodox" to refer to the interpretation of Islam promoted by Wahhabi reformers, opposing it to the word "heterodox," which referred to specific local Muslim traditions. She writes: "Wahhabi authority defined itself very specifically in opposition to saint worship, praying at graves, votive offerings, and Sufi *zikr* chanting and dancing, as well as fortune-telling, spell making, truth divining, and amulet wearing."[17] In the work of both Asad and Duomato, I found important parallels with the Bulgarian case.

As I solicited feedback on early drafts of the manuscript, however, I learned that many experts outside of the field of anthropology were very dubious about the term "orthodox." Edward Walker, a political scientist at Berkeley whose specialty is Islam in the post-Soviet context, objected to the word on two grounds. Firstly, the etymology of the word is from the Greek *ortho* (correct) and *doxa* (belief), and implies a theologically correct version of a religion as determined by some overseeing person or body. Walker felt that because Islam had no overseeing body, there could be no orthodoxy. Secondly, much of the "correcting" of Islam is about proper devotional practices rather than belief, so "orthopraxy" (correct practice) would be more appropriate than "orthodoxy."[18]

I was also fortunate to get invaluable feedback from the esteemed historian of Islam, Nikki R. Keddie.[19] She quite vehemently objected to the term "orthodox," because she felt that there could be no "correct" belief in a religion as diverse and complex as Islam, particularly when one considers the fundamental divisions between Sunni and Shi'a Muslims and the long history of conflict over what is "correct" belief and practice. Keddie also felt that I might, as an author, be interpreted as endorsing this specific form of Islam as the "correct" one. Finally, my colleague and mentor, Gail Kligman, felt that the word "orthodox" was too analytical for an ethnographic text, and that, as an ethnologist, I should use the terminology of my informants.[20] This would be either "Arab Islam" (*Arabski Islyam*), if my informant did not embrace it, or "true Islam" (*istinski Islyam*), if he or she did.

From these comments, I began to have reservations about using Asad's terminology, despite its wide acceptance in anthropology. The problem was what to replace it with, particularly because I wanted to be sensitive to the Bulgarian context and how the media there has deployed different terms. I ruled out "fundamentalist" Islam or even Olivier Roy's "neo-fundamentalism"[21] because of their very negative connotations in Bulgarian, where "fundamentalists" are synonymous with "terrorists." The term "Wahhabism" conflates radical Islamic movements such as Al-Qaeda with the official religion in Saudi Arabia, and since the 2002 publication of Stephen Schwartz's *The Two Faces of Islam*[22] has become a placeholder for "bad" Islam in opposition to "good" Islam. "Salafism" is an Arabic word that refers to the "ancestors" and connotes a version of Islam to be practiced as it was practiced at the time of the Prophet. The problem with this term is that it is distinctly backward-looking and rooted specifically in the Arabian Peninsula. The new forms of Islam in Bulgaria seem to be much more forward-looking and supranational, in the sense that their adherents are advocating a newer, more inclusive form of Islam, stripped of its local variations and cultural particularities, as in Olivier Roy's idea of "globalized Islam" or what one Bulgarian Islamic Studies scholar preferred to call "universalist" Islam.[23] Furthermore, both "Salafism" and "Wahhabism" denote a form of Islam that is seemingly fixed and unchanging, whereas in Bulgaria it was still rather vague and undefined. Dale Eickelman and James Piscatori have reminded us that "religious communities, like all 'imagined communities,' change over time. Their boundaries are shifted by, and shift, the political, economic, and social contexts in which these participants find themselves."[24]

Then there were the terms "Islamist" and "Islamism," which connote a political form of Islam, one that includes a focus on gaining political authority in order to promote morality (or deploying a discourse of morality to gain political power). In the Bulgarian context, at least during the time of my fieldwork, the promoters of this new Islam distanced themselves from politics and in fact were quite critical of the Turkish Movement for Rights and Freedom party for mixing religion with statecraft. There were also the terms "objectified" Islam or "authenticated" Islam (used in the Shi'a context),[25] which denoted a continual process of defining and distilling Islamic beliefs and practices. These terms better described the theological negotiations surrounding what this new Islam would look like among the Pomaks, and why it was considered "purer" or more "authentic" than the local beliefs, but they were rarely used in the Bulgarian context. Finally, Nikki Keddie suggested simply calling this new form of Islam "Saudi-influenced Islam," since it relied so heavily on Saudi resources, but I felt that this term ignored the important Jordanian influence, particularly that of the Muslim Brothers.

After much debate and rumination, I will continue to use Asad's terminology because it accurately reflects the attitude of Bulgarians embracing this new Islam, who claimed that their version of the religion was the "correct belief" and that the overseeing body to which they deferred was the Qur'an itself. I will keep the word "orthodox" in quotes throughout the text, however, to make it clear that I am not endorsing this version of Islam (or any other) as the correct one. I will also occasionally use "Saudi-influenced Islam" (without quotes), because it is accurate to say that this form of Islam is largely promoted in Bulgaria with monies derived from Saudi-funded Islamic charities, even if the ideas themselves are of more diverse origin.

This objectified form of "orthodox" Islam mounts a direct challenge to traditional Muslim practices, which come to be characterized as forbidden innovations, even if these practices were a part of local Muslim culture for centuries. Here I also follow Asad in his definition of "traditional" Islam, not as a fixed and stagnant ritualistic practice of the faith but rather one where the legitimacy of the interpretations of Islamic belief and practice is rooted in local histories.[26] Saba Mahmood further argues that in traditional Islam "the past is the very ground through which the subjectivity and self-understanding of a tradition's adherents are constituted."[27] Thus, "orthodox" Islam often comes into conflict with traditional Islam as the former tries to claim discursive hegemony over the latter by propagating the idea that it is more "authentic." This often results in a situation where widely varying local attitudes regarding mandatory Islamic practices (such as fasting, abstinence from alcohol, and head-covering) are criticized and targeted by "orthodox" reformers who claim there is only one "true" or "pure" Islam.

In Bulgaria, traditional Islam spans a very wide spectrum of belief from mainstream Hanafi Sunnism to Sufism to other forms of locally defined folk Islam. What they all share in common is that their collective practice is seen as a permanent part of the fabric of local Muslim communities, which have a centuries-long presence in the Balkans. Throughout Bulgaria there are remnants of mosques and other reminders of Muslim Ottoman culture that legitimate local interpretations of Islam—Bulgarian Muslims have been doing things their own way for a long time. Efforts to objectify Islam in Bulgaria, therefore, will inevitably meet resistance by those who want to preserve some form of continuity with the past, even if this is a past in which Muslim practices were banned by a communist government. A few examples of the shape of recent tensions between "orthodox" and traditional Islam in Bulgaria will help to sharpen the analytical focus around these two concepts.

One interesting example is the attempted prohibition of a Bulgarian Muslim holiday, Hadrales, which coincides with the Orthodox Christian holiday of Georgiov Den (St. George's Day). A Pomak and the Bulgarian chief mufti, Mustafa Hadzhi, explained in a 2005 interview that the celebration of Hadrales marked "the boundary between winter and summer" and came into Bulgaria through the Ottomans from the Persians who also celebrate a holiday by the same name. The mufti then went on to explain that Hadrales was a *pre-Islamic* holiday of the Persians and therefore, even though it has been celebrated for perhaps half a millennium, its celebration should be eradicated from local Muslim practice in Bulgaria.

> The celebration of a holiday such as St. George's Day or what the Muslims call "Hadrales" does not agree with the principles of the Islamic religion, because it is very clear on this issue—there are two holidays in Islam [Kurban Bayram and Ramazan Bayram] . . . As for other holidays, including "Hadrales," the celebration of such holidays is in no way allowed for the Muslims . . . the Islamic religion fully distances itself from the traditions and all other holidays of the other religions. We are not against the non-Muslims celebrating their own holidays, following their traditions . . . but we ourselves cannot accept them as ours and we cannot observe any rituals connected with them; this cannot be allowed

by the Islamic religion . . . Islam is first of all an order from God, and it is the last religion, and because of this its religious principles should be observed, not old traditions and rituals.[28]

Although the chief mufti officially condemned Hadrales, many Pomaks continued to celebrate the holiday, braving the disapproval of their newly devout Muslim neighbors.

Another extreme example of an attempt to eradicate local Muslim practices was that of Ali Khairaddin, a Pomak who was part of the official Muslim leadership (the regional mufti of Sofia and all of Western Bulgaria) before starting his own National Association of Bulgarian Muslims in 2006. Khairaddin argued that there should be severe punishments for Muslims who claim to be able to divine the future. It was not an uncommon practice among the Pomaks in the Smolyan region to seek out local "fortune tellers" in times of confusion and uncertainty, and then to ask for amulets from local hodzhas in order to protect themselves from the dangers predicted for them. In a 2005 interview, however, Khairaddin openly condoned the traditional Islamic punishment for fortune-tellers: death by decapitation. He said: "This extreme measure is right and it considers the psychology and the nature of man, because a man who has been tempted by this activity [fortune-telling] and makes an easy profit will have a hard time giving it up. Giving it up happens through the Islamic court."[29]

Both of the previous examples show religious leaders trying to cleanse local Islam of un-Islamic practices, often against the desires of local Muslim communities. On a more everyday level, few Bulgarians who would call themselves Muslim refrain from drink or pork, and most generally ignore a variety of practices associated with being a proper Muslim. The proponents of "orthodox" Islam trace the roots of this laxity in the local Muslim culture to lack of education and lack of critical reflection on what it means to be a Muslim in Bulgaria. These debates between "orthodox" and traditional Islam in Bulgaria are inevitably mapped onto ethnic divisions and intergenerational conflicts, and as we shall see in this book, also piggyback onto the country's forty-five-year history of Marxist-Leninism and its preoccupations with social justice and the "common good."

The discourses of "orthodox" Islam touched almost all Muslim communities in Bulgaria in the period after 1989, but what is fascinating from the point of view of the present study is the way in which this new and "foreign" form of the faith took root in a specific region of the Rhodope. The central question of this book is how and why this took place, and what we can learn from it about the process through which religious communities shift and refashion themselves in response to both internal and external stimuli. More importantly, in the European context, how are local, eclectic, traditional forms of Islam being shaped by the cultural, political, and economic context of postcommunist societies? And why are these local forms of Islam being displaced by externally defined versions of the religion? Are these imported "orthodoxies" becoming hegemonic or are they only selectively appropriated and strategically redeployed to support specific local ideological needs? As of 2008, the embrace of this externally defined Islam in Bulgaria was still very localized and far from complete. But attempts to promote the "true" Islam, particularly with regard to the dress and behavior of women, have precipitated increasing tensions not only between the traditional Muslims and their more "orthodox" neighbors but also between Bulgaria's Muslim minority and its overwhelming Orthodox Christian majority.

Theories to Explain "Orthodox" Islam in Bulgaria

For more than twenty years before she began selling Avon, Silvi worked as a teller in the local branch of the Bulgarian People's Bank in Madan. By the mid-1990s, the economy had been devastated by the collapse of the lead-zinc mining enterprise, and Silvi lost her job at a time when her family most needed her income. Her husband, Iordan, was traveling around Bulgaria in search of construction work. Her two sons were still in school, one at the university and the other at the *gymnasium* (academic secondary school), and she was determined that they would finish their studies, for she believed that education was the only pathway to success in the new market system. No matter how much money Iordan sent home, there was never enough, but Silvi gave as much of it as she could to her sons.

"Avon saved my life," she explained. "Without Avon, I cannot say what would have happened to us."

Armed with her monthly catalogues, Silvi eked out a meager salary and, more importantly, found a reason to get up in the morning and leave the flat. During almost fourteen months of unemployment, she had stayed at home, "stuck to the couch like Velcro." A naturally social person, she remembered that period with great frustration. "I did not even want to go out to spend thirty stotinki[30] on one coffee. In truth, I did not have one stotinka to spend. I could not believe that something like this could happen to me."

Slowly, she managed to build a client base and hired some distributors below her on the pyramid. She soon became an astute businesswoman. Because her livelihood depended so much on peddling beauty products, she was quick to realize potential threats to her business interests. At some point, she had determined that this new form of Islam was one of them, and she tried to make sense of what was happening around her. Her view of religion was a decidedly Marxist one, like that of most Bulgarians of her

generation, who were schooled in the philosophy of dialectical materialism and taught to equate modernity with atheism. According to Marx,
"Religious suffering is, at one and the same time, the expression of real
suffering and a protest against real suffering. Religion is the sigh of the
oppressed creature, the heart of a heartless world, and the soul of soulless
conditions. It is the opium of the people. The abolition of religion as the il-
lusory happiness of the people is the demand for their real happiness."[31]

For people like Silvi who were raised under communism, this was a
familiar and compelling analysis of the resurgence of religiosity in their
communities, and on the surface, the structural argument had plenty of
evidence to support it. As the local economies of remote areas like Madan
collapsed, the rural educational infrastructure crumbled, populations declined, teachers left, and schools closed. There was an empirically significant regression in the material conditions of people's lives after the end
of communism.[32] Marxists believed that people were more susceptible
to religion when they were poor and uneducated, particularly if the religious authorities had power and resources. It was a simple and mechani-
cal explanation for a more complex phenomenon in Bulgaria, but it sat
comfortably with the relatively accurate observation that destitute, rural
populations tended to be more religious than affluent city-dwellers.

But there were other explanations for this Islamic revival as well, explanations that Silvi did not consider but which were posited by various
experts I consulted as I grappled with the larger theoretical questions that
were raised by my examination of daily life in Madan. Western missionaries and evangelists, for example, held that communist-imposed atheism
had created a mass of godless souls in need of salvation following the fall
of the Berlin Wall: "Capitalism alone is not able to fill the 'spiritual vacuum' left by Marxism's collapse."[33] According to this argument, Marxist-
Leninism was an ideology that artificially filled in for the more spiritual
needs of the people, and the implosion of that ideology left a great exis-
tential void in the hearts and minds of former communist citizens which
religion could then fill.[34] Indeed, these convictions inspired the mad rush
of Mormons, Moonies, Hare Krishnas, Seventh Day Adventists, Jehovah's
Witnesses, Wahhabis, Ahmadis, Scientologists, Baha'is, and evangelical
Protestants of every kind into the former socialist countries in the immediate aftermath of the events of 1989.[35] The spiritual free-for-all in Bulgaria
led even the American magazine *Christianity Today* to claim in 1992 that
the country had become a "fertile ground for false teaching."[36]

A third explanation came from the local religious leaders. Officials from
the chief mufti's office (theoretically the spiritual authority over all Muslims
in Bulgaria) and the regional muftiship in Smolyan argued that religious
activity among Muslims in Bulgaria after 1989 was merely the reemergence of a piety that had flourished in the country before communism.

Forty-five years of heavy-handed oppression had forced many otherwise devout Bulgarian Muslims to abandon their traditions, lose touch with their faith, and, most importantly, forfeit connections that they would otherwise have had to the Muslim world. From this perspective the religious resurgence in places like Madan was a sort of spiritual restitution. New Islamic practices were being promoted by those interested in reinstating Bulgaria's long Muslim past, even if these supposedly "traditional" practices were taking on forms quite different from those preserved by old hodzhas such as Lili's father. These tensions were mapped onto significant generational divides, pitting young against old in a battle over the "proper" practice of Islam.

Some Bulgarian intellectuals,[37] and the deputy chief mufti in Bulgaria,[38] believed that the Islamic "revival" in the country was being driven by the Pomaks, who were having somewhat of an identity crisis. Because most (though not all) Pomaks believed that they were ethnic Slavs, they had always found it difficult to find their place in the Bulgarian cultural mosaic, to classify themselves in a way that expressed their political interests. The larger Muslim community in Bulgaria was made up of ethnic Turks, Slavs, and Roma, with the Turks accounting for the vast majority. While some Pomaks actually claimed that they were Turks, others argued that they were ethnically Arab, and still others said they had a unique ethnicity of their own.[39] The Greeks claimed that the Pomaks were Greek, and the Macedonians said they were Macedonian (which neither the Greeks nor the Bulgarians recognized as a separate ethnicity). This situation, so indicative of the complicated ethnic politics of the Balkans, supported the identity-crisis argument: the hybridity and fluidity of Pomak identity and the political powerlessness that accompanied it caused some Pomaks to embrace forms of Islam that diverged significantly from those practiced by the Turks. Some Pomaks did this to distinguish themselves from the Turks and make the claim that the Turks should not represent them politically (as had been the case between 1990 and 2008). By establishing closer links (even through an imagined ethnicity) to the Saudis or Gulf Arabs and practicing more "orthodox" forms of Islam, the new Pomak religious leaders also strategically positioned themselves to take advantage of the generous resources available from wealthy Saudi charities or other foreign sources of Islamic aid.

There was also the issue of faith, and indeed many young men and women embracing the new ways claimed that they had experienced a type of spiritual awakening that had been lacking in their lives. But why, I asked, would these spiritual awakenings be so geographically specific? Indeed, while each of the proposed explanations could account for a part of the story, none could fully explain the observed variability between almost identical populations. Many postsocialist communities were affected by similar conditions, yet the embrace of this "orthodox" Islam was very uneven and concentrated in specific regions.

Communities throughout the postsocialist world experienced similar rapid rural declines and stunning increases in poverty since 1989; this situation was by no means unique to Bulgaria. Moreover, most rural areas in Bulgaria had experienced a severe decline in their living standards.[40] Rural industries had been closed down, populations had fled, and access to education had been severely crippled by the shrinking of social welfare provisions. Religious missionaries of all faiths traveled throughout the country trying to entice potential believers with promises of food, financial aid, and religious education alongside spiritual salvation. And although the Pomaks may have been particularly targeted for conversion because of the perceived ambiguity in their ethno-religious identity, not all Pomaks have turned to "orthodox" Islam, and many have actively resisted it.

The more formal explanations could also be applied to a wide cross-section of Bulgarian society. If religion had simply rushed in to fix a problem created by Marxist atheism, it would have applied to all Bulgarians, particularly since social mobility before 1989 was linked to joining the communist party and rejecting religion.[41] The so-called "spiritual vacuum," if it existed, would have engulfed the whole postsocialist world, not just Madan and Rudozem. In Russia, two prominent sociologists of religion found that while "belief in supernatural forces" increased in the early 1990s among Russians, this trend was not sustained.[42] Although the young were initially among the first to embrace religion as a rebellious act against the Soviet regime, they were also the first to abandon it. The Russian communists were more ruthless in their oppression of religion than their Bulgarian counterparts, but the postsocialist "spiritual vacuum" existed equally in both nations. The sociologist Dimitri Yefimovich Furman argues that the majority of younger Russians lived in a morally, philosophically, and intellectually ambiguous universe filled with what he calls "postmodern eclecticism."[43] He notices an increase in situational morality, an unwillingness to define right or wrong in absolute terms. Social rules and norms were flexible and fluid and able to accommodate all of the uncertain exigencies of the postcommunist era.[44]

This moral relativity also engulfed Bulgarians, who were raised under communism to believe that capitalism was by definition an immoral system, where hereditary privilege and brute force perpetually subjugated the toiling masses, and where theft, corruption, and exploitation were rewarded with power and wealth. With the fall of the Berlin Wall in 1989, many Bulgarians hoped that the communists had been wrong, and that open multiparty elections and free markets would bring liberty, prosperity, and greater opportunities for those willing to take individual initiative and work hard in the new competitive system. Instead, they watched as corrupt politicians, disingenuous foreign investors, international financial institutions, and a new Mafia elite that terrorized the population into submission ransacked and pillaged their country. Valuable state-owned enterprises, which technically belonged to the Bulgarian people, were sold for a song to both foreign and domestic vultures that stripped their assets and ran them into bankruptcy in explicit violation of carefully prepared privatization contracts. The fire sale in Bulgaria left thousands unemployed; many experienced real poverty for the first time in their lives. The accumulated wealth of the country was concentrated into the hands of less than 5 percent of the population in just over a decade. There was no way to fight back. Judges were bought and sold, the police were thoroughly corrupt, and the West's cheerleaders for democracy supported privatization at all costs, despite the clear evidence that state-owned assets were falling into the hands of gangsters and thugs, who shot first and asked questions later.[45]

In spite of the chaos of the transition, few Bulgarians found comfort in faith, as many Russians did. Nationally representative surveys found a lack of religious interest in Bulgaria despite the influx of missionaries and the surge of religious activity in the early 1990s. In 2006, Bulgaria ranked seventeenth out of the fifty most atheist countries in the world (Sweden was first, the Czech Republic sixth, Russia twelfth, Hungary fourteenth, and the United States forty-fourth).[46] This study found that 34–40 percent of the Bulgarian population was atheist, agnostic, or nonreligious.[47] Another nationally representative survey, conducted in 1999, found that although 96 percent of ethnic Bulgarians claimed that they were Christians and 86 percent defined themselves as Bulgarian Orthodox Christians,[48] only 10 percent of those who declared themselves Orthodox said that they followed the prescriptions of the Church, with 49.3 percent claiming that they were religious "in their own way."[49] The survey also found that 30.5 percent of the Bulgarian population never attended church or mosque, with the same percentage saying that they only went on the big religious holidays, once or twice a year, demonstrating that Bulgarians are prone to defining religion as an aspect of ethnic identity, rather than a declaration of belief in the doctrines of a particular organized spiritual community. Furthermore, in an international study correlating wealth and religiosity, Bulgaria was a clear outlier. Although Bulgarians were relatively poor, they showed almost the same indifference toward religion as the Swedes and French.[50] In an overall culture of religious indifference, the resurgence of Islam in Madan and Rudozem was quite anomalous.

And while there was some sense of continuity with the precommunist past, this mainly applied to individuals and communities that were oppressed by the communists and fought to maintain their religious traditions and practices. Indeed, throughout the Pomak region and elsewhere in Bulgaria men and women reembraced the religions that they had practiced prior to 1945 or in the early communist years. But these populations tended to be older, and their return to traditional Hanafi practices could not explain why the younger Pomaks in Madan, Rudozem, and Smolyan were latching onto imported interpretations of Islam promoted by new nongovernmental organizations (NGOs) such as the Union for Islamic Development and Culture (UIDC). Proponents of these imported versions of the faith claimed that Bulgarian Islam was corrupted by forbidden innovations. Indeed, this was part of the draw of the new Islams: young people specifically wanted to distance themselves from what they deemed the incorrect practices of their elders and thus claim superiority over them. The young gained a newfound authority from the presumed purity of their own practices, adapted "directly from Arabia," the birthplace of Islam.

Finally, there were Pomak villages spread throughout the Rhodope, and while it was true that their inhabitants were becoming more religious than the Turks of Bulgaria, it remained unclear why the two largest postsocialist mosques in Bulgaria were built in Madan and Rudozem and not in other parts of the Rhodope where Pomaks lived. Some Pomaks embraced a Turkish identity, and others converted to Christianity or remained staunch atheists like Silvi and Iordan. But why were those who chose to reach out to the newly imported forms of Islam concentrated in just a few cities when the larger Bulgarian society seemed to be moving away from organized religion in general? And although intergenerational conflicts are apparent, the youth population here was not significantly greater than in other regions. All of the reasons discussed above play an important part in setting the stage for our story, but there are other factors as well.

One crucial factor, unique to these communities, was the collapse of the lead-zinc mining enterprise and the massive male unemployment that followed in its wake. Because miners, and especially lead and zinc miners, had been among the most respected and best-paid workers in the entire Bulgarian communist economy, the dominance of this industry had shaped the construction of masculine identities in this region more than perhaps any other external factor. The social project of communism had asked men and women to radically reshape existing conceptions of family, particularly in Muslim regions of the country, where patriarchal gender roles were deeply entrenched. Under communism, men were encouraged to allow women to leave the home, obtain formal education, and take up employment in the public sphere, but this solution to what the communists called the "woman question" was not about women's rights or about their individual fulfillment or personal emancipation. Instead, the dramatic change in women's roles between 1946 and 1989 was seen as a

collective sacrifice that both men and women had to make for the good
of society. Women's labor was required to realize communist industrialization, and their legal equality with men (although only theoretical) was
considered the hallmark of a modern society.

In her study of women healers in Saudi Arabia, Eleanor Abdella Doumato[51] argues that it was Muslim women who lost out the most in the
Wahhabi reforms. This was not because the Wahabbi reformers targeted
women's practice of Islam specifically, because men also participated in
these "heterodox" rituals. But as the focus of Muslim spirituality began
to center exclusively on the mosque, women were excluded from this new
space and became increasingly isolated. Thus, women lost power and
public presence in the process of reforming "heterodox" Islam to make it
conform to what the Wahhabis imagined to be a more "orthodox" interpretation of the religion. Similarly in Bulgaria, there are important gender
repercussions of the shift to more "orthodox" interpretations of Islam
that must not be ignored. But the importance of gender as an analytical
category is not only in the realm of effects. In the Bulgarian context, I
will argue that shifting definitions of masculinity and femininity might be
one important factor fueling the post-1989 embrace of these new forms
of Islam.

With the closing of the mines came a crisis in the way men and women
understood their place in the local system of gender relations. In many
families after the mid-1990s, men who had been miners stayed home
while women went out to work in the garment factories. For the first time,
wives had to give their husbands spending money. Some families just sank
into poverty because neither husband nor wife could find work; others
scratched out a living by growing their own food and collecting their own
wood. Men turned to alcohol and spent what little pensions they had on
rakiya. In many ways, the emergence of a more "orthodox" form of Islam
in Madan also promoted the idea that existing gender relations would
have to be arranged for the greater good of the community, a discourse
that was very familiar and perhaps had appeal following the gender role
reversals that accompanied the closure of GORUBSO. This new ideology
was supported by a generous availability of Islamic aid from abroad.
These were resources dedicated to helping Muslim communities find their
way back to the "true" Islam, an Islam which imagined a different gender
system than the one previously established in these rural cities during the
communist era. Gender instability, at a time of political and economic
tumult, may be one important, and often overlooked, factor in helping to
explain why "orthodox" Islam began to take root in this region and not
in other Pomak or Muslim communities throughout Bulgaria.

Furthermore, Islamic discourses of social justice[52] and community may
resonate differently in societies shaped by social-democratic systems ver-

sus those once engineered by Marxist-Leninism. I also want to explore
what happens to Islam when it enters a post-Marxist space, and how it is
shaped by the historical realities of protocapitalism in a country that by
2008 had still not reached the standard of living it had once enjoyed under
communism. In this interstitial Bulgarian limbo between two seemingly
contradictory economic systems, it is important to look for continuities
between the newly imported Islamic theologies and familiar, old communist ideologies. Both epistemologies share a moral challenge to the ex-
cesses of kleptocratic capitalism. Both place communities over individuals,
and both share a totalizing metanarrative of social justice. This is not to
say that Islam in Bulgaria has merely replaced Marxism, but only that its
discourses may be picked up and mobilized by post-Marxist subjects in
unique and interesting ways that demand further exploration.

And this would not be the first historical moment wherein Islam and
Marxism find themselves in dialogue with each other. In examining the
modern condition of Central Asian Muslims, the historian Adeeb Khalid
reminds his readers to not forget the important continuities between these
two seemingly opposed metanarratives, pointing out that even the early
Muslim Brothers found much inspiration in the success of the Russian
Revolution: "the political goals of Islamist movements owe a great deal,
in their formulation, to modern revolutionary ideologies, and to Marxist-
Leninism in particular. During the Cold War, Islamists tended to be rabidly
anticommunist in their stance because communism was a rival ideology,
one that rested on universal principles and was hostile to all religion
besides. That stance should not blind us, however, to the fascination that
Marxist-Leninism had for Islamists and the model it provided for successful political action."[53] In the Bulgarian context, the general cultural
memory of life under communism cannot be ignored, especially since
a growing number of Muslims have come to feel nostalgia for an economic system they believe to have offered more material security, despite
its recognized political disadvantages. The dynamic interaction between
these two ideologies provided a fascinating window onto the situation in
Bulgaria in the dawning years of the twenty-first century.

The case of the Pomaks in the Central Rhodope demonstrates that the
influence of "orthodox" Islam in this postsocialist country is not just another manifestation of a general European trend but has its own unique
set of circumstances and justifications, different from those in the French,
German, or British contexts. Thus, although social scientists and policy-
makers often want to find one or two generally applicable and empirically
demonstrable reasons why traditional Muslim communities are pursuing
new avenues in the practice of Islam, local political and economic contexts
cannot be ignored when trying to determine how people find their faith
in an era of rapid social change.

Understanding Faith in Context

I would like to make clear that I am not arguing that all spirituality is economically determined. I am, however, proposing that it would be erroneous to examine questions of faith and growing religiosity divorced from their social, political, historical, and economic contexts. It is perhaps important here to point out that I did not set out to study Islam, and indeed, beyond my own personal experience as the daughter of a "cultural" Muslim,[54] I came to the field with only a general knowledge of Islamic belief and practice. My initial intention was to begin research on the development of rural tourism in Bulgaria. The Rhodope was the ideal setting for this endeavor, with its natural beauty and geographic proximity to Greece. But one conversation would set me on the path to a very different project.

In the summer of 2004, a woman from the town of Devin was describing the prospects for rural tourism development in a small village with a mixed population of Christians and Muslims. Things had been going quite well there, she said, "until they built the mosque." Apparently, a brand new mosque had been constructed in the center of the village, and many residents (both Christian and Muslim) were upset because they believed it had driven the tourists away into "quieter" villages. "Who wants to wake up at five o'clock in the morning to the hodzha shouting from the minaret?" she explained.

Once I started asking about them, I found that new mosques were appearing in many villages throughout the Rhodope, some of them quite impoverished. No one really cared where the money was coming from, because the local men were only too happy to have work for a few months while the mosques were under construction. In some villages, the local Christians were up in arms. In other villages, it was the hodzhas who tried to fight the new mosques once the local preachers realized that new imams from outside of their communities would staff them. In Trigrad, an innkeeper explained that the conflicts were being fueled by money from abroad. While the hodzhas supported themselves by collecting contributions from local Muslims, the imams were giving money away—promising jobs, education, and travel abroad to frustrated youth tired of poverty and unemployment. Older Muslims were suspicious of the new mosques and their seemingly endless resources, but the young were easily swayed. Families were being torn apart by conflicting allegiances to old and new, or "right" and "wrong," ways of being Muslim. This innkeeper placed great hope in the ability of a thriving local tourist industry to provide work for the young and bring her community together again.

It was around this time that the mayor of Madan announced that he would try to develop mining tourism to revive his city's ailing economy.

When I arrived there in June of 2005, there was indeed much talk about developing some kind of tourism in light of a new border checkpoint with Greece to be opened less than twenty kilometers to the south. But little was being done. There was also a gigantic new mosque, larger than any of the others I had seen in the Rhodope, and a significant number of women dressed in what I would later come to refer to as the "Arab style." I did in fact begin my fieldwork doing interviews with local officials about tourism and the potential use of EU funds, but the longer I stayed in Madan the more I realized that there was something unique going on in the region, a resurgence of Islam that would eventually put Madan, and the nearby cities of Rudozem and Smolyan, in the national spotlight when two teenage girls insisted on wearing their Islamic headscarves to public school in the summer of 2006. Thus, as is often the case with ethnography, where research questions are reshaped by the shifting contours and unpredictable rhythms of everyday life, I went into the field with the intention of studying one thing but emerged from it having studied something entirely different.

Research for this book was carried out between June 2005 and August 2008, a period during which I spent a cumulative total of thirteen months conducting fieldwork in both the Rhodope and the Bulgarian capital city of Sofia. In addition to participant observation and countless informal interviews with Muslim religious leaders and laypeople, I spoke with Bulgarian politicians, public officials, and members of local nongovernmental organizations concerned with protecting religious freedoms and the rights of ethnic minorities. Over the three years that I conducted this research, I also amassed a rare collection of publications produced by and for the Bulgarian Muslim community. These books, brochures, newsletters, and magazines were usually only for sale through the local mosques and very few of them could be found in bookstores or libraries. I was also an avid reader of several Bulgarian Muslim websites, particularly the Islam-bg website (before the government took it down in March 2007). It was in these publications that debates about defending traditional Islam from the incursions of the new interpretations played out, and that the justifications for new Islamic practices were promoted. Thorough discourse analysis of these sources enriched my participant observation. Finally, in order to attempt to make sense of the complicated web of foreign funding supporting local Muslim NGOs and to find connections between different Muslim organizations in the country, I made extensive use of Bulgarian public tax records and the legal documents used to register commercial firms and nonprofit organizations.

What emerges from this research is an in-depth case study of a cluster of Muslim cities and villages in the south-central part of the Rhodope Mountains. But in order to understand the wide spectrum of factors influencing local events, I have also spent some time describing the national political and economic context of Bulgaria after the collapse of communism in 1989, as well as the rise of the international Islamic charitable establishment and its influence on Muslim communities in the Balkans following the Bosnian War.

In chapter 1, we meet Silvi's husband, Iordan and explore the ways that ordinary Bulgarian-speaking Muslims lived during the communist period. In order to understand why "orthodox" Islam has taken root among the Pomaks but not among the ethnic Turks of Bulgaria, it is essential to examine in detail the continually contested history of the Pomaks as an ethnic group. Understanding this history also helps to make sense of the communists' efforts to modernize the Pomaks and to return them to the Bulgarian national fold. The rural-industrialization program that built cities like Madan and nearby Rudozem was part of a larger plan to limit the lingering influence of Islam.

Chapter 2 begins with a walk through the Mining Museum, and here the tale of GORUBSO, Bulgaria's lead-zinc–producing behemoth, is retold, in addition to how the proletarianization of the previously peasant labor force reshaped local definitions of appropriate masculinity and femininity to meet the needs of rapid modernization and rural industrialization. The long and tortured demise of GORUBSO and how the miners became pawns in a power struggle between Bulgaria's new political elites is explored. The rise and fall of the lead-zinc mining enterprise is unique to this region, and new "orthodox" Islamic discourses began to take root in these communities around the same time that local social and economic relations were turned upside-down by the massive unemployment that followed GORUBSO's implosion.

The devastating effects of the privatization and liquidation of the lead-zinc mines on the individual lives of the men, women, and children of Madan is the subject of chapter 3. At exactly the historical moment when previously well-off families were plunged into unexpected poverty, religious workers from around the world who promised both aid and salvation targeted Bulgarians. In this chapter, we meet a host of individuals from Madan, including Donka, a woman working two jobs and making just enough to buy six loaves of bread to fill the stomachs of her unemployed, alcoholic husband and her two teenage sons. During this period, many were struggling to survive the demise of communism and its ideological commitments to protect the working classes. Some of them, like a young Muslim woman named Hana, reached out to new interpretations of Islam that brought comfort and happiness into their lives.

Chapter 4 briefly takes us away from Madan to explore the wider social, political, and economic context within which recent events in Bulgaria are embedded. I examine the changes that occurred in Bulgaria after 1989 and hone in on the internal structures and power dynamics of Bulgaria's Muslim denomination. I look at the rivalries over the leadership of the Muslim community and how different factions emerged in the 1990s. This history of the Muslim leadership will be essential to understanding how foreign Islamic aid became so influential in the Bulgarian-speaking Muslim communities in and around Madan, Smolyan, and Rudozem.

Chapter 5 begins with a lecture I attended in Madan—"Islam: Pluralism and Dialogue"—sponsored by a local Muslim nongovernmental organization that was a proponent of what many locals called the "new ways." Here, I investigate the influence on the Balkans of "orthodox" Islamic aid after the outbreak of the Bosnian War in 1992. Specifically, I explore how rifts in the Muslim community created a competition for resources, which opened the doors to Saudi and Kuwaiti funds and the "orthodox" version of Islam promoted by both charities and individuals from these states. This chapter is essential to understanding how local Muslim reformers were able to harness resources from international Islamic charities, resources that allowed them to promote their message through an increasing number of publications and public events aimed at displacing Bulgaria's traditional forms of Islam.

The wealthy shopkeeper Higyar helped me focus specifically on the issue of headscarves and the changing gender expectations in Madan and the surrounding areas. In chapter 6, I examine the arguments of the women who follow the "new ways" despite a history of relative gender equality in the region produced by decades of communist rule. Islamic publications promoting new forms of dress and behavior for women help demonstrate the kinds of discourse deployed by those who would promote "purer" forms of Islam among the Pomaks in Madan and the surrounding regions. Here we can see the replacement of traditional Islam with "orthodox" Islam most obviously, as locally defined ideas about the proper place of women in society are reshaped by imported Islamic discourses.

In the concluding chapter, I will reexamine the larger theoretical question of why "orthodox" Islam, in particular, appealed to Bulgarian Muslims, and why it appealed to them at precisely this moment in their history. The Bulgarian case study can help us understand two overlapping geographies: Western Europe and Eastern Europe (or what is increasingly becoming known as "Eurasia"—the former communist world stretching from Eastern Europe to the Sea of Japan). Both of these geopolitical constructs were significantly impacted by the collapse of communism and the subsequent gutting of command economies, communist states, Marxist ideologies, and their explicit (if only theoretical) commitments to social equality. The immediate postsocialist period opened up an intellectual window onto how capitalism would be built in communist societies that had had no previous experience of it and how it might be modified by the almost fifty-year (in the USSR, seventy-year) experiment with Marxist-Leninism.

As late as 1999, the philosopher Slavoj Žižek proposed that out of the ashes of communism would rise a new social and economic system, created by those who had lived under both capitalism and communism and intimately knew their advantages and disadvantages.[55] But by 2008, the hope for the emergence of what he had called a new "SECOND way" seemed occluded by the incorporation of many of the former communist states into the political project of the European Union. As the EU became more concerned with its internal relations with Muslim minorities, concerns for social equality were trumped by widespread worry about the failures of cultural assimilation.

Thus, it is very important to recognize that the changing practices of the Bulgarian-speaking Muslims are but one part of a larger trend that includes a general proliferation of Islamic literature and culture throughout the world, despite the worldwide increase in Islamophobia that has followed in the wake of the terrorist attacks of 11 September 2001. I examine the possibility that these new forms of Islam are becoming the oppositional discourse of choice among those frustrated by their continued exclusion from the wealth and privileges generated for increasingly remote elites of global capitalism. I investigate what on the surface seem to be striking similarities between Muslim theology and Marxism in Bulgaria, with their communalist challenges to the logics of neoliberalism and individualism.

But the possibilities of a universalist Islam are different in Western Europe than they are in postsocialist contexts. In the absence of a secular ideology that addresses the inequalities and injustices of the way (Mafia) capitalism has been built in Bulgaria, religion, and specifically a denationalized form of universalist Islam, may provide people with a new kind of internationalist metanarrative that helps them challenge the pervasive immorality of a world based on the most ruthless interpretations of survival of the fittest and neoliberalism. Whatever promises capitalism and democracy held out in the early 1990s, they have been lost in the fetid cesspool of murder, racketeering, theft, embezzlement, corruption, money grubbing, and power grabbing by the country's unscrupulous political and economic elites, leading many to look back with fondness and nostalgia to the moral absolutes of the totalitarian past. Olivier Roy and Gilles Kepel both propose that Islam in the Western European context is being individualized, secularized, and democratized by its contact with liberal multicultural societies. If this is true in France, Germany, Spain, and the United Kingdom, then perhaps in the former communist world, and in Bulgaria specifically, Islam may become "postsocialized" by its contact with societies shaped by decades of communist rule. Latching on to new

Islamic discourse may provide men and women with the tools for a revived critique of capitalism, consumerism, and exploitative relations of production, a language of morality and abstinence to transcend the crass materialism of the free market.

One task of this book is to understand how Islam's contact with differing social, cultural, political, and economic influences shapes the inner contours of its own logic in unique and unexpected ways. This is not to relegate religion to its hackneyed status as the "opiate of the masses," only to point out that the masses are still there, with or without their opiates, and they coopt and subvert religious discourses in a wide variety of ways. In the current polarizing geopolitical climate that pits Islam against the West in an apocalyptic clash of civilizations, the much more complicated worldviews of ordinary people too often fall by the wayside.

In Madan, what really mattered to most people was how to mitigate the worst social blows dealt by the so-called invisible hand of the market. Since the "visible fist"[56] of the working class no longer had any clout, the only resource, at least for the time being, may have been the invisible finger of God.

Chapter One

Names to Be Buried With

IORDAN THOUGHT FREQUENTLY about his own death. This was not because he was afraid to die. This was because he did not know what would happen to his remains when he did. Because of his name and who his parents were, no one in Madan would bury him. Iordan was a Pomak, and his name was changed when he was sixteen years old. He was born with the Turkish name Fikret, not because he was a Turk, but because his parents lived in a village near the Turkish minority region and they liked the name. As a child Fikret spent his days helping his mother string tobacco leaves to dry and tending to his parents' sheep. But the communists had plans for him; they intended to tear him from the tobacco and make him "modern."

Fikret became "Iordan," a good Bulgarian name. He was sent away to school to learn a trade, to join in the economic development of Madan and the building of the "bright socialist future." As Iordan, he did his apprenticeships, earned his certificates, went to the army for his two years of mandatory military service, got married, had two sons, bought his own apartment, and worked for over fifteen years for the state mining enterprise until communism's sudden and unexpected collapse in 1989. All of his documents—his national I.D. card, his driver's license, his diplomas, his military discharge, his marriage certificate, the birth certificates of his sons, the deed to his apartment, his pension card, his medical records, his bank accounts—were all under the name Iordan. After more than thirty years of being Iordan, he had almost forgotten that he was ever Fikret.

But no one would bury him if he remained Iordan.

He ran a tanned and weathered hand through his thick white hair, shaking his head. He had just returned from the nearby city of Zlatograd, where he recently found work fixing cement trucks for a large construction job. His blue overalls were covered with oil and dust, and his shoulders were slumped over with exhaustion. A former classmate of his had died that day, and Iordan was feeling all fifty-two years of his age. His Pomak friend had died suddenly of a heart attack. He had died with his Bulgarian name.

Although some of Iordan's former classmates and neighbors had re-
taken their original Muslim names after 1989, when it became possible to do so, the vast majority of men and women in Madan kept the
Slavic names the communists had given them. This was particularly true
for men like Iordan who were forced to leave the Rhodope after the
implosion of GORUBSO. In a society historically hostile to Turkey, it
was much easier to find work with a Bulgarian-sounding name. Since so
many Rhodope villages were mixed, prospective employers could only
tell the Muslims from the Christians by their names. There were real economic advantages to being "Iordan" rather than "Fikret," at least until he
died.

Iordan explained that the state-run mortuaries had closed in Madan,
and only the church and mosque handled the bodies of the recently de-
parted. Iordan was a Christian name, but the priest that serviced the
local Orthodox Christian Church would not bury him because Iordan
was a Muslim. Iordan was an atheist, but his parents and grandparents
were Muslims. That made Iordan a Muslim, too. The priest only buried
Christians.

The new, foreign-schooled imam in the mosque refused to bury Muslims with Christian names. Although the procedures were complicated
and it took time and money to have all the important documents in one's
life reissued under one's original name, the imam insisted that all Muslims must have a Muslim name. He would not perform funerary rites
for Pomaks who kept their Christian names. The young imam in Madan
had grown more influential with each passing year. His position was
strengthened by the funds he received from both domestic and foreign
foundations to promote a more "pure" version of Islam, one that was
not contaminated by contact with Christianity and communism. Iordan
dared not challenge him. When the time came, most likely Iordan's wife,
Silvi, would have to travel to a Turkish village to find an entrepreneur-
ial hodzha willing to perform the necessary procedures, and he would
charge a hefty fee for the service. Or Iordan could change his name. But
the bureaucracy was so cumbersome and inefficient, and the hostility to
Muslims in Bulgaria so deep-seated, that it would be easier for him to convert to Christianity, he told me, than to change his name. "And cheaper,
too."

We were sitting in Saramov's drinking draught beer. The restaurant was
having a special that was quite popular with the locals: order two large
Ariana beers and get a free plate of French fries. The evening was warm,
and we were happily munching on potatoes while we waited for Silvi
to join us for a light dinner. We were sitting at a table overlooking the
Madanska River, and I asked Iordan if he would tell me about his parents.
He drained the contents of his first glass and waved to the waitress to

bring two more. I wiggled the fingers on my right hand, preparing to take detailed notes while also enjoying the tasty Bulgarian brew. Iordan stared for a while at a dark age spot on the back of his left wrist, scratching at it tentatively with a blunt fingernail, underneath which there was still the visible trace of black machine grease. I guessed that he was trying to figure out where to begin.

Although the details of Iordan's upbringing are unique to him, his life story is quite typical of many men of his generation, men who were born in the late 1950s in the villages surrounding what the communists would make into the city of Madan. The Rhodope region had always been poor compared to other parts of Bulgaria, until GORUBSO was founded and the communists launched an ambitious project of rural industrialization.

Fikret was born in 1956 in a small village in one of the most rural parts of the municipality of Madan. He was the seventh of nine children and lived in an extended household that included a total of twenty-nine, counting his grandparents, uncles, aunts, and cousins. His earliest memories were of sharp, persistent pains in his stomach and the dizziness and disorientation that inevitably followed long periods of hunger. "When I ate, I ate with my hands and swallowed large pieces of bread without chewing. I ate fast so that my older brothers could not take my food. We were like animals, and my mother prohibited us from going to visit the homes of other children because we did not know how to behave around food."

All of his brothers and sisters had to work for the family to survive. "My older brothers cut wood and my sisters helped my mother with the tobacco. My job was to take the sheep down to the river in the morning and in the evening, and to help my mother. When I came back with the sheep, there would always be a big basket of [tobacco] leaves for me to string. We were always stringing."

Fikret and his family called themselves Pomaks, a local term he specifically used to distinguish Bulgarian-speaking from Turkish-speaking Muslims. He believed that his ancestors were Bulgarian Christians who converted to Islam or married into Muslim families during the Ottoman period, and this was the generally accepted view among most Madanchani. But there were competing histories, and understanding these contested origins is the first step in making sense of the unique ethnic identity crisis that faced the Madan Pomaks in the post-1989 era. Because the new "orthodox" Islam took root largely among the Pomak population, it is important to untangle who the Pomaks thought they were and how their Muslim identities were shaped and changed by their experiences under communism. Debates about Pomak identity continue to have real world bearing on the lives of individual Pomaks like Iordan, and so it is essential to explore them in some depth, even if it means leaving the beer and French fries for a few pages.

Who Are the Pomaks?

The entire territory that now includes modern Bulgaria fell to the invading Ottomans in 1396, and the region was part of the Ottoman Empire for the better part of five centuries. By most accounts, Islam followed the conquering Ottoman armies, having already undergone many mutations and modifications in its long journey from Arabia to Anatolia and evolving still further as it moved, eventually, into the Balkans.[1] When Ottoman Islam arrived in Bulgaria, it was already quite distinct and more amenable to local Christian traditions.[2] This led to the rise of various forms of "folk Islam" that were based on Islamic principles but blended with Christian and pagan practices. Various Sufi mystical orders also spread throughout the country.[3]

In part because of the wide variety of religions represented in their territories, the Ottomans instituted the *millet* system, a kind of religious federalism. Under this system, each confessional community was subject to the autonomous rule of an "ethnarch" or denominational leader.[4] There were four millets officially recognized under the Ottomans: Muslim, "Rum" (Christian), Jewish, and Armenian. All Christians save the Armenians[5] were lumped together into one millet, no matter how vast their ethnic or linguistic diversity. Similarly, all Muslims were considered part of the Muslim millet, whether they were Sunnis, Shi'as, Sufis, or former Christians that had converted to Islam. Members of this millet had the highest status in society and enjoyed many privileges, particularly with regard to taxation.

Despite the diversity of Islam in the Balkans, it is important to remember that Islam in some form has been present there for at least six hundred years. The first Muslims in Bulgaria are believed to have been nomadic Turkmen stockbreeders who moved their herds into the Rhodope after the Ottoman Empire had done away with internal borders.[6] They were followed by Turkish settlers from Anatolia. The descendants of these Turkish settlers today make up the largest group of Muslims in Bulgaria. There was, however, an indigenous population living in the Rhodope Mountains before the Turks arrived, and it is generally argued that some of them were either forcibly converted or voluntarily accepted Islam in the centuries that followed. The ethnic identity of this population and the process of their conversion remains highly contested both by historians and by ordinary people. These unsettled historical debates may have made the Pomaks vulnerable to both Arab and Turkish foreign influences, as well as making them the ongoing targets of Protestant evangelism and Christian Orthodox attempts at (re)assimilation.

The only two relatively uncontested facts are that the Pomaks (who go by different names in different countries) are a Bulgarian-speaking people who profess the Muslim faith. Today they are spread out among five nation-states: Bulgaria, Greece, Macedonia, Turkey, and Albania, with by far the largest number concentrated in Bulgaria. Each of the countries tries to claim this group as their own, and the matter of ethnicity is taken very seriously in a region where national boundaries were historically fixed by the ideals of ethnic self-determination. The Pomaks in Greece live on the other side of the border from the Bulgarian Pomaks and speak a Slavic language that is essentially the same Bulgarian dialect spoken in Madan and Rudozem. The Greeks argue that the Pomaks are descendants of the Thracians (an ancient people who inhabited the Rhodope before the Slavs) who gradually intermarried with their Greek neighbors. These Thracian Greeks were then Slavicized and Islamicized during the course of the Ottoman period.[7] Some Turkish scholars claim that the Pomaks are the descendants of Kuman Turks who settled in the Balkans before the Ottoman conquest and who were linguistically Slavicized by their daily contact with the Bulgarian Christian population.[8] The Macedonians believe that the Pomaks are ethnic Macedonians who were forced to convert to Islam by the Turks. Another theory is that the Pomaks are a distinct ethnicity of their own, unrelated to any of the other peoples in the region, who speak Bulgarian because of regular contact with Christian Bulgarians.[9]

One controversial theory holds that the Pomaks descend from a group of the Prophet Mohammed's most loyal followers, who were charged with spreading Islam beyond the Middle East. Some of these missionaries supposedly settled in the Balkans in the seventh century and were eventually Slavicized by intermarriage with local Slavic women.[10] In other versions, the Pomaks are the descendants of Arab traders or of exiled sectarian leaders.[11] These theories all share the thesis that the Pomaks were already Muslims before the Turks arrived. The historian Maria Todorova has argued that "this Arabic origin theory for the Pomaks was imported directly by Muslim missionaries sent from Saudi Arabia, Libya, and Pakistan,"[12] and the ethnologist Tsvetana Georgieva found that the "proof" of this theory in the Rhodope came usually in the form of an inscription found on a local tombstone or mosque by a visiting Arab missionary, which then disappeared.[13] Her informants told her that "they wanted the terms *Arabs* and *Pomaks* to become identical so that they could rely on the Arab community for protection."[14] In Madan and Rudozem, this theory was the topic of two books circulated through the local mosques, one in 1999 and one in 2006.

In my own interviews with local Muslim leaders and laypeople in the Rhodope, I also encountered various versions of this theory that the Pomaks were Arabs. In March 2007, the regional mufti (Muslim leader) of Smolyan explained that Islam had come to the Rhodope before the Turks, and that the reason that the communists had destroyed all of the old Muslim graveyards was because the tombstones had dates on them that proved this to be true.[15] "Islam came to this region directly from Arabia," he said. When I asked him if it was possible that the Thracians had been Muslims, he merely answered, "Why not?"

This idea was also to be found in *The History of the Pomaks*, a book written by a local businessman in Madan but allegedly published and distributed with support from a Saudi foundation.

> I believe that the Pomaks are an Arabic minority that settled in the Rhodopes because of Byzantine policies responding to the increased strength of the Slavs to the north. Byzantium had a long-term policy of settling Arabs along its northern borders and moving Slavs to the Near East, since the Arab *Halifat* was dominant in the Mediterranean for 500 years after the appearance of Islam . . . That is how the Muslim community that lived in the Rhodopes in the 7th and 8th centuries was formed.[16]

The most accepted argument among scholars for the origin of the Pomaks, however, is that they were ethnically Slavic, Bulgarian-speaking Christians who adopted Islam.[17] During the socialist period, historians and ethnologists amassed extensive evidence in support of this thesis,[18] but because the communists had funded this research to pursue their nationalist agenda, contemporary scholars have questioned its objectivity. Despite the continuing academic debates, however, this theory was the dominant belief of people like Iordan and the theory preferred by Bulgarians as a whole.[19] The big issue within this school is whether the conversions were forced and mass or voluntary and individual. Those who believe the former propose that the Ottoman authorities gave their new subjects the choice between conversion and death, and that entire villages were Islamicized in order to avoid a massacre. This argument also tends to focus on the understandable Christian aversion to the Ottoman "blood tax," whereby the sons of Christian families were taken by the Ottomans and trained to become an elite corps of Janissary troops fiercely loyal to the sultan. While some scholars[20] and many Bulgarians still believe in the mass conversion theory (which was actively promoted by communist propaganda before 1989),[21] many recent studies have called into question the historiographic evidence that supported these claims.[22]

Bulgarian historians, using archival materials from Russian, Western European, and Ottoman sources, now tend to promote the idea that the

Pomaks' conversion to Islam was made willingly, for political and economic reasons. After all, only a small percentage of the Bulgarian population converted to Islam, and they were concentrated mostly in one geographic area: the Rhodope Mountains. Evgeni Radushev, in his careful analysis of Ottoman tax registers, proposes that both geographic and material reasons lay behind the Pomak conversion. He argues that since the Pomaks lived in mountainous areas, their access to fertile lands was limited and agricultural production was two to three times lower than that of Bulgarians who lived in the plains and piedmont areas in the sixteenth, seventeenth, and eighteenth centuries. Furthermore, because members of the Christian millet were taxed at much higher rates than those in the Muslim millet throughout the empire, the Ottoman tax system was particularly detrimental to mountain-dwelling populations, which faced severe food shortages once they paid their tributes. Radushev argues that the Christian standard of living in the Rhodope Mountains was roughly two times lower than that of Muslim households, and that this disparity in living standards accounts for the concentration of conversions to Islam in the mountainous areas where most of the Pomaks continue to live to this day: "in regions where the repressive centralized economic system of the Ottomans is combined with unfavorable climactic, natural and geographic conditions, Islam easily gains new ground."[23] Thus, although they were not overtly forced to convert, the real prospect of starvation would have provided ample incentive for embracing Islam.

Even more interesting is Radushev's claim that Pomak conversions were concentrated in villages where the Ottomans had built charitable trusts (*vakif*). These complexes could include mosques, schools (*mekteb* or *medresse*), libraries, baths, or hospitals—facilities that would otherwise not have existed in impoverished rural mountain areas. The trusts would have also had access to a steady stream of resources as Ottoman notables continuously made theologically mandatory charitable (*zakat*) contributions in order to promote the spread of Islam. Radushev argues that "the waqf, with its social institutions and monumental buildings in every Balkan town and village, showed the Christian *reaya* what economic and cultural benefits it would enjoy once converted to Islam."[24] The historians Rositsa Gradeva and Svetlana Ivanova have also argued that the *vakif* and its associated institutions, as well as the Ottoman courts and "proselytizing preachers from one or another order," were important factors in Christian conversions to Islam in Bulgaria during the Ottoman period.[25]

Modern Bulgarian historians have also argued that the form of Islam adopted by this population was, from the very start, relatively lax. The historian Stoyan Raichevsky has amassed a considerable amount of archival material demonstrating the rather tenuous embrace of Islam by the Rhodope mountain dwellers during the Ottoman period; their knowledge of the Qur'an and proper Islamic ritual was weak, and they did not adequately regulate the behavior and dress of women.[26] He cites multiple Western European and Russian travelers who observed that many Bulgarian Muslims drank wine, kept their Christian names, raised swine, spoke Bulgarian, practiced monogamy, shared Christian superstitions, and did not cover or sequester their women. In one example, a group of young Pomak theologians brought a petition to the Ottoman chief of police in 1868, signed by more than a hundred Pomak imams, requesting that Bulgarian Muslims in mixed Muslim-Christian villages be allowed to behave in the manner of their neighbors. Specifically, they did not want their wives to have to cover their faces and wanted their women to accompany them to weddings and other village festivities.[27]

The origin and conversion of the Pomaks became unimportant, however, when the Ottoman Empire finally began to fall apart in the late nineteenth century. Bulgaria officially obtained its independence in 1878, and the territory that included the Rhodope was incorporated into the still new Bulgarian state in 1912. At that time, the Bulgarian-speaking population of the Rhodope was thought to consist of Bulgarians who had been forcefully converted to Islam. In 1912 and 1913, the government launched a massive campaign to rebaptize the Pomaks and give them Christian names.[28] The Pomaks resisted these attempts vigorously, and a subsequent government reversed the policy of forced Christianization. In the 1930s, young Pomak intellectuals in the southern city of Smolyan founded a new organization called Rodina, whose stated goal was to increase the Bulgarian ethnic awareness of the Pomaks while also supporting their Muslim identity.[29] This organization was responsible for creating Pomak educational institutions separate from those serving the Turkish population.[30] Rodina tried to create an appropriate form of Islam for the Pomaks, one that did not undermine their Bulgarian national identity. The organization introduced Bulgarian translations of the Qur'an, and use of Arabic in religious services was discouraged in favor of Bulgarian.

Rodina also wanted to modernize those Pomaks who held on to what were considered "backward customs," and in particular to improve the position of Pomak women. They actively sought to stop the practice of circumcision and the wearing of traditional Muslim garments: fezzes for men and headscarves and *shalvari* (baggy Turkish trousers) for women. These campaigns culminated in another attempt to Bulgarianize (though not Christianize) the names of the Pomaks in 1942. This second campaign was more successful than the first. Thus, even before the communists came to power in Bulgaria, Islam among the Pomaks had undergone significant changes, with many of the more "Eastern" customs weeded out of daily Muslim practice. The communists classified Rodina as a fascist organization and reversed the name-changing policy once again, but it only took a few years before they too felt the need to (re)integrate the Bulgarian Muslims into the national (now communist) fold by convincing them of their indisputable Bulgarian origins.

The communists not only targeted the Slavic Muslims for assimilation, but also set out to limit the influence of all religions, including Orthodox Christianity. The government embraced a Marxist worldview with a dogmatic rejection of religion. Marx believed that religion blinded the people to the material deprivation of their lives with promises of a heavenly reward in exchange for submission to the exploitative relations of production in this world. Spiritual desires were considered anathema to socialist projects for modernization.

In the first years after the Second World War, however, the Bulgarian communists were busy consolidating power. All religious populations, including the Pomaks, enjoyed a short time of relative noninterference in their spiritual affairs.[31] During this period, the government formalized the separation of Turkish and Pomak religious institutions that had been started before the war. The Pomak and Turkish Muslims were to have different religious leaders, schools, and mosques so that Islam could not be used to forge a shared ethno-religious identity between the two groups, which might pose a threat to the integrity of the Bulgarian state if Turkish populations tried to secede and join Turkey. This formal division only reinforced a division that already existed in practice; Turks and Pomaks were clustered in separate villages, where the local hodzhas and imams spoke either Turkish or Bulgarian.

As I drank the light, pleasant lager with Iordan, I listened carefully to his recollections of the past and saw that many of his childhood memories of the practice of Islam in his village coincided with the historical narratives. Few men in his village had read the Qur'an; most relied solely on the local Muslim leader, the hodzha, to interpret it for them. Although they did not keep swine, his father and the older men ate pork, drank *rakiya*, and married only one wife. The women carried small rolls of paper with Arabic words written on them by the hodzha for health, wealth, and good luck, and many of them made the pilgrimage to worship at the grave of a Muslim "saint" in Smolyan. For his part, Fikret memorized one or two lines in Arabic from the Qur'an but no longer remembered what they were or what they meant. The only thing Fikret/Iordan remembered was that stealing was absolutely forbidden. This was drilled into him from a young age, and the fear of God's punishment was used to frighten all of his brothers and sisters. But other than that, he could not recall learning anything more specific about Islamic teachings.

Eight years before Fikret was born, state repression against religious institutions had begun in earnest. The 1949 passage of the Law on Religious Denominations gave the communist state complete control over all spiritual affairs in Bulgaria.[32] During the years that followed, the government closed down all religious educational establishments and confiscated Church and *vakif* (Islamic charitable trust) properties. International Muslim, Catholic, and Jewish organizations were banned from opening missions or charity institutions in Bulgaria, and foreigners were forbidden from leading services in Bulgarian mosques, synagogues, and churches. The 1949 law saw the creation of a Department of Religious Denominations, which had the power to supervise and regulate almost all religious activities in Bulgaria and to censor any religious literature published there.[33]

Despite their distaste for religion, however, the communists did not abolish the existing religious structures; they subverted them instead for their own causes. Both the Orthodox Christian and the traditional Muslim religious establishments were heavily infiltrated by communist appointees and for the most part cooperated with the government. The Chief Muftiship (the spiritual authority for Muslims in Bulgaria) and the sixteen regional muftiships were considered useful tools in spreading the message of communism to Bulgaria's Muslim minorities. Local imams and hodzhas were also recruited.[34] In addition, the communists combined their propaganda with an aggressive form of "affirmative action" where Pomak children, especially girls, were given preferential treatment in admissions to prestigious secondary schools and universities in the hopes that access to higher education would more quickly integrate them into Bulgarian society.[35] Transcripts from early communist hearings on the question of the "Bulgarian Mohammedans" demonstrate that education was the weapon of choice against "religious fanaticism"; extensive efforts were made to train a local intelligentsia that could then take responsibility in the further integration of the Bulgarian Muslim population.[36]

With a change in the communist leadership in 1956, the government committed itself to quickening the pace of modernization and focused even more fervently on the eradication of "backward" traditions and beliefs among Muslims. The state production of anti-Islamic propaganda and the active recruitment of Pomak cadres were systematized and intensified throughout the 1960s and 1970s. Every aspect of life was targeted, as historian Mary Neuburger explains, "The total collectivization of agriculture and the cultural revolution that accompanied it focused on the material base which theoretically determined the superstructure of Muslim consciousness. Every material thing that Muslims touched, wore, ate and slept on—as well as the names that labeled and defined them—had to embody socialist advancement in order for progress to permeate their consciousness."[37]

In Fikret's village, this meant a new school and a communist schoolteacher. Fikret's mother was not happy when the communists built the primary school in the village. Before, it was easy not to send the children to school because the nearest one was too far for them to walk to. But then a small school was placed right in the center of the village; a notice was posted saying that it was now mandatory for all children, boys and girls, over the age of six to attend school. When the authorities realized that few people in the village could read, they sent a young man in a police uniform to all of the houses to tell the parents that the school would teach the children how to read and write and how to calculate. Fikret remembered that the man also said the students would be given lunch. At first, most of the people in the village did not send their children to school, but then the young man in the uniform came around again and told them that each family would be fined one sheep for each child who was not sent. When the big olive-green truck came to collect three sheep from one of Fikret's neighbors, he and his brothers and sisters were finally sent to school.

Although he liked going to school, Fikret recalled that he was always falling asleep in class. Once he started his lessons, he had to wake up at 4:00 a.m. and take the sheep to the river with his older brother. He would come back and string tobacco for a while before going to school, where the only thing he remembered learning was how to eat with a fork and spoon. In the afternoon, he went back to the river with the sheep. It was usually too dark when he got home for him to practice reading. Sometimes he could share a candle with his older sister, but usually he just strung tobacco leaves until he fell asleep. As a result, he never really did well at his lessons. "If I had different parents, I could have been a great man. But I was born the way I was. I am an *obiknoven rabotnik* [ordinary worker]. I wish I had more schooling. But I have a mind and an opinion, and I did well for who my parents were and where I started."

About the time the school was opened, some communists from Madan came to their village asking the men if they wanted to work in the mines. They came to explain about building communism and how they were going to make everyone rich and give them electricity and bring the water from the river into their homes. Fikret recollected that the local hodzha told the men in the village that only *gyauri* (unbelievers), or non-Muslims, worked underground and that it was forbidden for Muslim men to take jobs in the mines. But the communists offered wages. Fikret's father did not like the hodzha, who regularly collected money from the villages to support his study of the Qur'an, so he and two of Fikret's older brothers were among the first volunteers for the mines. Many other Muslim families followed them.

Life for Fikret and his family began to change after that; he remembered not being so hungry. Although he was never a good student, Fikret graduated from the eighth grade. He learned how to read and write and calculate, just as the communists had promised. Fikret was proud when

Figure 6 A postcard showing the village of Madan in the 1950s

he read the party newspapers to his parents at night under the shine of the single, uncovered light bulb hanging above the table in their small kitchen. Madan was growing and changing; the mines had brought wealth and development to the region. Fikret believed that the communists had kept their promises. His village now had electricity, and regular buses brought the miners to and from the village to the now burgeoning city of Madan. True, some in the village were very upset when the hodzha was arrested and sent away because he refused to work, and others disliked the communists' disrespect for Islam. But most could not resist the tangible material benefits of modernization, especially the young.

Fikret was learning to be a miner. He did not attend the newly built academic secondary school, but his quasi-apprenticeship at the mine in Borieva guaranteed him a position there once he finished his mandatory military service. His older sister, who was at university, bought him a guitar. When he took the sheep down to the river to graze, he would strum and pick at the strings with his calloused fingers, dreaming about becoming a rich miner after he did his military service and could take up full-time employment with the state mining enterprise, GORUBSO.

"The city was full of people," Iordan explained over his beer. "There used to be two families for each apartment. At the worker's cafeteria—you used to have vouchers for meals—you always had to wait for a place. And there was always work. If a policeman saw a man sitting in a café or around on the street on a workday, he would ask him, 'Why aren't you at work?' If you had no job, he would find you one, and send you there immediately. We all had real work."

Despite these initial steps at changing the material conditions of the Pomaks' lives, the communists continued to target the areas around Madan and Rudozem as strongholds of Islam because of what they believed to be the continued influence of the hodzhas on the local population. The Pomaks paid these hodzhas to circumcise their sons, to make amulets, and to recite verses for special prayer sessions (*mevlidi*) to celebrate important occasions.[38] Men in Madan also continued to attend Friday prayers at the mosque, and Pomak women were still largely sequestered in the home. Even worse, the communists feared that the Pomaks continued to share ethnic allegiances with the Turks.[39]

In order to fight the perceived entrenchment of Bulgarian Islamic traditions in these areas, the communists mobilized teachers, medical doctors, archeologists, ethnologists, and "scientists" of all sorts with the goal of returning the Pomaks to the national fold. The activists were particularly concerned with how to deal with the Pomak women, who were seen as the deepest repositories of religious "fanaticism." Indeed, one reason that the communist government continued to target Islam was its perceived negative treatment of women. It was crucial to reeducate the Pomaks and Turks because Muslim women were seen to be the "ultimate proletariat,"[40] oppressed by both patriarchy and capitalism. While the communists ruthlessly attempted to abolish religion, they also strove to emancipate women, using a similar strategy of coercion, "affirmative action," and administrative decree.

The 1947 Georgi Dimitrov constitution of the new People's Republic of Bulgaria had been exceptionally generous in its provisions to promote the equality of the sexes. Article 3 of this constitution guaranteed women the right to vote and stand for elected office for the first time. Article 72 proclaimed:

> Women are equal with men in all spheres of public, private, economic, social, cultural and political life. . . . Equality of women is realized by guaranteeing equal right to work, equal pay, right of annual holidays, right of social security, old age pensions and [the] right to education . . . Women-mothers enjoy a special protection in terms of conditions of work. The state takes special care of mothers and children by [the] setting up of maternity hospitals, day care centers and dispensaries, women are guaranteed paid leaves from work both before and after giving birth, and free obstetrical and medical service.[41]

This constitutionally enshrined commitment to the complete equality of men and women was unprecedented in Bulgaria, and paved the way for rapid changes in women's participation in public life. From the beginning of the communist period, efforts to combat Islam were intimately bound up with projects to promote the equality of men and women.

The communist propaganda campaigns in the Rhodope reflected the priority of women's rights over religious rights. A lesson plan from 1961 demonstrates the extensive educational programs to help incorporate Pomak women into the state socialist project.[42] This outline for "forty-five day courses for Bulgarian Muslim women activists of the Fatherland Front"[43] included a variety of lectures. Four hours were dedicated to Bulgarian and world geography and four to personal hygiene for women and how socialist women should dress (without headscarves, of course). Two hours each were set aside for the "unscientific and reactionary essence of religion," "religion and the woman," and "the harm of observing religious holidays and traditions." These lectures were followed by eight hours of lectures on the "morals of the socialist family," the work of the Fatherland Front among women, the responsibilities of women activists within the Front, and the role of women in building socialism more generally. The propaganda lectures were then mixed in with more science lectures, including short primers on physics and chemistry.[44] In addition to making them more educated and productive workers, these courses were aimed at convincing Muslim women to renounce their allegiance to Islam and to embrace scientific socialism in their private as well as public lives.

The communists also published a variety of propaganda materials focusing on the improvement of living standards among the Bulgarian Muslims. One such book, published by the Bulgarian Communist Party Press in 1960, targeted the Pomaks and was filled with lectures describing the ever-improving material conditions of life in the Rhodope, complete with before and after pictures of cities like Madan and Rudozem.[45] The book also included a series of before and after cartoons that tried to visually depict socialism's superiority over Islam. One such cartoon showed a man smoking a cigarette and riding a donkey while his wife, a barefoot figure wrapped up like a mummy and carrying several large parcels, a baby, and two hoes, walks behind him. The bottom panel shows a modern woman holding the hand of a young boy with a helium balloon. She is followed by her husband who is carrying a large household appliance out of a department store[46]; socialism not only brings material progress, but improves the position of women in society. Another cartoon shows an angry-looking man in a turban standing on the balcony of a minaret and holding an open book and prayer beads. The caption reads, "Builder of Paradise in the Sky." The bottom panel shows people working together to build a modern socialist city in the mountains, and the caption reads, "Builders of Paradise on Earth."[47]

Although the communist propaganda was somewhat successful in winning Pomak converts to scientific socialism, Islam proved to be more

Figure 7 A Pomak girl in the 1950s. Photo courtesy of one of the author's informants.

tenacious than anticipated. A 1971 book, *New Cities in the People's Republic of Bulgaria*, proclaimed that economic development had been so successful in Madan that the Pomaks had voluntarily changed their names back to Bulgarian ones, that the men no longer wore fezzes, and that the women had cast off their headscarves.[48] But "progress" was not as extensive as the communists portrayed it. For the communists, modernization required the most radical form of secularization: the abandonment of all religious practices in both the public and private sphere and the "rational" embrace of atheism. The early attempts at educating select Pomaks to help sway their neighbors to the benefits of modernization were not enough to eradicate persistent local Muslim traditions. The intransigence of these local forms of Islam caused the communists to step up their assimilation campaigns, and as the 1970s wore on, they began to ban certain Muslim rituals.

Rather than just implementing an outright ban, at first the communists put forward their version of rational arguments against Islamic practices.[49] For instance, fasting during the month of Ramadan was said to inhibit the immune system, making Muslims more susceptible to sickness. This self-inflicted predisposition to illness and the general weakness that accompanied fasting was also said to make workers less productive on the job. The ritual sacrifice of lambs during the Kurban Bayram (the Feast of the Sacrifice) was said to be unhealthy for Muslims, who could suffer from severe stomach upsets from eating too much fatty meat at one time; it was also economically wasteful because the lambs could be sold for hard currency abroad. Circumcision was considered a barbaric process only practiced by the most "backward" (read nonmodern) of peoples, and the communists argued that it was unhealthy and dangerous for boys. Headscarves and *shalvari* (Turkish trousers) for women were considered signs of their subservience to men and therefore had to be replaced with more modern attire.[50]

These hygienic and social considerations provided the justification for a variety of laws that were passed to outlaw the "backward" practices associated with local forms of Islam. The communists prohibited the celebration of the two big Muslim holidays Kurban Bayram and Ramazan Bayram.[51] They also outlawed circumcision and the wearing of Muslim clothing. Minarets around the region were torn down and destroyed; mosques were either closed or converted into cultural houses or museums. Islamic burial practices were made illegal, and in 1978 the government created and disseminated new guidelines for "socialist rituals" to be performed at funerals and other important life events.[52] Local imams and hodzhas who defied these new rules could be arrested and imprisoned.[53]

Another heavy-handed communist policy toward Muslims was the forced name changes that began in the 1960s and were not reversed until almost thirty years later, when communism came to an end in 1989. The process began in targeted villages throughout the Rhodope and continued through the mid-1970s until almost all of the Pomaks had been renamed. For centuries, most Pomaks had been given Turkish or Arabic names at birth. Names such as Mekhmed, Ahmed, Mehdi, Hasan, Shokri, Osman, Ramadan, Mustafa, Hairi, Ali, or Raif marked the bearers as Muslims, but also as distinctly non-Slav, a fact which was unacceptable to the communist government because they considered the Pomaks Bulgarians (i.e., Slavs). In fact, the communists went to great efforts to emphasize the Slavic roots of all Bulgarians in order to justify their "natural" affinities with the Russians and the other Slavic peoples of the Eastern Bloc. Pomaks would accept their Slavic ethnicity and embrace socialist modernism if only they had good Bulgarian names like Ivan, Andrei, Mikhail, Petar, Aleksander, Lyubomir, Vladimir, Dimitar, Todor, or Georgi. For women, Turko-Arabic names like Fatme, Faike, Hairie, Higyar, Emel, or Ayten had to be replaced with Bulgarian names like Desislava, Svetla, Veneta, Ana, Anelia, or Gergana. Muslim names in Bulgaria were a marker of difference, of ethnic and religious heterogeneity,[54] which the Bulgarian communists wanted to erase first from the Pomaks and eventually even from the Turks.[55]

Initially, the communists imagined that the name changes would be voluntary, that the Pomaks would willingly embrace their new names. And there were some Pomaks who did freely change their names, mostly communist party members and activists in the Fatherland Front, who had already been coopted by the authorities. But the vast majority of Pomaks did not cooperate, and the entire coercive power of the state—the army, the police, the secret services, and paramilitary troops—was mobilized to see that the changes went into effect in even the most rural of villages.[56] The two most focused campaigns occurred from 1962 to 1964 and 1971 to 1974.

With the total efficiency that only a centralized state can exercise, all traces of Turko-Arabic nomenclature were removed from the physical and administrative space of the country.[57] Every single document or legal record of an individual was changed to reflect his or her new name: internal passports, driver's licenses, and other essential documents were reissued. The dead were renamed posthumously: Arabic engravings on tombstones were erased and replaced with new Bulgarian text; some Muslim graveyards were just destroyed altogether. Newborn babies could not be registered with Muslim names; wages, pensions, maternity leave support, child allowances, and other forms of social assistance could not be collected without a document that bore a "proper" Bulgarian name.

The most well-known resistance to the name changes occurred in the village of Ribnovo in March of 1964, when the army was called out and several villagers were killed. These protests spread to other villages in the Rhodope, including Yakorudi and Satovcha. The residents of Madan and Rudozem got their turn in 1970, when thousands of Madanchani took to the main square over the course of a few days to protest the communists' policies.[58] These demonstrations spread to Rudozem, where a crowd, consisting mostly of women, gathered in front of the municipal administrative building for three days. Some of the participants in these demonstrations were interned by the local authorities, and according to Mary Neuberger there were reports of isolated killings.[59] In the end, however, the resistance proved futile, and all of the Pomaks in these cities and villages were officially renamed.

Fikret was sixteen years old in 1972 when the police came in jeeps to his village to change his name. Everyone had heard about what had happened in Madan two years earlier; those who had tried to avoid the authorities were inevitably caught and punished. Some months later, some families from a nearby village arrived in the middle of the night to hide with relatives near Iordan's parents' house. He heard that there were even people living in the forest to avoid the police and evade changing their names. But in the end the communists were very efficient, and many locals collaborated with the police. Those who tried to run were sanctioned by wage deductions, work reassignments to less desirable jobs, or prison sentences. The men and women who worked for GORUBSO were particularly vulnerable: if they did not change their names, they would not receive their salaries or could be transferred to a less desirable part of the enterprise or lose their positions all together. Iordan remembered that some men were sent away to labor camps, and that the communists had particularly targeted the hodzhas. With their own hodzha already gone, Fikret's mother complained that after the name changes it was harder to find another hodzha to celebrate the birth of a new child or to officiate at a funeral.

The police came on a Sunday in the spring when everyone was working in the village on their garden plots. Three men set up a desk in the center of the village. They had a list of everyone who was registered as living in the village, and whole families were called in at once. Fikret's father and his brothers had already changed their names at the GORUBSO headquarters in Madan. Fikret went with his mother and sisters to the police station, and waited in line for his turn.

"When I got to the desk, the man asked me my name. I said, 'Fikret Hadzhiev.' Then he told me to choose a name. He gave me a list of approved names to choose from. I just looked at it." Although he knew that he would have to change his name, Fikret had never given much thought to what he would want his new name to be. He did not think he would have a choice. His father and brother had been given their new first names by the administrator at GORUBSO. All of the names on the list were arranged in alphabetical order.

"There were so many names on the list. And the man said that 'Boyan' was a good name for me. But then I looked at the list and saw 'Iordan.' And I told him that I liked Iordan better. So he made me Iordan."

They reissued his identity card and birth certificate within a week, and all school records referring to Fikret were changed to reflect his new name. With incredible efficiency, the Bulgarian Communist Party (BCP) just erased the past of individual Pomaks, rewriting their lives from scratch in all official documents and registers. Although Iordan later became a member of the BCP and was still an avid supporter of communism in 2005, he believed that the name changes were a terrible misjudgment. "This is the name you have from your parents, the person you have always been. This was a big mistake of the BCP. Because the people started hating the party instead of believing in it and loving it. I told them [the communists], if the people want to build a little *paraklis* [chapel], give them some cement, let them do it; they will love you more for it. But they had their own way, and this was a big mistake."

The BCP deeply believed that it was liberating rather than persecuting the Pomaks and underestimated the resistance it would meet. The communists were ideologically driven by the belief that they were helping the Pomaks achieve a socialist modernism that all Eastern Bloc countries, and in particular the USSR, considered highly desirable for nations trying to move through what were then accepted to be certain required and linear stages of economic "development."[60] Moreover, Islam was an unwelcome reminder of Bulgaria's perceived subjugation to Ottoman feudalism at a time when the rest of Europe was "advancing" to the stage of capitalism.[61] The communists thus blamed the persistence of feudalism in Bulgaria on Muslim culture (still thriving among the Turks and Pomaks). Long after the rest of Europe had moved on, Bulgaria had remained economically and industrially underdeveloped, and the feudal mentality (of which Islam was undoubtedly a part) needed to be erased from the popular psyche if Bulgaria and the Bulgarians were to progress. Thus, the BCP actively combined their propaganda campaigns with real commitments to improving the material conditions of Pomak life. They were convinced that in the regions where there had been economic development in the Rhodope, there had also been progress away from the traditional practice of Islam. They strove to spread the benefits of socialist modernization as widely as possible.[62]

In fact, if religion was the disease, modernization and rising living standards were seen as the cure. The communists strategically committed resources to the development of different industries in Muslim areas,[63] particularly in Madan and Rudozem, where the population was even

Figure 8 A postcard showing Madan developed as a communist city

more isolated than most Muslim communities and where the local traditions of Islam were considered particularly durable. These cities also fell
within the internal border zones that the communists established to control the movement of Bulgarians trying to escape into capitalist Greece.
In order to enter into these border zones, one had to cross an internal
police checkpoint, present one's documents, and give a reason for visiting.
Despite being thus cut off from the rest of the country, the region received
special funds from the central government to support its rapid economic
development. Although many Bulgarian Muslims clung to their traditions,
some Pomaks were also eager to embrace the material accoutrements of
modern living. The Bulgarian government certainly used the stick, but
they also generously dangled the carrot.

Despite the disruptions caused by the name changes and the sometimes
violent resistance to them, life continued. The increasing economic prosperity of Madan swept many young people like Iordan into the dream
of prosperous modernity. Fikret was already Iordan for a year when he
met Aysel, who was already Silvia. They met after Iordan had joined the
communist youth organization (the Komsomol), and they were sent on
a summer work brigade to harvest roses for a week. Silvi liked the way
Iordan played the guitar; he fell in love with her long, dark hair. Silvi
was from one of the mining villages outside of Madan and was studying
at the secondary school. She became a teller at the local bank when she

Figure 9 A postcard showing the Central Department Store in Madan

graduated. A communist official married them in the municipal building two weeks before Iordan went to do his two years of military service in the construction corps of the Bulgarian army.

After they got married, Iordan and Silvi had two sons, bought a car, and moved into their own apartment in one of the brand new GORUBSO apartment blocs. With Iordan's wages as a miner and Silvi's salary from the bank, they enjoyed the fruits of communist modernity: a refrigerator, a gas stove, a washing machine, a television, and a *magnetafone* (reel-to-reel tape player). Iordan, whose passion for music and guitars continued to grow, spent good chunks of his salary buying black-market rock music from the West. During her four years of maternity leave, Silvi helped Iordan go to night school so that he could earn a secondary school equivalency. Although there were certainly many down sides to communism, like consumer shortages and restrictions on travel, Iordan had what he considered a normal life. He and his family were healthy and had all of the basic necessities, even though he sometime felt "like an animal in a zoo park." He once or twice considered the possibility of defecting into Greece, but he was unwilling to leave his family behind and feared the omnipresent secret police. Outside of defection, there were few ways to resist a government that controlled so many aspects of daily life. Iordan, like so many others in Madan, simply accepted the way things were and became a relatively comfortable communist citizen. What could he have done to change anything?

Back in Saramov's restaurant, we have consumed two plates of potatoes and four large beers. "That was my life," he said. "I sometimes hated it and wished that it was different. I wish I could have changed things. But now, all I wish is that I could go back to that life again. I never understood how important work is to a man. I had work, good work, for almost my entire life. It has not been the same for my sons. A man is not a man if he does not have work."

I looked around Saramov's restaurant and noticed that it was starting to fill up. Most of the customers were men, although there were also a few women, with young, gap-toothed boys who yelled "*Tati! Tati!*" (Daddy! Daddy!) when their fathers walked in. Taking my cue, Iordan looked around as well, nodding at acquaintances, who were obviously very curious about whom he was speaking to and why she was taking notes.

"We were all GORUBSO men once," Iordan said, glancing at two men in blue work overalls sitting down together at a table. "We were not Muslims. We were not Christians. Not even communists. Just men doing a job."

He sighed and drained the last of the beer which he had been sipping while I wrote.

Chapter Two

Men and Mines

IN THE CENTER OF THE CITY of Madan, across from the entrance to the new mosque, there was a hidden doorway that led into the GORUBSO mining museum. After the GORUBSO Company was privatized in the late 1990s, the municipality of Madan bought the museum, along with the Crystal Hall, which displayed the choicest specimens of minerals extracted from the area's mines. Visitors seldom came to either of these two museums, and if you wanted to go inside, a small note on the door instructed you, in Bulgarian, to call a mobile phone number and ask someone to come and let you in. On the hot, midsummer afternoon that I called, the friendly man on the other end of the phone told me that he was having dental work done in a nearby town. He instructed me to sit in the café of the mosque and have a coffee until he could meet me, in about forty-five minutes.

All stories in Madan somehow led back one way or another to GORUBSO. Everyone in the city or the villages around it had been affected by the meteoric rise or the convoluted and prolonged death of communist Bulgaria's nonferrous metals powerhouse. As went the fortunes of GORUBSO, so went the fortunes of the entire region. All personal narratives in Madan and the surrounding areas were told in terms of three distinct eras: before GORUBSO, during GORUBSO, and after GORUBSO. This was the primary temporal reference point for most of my informants. The word was like a mantra spoken over and over again, as if by summoning it with constant verbal repetition the residents of Madan could will it back into existence.

It would be difficult to tell the story of the growing embrace of "orthodox" Islam in Madan, Rudozem, and the surrounding regions without first telling the story of GORUBSO, and the way the communists used the lead-zinc mining industry as a catalyst to modernize the Pomaks. The entire history of the city for the last five decades was intricately bound up with the mines and the importance of mining as a profession within the communist worldview. More importantly, in this region, the mining industry was heavily gendered, with almost all male labor required underground or in masculinized supporting jobs in metallurgy. The development of the mining industry in this region also precipitated the massive mobilization of women's labor to fill all of the other positions in the growing local economy. It was to understand this history from the point of view of the people in Madan that I felt compelled to visit the Mining Museum.

The man I spoke to on the phone arrived at the museum just under an hour later, apologizing for his delay. He introduced himself to me as Yavor. "So few people come here," he said in English, searching for the correct key on his key ring, "especially not foreigners." He pushed the heavy door open with a lowered shoulder. "There really is not much to see here. The Crystal Hall is much better."

The heavy smell of mold permeated the thick, humid air inside the small museum, which was completely dark except for the light pouring in through the doorway. Yavor ducked inside, and sterile, white fluorescent light illuminated the rooms after several moments of prolonged flickering. The museum itself was in considerable disrepair; the décor and color schemes were reminiscent of the late 1970s. The burnt-orange carpet was heavily worn and frayed; a thin layer of dust visibly blanketed almost all of the horizontal surfaces. Some of the lights in the glass cases had burnt out, leaving part of the displays in shadow.

The first room of the exhibit was filled with old, enlarged photographs dating back to the early twentieth century and examples of antique mining equipment. One large photo showed the first geological team to have surveyed the area for mineral deposits in 1927—a group from the Soviet Union, all male except for one woman. In fact, modern mining in the Madan and Rudozem region began in the 1920s with Russian support, followed by the heavy investment of the Nazis during the 1930s and early 1940s. After Germany's defeat, Bulgaria became an official People's Republic, embracing centralized communist-party rule and command economics. Inheriting a relatively backward peasant economy, the new Bulgarian communists were eager to follow in the Soviet Union's footsteps and begin a project of accelerated industrialization. The extraction of raw materials to feed the engines of rapid economic growth was a top priority from even the earliest days of Bulgaria's socialist experiment. GORUBSO was formed on 3 May 1950 through an agreement between the Bulgarian government and the government of the Soviet Union (USSR).[1] In addition to the lead and zinc mines in Madan, the enterprise included a flotation factory[2] and ore-processing plants in Rudozem, as well as other support industries and mines in the cities of Zlatograd, Lŭki, and Kŭrdzhali. Madan, however, was the administrative seat of the enterprise and the home of the richest lead-zinc mines.

As an ideology, Marxist-Leninism favored industrial production over all other types of economic activity, and was as committed to industrialization

Figure 10 A statue of a GORUBSO miner as
a symbol of communist masculinity

as it was to the eradication of "superstition." Communism also idealized
the image of the honest, noble proletariat, the toiling masses that had been
so mercilessly exploited by the universally deplored fascists. No group of
workers better embodied this image than that of the miners, daily risk-
ing their lives in the deepest caverns of the earth for less than subsistence
wages while the wealth produced by their labor went to capitalists and
speculators whose hands had never held a shovel or a pick. For the Soviets, the image of the miner became synonymous with an ideal virile and
pure socialist masculinity, embodied most famously by the Soviet miner
Alexei Stakhanov.

Stakhanov was a coal miner in the Soviet Union who came to stand for
the superiority of the Soviet economic system at a time when the United

States was struggling through the Great Depression. His face appeared on the cover of *Time* magazine on 16 December 1935, and popular images of him, often posing with a jackhammer, emphasized his rugged manliness. In the Soviet Union, Stakhanov was awarded multiple medals and became a hero of socialist labor for his exceptional productivity, and those who strove to follow in his footsteps would be called "Stakhanovites."[3] Thus, from the earliest years of socialism in Bulgaria and the USSR the physical strength and hard work of the miner was contrasted to the sloth and leisured life of the cigar-smoking, overweight capitalist. Soviet masculinity and the socialist economic system was thus intimately bound up with popular representation of miners' bodies. To be a miner under communism meant that you were a real man, and cities like Madan were filled with statues and monuments celebrating their labor.

The display cases in the now unkempt GORUBSO museum were filled with photos of the men working in the mines. Yavor noticed me staring at one photograph of two young men in hard hats, their muscular arms flexing as the camera caught them about to swing their picks. "Those men are real men," Yavor said. "Mining is a job for real men."

Because the communists so highly valued industrialization and the resource extraction required to fuel it, mining was one of the most highly respected and well-paid professions before 1989. In fact, lead-zinc miners were in the highest category of wage earners throughout the socialist period, earning more than any other laborers save the coal miners (see table 1 in appendix A). The black and white photos of the GORUBSO miners gazing at the camera with their shoulders back and their chins angled upward seemed to embody the communist system, where hard physical labor was always valued over desk jobs. The miners in Madan earned a higher monthly salary in 1988 than a Bulgarian ambassador to the United States. Mining was difficult and dangerous work, and communist Bulgaria had accepted that miners should be justly compensated for it. Some of the images of male camaraderie also reminded me of the vibrant social space now provided by Madan's new mosque. After the mines closed and miners lost much of their social status, being a Muslim who attended Friday prayers must have allowed some men to regain a bit of their dignity.

Another display case further on focused on the types of ore that were extracted from the GORUBSO mines: lead, zinc, and silver. The display explained how the metal was extracted and processed, and gave geological details on the metal content of the different ores mined in Bulgaria. Because of GORUBSO, nonferrous ore extraction in Bulgaria increased exponentially between 1955 and 1966, and over the course of eleven years metallurgical production increased by a factor of twenty-three.[4] In 1963, GORUBSO-Madan alone employed approximately 20,500 people,[5] drawing in workers from the surrounding villages as well as from Smolyan and

Figure 11 Miners in Madan. Photograph on display in the Mining Museum.

other cities throughout the country. Between 1950 and 1962, GORUBSO's
yield of concentrated lead grew from 27,333 tons to 105,973.[6] The yield
of zinc increased from 19,077 tons to 112,192 in the same period. By
1963, the Bulgarian communists claimed that GORUBSO produced the
largest amount of lead and zinc ore in the world after the Soviet Union.[7]

The next display was an elaborate chart demonstrating how many millions of Bulgarian leva GORUBSO had earned in different years. In the
display cases near this chart were copies of articles from magazines all
over the world lauding the success of the Bulgarian nonferrous-metals
mining industry. Indeed, world prices for lead and zinc skyrocketed in the
1970s and 1980s. This, in addition to Bulgaria's own domestic consumption and the country's barter agreements with the Soviet Union and the
other members of the Council for Mutual Economic Assistance (CMEA),[8]
guaranteed that GORUBSO's metals were always in high demand. Furthermore, because the government placed such a high priority on the mining sector and there was such widespread societal respect for the work of
miners, the communist government also lavishly subsidized GORUBSO if
there were any production shortfalls in a given year, even if the shortfalls
were the result of lower productivity among the miners, who collected
their wages regardless of their output.

Lead and zinc were important industrial components throughout the
twentieth century. For a long time lead was an important additive to au-

tomotive fuel, and many paints, glazes, and other protective coatings were lead-based. Lead was also used in the production of bullets, water lines and pipes, brass, pewter, and crystal. The most important use of lead was in lead-acid automobile batteries, and the fortunes of the international lead market were and remain heavily dependent on automotive and replacement battery sales. During the 1980s, the environmental hazards of lead became widely publicized in the West, and leaded gasoline and lead-based paints were rapidly phased out. In Eastern Europe, however, environmental standards were much lower, and lead was used widely in fuels and paints until the end of communism.

Zinc is lead's more glamorous cousin and is used primarily for galvanizing steel to protect it from corrosion. Zinc has few substitutes, and the market price of zinc traditionally fluctuated with the state of the advanced industrial economies. When industrial and infrastructure investment increased, demand for zinc increased, and its price rose. But as more countries began to produce and process zinc (especially China), downward pressure on prices eventually made Bulgarian zinc too expensive on the international market.[9]

In the capitalist world, lead and zinc have historically been traded as commodities on the London Metals Exchange, but the whims of supply and demand have led many countries to control their prices. In the United States in the 1960s, lead and zinc were considered so important to the economy that the government passed Public Law 87-374—the Lead and Zinc Mining Stabilization Program—so that the price of lead mined in the United States would never fall beneath a fixed amount, no matter what international markets did. Price controls in the early 1970s in the U.S. gave way to a post–Vietnam War boom in lead and zinc. The international prices of the metals reached all time highs, to the great benefit of GORUBSO and its miners.

As a communist country, Bulgaria's zinc and lead production was not primarily traded on the London Metal Exchange but used domestically or bartered for other goods with CMEA countries in the Eastern Bloc. When the prices rose high enough, however, the Bulgarian government could choose to trade the metals on the open market in order to generate hard currency. The higher value of the metals also allowed Bulgarians a better bargaining position with their fellow socialist countries. But whether the metals were bartered or sold, the 1970s and early 1980s were a high time for GORUBSO, and the enterprise grew exponentially.[10]

The wealth generated by GORUBSO was largely funneled back into the enterprise, with particular attention to the betterment of the Muslims'/miners' living standards: people like Iordan and Silvi who were the ultimate beneficiaries. The meteoric rise of Madan illustrates the rapid economic development that the communists were able to achieve. In 1960, the old mosque in the center of the city was bulldozed, both literally and figuratively cutting the link between the village and its Muslim past. In its place, a shining, new, nine-storey high-rise was built to house the executive offices of the lead-zinc enterprise.[11] Between 1950 and 1978, GORUBSO built and owned 6,300 apartments and 65 residence halls in Madan, which housed 5,400 families.[12] In 1956, the communists began construction on the city hotel, a branch of the Bulgarian People's Bank (where Silvi later worked), a local office for the Ministry of the Interior, and a four-storey complex that housed the secondary school. Between 1957 and 1962, the communists also built a technical high school, a city library, and the Ivan Vazov Kulturen Dom (culture house or community center), which included a cinema and a large auditorium. GORUBSO had its own soccer team, which competed internationally for the Soviet Army Cup. There was a GORUBSO hotel on the Black Sea where the miners could stay in the summers, and GORUBSO hosted the yearly town festival for all of its residents, aptly called "The Day of the Miners."[13] By 1963, there were twenty-five schools throughout the municipality of Madan, including the secondary school and primary schools in all of the larger villages around the city.[14] The secondary school employed 240 teachers in 1978 and had more than 2,700 students. In a region where most educational opportunities for young people had come under the aegis of one religion or another, the rapid expansion of communist education, mandatory for all children up to the eighth grade, meant that an entire new generation of Pomaks was being officially indoctrinated into an atheist worldview.

All of these developments drastically changed the demographics of the small city and created a seemingly endless number of jobs. Mining was a uniquely masculine profession requiring a huge labor force, which the communists endeavored to supply by resettling Christian Bulgarians from other parts of the country into Madan. The cohabitation of Christians and Muslims in new communist cities was another strategy to reduce the continued importance of religion in everyday community interactions. As male labor was concentrated in the mines, the metallurgical factories, and the various support industries associated with mining, there was a great demand for women's labor in the administrative and social service sectors. This push for women's labor in Madan mirrored a national trend that sought to liberate women by including them in the labor force. It also solved the potential labor shortages that threatened to slow down the Soviet-style command-economic industrialization.

Between 1961 and 1988, the number of women in the Bulgarian labor force as a whole increased from 33.5 percent[15] to 49.9 percent.[16] In order to facilitate the formal employment of women, childcare became widely available. The number of full-day childcare facilities grew from 289 in

1948/49[17] to 3,619 in 1985.[18] The number of teachers in childcare facilities increased from 5,560 in the late 1940s to 28,864 in the mid-eighties.[19] Women also got generous maternity leaves and fully paid days off when looking after sick children. In 1985, the Bulgarian government claimed that its women received six months of paid leave for their first child, seven months for their second, and eight months for their third. While on leave they received their full salaries.[20] They also had the option of extending their maternity leave up to two years for each child, during which time they were paid at the current minimum wage for the country.[21] Moreover, their jobs were waiting for them when they were ready to return to the workforce. This was how Silvi got four years of paid leave to look after her sons until they were old enough to go to the full-day, subsidized nursery school, where from an early age they were taught to admire scientific socialism and to look down on "superstition." In Madan alone, there were two half day and nine full day kindergartens by 1963, of which one was a week-long facility where mothers could drop off their children on Monday and pick them up on Friday. This was in addition to another five boardinghouses for older children from the surrounding villages who were attending school in the city.[22] Again, the state's provision of childcare achieved two purposes: it allowed women to work outside the home, and it prevented children from being left with grandparents, whose religious values might be passed on to them.

The development of nearby Rudozem followed a pattern similar to that of Madan. The small village was once called Palas and had a population of approximately 200 people in 1946. Employment opportunities created by GORUBSO and the development of nearby Madan fueled population growth; by 1956, the village had a population of over 6,000, which it also drew from the rural areas, from larger cities like Smolyan, and from Christian villages and towns around Bulgaria. The communists officially declared Rudozem a city in 1960, and just ten years later the new *grad* (city) had 9,100 residents, making it the largest single settlement in the mining region.[23] Like Madan's, Rudozem's economy was heavily dependent on the lead-zinc mines, the flotation factory, and the peripheral services associated with metallurgical production. In 1971, about 93 percent of the economic activity in the city was connected to GORUBSO,[24] where the majority of male labor was employed. As in Madan, the wealth generated by GORUBSO contributed to the rapid development of the town: schools, sports facilities, cinemas, stores, restaurants, a culture house, etcetera.[25] The communists also built modern apartment blocks near the factories, complete with canteens and other facilities for the workers.

Many women in Rudozem were employed in garment manufacturing, and by 1989 there were approximately 400 local women employed in the Rubella cosmetics factory.[26] To support women's labor there were five full-day and eight half-day kindergartens, and all children over three were expected to attend nursery school. Rudozem was unique in that secondary education was mandatory for all young people, and the city also had a good network of boarding houses where students slept during the week while their parents worked. The standard of living in Rudozem improved dramatically during the communist period, and party leaders were convinced that Islam would simply wither away and disappear under the onslaught of economic development.

In both Madan and Rudozem, the communists were also relatively successful with their emancipation project for Pomak women. The anthropologist Katherine Verdery has argued that the communists lessened women's dependence on men by making men and women equally dependent on a paternalistic state,[27] and this was certainly true in the Rhodope region. Formal employment in these cities meant that women earned their own salaries and pensions and had access to generous social services provided by the state. For the first time, Pomak women were able, indeed encouraged, to exist outside of the rigid structures of rural Muslim family life.

One of Silvi's first memories as a working woman poignantly illustrates this point. After her first month of working in the bank, she received her salary. It was the first time in her life that she had been officially paid for her labor; the pay slip had her own (new) name written on it. "I went straight from the bank to GUM [the central department store] and just walked around looking at all the different things that I could buy. It was not my father's money. It was not my brothers' money. It was not Iordan's money. All my life, if I wanted anything, I had to ask for it. For the first time, I did not have to ask anyone. So I bought myself a light green blouse with white plastic buttons from Eastern Germany. Before, my clothes were always sewn, or I wore a uniform. Truly, it was not a very nice blouse, but I was happy to buy it without asking [someone]."

Many other women in Madan and Rudozem shared Silvi's pleasure at working in the formal sector and were told that they were contributing valuable labor to the communist project. It should be remembered that most Pomak women were traditionally employed in agriculture, growing vegetables or tobacco. Rural Christian families encouraged their daughters to go to school and to try to find jobs in the "modern" economy. They stigmatized agricultural work with tobacco as both Muslim and "backward." Agricultural work was tiring and repetitive, especially on tobacco farms, where long hours were spent harvesting and stringing leaves to dry. With paid maternity leaves and compulsory nursery schools, it was much easier for women like Silvi to combine working life and motherhood than it had been for their peasant mothers.

The high standard of living and the emphasis on modernization also helped to mitigate any anxieties that Pomak men had about their wives, sisters, mothers, and daughters joining the formal workforce or about the breakdown of the traditional gender roles prescribed by Islam. Furthermore, because the men were mostly employed in the more highly valued industrial sector of the local economy, earning higher wages and enjoying higher social status, there was little threat to their role as breadwinners if women became teachers, nurses, or bank tellers. Although there were a few token women employed as engineers or mechanics, for the most part women in Madan and Rudozem worked in the service sector or in light industries: garment manufacturing, food processing, or cosmetics production. All of these jobs paid significantly lower wages and were heavily feminized. So although Pomak women were experiencing a form of "emancipation," they never actually became the equals of men as the communists claimed they would. In this way, women entered the workforce without fundamentally upsetting the local system of gender relations. Since formal employment was mandatory for many women, their labor became a symbol of Pomak progress toward modernity even if the miners could have afforded (or would have preferred) to have their wives stay at home.

As I made my way through the exhibits in the mining museum, I could hardly imagine that the Madan I knew in 2005 had ever been such a vibrant city. Yavor had disappeared into an office as I finished reading the last of the little placards in the exhibit. He returned with a photo album. "This is Madan the way it used to be. Before the changes. Before everyone left."

The first photo was a black and white image of the old mosque at the center of the village. There were only a few buildings of any size clustered around it and about thirty low houses. Beyond this small circle were only trees and mountains. The album chronicled the steady growth of the city, a stark black-and-white photo capturing each new building soon after it went up. I recognized some of the buildings as structures that had already fallen down, their roofs caved in and their walls crumbling. Others I did not recognize at all, and Yavor told me that these were the ones that had been completely demolished.

I thanked him for meeting me on such short notice and promised that I would go to see the Crystal Hall the next day. We left the dark and damp building and emerged back into the hot summer sun. The new mosque loomed in front of us.

"That is where the heart of Madan is now," Yavor said, pointing to the minaret. He locked the door behind him. "If you want to know more about GORUBSO, you should speak with Lyubomir Dimitrov and the other miners in the pub."

The Fall of GORUBSO

The following day I went early to the pub called Sonic, knowing that the miners started drinking first thing in the morning, and that it would be good to talk to them before they got too drunk. Sonic had once been a nice bar right in the center of town, but its new private owners had let it fall into disrepair. The once luxurious upholstery of the dark orange chairs was frayed and torn, and bulges of brownish-yellow sponge spilled out through the velour fabric that had been the height of fashion in the late 1970s, when the chairs were originally made. The bare cement walls were painted a bland ochre. The light bulbs that hung from the ceiling were dim and uncovered. The lavatory consisted of two filthy stalls with squat toilets that reeked of sulfur, urine, and vomit. The ceiling of the room was covered with cobwebs, mold, and discolored water stains, and the drunks never bothered to close the doors behind them when they went in to relieve themselves. There were no separate toilets for women; the one female regular used the bathroom next door in the pizzeria. Most women in Madan did not want to be seen inside Sonic.

The men in Sonic were between the ages of forty-five and sixty-five. They were mostly dressed in tracksuits or inexpensive polyester pants and old sweaters. They were all gray-haired and in various stages of baldness, and had deeply lined faces. On the morning I went to find Lyubo, two men sat in one corner playing backgammon while a third looked on. There was a group of four men sitting together at one table. Two other men sat alone at separate tables, drinking and staring out the window onto the town square.

Lyubo was a brawny man of fifty-seven with wide shoulders and a deep, booming voice. He was one of the four men sitting together, and they were already into their *rakiyas*. Although he was a Muslim, he could almost perfectly imitate the baritone chants of the Orthodox Christian priests when he got drunk, which was often. I had been introduced to Lyubo once or twice before but had been reluctant to engage in an extended conversation with him when he was clearly inebriated. On this day, I asked him if he would tell me about GORUBSO, and he pulled me up a chair and waved at me to sit beside him. I declined his offer of a drink since it was only ten thirty in the morning.

"During communism we used to say that there were two seas in Bulgaria, the Black Sea and GORUBSO, because GORUBSO could feed a thousand families. There were more than twenty thousand of us. At the end of each shift, the streets were full of miners—from one side to the other. The bus for the first shift left at eight, for the second shift at four, and the night shift started at twelve. We worked three shifts a day."

The other men sipped their *rakiyas* and nodded in agreement. A man beside Lyubo added, "People came from all over Bulgaria to find work. And from China and Vietnam."

"How many mines were there?" I asked.

"Nine," one man said.

"No, there were more than that," Lyubo corrected. "But they were not all in Madan."

"There were nine," the first man repeated.

Lyubo started naming them. "Ninth of September. Spoluka. Borieva. Konski Dol . . ."

"Krushev Dol," the first man interrupted.

"Krushev Dol," Lyubo continued. "Petrovitsa."

A third man chimed in. "Gradishte. Strashimir. Gyudyurska. Spoluka."

"I said Spoluka," Lyubo interjected.

"Androu-Shumachevski Dol," said the third man.

"How many is that?" asked Lyubo.

The man beside Lyubo interrupted, "And there was a twenty-four-hour *sladkarnitsa* [sweet shop] upstairs so that we could always go and have coffee and cakes before and after our shifts. Even at midnight."

"They had the best strawberry ice cream," the third man added.

Lyubo, now following the thread of the conversation and abandoning the enumeration of the mines, scratched his head and nodded. "And it didn't matter if we were dirty in our boots and helmets. We had so much money."

"There was nothing to buy, but . . ."

"But we had money," Lyubo sighed. "And we had real work."

"So what do you think happened?" I asked. "To GORUBSO?"

At this, Lyubo sighed again, and called for another round of drinks. He began to drink in earnest—gulping rather than sipping. His recollection of events was clouded with emotion, and his explanations for why certain things happened were often shot through with detailed conspiracy theories. In the several hours I spent listening to him and the other miners tell their version of events, however, I came to understand how utterly devastating the closure of the mines had been for these men. GORUBSO's postcommunist history was a sad tale that combined all the necessary ingredients for economic disaster: corruption, greed, mismanagement, miscalculations, deindustrialization, capitalist market volatility, and foreign intervention in the local process of change. In order to understand why "orthodox" Islam found such fertile soil in this particular region, it is essential to understand how badly the various postcommunist governments handled the restructuring of the lead-zinc mining industry, and how the livelihood of an entire city fell victim to an emerging market economy gone seriously awry.

Figure 12 One of the GORUBSO mines in 2005

In 1989, Lyubo had spent his entire life under the rule of one political leader: Todor Zhivkov had been Bulgaria's secretary-general to the Politburo and chairman of the State Council of Bulgaria for three and a half decades.[28] On 10 November 1989, Zhivkov unexpectedly resigned, and the Bulgarian Communist Party found itself under new leadership.[29] Although support for his leadership had been quite strong among the country's *nomenklatura* (communist elites), the communists were able to hold on to power after Zhivkov's resignation because they convinced the population that he was solely to blame for what they had suffered under communism, particularly the heavy-handed suppression of Islam. At a party congress held early in 1990, the new leadership of the Bulgarian Communist Party (BCP) changed its name to the Bulgarian Socialist Party (BSP) and called for new elections. Two other political parties quickly emerged on the post-1989 scene, the Union of Democratic Forces (UDF), a coalition of more than ten different opposition groups, and, most importantly for our story about Bulgarian Muslims, the Movement for Rights and Freedoms (MRF).

The MRF was founded by one of Bulgaria's few real dissidents, a Turkish professor of philosophy by the name of Ahmed Doğan. It was essentially a secular Turkish party created to make sure that the voices of Bulgaria's ethnic minorities would be represented in the postcommunist political landscape. Doğan's party and political importance had been legitimized by huge Pomak rallies[30] against a law passed by the BSP in March 1990 that made it easier for the Turks to reclaim their original names than for Pomaks.[31] Doğan spoke openly in favor of harmonizing the procedure for both the Turks and Pomaks, promoting himself as the defender of all Muslims even though his party was explicitly secular.[32] Although it would have made sense for the MRF to join the UDF coalition, UDF leaders feared a nationalist backlash against them if they were seen as allied with the Turks.[33]

Partly because of this division, neither the UDF nor the MRF was able to displace the BSP in the elections held in June of 1990. Bulgaria became the first Eastern Bloc country to return its communists to power through free, multiparty elections. Doğan's fledgling party, however, garnered enough votes to make it into parliament, and he busily set about consolidating his base and expanding his party structures throughout the country. He focused on the Turkish and Pomak regions and used Turkish nationalism and Islam as his dual rallying points. Thus, with their small victory in 1990, Ahmed Doğan and his MRF party firmly established themselves on the Bulgarian political scene and remained a persistent player in every postcommunist parliamentary election to occur in Bulgaria right up to 2005, despite the many attempts made to dismantle, discredit, or divide the party. The deepest division was between the BSP and the UDF, and power traded back and forth between these two political forces throughout the entire decade of the 1990s. The BSP was essentially the heir to the communist party and claimed to stand for continuity and gradual reform, whereas the UDF was radically anticommunist and demanded a fresh start for Bulgaria as a democratic and capitalist country.

Under communism there had been one national organization that represented the interests of all of the trade unions, and it was under the direct control of the communist party: the Confederation of Independent Trade Unions in Bulgaria (CITUB). After 1989, however, the trade union movement split into two separate factions, one associated with the BSP and one allied with the democratic forces of the UDF. The UDF trade union movement was called Podkrepa (Solidarity) and was clearly modeled on its Polish namesake. Because of Solidarity's supposed success in defeating the communists in Poland, there were high hopes that the trade unions would play a similar role in Bulgaria. In November 1990, Podkrepa supported a general strike that included the miners and was at least partially responsible for bringing down the BSP government. It was the first of a series of strike actions in which the miners were important political players on the new democratic landscape.[34]

Less than a year later, Podkrepa organized more than 21,000 miners to go on strike in August 1991,[35] some of them on a hunger strike underground in the mines, to demand higher wages and better working conditions.[36] One of the key issues of the strike was the financial sanctions (wage deductions) that were being imposed on mining shifts who did not meet their pre-set production targets. The miners resented these sanctions even through they were often well deserved. Since salaries were not linked directly to productivity, the miners had little incentive to exert themselves and often sat idly underground until their shifts were over and then substituted rock for ore. Many miners also reported "injuries" that allowed them to recuperate while receiving their full salaries. Local doctors were only too willing to provide a diagnosis in exchange for a beautiful piece of crystal or a good bottle of *rakiya*.

On the other hand, the miners endured atrocious conditions; some of them were working over 250 meters below the earth with outdated or substandard safety equipment. They risked their lives, and there were plenty of real accidents to remind them that each day underground could be their last. As the government was forever telling them, their labor was essential to the Bulgarian economy, and they felt that they should be amply compensated for the many dangers they faced on a daily basis. As a result, Madan was at the center of a 1991 strike action organized by Podkrepa. The hunger strike, and the eventual participation of coal miners, threatened the whole country's electricity supply.[37] Public sympathy with Bulgaria's miners was high, and the Madan strike could have easily escalated into another nationwide general strike. The government finally made concessions, including the promise of a job creation program for any miners who were made redundant with the closing of obsolete mines, particularly uranium mines.[38]

On 13 October 1991, the socialist government lost its majority in parliament, and the UDF, planning to restructure GORUBSO, came to power in a coalition with the MRF. Much anticommunist opposition before 1989 had revolved around an environmental movement based in the northern city of Ruse, and environmental concerns were partially responsible for mobilizing dissent in the late 1980s.[39] Because of this, antipollution and environmental preservation measures were an important part of the UDF platform. The uranium, lead, and zinc mines (along with other industries) had been identified as serious polluters, and in 1991 there was increasing pressure to close down environmentally dangerous communist enterprises. Another important factor informing the economic context of the Bulgarian mining industry was the collapse of the Soviet Union in 1991 and the official breakup of the Council for Mutual Economic Exchange.

The collapse of the CMEA was devastating to GORUBSO. Whereas the socialist countries had once absorbed all of Bulgaria's production of lead and zinc, after 1991 the country's nonferrous mines had to compete on the open market for the first time.[40] Once the mining industry was exposed to international competition, it became clear that Bulgarian lead and zinc were relatively expensive to produce due to higher labor costs and a poorer quality of ore. The loss of the generous barter agreements with the Soviet Union and the declining international price of lead meant that GORUBSO went from being an important source of national income to a loss-making, state-owned enterprise in need of restructuring. It fell to the new UDF government both to take up environmental concerns and to oversee the painful marketization of the command economy.

The miners in Madan fought the UDF's agenda fiercely, even though they had been partially responsible for bringing the reformist government into power. In March 1992, the Madan miners announced that they were prepared to strike again over unpaid wages and the government's plan to close down certain mines or cut production at mines producing uranium, lead, zinc, and iron ore.[41] The Central Strike Committee of the Podkrepa Miner's Federation was set up, and Madan became "the heart of the strike."[42] Although this time the coal miners decided not to support the strike action of their lead- and zinc-mining colleagues, the Madan miners still had the full support of Podkrepa as well as broad public sympathy.[43]

A day before the strike was to begin, the prime minister and the minister of labor and social affairs left Sofia for Madan in order to negotiate with the miners. The UDF government had made a commitment to cut subsidies to "unprofitable" enterprises, but the strikers were demanding that the new government honor the pledge of the previous one, that is, that miners displaced by the closing of mines would be guaranteed alternative employment. The strikers threatened to bring their families down into the mines and conduct a hunger strike until the government met its demands.

Late Friday night on 27 March, about 20,000 of Bulgaria's 50,000 miners went on strike, most of them employed by GORUBSO.[44] They had not even waited for the prime minister and his delegation to arrive in Madan. When I asked about the 1992 strike, most Madanchani remembered it bitterly even though it was so successful. Their joy at effectively holding the government hostage for higher wages during this strike was overshadowed by the many failed strikes that followed. "We thought we were so important," Lyubo explained. "We thought the country could not survive without us."

Because of the ideological importance of GORUBSO under communism and the high social status accorded to the miners, Lyubo and his colleagues were led to believe that the lead and zinc they mined was central to the long-term survival and sustainability of Bulgarian domestic industries. They had little sense that their enterprise was subsidized by the state budget, and they did not understand that an important part of its original purpose was to help modernize the Pomaks by providing them with industrial employment. Lyubo continued, "No one ever thought they could close the mines. We did not understand the market economy. We asked for one hundred. They agreed to fifty. They gave us twenty-five and closed the mines. That is how it is in the market economy!"

When the prime minister arrived in Madan in 1991, he made it clear that he would spare no effort to reach a compromise with the miners. Several representatives of the strikers returned to Sofia with the prime minister to meet with the Council of Ministers.[45] After a few days, the negotiations broke down when the miners' representatives refused to compromise on any of their positions. The members of the Central Strike Committee returned to Madan and voted to intensify the strike actions. Dimitŭr Dimov, the president of the miners' section of Podkrepa, stated boldly, "We want bread and freedom. We are all together—irrespective of race, sex, age, belief. We are all the same, because this region must live. We will win!"[46]

At the same time, the strike began to spread across the country, radiating out of Madan like the ripples on a lake. Workers of the Balkan Mines Shareholders Association and many members of the Confederation of Independent Trade Unions in Bulgaria (CITUB) joined the action, as well as workers in a number of smaller mines across the country. Photos of the hard-hat–wearing, steely-eyed miners graced the front pages of the Podkrepa newspaper, symbolizing masculine resolve and solidarity.[47] Furthermore, there were reports that the Madan miners were threatening to use violence against anyone who prevented them from taking their wives and children into the mines.[48]

The miners persevered and forced the UDF government to meet almost all of their demands. The commercial banks servicing Bulgaria's mining enterprises met to figure out the total amount of debt owed to other Bulgarian state enterprises by companies like GORUBSO. In attendance at this meeting was then finance minister, Ivan Kostov, who became prime minister when GORUBSO was finally broken up, privatized, and run into bankruptcy. He drew up a three-year program for the liquidation and conservation of the unprofitable uranium, lead, and zinc mines, with guarantees made to the miners for elaborate retraining and reemployment programs. The government also agreed to pay the miners their overdue wages, speed up wage payments in the future, and set up several committees to examine the problems associated with the mining industry.

The strike ended on 4 April, and the miners celebrated what they thought was a wild success.[49] Ahmed Doğan, the leader of the MRF, assured the miners of his political support, positioning himself, against the wishes of his coalition partners in the UDF, as a champion of Madan's continued economic importance. He proclaimed, "There must be one principle which regulates our political life from now on. I give you my honest word—there will be mines. No one can deny your right to work."[50]

In 2005, people often discussed the strikes of the early 1990s with regret, feeling as if they had been used to fight political battles at the national level that had nothing to do with the mines. "Podkrepa played us like [chess] pawns," Lyubo reflected while sipping his third tall *rakiya*. "But we kept fighting. We kept asking for more money because we deserved more money." For a brief moment in April 1992, the triumph of the Madan strikers filled all of the national newspapers, becoming a testament to the will and backbone of the miners and their ability to destabilize the political elites. They still had Bulgarian popular opinion on their side. "We knew about Solidarity in Poland, and we were told that the strikes were part of democracy," Lyubo said. "We were fighting for higher salaries, but we were also fighting for democracy. We believed that democracy was good."

The unstable political environment at the national level meant that their victories would be short-lived. Later in 1992, the MRF broke its coalition with the UDF and formed a government with the Bulgarian Socialist Party. Doğan's support of Podkrepa and the miners' strikes in the face of UDF disapproval was at least partially to blame for the split.[51] Furthermore, all of the strikes and labor disruptions had drastically reduced productivity. Between 1985 and 1992 lead production declined by 46 percent, zinc by 37 percent.[52] The miners compromised their own bargaining position with each drop in production.

By December 1993, the miners in Madan were on strike again with a list of wide-ranging demands, from a parliamentary vote on specific legislation regarding the mining industry to guarantees on miners' pensions.[53] This time there were about 10,000 miners on strike, and although the government did make some concessions, the miners were beginning to lose public support as Bulgarians outside of the Rhodope became more and more caught up with their own problems.[54] They saw the rapid succession of strikes caused by the miners as partially responsible for the political and economic instability in the country.

The Bulgarian socialists were reelected on 18 December 1994. Zhan Videnov, a hard-line leader of the BSP, became prime minister. He promised to build closer relationships with Russia and to try to reduce the economic hardships associated with the marketization of the Bulgarian economy by focusing on social welfare issues. As part of Videnov's project to reduce Bulgaria's international debt and restore its creditworthiness, the BSP government closed about seventy losing enterprises by May 1996 under pressure from the country's external creditors. The BSP government also began imposing fines of 100,000 leva per month on polluting enterprises, including GORUBSO.[55] These fines from the Ministry of the

Environment placed an added burden on unprofitable enterprises to close down, and GORUBSO found itself sinking further into debt.

At the same time, the Bulgarian currency lost more that 25 percent of its value during the first four months of 1996. A total banking collapse ensued wherein more than two-thirds of the banks in the country declared bankruptcy. Tens of thousands of Bulgarians lost their life savings as a new class of Bulgarian "entrepreneurs" fought for the most valuable pieces of Bulgaria's economy. The emergence of the Bulgarian Mafia during this period meant that skyrocketing violent crime rates were added to the list of postsocialist ills plaguing the Bulgarian people. It was during these increasingly dire circumstances that foreign religious workers became more active in the country. Christian missionaries from the United States and Western Europe had rushed into Bulgaria after 1989; in the mid-1990s religious emissaries from the Middle East also arrived.

Throughout 1995 and 1996, the political situation in the country steadily worsened, and it became clear that the economic program of the BSP was unsustainable. In December of 1996, the Union of Democratic Forces boycotted parliament and demanded the immediate dissolution of the National Assembly and new elections. They were supported by widespread strikes and student demonstrations as masses of Bulgarians took to the streets. The Socialists refused to dissolve parliament since they still held a majority, offering instead to form a new BSP-led government. The trade unions responded to the BSP proposal by calling a general strike on 30 January 1997. Tensions in the country were at an all-time high. Hyperinflation was rampant. The dollar went from buying fewer than one hundred leva to buying more than two thousand. Religious workers with hard currency could get more and more proverbial bang for their charitable buck; Bible centers and mosques began sprouting up throughout the Rhodope.

During the economic chaos that led up to the new elections in 1997, the government did not adjust wages to hyperinflation and did not pay many state wages at all, even after people had returned to work. In February of 1997, both teachers and miners went on strike to demand that their wages be increased and denominated in U.S. dollars rather than leva. The Madan division of GORUBSO (though no others) participated in the strike, with the miners demanding a monthly wage equivalent to one hundred dollars and weekly wage payments. But GORUBSO, which remained wholly owned by the state, countered that it would raise wages only if output increased, and refused to make any concessions. Moreover, since the miners in the other divisions of GORUBSO did not join the strike, the Madan action was undermined and overshadowed by the parliamentary elections that returned the UDF to power.

The new UDF government promised to reduce crime and corruption and to accelerate the privatization process. It set up a currency board to stabilize the currency and inflation rate, and largely subjected itself to the economic policy prescriptions of the IMF and the World Bank, which were eager to see Bulgaria service its mounting foreign debt. The privatization process was the government's quickest way to generate the hard currency needed to repay its loans by attracting foreign investment. The UDF was also keen to start reforms, and the Bulgarian public seemed more ready to accept the negative social consequences of marketization after the total failure of Videnov's BSP government to manage the economy. But it soon became clear that restructuring the Bulgarian economy would result in massive unemployment, particularly in the mining industries.

Before 1989, the entire economy had been under the control of the communist state, and the budgets of individual enterprises were part of the national budget. Although the GORUBSO enterprise required electricity, it did not buy it. The National Electricity Company (NEC) was required to transfer some of its output to GORUBSO, as outlined in a five-year plan carefully crafted by central planners. Similarly, if GORUBSO required special equipment from abroad, either the government arranged to obtain it from another socialist country or GORUBSO could get a loan from the Foreign Trade Bank in order to purchase it from capitalist countries. But the Foreign Trade Bank was also owned by the state, and all transactions between enterprises were like moving money from one pocket of the national budget to another. If an important or strategic industry like GORUBSO incurred losses, these were automatically covered by shifting profits from another, more successful sector of the Bulgarian economy, such as tourism.[56] This was a kind of hidden subsidization: enterprises bartered their end products with each other to ensure the growth of the Bulgarian economy as a whole rather than the success of individual enterprises within it. Since the communist government measured progress through the extent of industrialization, heavy industry was valued over all other forms of production, and inefficient enterprises were often subsidized in bad years for the sake of national pride. But none of this mattered before 1989, because Bulgarian products and raw materials were barter traded with other countries in the CMEA.

For many reasons it should have been obvious that GORUBSO's days were numbered. First, in the general distribution of assets and liabilities among the communist-era enterprises, GORUBSO ended up with what seemed to be a disproportionate amount of debt to the National Electric Company, to several banks (which were the successors to the Foreign Trade Bank), and to the Bulgarian government in the form of taxes and environmental fines. Second, GORUBSO was a heavily polluting industry. Third, four of the five divisions of GORUBSO were located in Turkish or Bulgarian Muslim regions of the country that were traditionally supporters of the Bulgarian Socialist Party (BSP) or the Movement for Rights and Freedoms (MRF). The UDF leadership did not consider this region of Bulgaria as part of its strategic electoral base, which was largely urban and educated. Fourth, the miners of GORUBSO had shown themselves to be successful troublemakers; in many ways they were the ideological embodiment of the communist era, when workers' rights trumped economic viability every time. Fifth, there was a sharp drop in international prices for lead in the last few months of 1997, compounding GORUBSO's already substantial losses.[57] Finally, the government had passed a new law that established a thirty-five-year concession for the private extraction of Bulgaria's mineral resources for both local and foreign investors, paving the way for the privatization of the mining industry.[58]

In February 1998, the miners from four of the five divisions of GORUBSO went on strike yet again to demand higher wages and better working conditions. Overall, about 1,800 miners struck, a sharp decrease from the 20,000 of the earlier strikes. More than 1,000 miners remained underground in Madan, Rudozem, and Zlatograd. About 500 miners went on a staggered hunger strike in Zlatograd. Miners actively picketed all three mines in Rudozem.[59] The finance minister, Muravei Radev, went to the region to negotiate with the strikers while Ivan Kostov warned that the strikers could only do more damage to the enterprise by pushing it further into debt. The National Electric Company had threatened to turn off the electricity if the enterprise could not pay its bills.[60]

Once again Madan was the center of the strike action, but this time the government had a much stronger hand in the negotiations. The strikers reiterated complaints about dangerous working conditions and low salaries. They argued that GORUBSO was being mismanaged by the state, and that its debts could easily be repaid under the right leadership. The government argued that the enterprise was inefficient and could not be sustained in its current form. Some of the mines had to be closed so that the remaining mines could operate profitably. The miners agreed to a restructuring in which the five divisions of GORUBSO and its peripheral enterprises were broken up into eight separate economic entities. The managers of the new enterprises were responsible for setting their own wage policy, based on their own profits. Administrative personnel in the GORUBSO headquarters in Madan would be cut back to free up money for raises in the miners' wages. The finance minister promised to lobby for a deferral of GORUBSO's tax dues and made the miners agree to work overtime to compensate for the revenue lost during the ten-day strike. He also said he would try to secure an interest-free government loan to help the new enterprises in their restructuring processes.[61]

The UDF government was quite pleased with the results of the negotiations, as they had been able to shift the burden of responsibility for GORUBSO from the state to the local managers.[62] The government negotiators must have known that it would be difficult to privatize any of the companies when they were saddled with so much debt; many of the eight new entities did not survive the privatization process. But the miners left the negotiations thinking that they had come out on top; local control over wages and working conditions sounded like an ideal solution for an enterprise that had constantly resorted to strikes in order to win concessions from a stubborn state. By the time the miners realized what self-sustainability meant in practice, and that repayment of the debts and taxes owed by GORUBSO took precedence over salary increases, it was too late. The restructuring process had been set in motion.

In May 1998, the Bulgarian press reported that productivity at GORUBSO had dropped more than 60 percent in the last few years.[63] The media claimed that one working shift in 1988 had the same production capacity as an entire GORUBSO division in 1998. The deputy minister of labor made a public statement that the Madan-based enterprise was no longer a productive entity but rather a social program for the miners. The UDF was trying to repaint the public image of the miners: once the vanguard of the old communist proletariat, they were now a group of helpless welfare recipients.

Once it became clear to the miners that the breakup of GORUBSO required the closing down of several divisions, they turned against the proposal. The employees of GORUBSO began to lobby the government to privatize the enterprise as a whole. The government refused to consider the employees' request since the miners had already agreed to the terms of the breakup in the February strike negotiations. It was easier to privatize smaller pieces of GORUBSO; thus only the viable parts of the enterprise would survive. This inevitably meant that thousands of miners would lose their jobs. The government did commit some funds to build and repair roads in the Central Rhodope region, arguing that these infrastructure projects provided jobs for former employees of GORUBSO.[64] But this was a short-term project; there was nothing in the region that could provide long-term, stable, and "modern" employment for the displaced miners. Agriculture and livestock herding were the only vocations available to absorb the miners' labor, vocations which would be humiliating for the men who had spent their lives symbolizing an idealized communist masculinity. The only other jobs were in the garment industry.

As the breakup of GORUBSO proceeded, frustration among the miners mounted. By November 1998, the miners of GORUBSO-Zlatograd were preparing to strike once again. The 200 percent pay increase the miners had expected after the February strike negotiations never materialized once it became clear that almost all of the GORUBSO divisions were deeply in the red. The government refused to raise salaries as the GORUBSO divisions in Madan, Rudozem, and Zlatograd continued to lose money.[65] From the government's perspective, the only viable solution for such large debts was immediate liquidation of the enterprises. Despite these fiscal realities, the miners in Zlatograd, who earned the equivalent of about a hundred dollars a month, were adamant about their negotiated pay raise and willing to fight for it. Once again, they threatened to bring their wives and children into the mines and conduct a hunger strike.

In the meantime, the UDF mayor of Madan, Valentin Gadzhev, in an attempt to save the mines, floated a proposal to the GORUBSO management and the Ministry of Finance. Gadzhev suggested that the eight separate entities be reorganized into two new entities. One of these entities could inherit all of the accumulated debts of the GORUBSO divisions, and the other would comprise the remaining viable divisions. The entity with the inherited debts could then be declared insolvent while the remaining entity continued operating with a clean slate.[66] Gadzhev recognized that it was the accumulated debts that were crippling GORUBSO and knew that the government could reorganize the enterprise to erase the debts by forgiving the taxes and paying the National Electric Company and GORUBSO's other creditors out of the state budget. But the government refused this option.

On 7 November, the GORUBSO administration paid half of the back salaries due to the Zlatograd miners (without the increase), and the miners decided to delay the strike despite the expiration of a seven-day pre-strike warning period.[67] But three days later the strike began, with only 250 miners joining the action.[68] Claiming that the local strike committee had failed to comply with certain regulations, the two large union bodies, Podkrepa and CITUB, withheld their support.[69] An analysis column in the newspaper *Kontinent* also demonstrated that popular opinion was turning against the poor miners. "It is strange that people with relatively low qualifications all the time strike with demands for pay rises while doctors are deprived of this right," wrote the paper.[70]

This description of the miners as "people with relatively low qualifications" was a radical departure from the communist image of them as the vanguard of the working class, those who earned and deserved the highest wages in the pre-1989 economy. The comparison with doctors is also very telling and demonstrates that a new capitalist hierarchy of professions was beginning to take root in the popular imagination. Under communism, medicine was a highly feminized profession, and doctors were not considered nearly as valuable to the economy as those who labored in heavy industry. After 1989, however, the economic restructuring that accompanied the onset of capitalism meant that previously devalued professions, such as medicine, law, and banking, became some of the most prestigious ones. On the other hand, professions like mining, which had been idealized under communism, were reimagined as unskilled and unattractive professions, remnants of an undesirable communist past. The miners themselves in some ways came to symbolize all that was upside down and illogical about the command economy, where uneducated laborers digging out ore from the earth were more respected than well-schooled professionals who saved lives or upheld the law.

The political affiliations of the miners were also working against the Zlatograd strikers. Most GORUBSO employees were rural, Muslim, and working-class, constituencies which consistently voted for the Bulgarian Socialist Party or the MRF. With a Union of Democratic Forces government in office, there was little incentive for the state to help the miners, despite the acknowledged local economic consequences of liquidating GORUBSO. If anything, the government had strong motivations for breaking the political backs of the miners. The UDF government had an ambitious plan to privatize and marketize the Bulgarian economy, knowing full well that this would require mass lay-offs. For the UDF, under the tutelage of the International Monetary Fund and the World Bank, this shock therapy had come too late already, and it was only after the collapse of the economy in 1996 under the Socialist government that the Bulgarian population was willing to stomach the necessary fiscal medicine required to allow the country to properly join the global capitalist economy. But the necessary belt tightening was difficult for many Bulgarians, and the miners of GORUBSO had proven themselves to be a loud and reliable voice of opposition to any restructuring projects that jeopardized the rights of workers.

When the Ministry of Finance refused to budge on the restructuring of GORUBSO in deference to the miners' requests, the strikers forwarded a plea to the Bulgarian National Assembly, hoping that the members of parliament would have more sympathy for their cause. But with the UDF in control of parliament, little opposition to the government plan could be expected. The miners threatened to take their cause to both European and international trade unions if the parliament did not intervene on their behalf.[71] In return, the government threatened that if the Zlatograd miners did not end their strike, GORUBSO would be immediately liquidated.[72]

"Bulgarian miners appear to have done themselves out of a job" read a story in the *Mining Journal* after the Ministry of Finance issued an order on 23 November 1998 to liquidate GORUBSO-Zlatograd.[73] This move came as a shock to the miners, who did not think it possible that the government would actually shut down the operation. "I did not believe that they would close the mines until they closed Zlatograd," Lyubo explained. "I had comrades in those mines—men who had worked there for their whole lives. Then they closed the mines and they had no work. We thought the government wanted to keep our salaries down. We did not believe that they would close a mine full of ore. They are still full of ore."

The miners immediately appealed to the prime minister to reverse the finance minister's decision, but Kostov refused. The miners attempted to speak with the president and the chair of parliament, but no one in the government would hear their pleas. The leader of the Podkrepa trade union, Konstantin Trenchev, finally spoke out on behalf of the miners, claiming that GORUBSO's losses were not due to the strikes or to the falling price of lead and zinc, but to inefficient management.[74] Although their strike was now almost meaningless, the miners held a public demonstration and were able to mobilize support among members of parliament from the Bulgarian Socialist Party. Socialist MPs were openly sympathetic to the miners and used the opportunity to hurl accusations at the UDF government for not taking into account the human costs of economic restructuring.[75] Perhaps stung by the BSP's criticisms, Kostov made a public statement claiming that the government would be able to reemploy the laid-off Zlatograd miners through large public works projects scheduled to start in the region.[76]

The workers continued to demand a 200 percent increase in salary and sought the support of the Bulgarian president, Petŭr Stoyanov. At the same time, the Madan and Rudozem divisions of GORUBSO were scheduled to have their electricity cut off because of outstanding debts owed to the National Electric Company. But the government relented, allowing these divisions to continue operation.[77] In Zlatograd, however, the finance minister insisted that liquidation was the only viable option for the division. Radev claimed that selling off the assets of the company would allow it to pay some of its debts, including unpaid back salaries to the workers. The option of privatizing the division became less and less feasible. There was no outsider investor interested in the enterprise, and a management-employee buy-out would only be possible if the government canceled the division's debts, which it categorically refused to do.[78] At the same time, a thirty-one-year-old miner was killed in a work-related accident in Madan, becoming the seventh worker to die in the mines in 1998. Safety measures were neglected, and lead and zinc mining became more dangerous even as wages decreased. Lyubo believed that this was an intentional tactic to weaken the resolve of the miners.

As 1999 began, it became clear that the GORUBSO divisions in Madan and Rudozem would follow the path of Zlatograd. Since GORUBSO-Madan had become independent in June, the division had incurred 1 billion leva in additional losses.[79] In fact, all of the divisions continued to lose money, even though the miners in Zlatograd had gone back to work. In Zlatograd, five miners began a protest underground at the end of January to demand the salaries that had not been paid to them since November.[80] The GORUBSO management continued to insist that the three remaining divisions be combined into two enterprises: one with all the debts and the other with all the assets. The CITUB leadership also suggested that the debts of GORUBSO should be canceled and that the remaining assets of the divisions should be sold to the managers and employees for one U.S. dollar. They also proposed that redundant miners should be compensated with twenty-four months' salary.[81] But the government refused these solutions, insisting that pipelines and power facilities be sold off to pay the enterprise's debts, and that the municipalities concentrate on generating alternative employment opportunities for the out-of-work miners.[82] Initial attempts by the workers to set up a private mining company that could inherit the viable assets of GORUBSO also failed.[83] Liquidation and privatization of the remaining viable assets loomed large for all three divisions.[84] But since there were no private investors interested in the Madan, Rudozem, or Zlatograd divisions, management-employee buy-outs seemed the only option if any part of the enterprises was to be saved.[85]

GORUBSO-Madan had the most valuable mineral deposits, but it also had been saddled with the majority of the GORUBSO debt after the breakup of the enterprise into eight separate entities. While the employees in Madan tried to raise the capital necessary for a management employee buy-out, a mysterious foreign investor appeared on the scene in mid-1999. Little was known about the Russian-Turkish consortium, Rodopa Invest, which made a successful bid for GORUBSO-Madan. Some questions were raised about its assets or whether it had previous managerial experience in the mining industry, but the ownership of GORUBSO-Madan was nevertheless turned over to the secretive consortium. There were rumors that the sale of the division was concluded through personal negotiations between the prime ministers of Bulgaria and Turkey before an open competition could be announced.[86] It was also rumored that the MRF had been involved in the secret deal. Rodopa Invest proved to be the final nail in the coffin of any hope of a viable mining enterprise in Madan.

As soon as it was announced that GORUBSO-Madan had been sold, the miners began to demand the wages that had not been paid to them while the company had been in liquidation. There was considerable confusion as to whether or not these wages were owed to the miners by the state or whether Rodopa Invest had assumed responsibility for all debts when it bought the company. The new owners initially claimed that they would pay the back wages once they assumed official ownership of the company in February 2000, but later it became clear that Rodopa Invest had no intention of carrying through on this promise. The workers then demanded their back wages from the government, while at the same time the new owners were demanding money from the state treasury to meet the workers' claims and to pay some of GORUBSO's outstanding debts.[87] Small amounts of money were initially transferred from the national budget to Rodopa Invest for the purpose of paying the back salaries. In July 2001, the minister of finance transferred about 493,000 leva to the municipality of Madan so that it could purchase the Mining Museum, the Crystal Hall, and a few GORUBSO sports facilities from Rodopa Invest—monies that could have been used to pay back salaries to the miners. Allegedly, 12 million leva were also transferred to the UDF mayor of Madan to help retrain the miners. But the miners never received any of their salaries from the new owner, and the mayor of Madan publicly called for an audit of Rodopa Invest's finances.[88]

In July 2001, parliamentary elections were held, and the UDF government was pushed out of power by a new political movement, led by Bulgaria's hereditary tsar, Simeon Saxecoburgotski. This new government inherited the problem of GORUBSO-Madan and immediately promised that it would investigate the terms of the privatization and the reasons behind the nonpayment of back wages, which by this time had been outstanding for almost three years. In August 2001, ten desperate Madan miners began a hunger strike, while the new government announced that it had initially found no problems with the privatization contract but promised to continue its investigation of Rodopa Invest.[89]

What emerged from this investigation was enough to lend credence to Lyubo's many conspiracy theories. The new owners were intentionally pushing GORUBSO-Madan into bankruptcy. The government reported that Rodopa Invest had taken over ownership of the enterprise in 1999 with a positive balance of 1.7 million leva. It had both received outlays from the national budget and sold off equipment and other material assets from the enterprise, but none of this money was used to meet the company's debts, which had been accumulating for years. Whatever money had been generated by the sale of the assets had gone into the pockets of the new owners as "profits." The new economy minister admitted that the former government had been aware of the losses incurred by the mines after their privatization but had done nothing to diminish them. The mayor of Madan once again argued that the government had to preserve the mines since there were plenty of ore deposits and a skilled labor force ready to turn GORUBSO-Madan into the profit-making enterprise that it had once been.[90] The Ministry of Economy also hired international auditors to determine whether the Bulgarian government had any liabilities to Rodopa Invest for the unpaid wages.[91]

What the auditors found revealed the depth of the corruption that had plagued the privatization of the Madan division of GORUBSO. Rodopa Invest had paid 175,000 U.S. dollars for 80 percent of the shares of the enterprise, of which only 50,000 was paid in cash.[92] The price was set so low because the "foreign" investor had promised to pay all of the enterprise's debts. But it emerged that none of this money had come from abroad. Rodopa Invest had never had any foreign capital but had purchased the mines with a loan drawn from a Bulgarian bank and collateralized by the mines themselves. If Rodopa Invest failed to repay its loan, the bank could simply foreclose on the mines and destroy the mining industry in Madan in one fell swoop.

From the local perspective, the biggest crime that Rodopa Invest had committed was the selling off of brand new mining equipment as scrap metal on the international market. "There were machines for digging and special equipment for sounding. It was Soviet equipment but it worked very well, and some of it was new. There was even a new elevator that had been put in one of the mines. And there were hundreds of meters of railway tracks underground. They sold everything for scrap," one of Lyubo's drinking buddies, a man who specialized in repairing mining equipment, told me. "There is a lot of that kind of equipment still working today, and if anyone wants to reopen the mines, they will have to buy all new equipment. And they sold it for nothing!" Rodopa Invest had generated more than 6 million leva by scrapping mining equipment, but the company still had debts of 4.65 million leva at the time of the audit.[93]

Finally, the auditors found that although the privatization contract had been violated in numerous ways, Rodopa Invest had never had a single sanction imposed upon it by the former government. In short, the whole privatization of the mines in Madan had been a scam designed to sell off the enterprise's viable assets and then have it completely liquidated by Rodopa Invest's creditors.[94] To add insult to injury, the new government announced that it had no responsibility to pay the miners their back wages.

The miners responded with more protests, continuing their hunger strike and eventually blocking the only road between Madan and the regional capital of Smolyan.[95] The minister of finance declared that GORUBSO-Madan was insolvent, and an official bankruptcy procedure was opened in the district court of Smolyan in September 2001, less than a year after the completion of the new mosque. If successful, the state would reacquire the remaining assets of the division, which had been considerably diminished since the first privatization, and prepare them for a second one.[96] The Smolyan court did not allow the bankruptcy, and since the government still owned 20 percent of the shares of GORUBSO-Madan, a state representative was appointed to the management of the enterprise. Eventually, the company was declared insolvent, but no buyers could be found to purchase what remained of it, and the government refused to purchase it back from the current owners, despite their record of fraud and breach of contract. Rodopa Invest renamed itself Rhodope Holding BG[97] and retained ownership of the mines, operating them at a minimum capacity and paying the remaining miners about 150 leva, roughly 100 dollars a month. The GORUBSO divisions in Zlatograd and

Rudozem were also eventually privatized and fared slightly better than the Madan division, but wages were still very low and working conditions did not improve under the new owners. By 2002, there was little hope that the lead/zinc mining industry could ever return to its former glory. Miners were grateful for whatever salaries they were paid. There were no more strikes. The miners' strength as a political force in Bulgaria was once and for all relegated to the dustbin of history. In December 2004, the mayor of Madan announced that the mines would be turned into tourist attractions.

The collapse of the Bulgarian mining industry was fast and furious. In 1990, there had been 46,301 workers in the nonferrous-metals mining and processing sector,[98] the majority of whom worked for GORUBSO. When GORUBSO was being liquidated in 1999, there were only 3,000 employees remaining in the Madan division. Within just twelve months, 2,800 of these lost their jobs and registered for unemployment in the municipality of Madan alone, a 72.7 percent increase in unemployment registration from the previous year.[99] In a municipality with a population of about 15,000 at the time, this meant that one in every five people was directly affected by the liquidation of the mines, not including the many miners who had already been laid off or had quit due to unpaid wages. The effects on the local economy were catastrophic, as we will see in the following chapter.

*   *   *

Back in Sonic, Lyubo and his pals were already on their fourth large *ra-kiya*, and their conversations—never exactly linear to begin with—started to meander off into memories of old friends and funny stories. Lyubo reminded his buddies of some miner named Mityo, who spent two days in a bucket suspended over the forest somewhere between Madan and Kŭrdzhali. There had once been a forty-five-kilometer skyline that connected GORUBSO-Madan with GORUBSO-Kŭrdzhali. The large buckets that traveled back and forth between the two cities were supposed to carry ore, but sometimes the miners would climb inside a bucket and use the line as transportation between the two cities. Between hacking guffaws, Lyubo recounted the story of poor Mityo, who unthinkingly tried to sneak a ride just before a national holiday when they closed the skyline down for three days. By the end of the tale, all of the other miners were laughing, slapping their thighs and holding their stomachs. I took the opportunity to excuse myself, leaving the men to their *rakiyas* and reverie.

I left Sonic and emerged out onto the main square of Madan just as the call to prayer began. "God is great!" the muezzin called out across the town, the voice echoing through the shallow valley. After everything this town has been through, I thought to myself, it is no surprise that people here might find comfort in that idea. Five times a day, the call to prayer punctuated the passage of time in Madan, broadcasting a message of hope in what otherwise seemed like a bleak and random existence for those still coping with the fallout of the collapse of GORUBSO. The implosion of the local economy had been swift, and the once vibrant city had been depopulated in fewer than five years. This dramatic turn in the fortunes of the city had coincided with the growing influence of foreign religious workers, whose messages of spiritual comfort were backed with the resources to provide real material benefits to a generation of Madanchani who had long forgotten how to live in rural poverty.

Chapter Three _____

The Have-nots and the Have-nots

"ISLAM IS A GOOD RELIGION. It is a religion of peace. And what brings people peace and happiness cannot be a bad thing," Hana told me in July 2005. "If a woman has a child and the child is sick, it is very helpful to know that there is someone who can assist you. And not just the doctor and the nurse. If you pray to God, God can help you."

Hana was a woman in her mid-thirties, and we often shared a bench at the playground behind the GORUBSO building. Her daughter and mine were only eight months apart in age, and although my daughter's Bulgarian was still rather rudimentary and Hana's daughter spoke no English, they somehow managed to communicate in the universal language of children: play. On this day, Hana wore a floor-length light blue gown, a *jilbab*, and a large headscarf that framed her perfectly oval face. Underneath the headscarf she wore a kind of underscarf of white cotton and lace. She explained to me that it was actually a kind of skullcap that kept the larger headscarf from slipping around during the day. "I am always running here and there and I don't have time to worry about my hair showing."

Hana and I met frequently, and she was always ready to speak about her newly revived Islamic faith. On some occasions, I believed that she was trying to convert me, and on others, I felt she was just happy to have someone to talk to. She was one of those people who talked with her hands, wrists waving to punctuate every thought. On this day, she was in a particularly chatty mood, and I did not have to ask many questions to keep our conversation flowing.

"How can anything be bad if it brings people happiness? Everything was permitted under communism, except you weren't permitted to be religious. They tried to prevent people from knowing God and from knowing our own ways. Look at the Muslims in Madan, they drink alcohol and eat pork and wear short skirts, and they call themselves Muslims. Communism is at fault. People put communist values and Islamic values in the same cup, but they must be separated. The people lost the way. They tried to make us forget about God. But we need God. Everyone needs God. Belief is the most important thing in life."

I nodded while our two girls chased each other around a lopsided tire swing, squealing and giggling. Hana's daughter liked to do the chasing and mine was only too happy to be chased. It was a game that required little communication.

"Most of us are ruined by communism," Hana continued, clenching her fists lightly. "But the younger generation—they are clean. They can learn to love God without doubt. I will teach my daughter the right ways of the Qur'an, and her generation will be raised in God's love."

Hana stopped and leaned back into the bench as the girls made a wider circle around the playground. "Don't go too far," she shouted.

"They are having fun," I said.

"Yes," she replied. "All I want is a good life for my daughter. To make sure that she has what she needs and that she is happy."

"*Razbira ce*," I muttered. "Of course." What mother does not want everything for her children?

Hana paused for a long moment, took a deep breath, then pressed her palms together and pushed them forward away from her chest as if driving a wedge into the air in front of her. "I know if I follow the right path, if I teach her to follow the right path, God will take care of her. God will protect her."

Sitting beside her on the bench that day, I was struck with how comfortable she was in her conviction. Her voice was steady and clear, strengthened by an inner certainty that I found myself admiring. It was rare to meet Bulgarians after 1989 that believed so strongly in anything. Hana's unquestioning faith was still a relative anomaly among the Madanchani in 2005, as was her distinctly negative assessment of communism. In that summer, even fairly religious people in Madan had admitted to me that despite the ban the communists had imposed on most religious practices, life had been qualitatively better before 1989. Hana was one of a growing number of men and women who were trying to forge a new path forward, to put the legacies of the communist past behind them, even as so many of their fellow Madanchani continued to live with an all-pervasive nostalgia for the not-so-distant past.

The last chapter described the rise and fall of the GORUBSO enterprise and the unique way in which the fortunes of cities like Madan and Rudozem were intimately tied up with the fortunes of the company. More importantly, the meteoric rise and expansion of the lead-zinc mining industry and the communists' commitment to rural industrialization and modernization also dramatically reshaped the texture of everyday life. Religious practices had been outlawed, names had been changed, and relationships between men and women had been rearranged. Being a "real man" meant being a miner and having a wife who also had a job. It meant sending one's daughters to secondary school, even away to university. Although many

people resented the communists' monopoly on power, the ubiquity of the
secret police, and the increasingly visible privileges of the *nomenclatura*
(the communist elites), few could deny that communism had in fact radically improved the material conditions of their lives, that their standard
of living was much higher than that of their parents. Thus, in order to
comprehend the context within which "orthodox" Islam took root in
these communities, it is important to understand what happened to the
Pomaks in Madan after communism unexpectedly fell apart.

Lost in Transition

Although the economic benefits of communism soon evaporated after 1989,
it left many social legacies. In conversation after conversation in Madan
and Rudozem, I was told that life for men and women like Silvi and Iordan had been much better under communism. It was not only Lyubo and
the former miners but a wide cross-section of Pomaks who believed that
democracy had brought nothing but poverty to their once prosperous
cities. This preference for communism, despite the brutality of the name-
changing campaign and the suppression of Islam, prevailed among the
Pomak population as a whole. A national representative survey of Bulgarians in 1994 found that Pomaks had the most positive attitudes toward
the communist period. Only 12 percent of Pomaks had a negative assessment of communism, compared to 17 percent of the Turks surveyed and
25 percent of the Christian Bulgarians.[1] The anthropologist Dimitrina
Mihaylova also found that the Pomaks she worked with believed that
communism had made much progress in lifting them out of their "inferior
positions through the results of socialist modernization, education policies
and local socio-economic development."[2] In my own interviews, I found
that although many residents of Madan and Rudozem did look back with
some bitterness at the repressiveness of the communist state, for the most
part those old enough to recall the socialist period remembered it as a time
of economic growth and social stability, even if secured at the cost of their
Muslim traditions.

In fact, the communists were rather successful in suppressing the influence of Islam, at least for a while. One study conducted in the early 1990s
found that 31 percent of the Pomak population claimed that they were
atheists, and another 4.5 percent said they were Christians.[3] Another 1994
study of religiousness among Bulgarians found that although most Pomaks
and Turks still believed in God, Pomaks were less likely to go to the mosque
or to pray than the Turks. Furthermore, while the Turks still observed the
fast for Ramazan, the Pomaks had largely abandoned this practice.[4] Other
researchers and ethnologists who have lived among the Pomaks found

very low mosque attendance among Pomaks throughout the Rhodope.[5] Silvi's opinion of religion, so unlike Hana's, captured a common sentiment among many Pomaks in Madan who were raised under communism: "I can't believe in anything unless I see it. I don't believe in God and I don't believe in *Hristos* [Christ]. I believe in myself. When I have a decision to make, my mother says that God will show me the way, but who is God to make decisions for me? I make my own decisions. I do not want anyone to tell me how to live my life. No one looks after me. I look after myself. I know what is right and wrong—not to steal, not to lie, etcetera. I don't need anyone to tell me what is right or wrong."

One result of the spread of atheism among the Pomaks in Madan was the increasing frequency of marriages between Muslims and Bulgarian Christians. In Madan, Bulgarian Christians were referred to as "Bulgarians" (*Bŭlgari*), Pomaks were referred to as "Muslims" (*Myusyulmani*), and the Turks were simply "Turks" (*Turtsi*). A local term for marriages across these different groups was *mish-mash*,[6] and Christian men were just as likely to marry Muslim women (traditionally forbidden in Islam) as Muslim men were to marry Christian women. Interestingly, in Madan both Christians and Pomaks were less likely to intermarry with Turks. Silvi explained that this was due to the language difference: most Bulgarian Turks retained Turkish as their mother tongue.

Before 1989, despite the risks associated with early widowhood, young women in Madan preferred to marry miners, for they had the highest salaries and social status. If a suitable miner was not available, many women were eager to marry Christian men, because interreligious marriages were also perceived as an avenue of social mobility. Many of the communist leaders in the city were "Bulgarians," and many of the technical engineers and specialists who worked for GORUBSO were Christians assigned to Madan for mandatory three-year internships (a kind of national service) after completing their higher education. Most of the Christian population came from outside of the Rhodope and was therefore seen as more "foreign" and worldly than the locals, even if some of these Christians came from smaller villages and cities than Madan.

Even in 2005, for many young women, wealth trumped religion in a prospective husband, despite the growing divisions between Christians and Muslims and between traditional and "orthodox" Muslims. Such was the case of Andrei, a young and very handsome Christian man whom all the girls in town were hoping to catch. Aside from his striking good looks, Andrei was a professional soldier with a good salary of 300 leva a month (about $200) working in Smolyan. More importantly, Andrei had served a five-and-a-half–month tour of duty in Iraq as part of Bulgaria's troop contribution to the so-called "coalition of the willing." For his services, Andrei was paid 82 dollars a day by the American government, and he had returned to Madan with over 13,000 dollars in savings, a phenomenal amount of money in the local context, particularly for a twenty-two-year old. He had already bought himself an apartment, a car, and a large gold cross, which he wore on a thick gold chain around his neck lest anyone mistake him for a Muslim. He could also be seen regularly going up to the small church behind the GORUBSO building to light candles for the Bulgarian soldiers in his unit who did not make it back. Despite his obvious self-identification as a Christian, when I asked him if he would marry a Muslim woman, he shrugged and said, "I'll marry whoever I love the most."

Although Andrei's parents were both Christian, the Christian families that stayed in Madan after the collapse of GORUBSO were mostly those who had married into Pomak families. The owner of the Regal Complex, one of the most powerful businessmen in town, was a Christian married to a Muslim woman from the nearby village. There were several other couples that were well-known "mish-mash" marriages. One of the reasons that intermarriages became so much more common during the communist era was that religious practices for both Muslims and Christians were banned and replaced with socialist life-cycle rituals. Tanya, the cook in Sonic, and Liliana, a woman who sold newspapers in a kiosk in the center of town, explained this over coffee one day. Both of the women were Pomaks, and Tanya's daughter and Liliana's son had once dated for several years. The Pomak son was now going to marry a Christian woman from Smolyan, and Tanya's daughter was engaged to a Christian man from Sofia who was working in Italy.

"Mixed marriages were easier before, when we did not have our holidays or religious education. We could not even choose our own names, so there was no reason for these things to keep the families apart," Tanya explained.

"But now it is more difficult," Liliana continued, "We have different kinds of weddings and celebrations for the new child. We have different names. I don't know what to do in a Christian house or how to celebrate a Christian holiday."

"My daughter will have to start making *kozunak* [a traditional bread made for Easter]," Tanya added.

I asked them if they approved of the marriages, and both women just laughed and said that it did not matter if they approved or not because their children would do whatever they wanted. Both of these women were in their mid-fifties, and neither wore a headscarf. Both women, sometimes, enjoyed a shot of vodka together in the early evening. They were more culturally than religiously Muslim.

In stricter Muslim families, however, there were a few parents who refused to allow their children to marry outside of their faith. The most well-known example of this in Madan was the case of a pizzeria waitress named Adriana. Adriana came from a Christian family. She lost her father in the mines when she was very young, and her older sister died when she was a teenager. Her mother was chronically ill, and Adriana had dropped out of secondary school to start working at seventeen. She was also the town beauty, with large blue eyes, wavy blonde hair, and long thin legs which she loved to show off by wearing skirts that barely covered the top three inches of her slender thighs. Soon after she started working at the pizzeria, she fell in love with the son of one of the richest Muslim families in town, a family that had rediscovered Islam in the years immediately following 1989 and was growing increasingly devout. When Adriana became pregnant, everyone in Madan thought there might be a fairy-tale ending—the richest young man marrying the prettiest young woman and living happily ever after. But because Adriana was a Christian, the parents of the boy would not allow him to marry her, even though the Qur'an does not forbid Muslim men from taking non-Muslim wives. The young man was sent away to live with an uncle in Varna. The family ignored Adriana, and she was forced to raise the child without their support.

But Adriana's case was an exception, and throughout the 1990s there was still much intermixing between the "Bulgarians" and "Muslims" in Madan. Many people told me that Christians had helped build the mosque and that Muslims had helped build the church. When I was in Madan for Georgiov Den (St. George's Day—St. George is the patron saint of the church), older Muslims openly joined in the celebratory feast after Mass,[7] and I was told that Christians also went to the mosque for sweets after sundown during the month of Ramadan. On Easter, I was surprised to hear my Muslim friends greet me and the other Christians in the city with a cheerful "*Hristos Voskrese*" (Christ has risen). On Christmas both Christians and Muslims greeted each other with "*Vesela Koleda*" (Merry Christmas). (Only rarely did people employ the Bulgarian equivalent of the politically correct American formula "happy holidays," *chestit praznik*.) But by 2005 these practices were starting to fade. The separation of Muslims from Christians, and of devout Muslims from nondevout Muslims, was increasing.[8] After 1989, an era of political and spiritual chaos began as Bulgarian society fractured and democracy opened the door to new actors and influences.

A Glance at Religion and the Bulgarian Political Scene after 1989

Although the spiritual liberalization that followed the collapse of communism could have led to a healthy revival of Bulgaria's traditional faiths, it led instead to greater chaos within religious denominations. After 1989, when freedom of religious expression for Bulgaria's Muslims was restored after more than forty years of state-sponsored atheism, those who had remained devout emerged to find themselves facing bitter internal disputes over who their proper leaders were. In the fifteen years that followed the onset of Bulgaria's political and economic transition, the leadership of the Muslim community split into three rival factions vying for power and control over the community's resources. This rivalry filled the local newspapers with a never-ending supply of stories about Muslim infighting and ultimately led to two lawsuits against the Bulgarian government, heard before the European Court of Human Rights, for its continuing interference in affairs of the religious community. Public accusations of being either "communist collaborators" or "Islamic fundamentalists" fueled a public anxiety about the allegiances of Bulgaria's Muslims. The conflicts that plagued the Muslim leadership undermined its authority. They created the conditions whereby foreign Islamic NGOs were able to promote a "superior" and more "authentic" form of their religion to those who were disgusted by what they saw as the political and material interests of those fighting for control of the chief mufti's office.

These divisions in the Muslim community occurred during the most chaotic and tumultuous periods of Bulgaria's recent history—a time of radical political and economic change that redefined the contours of Bulgarian society in less than a decade. From a totalitarian state that controlled all aspects of the polity and economy as well as having a monopoly on religious and spiritual structures and discourses, Bulgaria became a fractured and unstable "democracy" under the sway of foreign capital, aid, political influences, and missionary zealots riding into the country under the banner of anticommunism. As the economy went into free fall and one government after another fell, American and Western European funds to support the creation of political pluralism and civil society flooded the country, as did foreign religious workers, who promised salvation for the relatively atheistic population. In a rudderless and increasingly immoral society characterized by corruption and organized criminality, indigenous religious institutions could have reasserted themselves as moral leaders, but they did not; they fell apart. At the exact moment when members of the former security services and the communist elite violently began carving up state-owned assets, religious leaders were preoccupied with internal divisions and a crass competition for material resources and political power. From the point of view of people hurt most by the transition, these internal struggles at the national level undermined the moral credibility of the very people who could have critiqued the emerging kleptocracy from a spiritual high ground.

The intense rivalry between the "Reds" (the BSP) and the "Blues" (the UDF) was responsible for internal chaos in both the Christian Orthodox and Muslim denominations. It was during the period of the UDF-MRF coalition in 1991–92 that the first cracks in the edifices of Bulgaria's Orthodox and Muslim denominations were operationalized by UDF party activists who wanted to challenge the authority of the communist-appointed patriarch and mufti. In the first instance, the 1971 election of the Holy Synod with the Bulgarian Maksim as patriarch (the highest authority in the Orthodox Church) was declared illegal by the UDF government. Charges were leveled that the patriarchate had collaborated with the communist regime and that many among the clergy were working for the secret police. As an alternative, the UDF and its leaders backed one of Maksim's close colleagues, Metropolitan Pimen of Nevrokop, creating an "Alternative Orthodox Synod" to replace the current Holy Synod, which had been in place for over twenty years and which most Bulgarian Orthodox believers deemed to be legitimate, despite its election during the communist era.[9]

The resulting schism, which lasted throughout the entire decade of the 1990s, undermined all the authority of the Church among Bulgarian Christians and prevented it from playing an active role in the rebuilding of Bulgarian society in the immediate postsocialist era,[10] when the country was undergoing unprecedented economic insecurity and was in dire need of leaders. There were severe food shortages, and temporary rationing was introduced because Bulgaria's hard-currency deficit did not allow for the importation of food or consumer goods to make up for the shortfalls.[11] Economic catastrophe deepened and spread throughout the 1990s. Between 1990 and 1997 (when the Bulgarian currency was finally stabilized by the introduction of a currency board and strict macroeconomic policies put in place by the International Monetary Fund), the economy was choked with hyperinflation, banking collapses, and rampant unemployment as local industries like GORUBSO imploded and national wealth was privatized into the hands of a new elite class of criminal nouveaux riches. In this seven-year period, gross domestic product declined in real terms by almost 25 percent, and consumer prices were twenty times higher in 1997 than in 1990.[12] Real household income had plunged by over 60 percent, and the vast majority of Bulgarians were sinking into a kind of poverty they had never dreamed of.

The schism in the Orthodox Church also coincided with an influx of foreign religious workers hoping to poach potential believers left without a functioning church. As early as 1991, the Jehovah's Witnesses registered themselves in Sofia.[13] The Pentecostal/Charismatic international missions began work in Bulgaria in 1992.[14] The first American missionaries from the Church of the Nazarene arrived in Bulgaria in May 1994, reaching Bulgarians through "sports evangelism."[15] The Presbyterian Church in America began its "church-planting" missions to Bulgaria in 1996.[16] According to the Presbyterians, the Mormons sent over 5,000 missionaries to Eastern Europe in the summer of 1991 and by the late 1990s had bought over 1,000 apartments in Bulgaria to house their religious workers.[17] In January 1992, Bulgaria was already home to the Mormons, the Hare Krishnas, the Religious Community of the "White Brethren," The Children of God, and the Unification Church of Sun Myung Moon.[18] The Mormons alone had fourteen centers throughout the country and about 2,000 young people had joined the Children of God in the capital.[19] Although many of these missionaries did make it down to the Rhodope and into cities like Madan and Rudozem, few of the locals took them seriously, and they found only a handful of converts. More dangerous to the religious identity of the Pomaks than any of the foreign sects, however, was the rise of Father Boyan Saruev and his "Ioan Predtecha" (John the Precursor) Movement for Christianity and Progress.

"This mountain will become a large temple of Jesus; the spirit of the Eastern Orthodox Christianity will pervade the mountain. The Rhodope will become a symbol not only of the Bulgarian spirit but of the Christian one as well,"[20] said Saruev in 1996, referring to his personal crusade to convert the Pomaks back to Bulgarian Orthodoxy. Saruev openly admitted to having been a member of the secret police involved in the 1985 name-changing action against Bulgaria's Turkish minority. But shortly after those events, he left the Ministry of the Interior and converted to Christianity. In the immediate postsocialist period, he claimed to have converted over 50,000 Pomaks[21] and became a virulent and popular Bulgarian nationalist, attracting the attention and support of MPs from both the UDF and the Socialist Party. When *Gori Gori Ogŭnche* (Burn, Burn, Little Flame), a dramatic television miniseries about the government violence used against the Pomaks during the name changes, aired on national television in early 1995, Saruev openly critiqued the film as part of a plot to create an independent Muslim nation in Bulgaria along the lines of Bosnia[22] and blamed the Americans for their unequivocal support of Muslims in the Balkans.[23] These sentiments reverberated throughout Bulgaria and touched a sensitive nerve in the popular imagination after the three-year bloodbath of the Bosnian War.

Saruev's work also raised the hackles of the MRF and its allies in Turkey. The larger Muslim world saw the attempted Christianization of the Pomaks as yet another installment of the assimilation process. The Iranian government threatened economic sanctions on Bulgaria if the mass conversion of Pomaks was not stopped, and at least one Bulgarian scholar believed that Pomak students studying in Saudi Arabia, Kuwait, Iran, and Syria were hastily returned to Bulgaria to work against Saruev.[24] For his part, Saruev claimed that converting the Pomaks was his "personal religious mission"[25] and that all Bulgarian Muslims who converted did so on a purely voluntary basis. Numerous foundations and associations, the Catholic Church, and the Union of Democratic Forces government that rose to power in 1997 supported Sarüev's work among the Pomaks. Through his efforts, new churches were built throughout the Rhodope, even in towns with insignificant Christian populations.

The first ten years of democracy were a very difficult time for the Pomaks of Madan and Rudozem. As the threatened privatization and liquidation of GORUBSO inspired consecutive strike actions and economic security grew more tenuous, missionaries of every denomination circumambulated the Rhodope looking for new converts. As living standards began plunging and poverty increased, the *evangelisti* were spreading the gospel of Jesus Christ to anyone who listened. The aggressive proselytizing of both the American missionaries and of Sarüev inspired local Muslims to try to preserve their own traditions and religious cultures, and attracted the attention of international Islamic organizations.

As the situation in these regions worsened in the first years of the twenty-first century, aid from Islamic charities began to grow in influence, and new mosques were built to counter the new churches.[26] A chaotic political situation at the national level allowed religious rivalries in the Rhodope to continue unimpeded and to intensify, and internal divisions within the Muslim community led to the formation of factions, which increasingly looked abroad for financial support to bolster their claims to leadership. And as this was going on at the national level, everyday life for most people in Madan was becoming unbearable.

The Aftermath of GORUBSO

When the mines closed, the families that had relatives or contacts in other cities fled Madan and the surrounding areas, abandoning their flats in the GORUBSO blocks. Even those who had been born and raised in Madan had to seek their fortunes elsewhere. The former miners looked for construction work elsewhere in Bulgaria, and many emigrated illegally to Greece, Spain, or the United Kingdom, where they worked as day laborers, taxi drivers, or other low-paid service personnel. In one case, a former miner paid 200 leva for a fake Greek passport and worked as a janitor in Thessaloniki for 8.60 euros an hour, about 138 leva a day, just slightly less than the remaining GORUBSO miners back in Madan earned in a month in 2005. One waitress who had earned 120 leva a month in 2006 left for the Netherlands, where she found work in a hotel earning more than 300 leva a day. There was a story of a village in Spain almost wholly populated by fleeing Madanchani. On the bulletin board in the mosque in Madan, a flyer announced opportunities for men between the ages of twenty-five and fifty to become truck drivers in Kuwait, where the monthly wage was

1,200 dollars. Other men hoped to find work in the United Arab Emirates
and in Saudi Arabia. When I first began visiting the city in 2005, almost
everyone I met had a relative or close friend living and working abroad in
Europe, North America, or the Middle East. In the neighborhood called
Batantsi, which had been one of the most vibrant and overcrowded quarters of Madan, row after row of six-storey blocks stood empty. Flats that
had once housed two families each stood bare, and it was possible to rent
one for about 12 leva ($8.00) a month if you did not mind being the only
resident of an entire apartment building.

Once the miners and their families left, many of the local businesses
began to shut down for lack of customers. The primary school was being
closed in Batantsi in 2006, and where there had once been a regular bus
service from Batantsi to the center of Madan every ten minutes, now only
two or three buses a day made the run. The football stadium built by
GORUBSO was dilapidated and overgrown with grass; the locals used
it to graze their cows and sheep. The factories and workshops that were
once teeming with workers all stood empty, their windows smashed and
their roofs collapsing. And not only in Batantsi, but in the neighborhoods
and villages all around Madan, it was as if a plague had decimated the local population. The closing of schools and businesses had a domino effect
through the local economy, and more people were forced to flee the city
and look for work elsewhere. An American Peace Corps volunteer who
lived in Madan between 2003 and 2005 told me that there was almost no
one between the ages of eighteen and thirty-five left in the town, and that
there was nothing for those who remained behind to do but bide their
time until they too could seek work in the big cities or abroad.

But the young were not the only ones to leave; men of middle years also
left, with few skills to compete in the new market economy. From the late
1990s until 2003, Iordan had traveled throughout Bulgaria looking for
jobs at various construction sites on the Black Sea or in Sofia and Plovdiv.
He worked in a total of nine different cities over a span of six years, returning to Madan only in the winters, when there was little construction
work. "If I worked in Madan or in Smolyan, I was paid only 150 leva a
month, but in Varna or Burgas, I could make more than 600. If I spoke
foreign languages, I could go to West Europe and make 600 leva a day!"
Iordan told me. "But life is very hard in a foreign country. And you cannot
see your family. There were two brothers, Nasco and Pesho; they were
always together. Then one went to Spain and the other went to England,
and they have not seen each other for more than five years."

Deepening poverty pushed even those left behind in Madan to find
their way out. Everyone in the town was obsessed with finding employment, and almost every conversation between friends meeting on the street
would start off with a casual *"Namerish li rabota?"* (Have you found

work?) or "*Rabotish li sega?*" (Are you working now?). In the fieldwork that I did for my previous book, it was always very difficult to get Bulgarians to talk about their personal finances, and wages and salaries could only be discussed with utmost discretion. Now, money was all anyone ever seemed to talk about in Madan. My field notes are filled with long discourses from my informants about how difficult it was to survive from one day to the next after the mines closed.

Vesela, a waitress who served the unemployed miners in Sonic, made 120 leva a month (about $80) for working more than forty hours a week. She received another 45 leva ($30) in social assistance from the municipality because she had a child. Her mother received a pension of 53 leva ($35), and all three lived together in a one-bedroom GORUBSO flat that Vesela's father had bought before his death. In total, they lived on 145 dollars a month, or about 50 dollars per person. This amount barely covered food, utilities, and medicine for Vesela's mother. But Vesela's son was twelve, and he wanted money for chips and soda and to play games in the internet café. Vesi dribbled away at least 40 leva in coins to keep him happy and out of trouble. But at least Vesela had work. "Even a job with a bad salary is better than no job," she said.

For women and men who were not employed, the municipality only gave 45 leva per month in social assistance for six months while individuals tried to find work. For most apartments, 45 leva was barely enough to pay for the electricity bill if you turned lights on in the evening or watched television. After six months, it became necessary to earn this social assistance by working for the municipality in some capacity. This was the situation of many women who tended the public spaces in Madan. A woman named Albena had once worked as a cook but had been unable to find work for over three years. She cleaned the streets for her 45 leva but had to support two children on her own with this money since her husband had long ago abandoned their family. The three of them lived in a small house in Borieva, and the children, who were seven and nine, went to bed with the sunset even in winter, when it got dark before 5:00 p.m., because she could not afford to pay for any electricity. When her older son got an abscess, it was left to painfully fester in his mouth for weeks before she could borrow the 15 leva necessary to have the tooth pulled out. The agony of the toothache combined with his persistent hunger made it impossible for him to concentrate in school, and he spent weeks at home sipping homemade *rakiya* because Albena did not have enough money for *analgin* (pain medication). She came home from cleaning the streets each day to find her nine-year-old boy red in the face from drunkenness, clutching his cheek and crying. "I will tell you a hundred times," she once told me, "communism is better than democracy. A hundred times better. For poor people, a hundred times better."

There were many others who shared this sentiment, especially those who had been most severely affected by the closure of the lead-zinc mines and the economic implosion that followed. In a country where access to electricity had been a right of all socialist citizens and health care was provided for everyone (no matter how substandard it might have been), it was very difficult for many people to adjust to the harsh reality of the market economy, where the have-nots really had nothing, even if they were employed. Unlike Albena, Donka had a job as a seamstress during the day and worked as an Avon distributor in the evenings and on the weekends. But she was the sole earner in a family that included an unemployed husband and two teenage boys attending secondary school. Her wages and commissions from Avon sales never totaled more than 250 leva a month. Her husband would occasionally earn some money by logging illegally, but he often preferred to sit in a café and drink beer all day (an expensive drink compared to *rakiya*). He often started drinking as early as 6:30 a.m.; Iordan would see him as he waited to catch the morning bus to Zlatograd. When Iordan asked him why he drank so early, Donka's husband would laugh and say, "One beer is worth ten *kifli* [breakfast pastries]."

And indeed, aside from beer, there was little variety in his family's diet. I often saw Donka in the store in the mornings buying six loaves of bread, which she apparently did every day. I later learned that bread was all the food she could afford to buy, and that everyone in her family ate one and a half loaves of bread a day to keep their stomachs full. Sometimes her boys ate two loaves each, and Donka only ate a half a loaf, smoking cigarettes instead to dull the pangs in her stomach. In addition to her two jobs, she also worked a plot at her mother's house in a village outside of Madan and was able to bring back some vegetables, beans, and yogurt to round out their diets. Her husband sometimes found berries and mushrooms in the woods while he was logging. When I ran into her buying bread one morning, I heard her tell the shopkeeper that it had been over three months since her family had had any meat. The last time had been during Kurban Bayram, the Muslim Feast of the Sacrifice, when the imam had distributed lamb donated from abroad to the local population. In fact, Donka relied on the mosque for meats and sweets during the month of Ramazan, even though she did not technically keep the fast. Although Donka was a Muslim, she admitted to attending Christian services on holidays because the church also celebrated by distributing lamb and bread during the feasts that often followed. She also told me that the confirmed cases of bird flu in Bulgaria in early 2006 worked to the great advantage of many residents in Madan. Because the price of poultry dropped so low, families like Donka's were able to enjoy chicken for several months before it once again became out of reach.

The deepening poverty into which many Madanchani sank resulted in a full-scale retreat from the official economy and a return to subsistence agriculture—the kind of life that Iordan had lived when he was young. I met another woman cleaning the streets for social assistance, and she took me to her house in Vŭrbina one day. Elena was thirty-two and had two children, one daughter and one son. She lived in a house with her mother, her aunt, her two brothers, a niece and her baby, and Elena's father, who was mentally ill. The house had five sparsely decorated rooms with hand-woven blankets and *kilims* (thin rugs) on the floors, beds, and walls. In the kitchen there was a wood-burning stove and a small kerosene-fueled burner for cooking in the summer. Elena explained that they had once had a television, a refrigerator, a radio, and a washing machine, appliances that her husband had bought before 1989, but in the summer of 2002, a thunderstorm had caused a power surge that irreparably damaged all of their appliances. Many families in Vŭrbina had their appliances destroyed in the same way, and few had the money to replace them. Elena's husband had long since gone to Germany to find work. She had not heard from him in over three years.

In addition to the 45 leva that she earned cleaning the streets, her mother had a small pension of 53 leva, and her niece received 18 leva a month from the state to help her look after her baby. Her father also received a disability pension, but he was a paranoid schizophrenic and he buried this money in the woods as soon as he received it. For a while, Elena sent her children on treasure hunts to find it, but her father flew into a horrible rage and beat the children if he realized that they had disturbed his "savings." She decided the money was not worth pursuing anymore. Altogether, then, the whole extended family of ten people lived on 116 leva a month, or 77 dollars—about 8 dollars per person per month, only enough money to keep the family in bread and cooking oil.

They only survived by producing what they needed by themselves. Everything in their home was produced by their own labor or was left over from the communist era. They grew potatoes, beans, tomatoes, peppers, cucumbers, onions, garlic, plums, apricots, and a variety of cooking herbs and spices such as dill and thyme. They raised chickens, cows, sheep, and goats. They preserved fruits and vegetables for the winter, made *rakiya*, spun their own wool, and knitted their clothing. They made their own butter, cheese, and yogurt. The children grazed the sheep while the women tended to the garden and Elena's father went out for firewood. The only thing they ever bought was kerosene, soap, bread, sunflower oil, and occasionally clothing or small toys for the children. Visiting them was like going back in time, and I was sad to learn that Elena's older daughter was not going to continue school beyond the eighth grade because she was needed to tend the sheep. "And if she goes to school," Elena told me, "she might get pregnant, and we cannot have another baby to take care of."

In fact, a baby meant disaster for most of the rural families. The state only gave 18 leva a month in child allowances, and a woman only received 160 leva a month during her maternity leave (if she was lucky enough to be employed when she got pregnant). If a mother was not able to feed her baby on breast milk, just a three-day supply of formula cost 12 leva and diapers were 50 stotinki each. Of course, most of the poor families had cloth diapers, but the time and effort of washing these was considerable and many families bought the disposable diapers even if they could not afford them. If the babies got sick or needed medicine, those expenses exceeded many household budgets and more and more often herbal remedies were resorted to—until the children got so ill that they had to be hospitalized.

Because of these costs, many babies were merely turned over to orphanages. I learned this one day while sitting with Silvi in front of the pizzeria. A sixteen-year-old girl who helped look after Silvi's mother often greeted us when we sat in the center of town, and she had gotten into the habit of asking me for cigarettes. One day Silvi chastised her for asking me once again by telling her that she should not be smoking "in her condition." It was then I learned that she was almost six months pregnant. I became upset that she had been smoking so much, not only because she was so young, but because it would hurt the baby. "It doesn't matter," Silvi explained. "She will just give it to a home. She does not care about it."

"What?"

"She lives with her mother on a 43-leva pension. How can they have a baby?"

Stupidly, I made a comment about having an abortion, which was still legal and easily accessible in Bulgaria.

Silvi almost spat at me. "Just pulling one tooth costs 15 leva—do you know how much an operation is!?"

I sheepishly took the opportunity to change the subject by asking Silvi about her teeth. Teeth were an obsession with most Madanchani, and Silvi was particularly worried about the state of her mouth. "I have to have ten teeth pulled in order to have *castaneti* [dentures]. That is 150 leva plus the money for the medicine, and then another hundred for the *castaneti*. I am too young for those, but to have bridges and crowns put in to fill in all these places will cost me more than 400 leva!"

It was in the context of this discussion about teeth that Silvi explained her entire financial situation to me in detail. By Madan's standards, Silvi and Iordan were relatively well off; she earned about 150 leva a month, and he earned close to 300. They sent about 100 leva a month to each of their sons to help with expenses and had to divide the remaining 250 between themselves. Iordan kept 100 leva for himself to take the bus each day to and from work and for lunch and cigarettes. With 150 leva, Silvi had to buy the groceries (although she too got vegetables and fresh milk from her mother in the village) and pay the bills for electricity, for the home telephone, for her and Iordan's mobile phones (which were essential for their jobs),[27] for the maintenance of the elevator, for the water, and for the property taxes on their flat. In some months they had to buy kerosene for their kitchen burner or a 36-lev bus ticket for one of their sons to come home for a holiday. Each month, there might be 10 or 20 leva left over after all of the expenses were paid, but this was never enough to do something like fix one's teeth.

Because even the relatively wealthy faced a constant shortage of cash, almost everything in Madan worked on an elaborate system of credit. Every store or restaurant in town had drawers or boxes full of running tallies of people's debts. Although it was always a risk to lend money with no collateral, it was the only way stores could stay in business. Particularly for holidays or special occasions like weddings or the birth of a new child, when families entertained relatives and neighbors at home, it was impossible for them to buy all of the necessary provisions without credit. Since Madan was such a small town and everyone knew everybody, these credit transactions worked on an honor system. And it was not only food that was bought on credit, but goods and services of all kinds, including beauty products from Avon. Silvi always complained about the clients or distributors who had not paid her. "When they want their stock, they are calling me every minute, but when they have to pay for it I cannot find them. I have to run after stotinki in Madan to live!"

Avon worked as a pyramid, and Silvi oversaw about thirteen subdistributors. They ordered their Avon products from Silvi, who ordered them from Sofia, and when the goods arrived, she gave the products to her distributors on a thirty-day credit agreement extended to them by Avon. If they did not pay for the goods in thirty days, there was a 10-lev fine for each week that they were late, which Silvi had to keep track of and collect in addition to the original value of the products. Because Silvi was always collecting cash from her distributors as well as from the women who bought products directly from her, everyone knew that she could pay their bills for them if they came up short before the deadline. Friends and distant relations were constantly asking her to borrow money for necessary expenditures, but Silvi had to be very careful not to run out of operating cash with which to meet her own needs and to pay her debts to Avon. Donka, the woman with the six loaves of bread, was constantly in debt to Silvi, as were a variety of other women who sold the Avon products in town but then used the money to buy food or medicine for their families, leaving Silvi to demand the money from them when she knew that they had already spent it. The 10-lev fine imposed by Avon for lateness was particularly harsh, and each month Donka tearfully begged Silvi to pay her bill for her so she could avoid the penalty. "I hate this work. I do not feel good when I see an acquaintance on the street, but she walks past me without greeting me because she must pay me money."

Another rumored source of cash was the imam, who was said to have access to vast resources for the daily operations of the mosque. Those men who went regularly to Friday prayers might be able to ask the imam for help in a dire circumstance. But the most common gossip was that the imam had money to pay women if they agreed to wear the headscarf, and this was the usual explanation for why a growing number of women were wearing the *zabradka* (headscarf) in the new style, as will be discussed in detail in chapter 6. Ofelia, a woman who worked in the Austrian-owned garment factory, told me that women in the factory had been offered 100 leva a month to wear the headscarf. I once asked Silvi why Donka did not wear the headscarf for money, and Silvi explained that the money was not only for the headscarf but for changing your entire life. Donka would have to stop smoking and start attending lectures and seminars. "We are poor," Silvi said, "but we are free." I also tried to bring up the topic with Albena, and it was clear that she had considered the possibility. "My boy is nine," she said. "They will want to take him away from me. He is all I have."

If there was no job and no other source of credit, another strategy for paying off debts was to try to barter one's own labor or to give over a valued possession. Seamstresses offered to sew, and the former miners offered to bring firewood. But these services were not in high demand since most women could already sew and anyone could go and collect wood. Labor alone was worthless. Many of the former miners illegally entered the mines and went hunting for crystals with which they could buy *rakiya* in the Hotel Balkan. Anyone who had jewelry had already sold it to the *zlatar* (goldsmith), so people tried to give away televisions or other household appliances instead. Many shopkeepers were offered toaster ovens or coffee machines as barter payments, which they had to refuse because their own creditors would only accept cash payments. A distributor once offered to give Silvi a washing machine to settle a debt, but Silvi already had one and needed the money to pay Avon, which would not accept a washing machine as payment.

The constant inability to collect the debts owed her meant that even Silvi and Iordan ran short some months. They always bought their groceries and other supplies at a small shop in their neighborhood run by a couple that lived in the same apartment building, Alexei and Ana. Alexei had also worked for GORUBSO, in one of the repair shops, and Ana had been a primary school teacher; they both lost their jobs in the late 1990s and converted a small garage into a store. Alexei knew that Iordan would always pay him, but he told me that he had more than 1,000 leva of outstanding debts to collect, a massive sum in Madan. Some people had no work and simply could not afford to pay him, while others maliciously avoided his store. He said that there was one man who ran up 150 leva in debt, and when he finally found work at a construction site in Madan, he started shopping at a different store—the ultimate affront in this small city.

In fact, people formed a type of fictive kinship relation with the people who ran the stores where they shopped, and even if prices were lower elsewhere, it was the gravest of betrayals to shop in another store if you already had a credit relationship established with your local shop (unless it was because you needed something that the local shop did not sell). These shopping loyalties were a topic of constant complaint when the prices in different stores varied for identical goods. Sonic's waitress Vesela often complained to me that produce was much cheaper in the *plod i zelenchuk* (fruit and vegetable shop) near the bar, but that she was obliged to buy her tomatoes and cucumbers in the store near her apartment, where she had a credit relationship, lest the owners find out and cut her off. "I want to buy a watermelon, but it is 12 stotinki more per kilo down there!" A few times, she gave me money to buy the watermelon for her and to deliver it to her apartment as a "gift."

Small tradesmen and shop owners could be forgiven for demanding loyalty from their customers, especially if they extended those customers unsecured credit. Everyone's ire, however, was directed at the local "businessmen." There were three or four groups of men who seemed to own everything in Madan, and they prospered while the rest of the town suffered. In many cases, they had privatized buildings or enterprises that had once belonged to GORUBSO, and many of these transactions were riddled with favoritism and corruption. One man owned several sewing workshops, which hired local women and paid them paltry wages to fulfill contracts from abroad. Another man had bought the entire complex of the Hotel Balkan—all of the rooms, the shopping arcade, the restaurant, and the bar. Another group of men had privatized the entire complex that had once been the central shopping and dining area of Madan, which included Sonic, the pizzeria, the disco, and three floors of retail space. In all three cases, the locals believed that these assets had been transferred from GORUBSO or the municipality through some back-channel deal. One of Vesela's bosses liked to flaunt his wealth by wearing thick gold chains around his neck and wrists while paying his employees 120 leva a month. He also drove a brand new Mercedes M-class Jeep and carried the most expensive Nokia N series phone available in Bulgaria in 2006. If you had money in Madan, you wanted everyone to know it. And the best way to show it was to imitate the style of the Bulgarian Mafia through conspicuous consumption.

In addition to those who had profited from the unfair transfer of former GORUBSO assets into private hands, there were a few men who had brought in capital from the outside. There was one family that had a very rich relation in the United States who had bought several businesses in town and built his relatives new homes. The owner of the Regal Complex was rumored to have connections with the real Bulgarian Mafia, and he had two personal bodyguards whose sole responsibility was to collect the debts owed to him. Lili and I sat behind these bodyguards one day in the Café Americana, and she told me that one was a local from Madan but that the other was from Smolyan and had some kind of degree from a "bodyguard" school in Plovdiv. Both were quite large and were certainly the most intimidating men I had seen in Madan. With their shaved heads, dark sunglasses, and Adidas track suits, they had "mobster" written all over them. The owner of the Regal Complex also must have had some special inside connection with the mayor and the municipal council because he had managed to secure European Union funds to build his complex, a transaction that had to have been approved by the local government officials.

In fact, the mayor was the target of universal resentment. He had served four terms, one as mayor in the village of Srednogortsi and three as mayor of Madan. According to the locals, the mayor shamelessly enriched himself at the expense of his constituents. Lyubo claimed that he had taken a municipal loan of 1 million leva to build a bridge. He contracted his father-in-law to do the construction, and everyone in the city agreed that the bridge could not have cost more than 300,000 leva. All of the municipal offices were staffed with his friends and relatives, and two different women told me that there was not a single employee with a university degree working for the city, although plenty of qualified people were available. Vesela complained that they only advertised jobs in the municipality after the position had already been filled. Even the American Peace Corps volunteer who had lived in Madan reported that all the municipality ever wanted her to do was write grant proposals, so that they could take a cut of whatever she brought into the city. One person's wealth was always seen as another person's poverty. And poverty was exploited to make the already wealthy wealthier.

Indeed, this fighting for crumbs destroyed all solidarity and made people feel hopeless. Hana blamed this on communism. "Communism treated people like children and told them how to live their lives. They have been spoiled by the communists," she told me at the playground. "People in Madan lack initiative because GORUBSO was everything for such a long time. People prefer to wait to see if someone else will do something, for someone else to take the initiative. They all think that the mines will re-open and that they will all have work again. They are waiting for something to happen from the outside, because no one here is used to doing anything for themselves. They want everything to fall from the heavens. No one wants to work for anything. But nothing good comes without hard work. We were spoiled by the communists because we ate well and had nice apartments and heat and electricity and took five coffee breaks a day. In other countries, people must time their breaks by the second, and then they only have time to eat something and to urinate because they won't get a chance later. People in Madan are only good at complaining. Everyone complains, but no one does anything. It is easier to wait for someone else to try to do something and then to laugh at him if he fails or say he is a criminal if he succeeds."

With so many people out of work, and no one willing to try to change things, time moved slowly. There were few clocks in Madan, and people often forgot what day of the week it was because they were not working and had nowhere they were required to show up. People only remembered when it was Friday because it was the only day when Madan came to life; it was the big shopping day and the time when all of the men from the surrounding villages came into town for Friday prayers. There was also a disco on Friday nights, which was the only thing for young people to do all week. Otherwise, people just wandered around, looking in store windows, with no money to buy anything. Or they ordered a 30-stotinki coffee and sat drinking it for hours just to get out of the house. Friends would meet and talk, but there was little new to talk about.

One result of this vacuum of time combined with the lack of money was increasing rates of alcoholism, abandonment, and domestic violence. I heard many stories about irresponsible men and abused women. First, there were the widows of alcoholics. Many men in Madan had died of liver diseases, and others had fatal accidents while drunk. A car had hit the husband of the woman in the hardware store, and the uncle of a waitress in the pizzeria had passed out on his way home in the winter and frozen to death. A former classmate of Lili's had fallen asleep and choked to death on his own vomit. Younger men and women were often the victims of drunk drivers; the local newspaper seemed to report another fatal car accident every week. Traffic deaths were morbid topics of conversation, but if the victim had been a resident of Madan, people at least had something new to talk about.

Then there were the men who chased women and left their wives for younger love interests. Teenage girls particularly targeted the older GORUBSO miners, because the miners had relatively large pensions. I heard about one woman whose husband left her for a secondary school girl whom he had promised to send to university, despite having two children of his own. Another woman complained that her husband spent all his money buying drinks for girls in the disco on Fridays. There were countless stories of women who had simply been abandoned by their husbands, who went abroad and were never heard from again. Many women, like Albena, Elena, and Adriana, were raising children on their own.

Then there were the stories of beatings, which women always told in hushed voices. Many women had been victims, particularly when their husbands were drinking, and on more than one occasion I heard it said that so-and-so would be better off if her husband died. When I tried to get information about the extent of domestic violence from the local police, I was told that they did not intervene in family affairs. Iordan confirmed that many men would hit their wives in order to take out their frustrations, but he did not seem too concerned. "They are not bad. They have too much to drink or something. It happens sometimes." When I asked the miner Lyubo about this, he just shrugged and refused to discuss it, only saying that many men suffered from "nerves." Only Lili seemed to know about all the women who had abusive husbands, because she had a good friend who worked in the hospital. She would sometimes point them out to me on the street, and they were often older women in their fifties. Once at the market there was a man violently beating a small boy for some misbehavior. Lili quickly led me away, simply muttering, "He is a bad one."

Less discussed, but no less obvious, was the stress that many men were under when they searched for employment but could not find it. Lyubo was the man who most openly expressed his frustrations, but only because his wife regularly came into Sonic to publicly berate him for drinking there with his friends. Like Iordan, Lyubo only graduated from the eighth grade before he went to work in the mines; he had been one of the last remaining miners employed by GORUBSO-Madan in 2000. Although he had managed to work as a painter on the Kulturen Dom project for a few months, he had not had a steady job in over five years. Luckily, he was granted a full miner's pension from the state because he had worked for so many years underground.

He collected his 300-lev pension once a month. Had he been on his own, he would have lived relatively well. But Lyubo had been a miner with a miner's high wages, and for many years he had been the provider for an extended family of women, who all still shared his two-bedroom apartment: his wife, his younger sister, his elderly mother, and a grown, but unmarried, daughter. His mother was widowed and his sister divorced, and ten years earlier he had been very proud to offer them support in their time of need. All of the women had gotten along fairly well, and his relatives were always grateful that he had taken them in. Now, he claimed that they descended on him like harpies whenever he walked into the house, blaming him for not being able to provide for them as he once did.

"All they want is money: my mother for medicine, my sister for food, my daughter for clothes, and my wife always for this bill or that bill. If I give it to one, the others start screaming. But I don't have enough, and then they say that I am to blame."

After Lyubo took care of the basic utilities and gave his wife 50 leva for the shopping, he only had about 150 left, not nearly enough to satisfy all of the demands made on his now meager income. His daughter got occasional work as a seamstress, his mother had a small pension, and his wife and sister often went walking in the forest to collect mushrooms to sell. But there was never enough money for all of their various needs, and the women now fought incessantly, complaining that he was playing favorites if he gave money to one but not the other. Lyubo had long since decided that he would spend his remaining pension on drinks for himself and his friends in Sonic. This infuriated the women even more, and his wife had gone into each of the bars in Madan and asked that he not be allowed to drink there. But Lyubo was a good drunk. He always paid cash, unlike the other men, who often drank on credit. When his wife would appear, sometimes even bringing Lyubo's mother along to scold him, the miner would just laugh and shake his head at them. Then he would drink more.

Sometimes I would see him returning from Friday prayers, obviously drunk and surrounded by friends and former colleagues. They would sit in Sonic, buying each other rounds and telling stories of their various near-death experiences in the mines. The men would listen intently as each one told about a mineshaft that almost collapsed or a battery that ran out, leaving someone stranded in darkness. Vesela, the waitress, felt sorry for Lyubo and the other men. "They have nothing else," she told me one day. "They used to have so much money, and everyone respected them. It is hard for a man to be without work. There is nothing for them to do. What can miners do without mines?"

As in Russia and other parts of the former Soviet Union,[28] alcoholism was rampant in Madan, and the men I met seemed to become more and more fragile as they swayed and slurred their way through the long, empty days. They drank to forget the humiliation of being unemployed in a society where their work was once the most central component of their identities, especially if their wives now supported them, which was often the case. Some days I would stop by Sonic in the late afternoon and see men slumped over the tables or just staring out the door in silence, their hand gripping a glass. Unlike the women in Madan, who shared their pains and sorrows in an endless and repetitive catharsis of chatting, men like Lyubo largely bore their disappointments in silence. In some ways, this was the greatest tragedy of all.

Hana would have liked to completely blame this state of affairs on the communists, but what happened in Madan happened well after Zhivkov had left power. No, the situation in Madan was largely the making of Bulgaria's postsocialist leaders and the phenomenally bad way in which the transition from communism to capitalism had been handled. And as we will see in the next chapter, it was not only the economy that they damaged, but the entire social fabric of society, including the emerging religious establishment. Muslims at the national level would be dragged into political and economic struggles for power, wealth, and influence, dividing its leaders, and opening the doors to international Islamic aid at a delicate and unpredictable time.

Chapter Four

Divide and Be Conquered

HASAN WAS A SOFT-SPOKEN retired miner who worked his way up through the ranks of GORUBSO from being an ordinary laborer to being the boss of the one of the mines. He worked in the café of the new mosque, serving tea, juice, and snacks and selling Islamic literature. He was a handsome man with a full head of thick, salt-and-pepper hair and a carefully groomed beard. There was an air of confidence about him, something almost benevolently patriarchal. Even though he had little in the way of formal education and had spent most of his life underground, he projected the wisdom and spiritual clarity of a sage. He was also a hadj, one of the thirty or so local men and women to be sponsored by international Islamic charities to make the pilgrimage to Mecca. He told me that they made the trip by bus through Turkey, Syria, and Jordan, which reminded me just how close Bulgaria was to the Middle East. He called himself a *tochen myusyulman*, a "precise Muslim," in order to differentiate himself from the other Pomaks in Madan, like the men who drank all morning, went to the mosque for Friday prayers in the early afternoon, and then returned to their *rakiyas* for the rest of the day. He did not drink alcohol, refrained from eating pork, observed the fast for Ramadan, and believed that his first duty was to God and his second duty to his wife and family. When I met with Hasan in the café, our conversations were often interrupted because he locked up and went upstairs to be ready for the *ezan*, or call to prayer, which he observed five times a day. When I asked him why other Muslims in Madan were not "precise Muslims" like himself, he replied: "They have lost their way. The communists wanted to take our belief away from us. They made it difficult to live our life as God wishes us to live. The old people hid their belief in their homes. The young people did not learn or were embarrassed by their parents being fanatics. Only now, after democracy, can we find the right path."

The mosque café had a variety of Muslim publications for sale, as well as home-Arabic courses on compact disc and recordings of Islamic lectures. Hasan often gave me Islamic literature in Bulgarian to read, and it was he who sold me my first Bulgarian translation of the Qur'an, making

me promise that I would take good care of the book before he would let
me take it home. "God gave the words to Mohammed," he said, "and
Mohammed put the words down in the suras of the holy Qur'an. These
are the words of God. It is best for you to read the Qur'an, so you can
know the true meaning of God's words. But it is sometimes difficult to
understand the language."

"I have a good Bulgarian dictionary," I told him.

"Some of the words will not be in the dictionary," he told me and then
offered to answer any questions if I had them.

He sold various magazines and newspapers as well, but most of the
men I saw in the café came in and merely read through them while they
drank their tea. These publications included the Bulgarian edition of the
newspaper *Zaman*, owned by the Islamist Gülen movement in Turkey, as
well as the Turkish culture and lifestyle magazine *Ümit*, published in both
Bulgarian and Turkish. Hasan also sold the locally produced Bulgarian
Islamic magazines *Ikra* (from Madan) and *Myusyulmansko Obshtestvo*
(from Smolyan). From Sofia, there were sometimes copies of an Islamic
magazine called *Selyam* (in Bulgarian). And there were always issues of the
official publication of the chief mufti's office, *Myusyulmani*, published in
both languages and distributed widely throughout Bulgaria. This was an
eclectic mix of literature, representing different interpretations of Islam
from different countries, and indeed the only thing some of them had in
common was that they were published in Bulgarian.

I was flipping through a copy of *Myusyulmani* one day when I ran
across a curious letter published among its pages. It was a plea for unity
among Bulgaria's different groups of Muslims, and it captured the tensions and frustrations plaguing ordinary believers as they watched their
leaders shamelessly scramble for power. The "Message from a Muslim
Woman" opined:

> The condition of the Muslim community in this country is upsetting.
> We are our worst enemy, we are infatuated with and blinded by the
> trivial aspects of things. Lust for power is dividing us; the sword of the
> ego rips the vestments of Islam with a skill that excels that of an agile
> fencing master. At what stage of our spiritual development shall we be
> able to speak about real Islamic unity? When will our hearts be full of
> the genuine feelings of fraternity that the Holy Qur'an mentions time
> and again, and that is a privilege of Islam and distinguishes us from the
> other communities?
>
> We are compartmentalized and it is enmity and intolerance that prevent
> our communication. Here is one example: those who have graduated
> [from schools] in Saudi Arabia sit in one compartment; those who have
> graduated in Jordan sit in another compartment; those who have gradu-

ated in Turkey sit in a third compartment. None of the compartments are open to people whose views are different from those of the men already in them. Each compartment has its philosophy and objectives, and as a result different Muslim organizations are created and each seeks to demonstrate excellence in rivalry with the others.

Dear Muslims, why don't all these organizations put themselves into the service of Islam? Why don't they complement and support each other in the hard effort needed to achieve the one and only goal: to make our religion known to people . . . ? Why should it be impossible for the leaders to sit at the round table of concord and find a common language—the language of our religion? The adversaries of Islam will be only too happy to watch us engulf each other, for this "cannibalism" will spare them the effort that they will have to make to annihilate us![1]

This letter to Bulgaria's Muslim community not only acknowledged the deep divisions within it but also recognized that these divisions were created by local allegiances to the different foreign countries that had sponsored the Islamic educations of rival groups of Bulgarians. Each group was mobilizing the resources of its sponsor nation to found its own Muslim organizations rather than join its efforts to those of other groups. The author was trying to warn Muslims that their internal disagreements would weaken them before those who would see Islam (in any form) eradicated from Bulgarian soil. In fact, those once-faceless Islamophobes now had political power, namely, a growing nationalist movement that found its voice in a surprising parliamentary victory in the 2005 elections.

This new right-wing party, Ataka (Attack), entered the race just months before the elections with a grassroots campaign and campaign posters that consisted of A4-size black-and-white photocopies of their platform. Their message was a straightforward insistence on ethnic and religious Bulgarian-ness to the exclusion of all other groups or faiths. It was an openly anti-Turkish, anti-Romani, anti-Muslim stance that garnered the nationalists enough votes to become the fourth largest party out of the seven that made it into parliament that year. At the exact moment when new forms of "orthodox" Islam in the Rhodope were gaining hold among the local population, Bulgarians voted for a party that would challenge Bulgaria's still tenuous commitments to religious freedom and multiculturalism.[2]

When I asked Hasan about the article, which I had read soon after the 2005 elections, he simply said, "Religion and politics must be separate. But unfortunately, in Bulgaria, religion is politics."

Hasan was merely relating what almost every Bulgarian already knew: that Bulgaria's two major religious groups, the Orthodox Christians and the Muslims, had been torn apart by their involvement in the political machinations of the immediate postsocialist period, when the first free, multiparty elections precipitated deep divisions in Bulgarian society. The political situation at the national level would therefore contribute to the multiple schisms in the Muslim denomination. These schisms facilitated the exclusion of certain groups from the power structures and resources of the Muslim community and forced some of them to look elsewhere for support. One of these groups was a small network of Pomaks who had been educated in Jordan and Saudi Arabia. They were based in the Smolyan region, and their insistence on promoting a "purer" form of Islam disentangled from Bulgarian politics and Bulgarian Turkish interests was one of the most important catalysts for the embrace of "orthodox" Islam in Madan and Rudozem. But before diving into a description of the multiple fissures within the Muslim community, one must have an idea of the structure of Islam in Bulgaria and how its leaders should (at least theoretically) be chosen by the country's believers.

The Structure of the Muslim Denomination in Bulgaria

Unlike Catholicism, Islam no longer has a transnational hierarchy that culminates in one individual believed to be God's representative on earth. Each country has its own unique way of organizing the structure of the Muslim communities within its borders, and the Bulgarian Muslim denomination has its own logic and structure, governed by internal statutes voted upon regularly by representatives of its leadership.[3] The problem with the structure and governance of the Bulgarian Muslim community is that each time there is a national conference, the statutes governing the denomination can be changed, and such changes are easily manipulated for political or economic reasons. Because of this constant flux in the rules governing the religious community and the perennial infighting among different factions, it is difficult to give an exact account of the inner workings of the Muslim community in Bulgaria.

At the time when I did the research for this book, a new statute was in place that had been voted upon at the contested national Muslim conference on 20 March 2005.[4] According to this statute and to the deputy chief mufti of all Bulgarian Muslims, whom I interviewed in August 2006, the structure of the Muslim denomination was organized from the bottom up along theoretically democratic principles. At the lowest level, every community of at least thirty Muslims could form a local Muslim board of governors that was either attached or unattached to a mosque. This board of governors (*myusyulmansko nastoyatelstvo* or *dzhamiisko nastoyatelstvo*) consisted of five elected members, with a designated chairman (*predsedatel*). Above this level there was sometimes a subregional Muslim council, which represented the Muslims of all local boards of governors in a conglomeration of between seven and fourteen different municipalities. Members of the local boards of governors were registered with local officials (the mayor or the local court) and served a term of four years.

Above the local level, choosing the leadership of the Muslim community got more complicated and entangled with local and national politics. From these local boards of governors, delegates were chosen to attend a regional Muslim conference (*raionna myusyulmanska Conferentsia*) where about every four years a new regional mufti (*raionen myuftiya*) and regional muslim council (*raionen myusyulmanksi süvet*) were elected to make up the regional muftiship (*raionno myuftiistvo*). In 2005, there were eleven regional muftiships in Bulgaria.[5]

The regional muftis technically had control over all of the Muslim "clergy" working in the mosques and attending to the needs of the Muslim population in their region. These spiritual workers included the imam, *hatib*, *vaiz*, *hafuz*, and hodzha. In Bulgarian, the term *imam* referred to a congregational prayer leader specifically linked to a mosque. He was the man who oversaw the daily prayers and led the important Friday prayers, reading the Qur'an in Arabic from the niche (*mihrab*). The imam was often the most educated person in rural Muslim communities, and in some cases he had been abroad after 1989 to study Islam in Turkey, Syria, Jordan, or Saudi Arabia. Imams also performed funerary rites. A *hatib* referred to a man who gave the Muslim equivalent of a sermon to the congregation during Friday services. The *hatib* delivered these religious lectures from the pulpit (*minbar*) in Turkish, Bulgarian, or Romani, depending on the audience, and usually addressed contemporary issues of relevance to the local religious community. The *hatib* also delivered lectures/sermons on the two most important holidays: the feast at the end of Ramadan (Ramazan Bayram) and the Feast of the Sacrifice (Kurban Bayram). When the Bulgarian government forbade the appointment of foreign-born imams, lecturers from abroad were still able to address Muslim congregations as *hatibs*. A *vaiz* was also an educated religious worker who could deliver lectures at the mosque in the local language, speaking on a variety of themes but usually on social problems and how to strengthen faith. A *vaiz* often traveled around the country from mosque to mosque. Unlike the *hatib*, who was always a man, a *vaiz* could be a woman, a specialist in issues related to Muslim women and families. Finally, there was the *hafuz*, a person who could recite the entire Qur'an in Arabic from memory. Before communism, different people theoretically filled these positions, but after 1989 the imam often served the function of the *hatib* and the *vaiz* and was sometimes also a *hafuz*.

After 1989 men and women could follow a variety of educational pathways into the Muslim clergy.[6] The High Islamic Institute in Sofia as well as
three Islamic secondary schools in Ruse, Shumen, and Momchilgrad were
accredited through the Bulgarian Ministry of Education to grant officially
recognized secondary school degrees. The curriculum of these schools
was directly controlled by the chief mufti's office, and they were funded
largely by the Turkish government. Outside of these schools, there were
imam courses that had no official accreditation and were often funded
by various religious foundations or foreign individuals. It was unclear to
what extent the chief mufti's office had control over the curriculum taught
in these courses, which had proliferated throughout the country since the
mid-1990s. Foreign organizations that gave money for the construction of
mosques also gave money for the training of imams to run these mosques
according to the Islamic traditions of the donor.[7] Finally, as referred to in
the article quoted above, many young Muslim men and women were sent
abroad during the 1990s to study Islam in Turkey, Jordan, Syria, Kuwait,
and Saudi Arabia, sometimes for as long as eight years. All of these different educational opportunities were fully funded, with room and board,
by money either from the Turkish government or foreign foundations, making them very attractive educational avenues for poorer youth.

But being a Muslim spiritual leader did not always require education,
and indeed, the vast majority of Muslim religious workers in Bulgaria,
even after 1989, were largely self-taught, since there had been little religious education under communism. Somewhat independent of these
Arabic-titled positions within the Muslim denomination was the *hodzha*,
a slippery Turkish word that simply meant "teacher." The hodzha, like
Lili's father, was often a folk preacher who had little in the way of official
Islamic education but performed the roles of the local spiritual leader
when there were no mosques and no imams, especially during the communist era. Hodzhas often worked outside of the official Muslim hierarchy,
and many of them tended to be aged men that clung to the old Muslim
traditions of Bulgaria even after 1989 and the influx of "proper" Islam.
It was the hodzhas who would also view "orthodox" Islam as something
distinctly foreign, and the Islamic charities and their local representative
organizations considered the hodzhas the purveyors of incorrect Islamic
practices. Hodzhas were very close to local populations and would be
called in to perform funerary rites when the local imam for some reason
refused to (for example, because the deceased lacked a proper Muslim
name). The hodzhas also read from the Qur'an during special prayer sessions (*mevlidi*) meant to bless a new house or the birth of a child and
were often called upon to make amulets (*muski*) for protection, good luck,
health, wealth, or love. In all cases, the hodzha charged clients directly
for his services, since he did not have access to the official *vakif* funds to

support his work. Since many of the new imams had been trained in Saudi Arabia, Jordan, or Syria, they looked upon these traditional Bulgarian practices as forbidden innovations in Islam. Because the official clergy were becoming more and more "orthodox" in their Islamic practice, it was still the hodzhas to whom most Bulgarian Muslims turned for their spiritual needs. Although he was ill, the services of Lili's father's were still in high demand.

This divide between the hodzhas and the foreign-trained imams also reflected an important generation gap. Most of the hodzhas were aged men who had taken significant personal risk to preserve traditional Islamic practices during the communist era and therefore had great authority among the older generation of Pomaks. The foreign-trained imams were usually much younger men who had been given scholarships to go abroad, where they had supposedly learned the true form of Islam. This relationship between the imams and hodzhas perfectly reflects Talal Asad's understanding of "orthodox" versus traditional Islam. The hodzhas, who rarely read Arabic, used their own age and personal histories to legitimize their understanding of proper Muslim practice. They argued that they were the only conduits to the "lost" traditions of Bulgaria's precommunist Muslim past. On the other hand, the youthful imams based their spiritual authority on the Qur'an, because they could read Arabic and therefore directly access the text. They also claimed superiority based on their contact with foreign Muslim scholars and the wider Muslim world. In Madan, Lili's father had been a hodzha but had felt his legitimacy decrease with the construction of the new mosque and the installation of the young, foreign-trained imam. Although he said he was retired, Lili's father continued to supplement his meager pension by making the occasional amulet. Although the *muski* were still in high demand, the imam refused to make them.

Above the local level was the much-contested national leadership of the Muslim denomination. Theoretically, a national muslim conference (*natsionalna myusyulmanska conferentsia*) was called every few years to elect a High Muslim Council (*Vish Myusyulmanski Sŭvet*) and a chief mufti (*glaven myuftiya*) that made up the Chief Muftiship (*Glavno Myuftiistvo*) based in Sofia. At some conferences, the High Muslim Council was directly elected, and then the council members chose the chief mufti. The biggest problem, as we shall see below, was who should convene the national muslim conference and who the delegates should be. By statute, all of the regional muftis, as well as the rector of the High Islamic Institute, were to attend, but below that level the composition of the participants was the subject of much controversy and dogged the legitimacy of more than one national conference. In theory, the convention included imams and chairmen of the mosque boards of governors, as well as members of Muslim communities, including the unofficially recognized hodzhas. In reality,

the choice of delegates was subject to much manipulation by different
factions within the Muslim community, but particularly by Ahmed Doğan
and his political party, the Movement for Rights and Freedoms.

Although controlling the Chief Muftiship often translated into control over the votes of Bulgaria's Muslims, the most attractive asset of the
chief mufti's office was its cash flow. When the Ottomans left Bulgaria in
the late nineteenth century, they bequeathed to Bulgaria's Muslims large
vakif (charitable trust) properties that had been amassed by the Muslim
denomination over the years. These charitable trusts included the land and
about a thousand mosques and other religious facilities, as well as residen-
tial properties in key urban centers and fertile agricultural lands. From the
rents paid on this real estate, the chief mufti's office was supposed to take
care of the needs of the Muslim denomination: restoring and renovating
mosques, paying clergy salaries, funding Islamic education, etcetera. Under communism, many of the *vakif* properties were nationalized, but after
1989, some of them were restored to the Chief Muftiship, particularly the
mosques which had been turned into museums or community centers. In
addition to this income from rents, there was also foreign Islamic aid to
Bulgarian Muslims, particularly after the outbreak of the Bosnian war in
1992. Taken together, a significant amount of money was flowing through
the accounts of the Chief Muftiship in Sofia, a very attractive revenue
stream for politicians and businessmen looking for cheap and easily accessible capital in the cash-starved Bulgarian economy of the transition
period. It was the desire to control these resources that began the initial
schism in the Muslim leadership.

"The Passion of the Muftis":[8] The Drama of a Modern European Muslim Minority

As discussed earlier, all religious life under communism was governed by
the 1949 Religious Denominations Act, which gave the state the right to
oversee and regulate all religious communities in the country. Although
the chief mufti was still elected by a national conference, all delegates to
the conference were vetted by the communist party, and the communists
anointed a chief mufti who kept the Muslim denomination under control
while at the same time representing the country's Muslims to Bulgaria's
Muslim allies and trading partners in the Middle East. Thus, if the government forbade religious education, prohibited Muslim rituals, destroyed
mosques, or forced Muslims to change their names, there was little the
mufti could do to protest, and worse, in the international arena he had
to pretend that communist Bulgaria was a tolerant and Muslim-friendly
state. If a chief mufti dared to speak out against the communists' policies,

he was summarily removed and replaced with someone more amenable to the Zhivkov government.

In 1988, Dr. Nedim Gendzhev was "elected" the chief mufti of all Bulgarian Muslims. Gendzhev was born in 1945 to an influential Bulgarian Turkish family. His father had been an atheist and a communist, but then left the party and grew very religious in his later life, becoming an important hodzha who was heavily involved in local politics among the Turkish population.[9] By Gendzhev's own account in a conversation I had with him in March 2007, he studied law at the university in the 1970s, and upon his graduation, the government placed him in a mandatory three-year internship, which was common practice for all university students in Bulgaria. He was assigned to the Ministry of the Interior, where he worked for the Bulgarian State Security Services.[10] Although he was later blamed for his complicity with the "rebirth" process that forced the Turks to change their names, he insisted that he was out of the country at the time (1984–85). One of his most important acts was to unify the Muslim denomination in Bulgaria under his leadership. He demoted the Pomak mufti to the status of regional mufti, accountable to the Muslim leadership in Sofia, merging the previously separated Pomak and Turkish institutions into one.[11]

After 1989, Gendzhev remained chief mufti and should have continued in that office until 1994. In the immediate post-1989 period, Gendzhev spoke on behalf of the Muslim community in support of the continued rule of the Bulgarian Socialist Party, assuring the world that Bulgarian Muslims now enjoyed freedom of religion and no longer faced state oppression.[12] Gendzhev's continued loyalty to the communists in their new guise as the BSP confirmed the view of many Muslims that he had been a collaborator. He had to be removed to make room for new, "democratic" leadership.[13]

By the end of 1991, the United Democratic Forces and the Movement for Rights and Freedoms formed their coalition and took control of the country. As soon as they were in control, the new government began agitating for Gendzhev's removal. In January 1992, Muslim clergy demonstrated in the southeastern town of Kŭrdzhali, a stronghold of the MRF, and students in Sofia called on all Bulgarian Muslims to demand Gendzhev's removal.[14] At the same time, the UDF launched an investigation into whether or not Gendzhev's election as mufti in 1988 was legitimate (it found it was not) as well as into his alleged misuse and embezzlement of funds given to the chief mufti's office in 1991.[15] Gendzhev claimed that the allegations against him were all coming from the MRF, in a bid to take control of the Muslim community for political purposes.[16]

Indeed, Ahmed Doğan had a great interest in who was in control of the spiritual life of Bulgaria's Muslim communities. Even though many of the top politicians of the MRF, including Doğan, were atheists, they understood that control of the Chief Muftiship could translate into representation in parliament. The majority of Bulgaria's Muslims were poor and rural, and despite the heavy-handedness of the name changes and the forced emigration of Turks in 1989, were still sympathetic to socialist principles. Furthermore, the mosques served as the political and social centers of most Muslim villages, and the imams and hodzhas were greatly respected for their education and mastery of the Qur'an. If the Chief Muftiship remained under the control of the BSP, many Muslims would continue to vote for the socialists in local and parliamentary elections, effectively cutting into the MRF's "natural" constituency. Aside from the resources that control over the muftiship could provide, the political survival of the MRF depended on consolidating the Muslim/Turkish vote.

In February 1992, the UDF/MRF government invalidated Gendzhev's election to the post of chief mufti in 1988, and he was removed from office. The government appointed three people to serve as a temporary governing body of the Muslim community until a national conference could be held.[17] Gendzhev appealed the decision, and the Bulgarian Constitutional Court supported him, arguing that the government had no capacity to void the 1988 election. In June, Gendzhev and his associates reoccupied the offices of the chief muftiship in Sofia. One day later, Muslims bussed in from Kŭrdzhali protested outside of the building, and the police (now taking orders from the UDF/MRF government) helped to evict Gendzhev. As early as 1992, Gendzhev warned that there were foreign Islamic "sects" in Bulgaria hoping to take advantage of divisions within the Muslim community. "There are forces wishing precisely this, but I will not allow any conflicts among Muslims," he said.[18]

In September, Gendzhev issued a statement claiming that his was the only High Muslim Council in Bulgaria and that the council that was trying to convene a national conference to elect a new chief mufti was illegitimately created by the MRF.[19] Since the entire Muslim clergy associated with Gendzhev was suspected of collaborating with the communists and subsequently of being allied with the BSP, new delegates to the conference had to be found, particularly those who were sympathetic to the UDF and MRF. On 19 September 1992, the national conference was held, attended by 665 delegates chosen by the alternate high council and foreign guests from Turkey, Greece, and Saudi Arabia.[20] Fikri Sali Hasan, the MRF's chosen candidate, was elected as the new chief mufti. Hasan was only twenty-nine years old, and many of the older Muslims considered him too young to be chief mufti of all Bulgarian Muslims. Nevertheless, his election was almost immediately recognized and registered by the UDF.

During 1993 and 1994, the dispute between the two rival factions continued. In effect there were two High Muslim Councils claiming to represent all of Bulgaria's Muslims, and each could convene a national

conference of chosen delegates and elect a chief mufti to its liking. Gendzhev and his supporters convened yet another national conference,[21] and
he was elected president of the High Muslim Council. A close associate
of his was elected chief mufti. Gendzhev and his followers immediately
applied for recognition from the Directorate of Religious Denominations,
the government body in charge of registering new religions. At the same
time, Gendzhev tried to forge greater connections with the Muslim world
to support his short-lived political party, the Democratic Party of Justice,
in the 1994 parliamentary elections.

When the BSP was returned to power, one of its first acts was to issue
a decree recognizing Nedim Gendzhev and his followers as the legitimate
leaders of Bulgaria's Muslims. Gendzhev took over the Sofia headquarters
of the Chief Muftiship by force. Hasan and his followers protested their
removal from office, and in 1995 convened yet another national conference, with their own delegates, which reelected him as chief mufti. They
reapplied to the Directorate of Religious Denominations for recognition as
a separate religious organization, but the government refused to consider
the application: the Muslims already had a chief mufti. Hasan appealed
to the Supreme Administrative Court, claiming that the government had
no right to impose one leadership on a religious community. Twice the
Supreme Administrative Court agreed with Hasan, but the directorate still
refused to recognize him. Following these events, Hasan and his followers
successfully sued the Bulgarian government in the European Court of Human Rights for the government's undue interference in the organization
of a religious community.[22]

As soon as the UDF was returned to power in 1997, Hasan petitioned
the new Directorate of Religious Denominations demanding the immediate removal of Gendzhev and his chief mufti. One of Turkey's former
prime ministers lobbied Bulgaria's president on Hasan's behalf.[23] Gendzhev tried to preempt his removal under the UDF government by proposing a "unification conference" where the two rival High Muslim Councils
would convene a national conference together and elect a chief mufti.

Elections were held throughout the country to select representatives to
the national unification conference, and local mayors were supposed to
certify the election results. Many local mayors, however, were members
of the MRF party, and Gendzhev claimed that the election process had
once again been influenced by MRF activists.[24] Gendzhev and some of his
allies in the Muslim community pulled out of the "unification" conference, and the congress was convened without them. Hasan's High Muslim
Council regained control of all of the organizational aspects and assets
of Bulgaria's Muslim community, and his close colleague, Mustafa Alish
Hadzhi, became chief mufti. The now UDF-controlled Directorate of Religious Dominations accepted the results of the unification conference and

removed Gendzhev from his position. The new leaders also voted to begin
a criminal investigation into the alleged unlawful activities of Gendzhev.
Gendzhev protested his removal and appealed the directorate's decision
through the Bulgarian courts all the way up to the Supreme Administrative Court. But the UDF government accepted the results of the unification
conference, dismissing numerous appeals.

The UDF was firmly entrenched in power with the strong support of
the United States, so Gendzhev began trying a different tactic. He began
lashing out against what he perceived to be a growing coziness between
the chief mufti's office and foreigners promoting Saudi-influenced Islam
in Bulgaria. In April 2000, more than a year before the terrorist attacks
in New York and Washington, DC, an organization of Gendzhev's supporters accused the chief mufti, Mustafa Alish Hadzhi, of having links
with Osama Bin Laden, the Islamic fundamentalist leader of Al-Qaeda.
The organization known as "The Straight Path for Bulgarian Citizens of
Turkish Origin" held protests in front of the chief mufti's office in Sofia,
threatening to take it by force.[25]

Several months later, the leaders of the Straight Path also accused Hadzhi of having intimate connections with the Movement for Rights and
Freedoms. Gendzhev's supporters claimed that Ahmed Doğan had received half a million U.S. dollars to ensure the election of Mustafa Alish
Hadzhi as chief mufti in 1997 by mobilizing its political operatives at
the municipal level.[26] Another 500,000 dollars was allegedly given to
a minister in the UDF government to support the activities of the new
mufti.[27] This money supposedly originated from Abdul Rakhman Takan,
a man who had been deported for having ties with the Muslim Brothers,
an Islamic organization officially banned in Bulgaria. The leaders of the
Straight Path demanded a financial audit of the chief mufti's office as
well as an investigation into its links with Islamic fundamentalists.[28] The
chief mufti's office denied all claims, although it was admitted that there
were emissaries preaching Islam in Bulgaria, particularly in the Rhodope
region.[29]

It was at this time that the Bulgarian security services also deported
several Muslims for their religious proselytizing, claiming that they were
a threat to national security.[30] In August 2000, the UDF-controlled Bulgarian security services deported a Jordanian, Ahmad Musa, for preaching Islamic fundamentalism and preparing Bulgarian Muslims to engage
in terrorism. The government claimed that it had evidence that Musa
was organizing seminars and summer youth camps that preached radical
Islam. He was also accused of having organized a Bulgarian cell of the
Muslim Brothers.[31] After Musa was arrested, the chief mufti came to his
defense by claiming that the Jordanian had not conducted any religious
activities in the country. When he was deported on 6 August, about two

hundred Muslims, including the regional mufti of Sofia, Ali Khairaddin, showed up at the airport to protest.[32] In the controversy that followed, it became known that Musa, as director of the Bulgarian branch of the Kuwaiti Social Reform Foundation, had given more than 1.5 million dollars in aid to the chief mufti's office. According to a press release from the Bulgarian Tolerance Foundation, a human rights NGO trying to defend Musa, "It is believed that the real reason for the expelling of Mr. Musa is the desire of the Bulgarian authorities to keep the control over the financial resources of the Muslim religion in Bulgaria. According to Mr. Musa, the foundation supported the activities of the Chief Mufti's Office. Thus, the Chief Mufti's Office could obtain some financial independence from the state."[33]

In the late 1990s, 1.5 million dollars was a considerable sum of money, given the exchange rate. In August 2000, a statement signed by about ten thousand Muslims in Bulgaria and submitted to the Bulgarian president and prime minister demanded an investigation into whether or not Chief Mufti Mustafa Alish Hadzhi was a proponent of what they called Wahhabism.[34] But this was before 11 September 2001, and warnings about Islamic fundamentalism in the Balkans were often read as Slavic anti-Muslim propaganda. In October 2000, Mustafa Alish Hadzhi convened another conference and Selim Mekhmed, yet another associate of Fikri Sali Hasan's, became the new chief mufti. The MPs from the Movement for Rights and Freedoms were apparently among the first to congratulate the new mufti.[35] The division between the two factions of the Muslim community deepened.

After the attacks on the United States in September 2001, the fear of Islamic fundamentalism quickly spread worldwide. The bogeyman of terrorism was picked up by both sides of the Muslim community in order to further their political goals. In the weeks following 11 September, Gendzhev's close allies claimed that at least sixty foundations operating in Bulgaria had links to Islamic fundamentalists, including Osama Bin Laden and the Muslim Brothers. There were schools throughout Bulgaria, Gendzhev charged, teaching young Muslims a form of Islam foreign to the country, and these schools were concentrated in the Rhodope region, where the Pomaks lived. The chief mufti responded: "Such a thing cannot exist in Bulgaria. These people are impudent and are taking advantage of the aftermath of the attacks in the USA to discredit the Chief Mufti's office and to force a split in the Muslim community."[36]

At the same time, however, the new chief mufti himself deployed the threat of Islamic fundamentalism to bolster his restitution claims. In January 2002, Selim Mekhmed argued that if the Bulgarian government did not make a greater effort to return the properties that had been confiscated from the Muslims under communism, the Muslim community in

Bulgaria might have to embrace Islamic fundamentalism because of the vast resources the fundamentalists had at their disposal.[37]

The chief mufti's office did acknowledge that there was a problem. In November 2002, Selim Mekhmed announced that all of the foreign funds would now be controlled by the state. All of the aid monies received by the chief mufti's office and the regional muftis would be placed in a special account within the Ministry of Finance until the origin of the money could be established. "This will block the access to Bulgaria of money of dubious donors, proponents of fundamentalism," the mufti said.[38] Furthermore, the mufti agreed to take precautions against the infiltration of Islamic fundamentalists by closely monitoring the activities of all Muslim clergymen and any contacts they might have with radical Islamists from abroad.[39]

But some of Gendzhev's accusations started to stick, particularly after the bombings in Istanbul in November 2003. Immediately following the attacks, Gendzhev once again accused the Chief Muftiship of not doing enough to prevent the spread of fundamentalism in the country. Gendzhev claimed that Mekhmed had been accepting bribes from foreign "Wahabbi" clerics and allowing them to operate illegal Islamist schools. He warned that the radical ideas were particularly penetrating an area that included Smolyan, Rudozem, and Madan. Finally, Gendzhev alleged that about a hundred students who had been sent abroad to study in Jordan, Saudi Arabia, and Kuwait were returning to Bulgaria to promote "militant Islam."[40]

Among the Bulgarian students retuning were Arif Abdullah and Selvi Shakirov, two young Pomaks who had received their Islamic educations in Jordan. For years they had given lectures and seminars in Smolyan during their university vacations, and now they immediately became active in the leadership of the Muslim denomination. At the Regional Muslim Council in Smolyan in 2003, attended by imams, chairmen and members of the boards of governors from the mosques throughout the region, Shakirov was elected regional mufti with 143 out of 145 votes, and Abdullah was elected chairman with 144.[41] Both men were devout Muslims, naive about the corruption and scandals that riddled the Bulgarian political landscape and unaware of the extent of the political machinations in the national leadership of their denomination. When the national conference was convened in December 2003, with delegates hand-chosen by the MRF, Abdullah and Shakirov were surprised at the degree of blatant external manipulation. "We expected that there would be a democratic election like the election we had at the regional level. But the choice of the chief mufti was already predetermined," Abdullah explained in a meeting I had with him in March 2007. "We had no choice but to do something."

During the 2003 conference, members of the Smolyan delegation left the room in protest against the election of Fikri Sali Hasan as the new chief mufti under the undue interference of the MRF. The Smolyan delegation not only protested the election but mounted a court case against Hasan and submitted documentary evidence of illegal activities conducted by him and his associates, including the disappearance of monies allocated to the Chief Muftiship.[42] Abdullah and Shakirov, as well as Ali Khairaddin, the regional mufti of Sofia, hoped that there would be a free and fair election. Quite independent of Gendzhev and his faction, the Pomaks in Smolyan supported the election of Ali Khairaddin, a Pomak, because they wanted to restore some spiritual integrity to the muftiship.

Khairaddin was certainly the most devout believer among the Muslim national leadership. "Islam is the middle path," he explained to me during an informal conversation in July 2005. "Judaism is too material. Christianity is too spiritual. Islam finds the balance between the spiritual and the material. Islam is a system for your whole life—it guides you through every step of the way, what to eat, how to dress, when to pray, how to treat your spouse. Islam is the only religion that can be a world religion. Judaism is a national religion of Israel. Christianity is too spiritual; everyone is just waiting for heaven. There is no guidance for this life. Buddhism is too inward-looking. Islam is the final religion, and the fastest growing. It will bring us all together in peace."[43]

By 2006, Khairaddin was arguing that Bulgarian Islam had been corrupted by national politics; he wanted to restore morality to the chief mufti's office. Despite ongoing objections, Fikri Sali Hasan took office after the contested conference. He immediately began accusing Gendzhev of illegally controlling commercial properties that belonged to the Chief Muftiship. At the same time, Gendzhev's High Muslim Council still claimed that it was the only legitimate representative of Bulgaria's Muslims. Because a new 2002 Denominations Act required the re-registration of all Bulgarian denominations, the conditions were ripe for a renewed conflict between Gendzhev and the faction represented by Hasan, Hadzhi, and Mekhmed. Both factions submitted documents to the government to register their group as the legitimate representative of the Bulgarian Muslim community. Both groups had High Muslim Councils that held national elections for the position of chief mufti; their documents were almost identical. Initially, the government allowed Gendzhev to register a parallel Muslim denomination that would be in charge of the disputed (and quite valuable) properties under his control.[44] Two more court cases were brought as Gendzhev and Hasan tried to sue each other, and the denomination plunged into chaos for months.

In the summer of 2004, the courts finally decided that the government could not register either faction. It was impossible to determine from the documents submitted which was the true representative of Bulgaria's Muslims.[45] At the same time, the evidence brought by the Smolyan faction that the national conference of December 2003 had been tampered with was compelling enough for the courts to question the legitimacy of Hasan's election. As an interim measure, the Sofia City Court removed Hasan from office and installed a temporary triumvirate to oversee the affairs of the community until the court came to a decision, which could take up to a year. One of these interim leaders, however, was Fikri Sali Hasan himself, and the other two were his close supporters. Although the three-person, government-appointed leadership was later declared unlawful, they remained in power. Having lost out in the battle for the interim leadership, Gendzhev lashed out, this time filling the international press with worries about fundamentalism in Bulgaria.[46]

"This religion is being divided and non-traditional elements are gaining command of various regions," Nedim Gendzhev told the international press in 2004.[47] Georgi Krŭstev, the expert on Muslim affairs at the Council of Minister's Directorate of Denominations also stated, "It is very likely that Wahhabism is being preached in Bulgaria. There are a number of young people [here] who graduated in Saudi Arabia and Jordan and who must have been influenced by these countries' conservative traditions."[48] General Atanas Atanassov, the director of Bulgaria's state security services from 1997 to 2001, emphasized that local Muslim groups were becoming dependent on money from the Gulf Arab countries, and that this aid was attached to more "orthodox" versions of Islam, including that of the Muslim Brothers coming from Jordan.[49] Even the Bulgarian Helsinki Committee, a human rights organization dedicated to protecting religious rights, acknowledged that rich, foreign Islamic foundations were helping Bulgarian Muslims rebuild mosques throughout the Rhodope,[50] and that this might cause conflicts with the local Christian population. Saudi money had probably been coming into Bulgaria since the very early 1990s,[51] and the return of Pomaks who had studied in Jordan provided new avenues to funnel this money into local communities.

In December 2004, the European Court of Human Rights found in favor of Gendzhev, declaring that the state had wrongly removed him from office in 1997.[52] Soon afterward, the Supreme Court of Appeal in Bulgaria found that Gendzhev's organization was the only legitimate representative of Bulgarian Islam.[53] Despite this decision, the NMSS/MRF government still refused to recognize Gendzhev's High Muslim Council and waited instead for another national conference to be convened by the three appointed caretakers of the Muslim denomination. Gendzhev accused Doğan and his followers of trying to maintain control over the Muslim community until the July 2005 parliamentary elections[54] and refused to attend the new national conference. At the same time, Abdullah, Shakirov, and Khairaddin came to the conference hoping that their court challenge would have reformed the national conference and made it more

Figure 13 An MRF campaign sign for the 2005 parliamentary election. It says "Togetherness" and shows pictures of a mosque, church, and synagogue.

democratic. All three of them had put their names on the ballot for chief mufti. Instead, when they arrived they found that Smolyan was the only region where the delegates had been elected by the mosque boards of governors and the imams. The other delegates were once again activists of the MRF, and the Smolyan faction accused the conference of grasping not the "rope of God" but the "rope of Ahmed Doğan."[55]

The day after the conference, Abdullah, Shakirov, and Khairaddin held a press conference and denounced the interference of the MRF in the Muslim denomination. They complained that five MRF members of Parliament had been present during the conference and that the chosen delegates did not represent the Muslims of Bulgaria. "Our biggest enemy is political intervention," Khairaddin said. "We are also to blame, we the Muslims, for allowing this intervention to happen. The guilt is on both sides. The reason for the chaos is those interests that are not religious ones."[56] In their magazine, *Muslim Society*, Abdullah and Shakirov made a similar point: "[We are] against the imposition of political force in religious matters. For more than fifteen years the Muslims in Bulgaria have been unable to elect a chief mufti. The MRF controls the choice so directly that the last time it ensured its cause with preselected delegates. The total political control over religious institutions is the reason for the economic, social, and religious stagnation in the Muslim community."[57]

According to a document prepared by Gendzhev and submitted to the court in opposition to the March 2005 National Conference,[58] out of the 1,351 delegates in attendance, 1,214 of them had no right to be there. Of the total number of delegates, only 137 were imams or chairmen, secretary-treasurers, or members of the mosque boards of governors. The rest of the delegates had no official leadership positions within the Muslim denomination of their regions, hence no documentation to legitimize their participation in the conference. Most interesting was the inclusion of fifty MRF village mayors among the delegates. Because of them, Mustafa Alish Hadzhi, the candidate favored by the MRF, was elected to the post of chief mufti. Both the Smolyan faction and the Gendzhev faction protested the election,[59] but the NMSS/MRF government recognized it.

Thus, what originally started as a rivalry between Gendzhev and the MRF slowly began to develop into a new three-way conflict between the two groups of Turkish Muslims and a group of Pomaks whose sphere of influence included Madan, Rudozem, and Smolyan. Immediately after the conference, Selvi Shakirov suspected that he would be removed from his office as regional mufti of Smolyan because he went against the election of Hadzhi. At that time, he proposed three alternatives for the Pomaks: (1) to separate themselves and form an autonomous muftiship (as they had been under communism); (2) to start a national association of learned Muslims in Bulgaria; or (3) to enter into a coalition with a political party which might protect them from the machinations of the MRF.[60]

The Pomaks from Smolyan allegedly allied themselves with the Democrats for a Strong Bulgaria, a UDF splinter party formed by Ivan Kostov, the former prime minister,[61] and also formed at least two Muslim associations. Arif Abdullah had already, in 2004, founded the Union of Islamic Development and Culture (UIDC), and in 2006, Ali Khairaddin started the Union of Bulgarian Muslims. Both nongovernmental organizations supported the spiritual development of the Muslim community but they promoted a more "orthodox" interpretation of Islam, one influenced by their contacts with Saudi Arabia and Jordan. This "Arab" Islam was theologically distinct from that practiced by Bulgaria's Turks, and thus its adherents distinguished themselves from the Turkish leadership and claimed a higher spiritual authority based on their stricter adherence to "pure" Islam. The Pomak leaders believed the Turkish Muslims to be lax in their Islamic observances and therefore completely vulnerable to political manipulation.[62] Abdullah, Shakirov, and Khairaddin wanted to wrest control of the denomination from the monopoly of the MRF once and for all. But because they were truly devout Muslims and regarded Gendzhev as only interested in the material gains that came with denominational leadership, no strategic alliances were forged between him and the Smolyan Pomaks.[63]

Since the opposition was not united against Mustafa Hadzhi, the chief mufti's office, together with its allies in the MRF, took revenge. The first casualties were Selvi Shakirov and Arif Abdullah, who were indeed removed from their offices in the Regional Muftiship of Smolyan. Even though they had both been democratically elected and maintained the support of the Muslims in the region, the right to serve as regional mufti had to be granted by the chief mufti and could be taken away at will.[64] While Abdullah and Shakirov were on a pilgrimage in Saudi Arabia, their rights were revoked, and Shakirov was replaced by Haireddin Hatim, a young imam from the city of Zlatograd.[65] Hadzhi appointed Hatim over the wishes of the local Muslims, who wrote to the chief mufti to protest against Shakirov's removal.[66]

Shortly after the removal of Shakirov in Smolyan, Nedim Gendzhev was arrested for allegedly embezzling money from the chief mufti's accounts.[67] The arrest of Gendzhev, carried out one day before he was scheduled to give a press conference about corruption in the chief mufti's office, caused a scandal.[68] Gendzhev explicitly told the press that he believed that Doğan was responsible for his detention.[69] He was eventually released on bail after more than two weeks in custody and continued to agitate for recognition of the higher court's decision in his favor.

In the summer of 2006, several high-profile incidents brought the Union of Islamic Culture and Development to national attention, and for several months Selvi Shakirov and Arif Abdullah were featured on Bulgarian radio and television and splashed across the national newspapers as they agitated for the rights of Pomak girls to wear headscarves in schools, an issue which will be discussed in depth in chapter 6. Their commitment to "orthodox" Islam grew in its intensity and was seen as a threat to the legitimacy of the chief mufti. Certainly, from the perspective of those within the chief muftiship, the Smolyan Pomaks were merely acting out because they lost the election and had a bad case of sour grapes.[70] Hadzhi did not support their case.

Just months after Gendzhev's arrest and the national headscarf case, the Muslim NGO set up by Shakirov and Abdullah came under increasing government scrutiny. On 19 September 2006, the regional prosecutor of Smolyan opened a personal investigation into the activities of the UIDC, requesting information from the national security services as to their sources of funding.[71] Abdullah himself told me that he believed that this investigation was started after the Smolyan representative of the MRF sent a letter to MRF headquarters in Sofia denouncing Abdullah and Shakirov as Islamic radicals trying to destabilize Bulgaria.[72] In fact, he was certain that the attacks were, once again, politically motivated: the

activism of Abdullah and Shakirov among the Pomaks in the Smolyan region threatened the MRF's near-monopoly of the Muslim vote in the lead
up to the 2007 municipal elections. After months of grueling scrutiny, in
March 2007 the Smolyan chief prosecutor finally admitted that Abdullah
and his organizations had committed no crimes under Bulgaria law.[73]

Tensions continued, however. Ali Khairaddin and three other Muslims
associated with the Union of Bulgarian Muslims were arrested in February 2007 for publishing two "radical Islamic websites," which were said
to be promoting Wahhabism and a holy war against all non-Muslims.[74]
In particular, one of the women working with Khairaddin was accused
of translating into Bulgarian Chechen Islamic literature advocating for
the Rhodope to become the next Chechnya. As this woman turned out
to be Khairaddin's "spiritual" wife, it seemed that the Union of Bulgarian
Muslims was also promoting polygamy. One of the websites, www.islam-
bg.net, was frequently visited by the young Pomaks in Madan, and the
local Muslim magazine, *Ikra*, relied on the website for a good portion of
its Bulgarian content. Furthermore, according to one press report, Khairaddin was fashioning himself as a political leader of the Pomaks and
advocating "orthodox" Islam, in opposition to the relatively more liberal
Hanafi Sunni Turkish form of Islam, as a way to distance the Pomaks
from the Turks.[75] He was rumored to have strong links with Saudi Arabia
and the Muslim Brothers in Jordan. He was also responsible for sending
many young Pomaks to study Islam abroad. Although Khairaddin and his
associates were released on bail soon after their arrest, the charges brought
against them were quite serious. They were accused of spreading antidem-
ocratic propaganda and potentially advocating for the partition of the Bulgarian state.

By the beginning of 2007, the great irony of the situation was that
Ahmed Doğan was assuring American diplomats that he would take care
of any "radical" Islamic threats in Bulgaria, and continuously asking the
United States for financial support to promote his endeavor of maintain-
ing ethnic peace and tolerance in the country.[76] From one perspective, however, the atheist Doğan and his MRF party could be held at least partially
responsible for the chaos and confusion in the Bulgarian Muslim denomination and the drift toward "orthodox" Islam. The struggle for control of
the Chief Muftiship and the resulting neglect of the needs of the Muslim
community led more and more Bulgarians to look outside of the country
for leadership. In 2007, Gendzhev claimed that most imams in Bulgaria
had not received salaries from the chief mufti's office in over four years,
and this had made them susceptible to "emissaries" who offered them access to resources and funds for their basic survival.[77] Indeed, neither Khairaddin nor Abdullah received official funding from the chief mufti's office
or from the Turkish government, which means that they had to derive

their income from elsewhere.[78] The many scandals and internal conflicts among Bulgarian Muslims were perhaps the most important factor in opening the door to external influences, in particular from foreign-based Islamic charities. Doğan's desire to monopolize the Muslim community for political reasons increasingly alienated all of those who supported the idea that Islam was a religion and not just a path to political power.

*   *   *

For believers like Hasan, these political conflicts undermined the spiritual message of Islam. Once more in the mosque café, Hasan was telling me about his pilgrimage to Mecca, and how hot it was in Saudi Arabia. "There were millions of people, and it was almost fifty degrees [Celsius]. The Saudis had booths with water everywhere. It was very interesting how much more water the European Muslims needed compared to the Africans and the Arabs."

He made us both a cup of tea and nodded toward one of the posters on the wall. "In those few days, I heard every language in the world; there were people from almost all countries, together to make the hadj. In those millions [of people] I felt the power of God. I thought I knew God before I made the hadj, but I only truly knew him in Mecca. God is unity among people who come together in peace to pray to him. I have brothers everywhere in the world."

Hasan shook his head slowly, looking down at the copy of *Myusyul-mani* magazine still on the counter in front of me. "Perhaps that is why God has such a hard time with us in Bulgaria. In Mecca, the millions can put aside their differences to pray together in peace. Here, brothers steal bread from their brothers."

Chapter Five

Islamic Aid

ON A HOT AND STICKY AFTERNOON in the middle of June 2006, I sought coolness in the main auditorium of Madan's Kulturen Dom, the newly painted building erected by the communists to educate the toiling masses and inspire them to build a glorious socialist future. The interior was considerably aged and worse for wear from many communist party meetings and state-sponsored concerts. I was there to hear a lecture that had been advertised around town for two weeks: "Islam: Pluralism and Dialogue."

The lecture was supposed to begin at 3:00 p.m., an hour obviously selected to attract the crowd from the mosque after Friday prayers. A steady trickle of people slowly filed into the auditorium, some in pairs, some in groups of five or six, men and women walking in together. At one point, a group of women in headscarves and long gowns that had initially tried to sit apart from the men, up in the balcony section, were discussing whether or not they would be able to hear the talk. After some consideration, they came back down to the orchestra level. With no direction from any ushers, the women self-segregated by taking seats in the last four rows of the theater while the men came down to sit toward the stage. I had spent ten years doing research in Bulgaria but had never seen this happen anywhere else in the country. As more women came in, they joined the already seated women in the back of the theater, creating a distinct separation between the sexes. With the exception of myself and two older women, all of the women wore headscarves and were fully clothed, down to their wrists and ankles, despite the intense summer heat outside.

When they finally closed the auditorium doors, there were well over 150 people in the audience—at least fifty women and more than a hundred men. The crowd was relatively young; most attendees seemed to be under forty. Very few events beyond the Friday prayers could draw such a huge crowd in Madan—a home soccer game might get 60 or 70 people, and the film *The Da Vinci Code*, which played right after the lecture, drew about 9. As I looked around at the faces, I recognized that some people had come from Rudozem and other villages surrounding Madan; this was not a purely local crowd. Still, there were quite a few people in the room to hear a man who was merely the director of a small, relatively new Islamic NGO in the region.

Beyond the unusually large number of men and women in the audience, there were two other surprises. The first was the quantity and quality of the audiovisual equipment the organization had set up to film and record the lecture. In front of the stage was a man with a digital video recorder on a tripod. The camera was connected to a new laptop computer, which was open and facing the audience. As the first men stood up to make the introductions and thank people for their attendance, the audience could see the speakers' images being recorded and displayed in color on the plasma screen of the laptop. There was also an LCD projector beaming the organization's logo onto a screen behind the stage, and two large Yamaha speakers on either side of the screen. The men also had two wireless microphones that were casually passed between them. Of course, none of this would seem out of place in the United States or Western Europe, but in a very poor community, where most bellies were full of cucumbers and white bread, to have so many expensive toys on display was to cultivate both envy and admiration from the audience. The equipment established for the organization the type of authority that comes with access to great resources.

As the young man singing verses from the Qur'an finished his opening performance and the formal program began, it was also impressive that the keynote speaker, Arif Abdullah, proceeded to lecture for over an hour without using any notes, a very rare occurrence in Bulgaria, where most speeches are meticulously prepared ahead of time and then read verbatim from the page. Furthermore, the intellectual tenor of the lecture was unusual for a nonacademic crowd. The theme was a critique of the Western concept of pluralism, starting with Socrates, Erasmus, Martin Luther, and Rousseau and ending with the American political scientists Samuel Huntington and Francis Fukuyama. He carefully enumerated all the reasons why the Western concept of pluralism was a failure and concluded that Islam was the only way that the many peoples of the world could live together in harmony and peace. But not just any Islam, the one "true" Islam of the Qur'an, one that had not been corrupted by centuries of contact with Christianity and decades of atheist distortion.

As I listened to the lecture, I tried to gauge the reaction of the crowd, whom I assumed had never heard of either Huntington or Fukuyama. Their attention was absolutely fixed on the speaker. Abdullah was a young and handsome man, just thirty-two years old. He wore his light brown hair and beard short and closely shaven, and heavy lashes framed his intense blue eyes. Having won a scholarship to study abroad, Abdullah held a master's degree in the Exegesis of the Qur'an from the Faculty of Shari'a at the University of Jordan. His knowledge of both philosophy and

Islamic theology was well honed. His Bulgarian was erudite and elegant without being haughty, and he spoke in a confident and clear voice, with a charisma that seemed to enchant the crowd.

Despite the difficulties of the subject matter, Abdullah never lost his audience. He spoke of Islam in the same way Bulgaria's old leaders had once spoken about communism: a bright future lay ahead through embracing a total belief system that regulated every aspect of life. All other political systems had failed. Islam was the only answer. It was the "final way." It was ironic that he was giving this lecture here in the very building that symbolized all the promises of the Bulgarian communists.

At the end of the lecture, Abdullah took questions from the audience, and several people accused him of trying to cause problems between the Christian and Muslims. "This Islam is against Bulgaria," one man said. "How can a Bulgarian be a Muslim in this way?"

Abdullah leaned into the microphone. "We are Bulgarians because we live in Bulgaria and speak Bulgarian. We are Bulgarian citizens. We cannot be Italians or Americans. We should never mix up ethnicity, nationality, and religion. They are different things. If you look at my *lichna carta* [personal identity card], it says, 'Nationality: Bulgarian.' Not Italian. Not French. I am Bulgarian, and I cannot be anything else. But that does not determine what we believe. We are Muslims. Integration is good, but enslavement is bad. There is no tolerance if people are asked to give up their culture and practices."

Abdullah took a few more questions, and then thanked the audience for its attention. After the lecture, I shuffled out among the chattering crowd, listening to a cacophony of conversations around me. Through the thick forest of voices, I overheard two male voices speaking almost directly behind me.

"This is not Bulgarian Islam. These are not our ways," the first male voice said.

"There is no Bulgarian Islam. There is only one *istinski Islyam* [true Islam], and we must learn it," replied a second voice.

"*Iskat da staveme talibani!* [They want us to become Talibans!]" exclaimed the first. "Bulgaria is not Saudi Arabia. We have our own ways."

A moment later, I emerged into the bright sunshine craving caffeine and someone with whom to share my thoughts. Because of the number of women in headscarves in the audience, I had assumed that Abdullah was speaking mostly to those who already agreed with him, but there were still clearly some dissenters. I wandered toward the steps in front of the Culture House, where there were some tables and chairs, shaded by red and white Coca Cola umbrellas, overlooking the main square. I found an empty table and sat down to enjoy a thick Bulgarian espresso coffee. I watched as the men and women from the lecture pooled into groups of two and three, some still discussing the lecture with each other and others heading off toward their cars. There was a minibus waiting on the narrow street, and about twelve of the women in headscarves boarded it; someone had obviously arranged transportation for them.

Lined with linden trees, the main square was bordered by a playground and the Madanska River to the left and a narrow street to the right. On the river's side of the plaza, the silver top of the minaret was just visible through the trees. Across the narrow street to the right were the main municipal administration buildings, the pizzeria, the bank, Sonic, the disco, and the small casino. At the other end of the square was a fountain with a young, naked, bronze woman lifting two outstretched arms up to the sky, a circle of thin streams of water bathing her. Four young Pomak women sat on the ledge of the fountain, watching the crowd from the lecture. One of the women wore a white bustier, a very short red skirt, and "Grecian" sandals that wound up her calves. Another wore a loose, flowery, spaghetti-strapped sundress that floated out around her half-bare thighs. The other two wore white pants and halter tops—one blue and one camouflage-printed. Three of them wore their brownish-black hair loose and long, and the fourth, a "dirty blonde," had hers up in a high ponytail and was exposing a wide swath of bare back beneath the thin band of the halter top around her neck.

The young women near the fountain were laughing and gesturing toward the women boarding the minibus and the others who wore head coverings, long sleeves, and floor-length skirts or gowns. It was a striking contrast, and I regretted immediately that I had forgotten my camera. Both groups of women occupied the same physical space of the main square, but they seemed to be from different worlds. They embodied all of the contradictions that were emerging in Madan in 2006. The conservatively dressed lecture audience and the new minaret represented one version of Madan, while the bar, the disco, the casino, the fountain, and the four young "fashionistas" represented another. These two versions had so far coexisted without conflict.

But over the last fifteen years, resources from the Muslim world had helped to build over two hundred new mosques around the country, in addition to free Qur'anic schools, Islamic centers, and free boarding houses for Muslim children. Foreign monies had also supported the translation of Islamic literature into Bulgarian and its publication and distribution as books, brochures, and magazines. Increasingly, this literature had begun to appear on newly launched websites targeting Muslim youth, such as Ali Khairaddin's two websites that were shut down by the government in 2007. A network of "orthodox" Islamic foundations and associations had sprung up to help train and support a new generation of Bulgarian Muslims uncorrupted by the theological distortions of the past. Stipends of more

than 1,500 leva were given to members of devout families to make the
pilgrimage to Mecca, and young people got scholarships to travel abroad.
And in this region, all of these developments had coincided with the privatization and liquidation of GORUBSO and the massive male unemployment that followed.

These activities, which the anthropologist Saba Mahmood calls "religious sociability,"[1] were financed by "Islamic aid,"[2] funds originating in
the Middle East to support *da'wa* (mission) work among Muslim populations around the world. Although this Islamic aid could take the form
of humanitarian assistance in times of crisis or of loans and grants for
general economic development, it was often linked to the specific Islamic
teachings of the donor state or organization. Many of the international
organizations associated with this form of aid had been operating since
the mid-1970s in Africa and South Asia, but it was only after 1989 that
their activities expanded to include Europe and Central Asia. The collapse of communism and the creation of a whole new crop of states with
Muslim majorities or significant Muslim minorities provided a bounty of
new opportunities for both development assistance and *da'wa* activities
in regions formerly dominated by state-endorsed atheism.

Although Bulgaria's Muslims received aid from Turkey and Iran, it was the
resources originating from Jordan, Saudi Arabia, and Kuwait that proved
to be the most controversial.[3] First, they were seen to be promoting a form
of Islam that was foreign to the Balkans. Second, while Turkish or Iranian
funds came directly from their respective governments as a form of bilat-
eral aid to Bulgaria, "orthodox" Islamic aid often arrived in the country
through unofficial channels, from private individuals or through NGOs.
Most importantly, however, it was the influence of the Saudis that was
scapegoated as responsible for the increasing radicalization of the Muslims in Bosnia, Kosovo, and Chechnya. The Saudis, it was felt, were pro-
longing or intensifying conflicts in these regions by providing resources
to separatist Muslim forces.

Supporting the *Ummah*

When conflict erupted in Bosnia in 1992, "orthodox"-Islamic aid organizations entered the country, ostensibly to provide humanitarian assistance
to displaced Muslim refugees. New local Islamic organizations were created to deal specifically with the Bosnians' plight, some under the aegis of
foreign governments that felt they needed to respond to the growing crisis
in the Balkans. Various organizations were set up or indirectly sponsored
by the Saudi Arabian, Sudanese, and Iranian governments to provide help,
all jockeying with each other for power and influence in the new European

Muslim states of Bosnia and Albania. At the beginning of the conflict, the secretary-general of the Saudi Arabian World Assembly of Muslim Youth (WAMY) sent an official letter to the Organization of the Islamic Conference (OIC) urging immediate military support for the Bosnian Muslims: "The very worth of the whole Muslim *Ummah* in general and the OIC in particular is now in question."[4] He supported the creation of an official Muslim rapid-deployment force to go into Bosnia to protect the Muslims, but such direct action was not supported by the OIC. Other forms of support had to be found.

During the conflict, it became apparent that many of the foreign states and their "nongovernmental" organizations and charities were providing arms and supplies to the Bosnian army and the *mujihadeen*, unofficial fighters (many from Afghanistan) who had been sent to Bosnia to battle on the Muslims' behalf. Their missions overtly included the "re-Islamization" of the Bosnian Muslims and support for the creation of an Islamic state in Europe. Jerome Bellion-Jourdan refers to organizations like the International Islamic Relief Organization (IIRO) as "so-called NGOs" and claims that they were merely "para-statal structures corresponding to the Saudi strategy in Bosnia."[5] Both the Muslim World League and WAMY were intimately tied to the Saudi royal family and charged with promoting "orthodox" Islam among Muslims around the world, including in the Balkans.[6]

Other examples were the Third World Relief Agency (TWRA) and the Al Haramain Islamic Foundation (AHIF). The TWRA was founded in 1987 in Vienna by a prominent member of the National Islamic Front party in Sudan. Its official mission was to oversee the spread of Islam to the countries newly emerging from communism.[7] Instead, it became the organization primarily responsible for money laundering and smuggling arms to the Bosnians during the weapons embargo. Its largest donors were Saudi Arabia, Iran, and Sudan. The Al Haramain Islamic Foundation was a subsidiary of the Saudi Muslim World League. The AHIF, created in 1988, aimed at protecting and assisting Muslims around the world while also promoting "orthodox" Islam to those most in need of material aid.[8] In Bosnia, the AHIF was also active in providing support for the "Afghan-Arabs" fighting alongside the Bosnians during the war and introducing Bosnians to the "pure" version of Islam. Other charities, such as the Islamic Relief Agency and the Saudi High Commission for Relief were implicated in providing money to arm the Bosnian resistance.[9]

These charities thus fueled the Bosnian war,[10] but what is more relevant to developments in Bulgaria is the extent to which they actively promoted forms of Islamic belief and practice that were at odds with the traditional Islam practiced locally.[11] In the aftermath of the Bosnian war, it became apparent that there were important differences between traditional and "orthodox" interpretations of Islam, and exponents of the latter were set on reforming what they saw as heretical Balkan innovations. The historian Isa Blumi writes: "The hallowed principle of Sunni Islam, according to which all those who profess the *shahada* [ritual act of belief] are Muslims, is therefore rejected by Wahhabis in favor of the necessity of struggling against all other Muslims who fail to accept Wahhabi teachings."[12]

Since Islam was supposedly brought to the Balkans by the Ottoman Empire and grew up side by side with Catholicism and Orthodox Christianity, the region was home to many types of Hanafi Sunnism and Sufism that included practices considered to be *bid'ah* (an innovation) to the Saudis. For instance, as in the Rhodope, many Balkan Muslims believed in amulets, small pieces of folded paper with verses from the Qur'an written on them, which were bought from local hodzhas.[13] Balkan Muslims also venerated local Muslim saints and went on pilgrimages to shrines (*teke*) at their graves. Similar practices could be found in other parts of the Muslim world and have been consistently targeted for "correction" through the *da'wa* efforts of Saudi-influenced charities.[14]

In fact, the collapse of the Soviet Union and the end of communism in Eastern Europe marked the beginning of a whole new era for the Saudi-funded charities. In the early 1990s, organizations such as the Muslim World League (MWL) were calling for all-out commitments to *da'wa* work in the former communist world.[15] Within the span of a few short years, new Muslim states sprang up in Europe and Central Asia that were in dire need of financial assistance and humanitarian aid. In these countries, as in Bulgaria, religion had in various degrees been suppressed by the state, and they were now eager to reach back and reclaim their traditional faiths as part of the project of recovering national identity.[16] But because the communist regime had been so committed to atheism, many populations had gone for decades without religious education and training. It was therefore quite easy for the Islamic charities to gain a foothold in these new states by claiming that they were providing access to the lost traditions of Islam.[17] In reality, these organizations were promoting their own version of Islam, one that had never existed in these nations before the 1990s. Balkan Islams had always had their own local characteristics, but "orthodox" charities discursively linked these differences with communism, thereby tying the acceptance of "true" Islam to a rejection of the recent totalitarian past.

After 1992, different forms of Islamic aid floated around in Bosnia, Albania, Macedonia, and eventually Kosovo. There is no question that Islamic charities provided much-needed humanitarian assistance during the Bosnian war, but like their Christian counterparts,[18] they often linked aid to proselytizing. Some Saudi-based Islamic charities went even further and openly conditioned the receipt of aid on whether or not individual Bosnians were "true" Muslims. Aid recipients had to forego pork, cigarettes, and alcohol. Additionally, men were required to attend Friday prayers and women to wear "proper" Islamic dress. In one case, women who wore miniskirts or revealing clothing were refused assistance until they dressed more modestly.[19] "Being Muslim the Bosnian way"[20] was seen as an aberration from the "true" Islam, and the Islamic charities that established themselves during the war continued thereafter in their efforts to correct traditional Bosnian Islam.

It was not long before another crisis erupted in Kosovo. The charities, already well established in the region, expanded their activities once again. The secretary-general of the Muslim World League was among the first to issue a call for international Islamic institutions to come help yet another group of European Muslims.[21] The Saudis set up the Saudi Joint Relief Committee for Kosovo (SJRCK), an umbrella for five Saudi charities, including WAMY, to deal with the refugees from the conflict—numbering in the thousands—which Bulgaria would not let in. By July of 1999, SJRCK was managing over 17,000 refugees at twenty-three camps.[22] Amid the fear and displacement of the massive evacuations, the da'wa section of WAMY was hard at work among the Kosovo Albanians, distributing more than 3 million copies of various Islamic publications and sending Islamic teachers trained in Saudi Arabia and Egypt out to teach Albanian children. They also had special Albanian-speaking female teachers to provide religious instruction to the refugee women.[23] In Kosovo, the Islamic charities also destroyed centuries-old mosques and religious complexes under the guise of "reconstruction." Mosques built in the Gulf Arab style replaced the old Ottoman mosques destroyed in the war. In other cases, journalists reported that humanitarian aid to local communities was made contingent on permission for the charity to rebuild the local mosques.[24] Gravestones, mausoleums, and libraries that were hundreds of years old were destroyed because they were considered idolatrous.[25]

After setting up refugee camps in Macedonia during the Kosovo crisis, the Islamic charities then began to work among the Albanian Muslims in that country as well. In 2000, WAMY had given funds to support a Muslim Women's Society in Macedonia and organized more than a thousand lectures, some by Islamic preachers from Saudi Arabia.[26] By 2003, the leadership of the Muslim World League was being sought to help renovate Macedonian mosques destroyed during Macedonia's own escalating ethnic conflict.[27]

When the conflicts subsided, the da'wa missions continued. Blumi has complained that Western aid agencies abandoned the local population to the relief efforts of faith-based Saudi organizations and ignored "the efforts of Arab NGOs to impose their Salafi practices on Kosovar Albanians."[28] He claims that the rural population in Kosovo was left in abject poverty after the conflicts, and that many families had become completely dependent on NGOs for their basic needs. This was problematic in his view because in addition to providing humanitarian aid—food, shelter, clothing, etcetera—one of the primary tasks of the Islamic NGOs has been education and the teaching of "correct" Islamic practices to the Albanian Muslims. In Prishtina (the capital of Kosovo) in 2005, according to Blumi, the Saudis held nightly "training" sessions for women, which included lectures on "the superiority of Arab culture and the need to return to the exemplary behavior of the first Muslims," which meant, among other things, that women should submit to men and wear the headscarf.[29]

In all three countries, reforming the dress and behavior of women was an important goal. In fact, the gender politics of organizations such as WAMY and the MWL were often at odds with the communist project of women's emancipation and the legal equality of the sexes that had defined gender relations in these Balkan states, including Bulgaria. For example, in an open letter to the secretary-general of the United Nations Fourth World Conference on Women in Beijing in 1995, the secretary-general of the Muslim World League, wrote: "Equality of economic participation will strain the role of women as mother raising her children and minimiz[e] her nurturing function and mak[e] her reproductive function an unbearable personal burden. Motherhood is an inherent and inalienable right of women. Neglecting the natural biological function, the innate skills and the acquired roles of women and pushing them out into the open labor market is a clear lack of respect of womanhood and motherhood."[30]

Such a position ran against the predominant culture of most postsocialist states in the 1990s, which still had some of the highest rates of women's labor participation in the world, where women had dominated key sectors such as medicine, law, education, and finance, and where the legal equality of men and women was constitutionally enshrined.[31] In the Balkans, communism never completely eradicated local patriarchies, but in practice women were active participants in the polity, society, and economy of their countries. Guaranteed employment coupled with generous social supports for mothers ensured that women could combine work and family responsibilities. Furthermore, women were expected to engage in formal employment and rather than being discursively constructed only as mothers, they were celebrated as full members of the working class and co-builders of communism.

Balkan Muslim women were the targets of Islamic reform efforts. A 2002 investigation found that at least 10,000 Bosnian war widows and orphaned children were sent letters in the late 1990s from Saudi charities. These letters offered women widow's pensions on the condition that they wear headscarves and send their children to local, religious schools. The charities strategically targeted rural women with little education and few job prospects; many of them accepted these offers of help out of desperation.[32] In the same year, the Bosnian deputy foreign minister claimed that poor Bosnian women were being paid to wear *burqas*[33] like those worn by women in Afghanistan under the Taliban.[34] Earlier in the 1990s, WAMY had, by their own account, handed out more than 14,000 Islamic cassettes and over 6,000 headscarves to Muslim women in Albania.[35]

Although their approach to Islamic practice, specifically regarding the role of women, was new to the Balkans, many of these charities and organizations continued to operate in Albania, Bosnia, Kosovo, and Macedonia, hoping to spread their particular version of "universal" Islam to Europe. Toward the end of the 1990s, their success in achieving this goal was still quite limited; Bosnia did not become an Islamic state, and most Albanians rejected the "orthodox" doctrines. But the aid organizations continued their work, expanding their *da'wa* efforts to include the Muslim populations in Bulgaria. Of the countries slated to join the European Union before 2010, Bulgaria was the only one with a significant Muslim minority.

Islamic Aid in Bulgaria

In 2005, Muslim schools in Bulgaria received money from three primary sources: the Turkish government, foreign foundations, and individual "businessmen."[36] The Turkish Directorate of Religious Affairs (Diyanet) made direct transfers to the office of the chief mufti in Bulgaria to run the three secondary schools in Ruse, Shumen, and Momchilgrad.[37] The courses to train imams that were officially acknowledged by the mufti's office in the towns of Ustina, Sŭrnitza, Bilka, and Delchevo were supported by Turkish-Islamic foundations based in Turkey, Austria, and Germany and by "radical societies primarily from Saudi Arabia," including the foundations Al-Waqf Al-Islami, Taiba, and Irshad.[38] In addition to these official schools and imam courses, there were a number of Qur'an courses, which were sponsored throughout the country and over which the chief mufti's office had little control. Each regional mufti could organize his own course and find sponsors for the students among the many foreign foundations willing to give money to support Islam. Even local imams could appeal directly to foreign foundations for funds to support Qur'an courses, to build mosques, to provide educational opportunities for youth, to give stipends for the hadj, or to distribute ritually sacrificed meats.[39]

Under communism there had been, in general, only limited contact between international Islamic organizations and Bulgaria's Muslim minority. Although the country had good political and economic relations with many countries in the Muslim world, and Palestinian "stateless persons" had been granted Bulgarian citizenship if they settled in the country, these strategic relations seldom extended into the realm of religion. After 1989, however, international Islamic organizations and Muslim states were quite active in forging ties with Muslim communities in the Balkans, including Bulgaria, even though its Christian population was much larger than those in Macedonia, Bosnia, Kosovo, or Albania. The confusion in the Islamic leadership meant that outside donors had no idea who the legitimate representatives of Bulgaria's Muslims were and could easily be manipulated into giving funds to rival groups with different political, economic, or spiritual interests from each other. And all factions of the Bulgarian Muslim leadership reached out to ask for aid and assistance from one of the wealthiest of the Muslim countries: Saudi Arabia.

It was in the Pomak region that resources from Jordan and Saudi Arabia had the most lasting influence. The Turks in Bulgaria were more secure in their Islamic traditions than the Pomaks and had a strong ethnic identity tied to a relatively powerful nation-state, which supported its diaspora through official channels. Moreover, Turkey was still a decidedly secular state, and support to Turks focused more on preserving the Turkish language and culture than on bolstering allegiance to Islam. In contrast, the Pomaks were relentlessly targeted by both Christian and Islamic missionaries because of a perceived ambiguity in their ethnic and religious identity and their high levels of atheism after 1989. They were both politically and economically marginalized throughout the long transition from communism, and Ahmed Doğan and the MRF had done little to help them. This made them a community particularly vulnerable to the promoters of "orthodox" Islam. Finally, the divisions within the Muslim community had largely cut the Pomaks off from the funds that originated in Turkey and Iran. Although in some parts of the Rhodope the Pomaks claimed a Turkish identity, in Madan and its surrounding areas they viewed themselves as a separate ethnicity altogether or a group with links to the Gulf Arabs.

As early as 1990, Nedim Gendzhev went on official visits to Jordan and Saudi Arabia, where he met with the secretary general of the Muslim World League.[40] Representatives from Saudi Arabia also came to Bulgaria to attend the national Muslim conference that elected Gendzhev's rival, Fikri Sali Hasan, in September 1992,[41] and began providing funds for the construction and restoration of scores of mosques throughout the country in 1993 and 1994 through the Islamic foundation Al-Waqf Al-Islami.[42] Exactly at the historical moment when the Gendzhev/Hasan conflict drove a wedge into the unity of the Muslim denomination, several local Islamic charities were set up, including the foundation Irshad in 1991. There were also representatives of the Muslim World League and the International Islamic Charitable Organization (a Kuwaiti organization with strong links to many Saudi charities)[43] at the national conference in August 1996 that returned Gendzhev to the leadership of Bulgaria's Muslims.[44] A few months later, he orchestrated an official state visit of Saudi dignitaries to the Socialist Bulgarian government. On 16 October, the deputy prime minister, Svetoslav Shivarov, received a delegation from the MWL in order to discuss Christian-Muslim relations and the "cultural and spiritual development of Bulgarian Muslims."[45]

The World Assembly of Muslim Youth was active in Bulgaria throughout the 1990s, but its presence was not recognized until the immediate aftermath of the attacks on 11 September 2001, when Nedim Gendzhev began to accuse his rivals in the chief mufti's office of helping to build a "fortress of fundamentalism in Bulgaria."[46] Gendzhev claimed that WAMY was among a number of "fundamentalist" organizations registered in Bulgaria between 1995 and 1999, and that they had sponsored seminars throughout the Rhodope in August 1995, July 1996, and July 1997, and in the summer of 1998. He asserted that the Saudis were paying the expenses of Muslims who made the pilgrimage to Mecca and also alleged that Saudi-based organizations, including WAMY, had links to the Muslim Brothers,[47] an organization that the government considered a threat to national security. In the summer of 2005, a collection of brochures, the *WAMY Series on Islam*, was translated into Bulgarian and was available in the mosque at Chepintsi, a village just a few kilometers south of Rudozem. These bore the WAMY logo but were published by the "charitable foundation Al-Manar," apparently a local affiliate of WAMY with an address and phone number in Sofia.[48]

Despite all these accusations, Gendzhev himself was also accepting funds from organizations and charities linked with Saudi Arabia.[49] Sometime in the mid-1990s, Gendzhev took money from the Third World Relief Agency (the same organization that was funneling arms to Bosnia) in order to publish and distribute a beautifully bound translation of the Qur'an with the Bulgarian and Arabic texts side by side. He was also personally involved as a "manager" with the International Charitable Islamic Organization "Hayatel Igasa" of the Kingdom of Saudi Arabia and the Kuwaiti International Islamic Charitable Organization. Both factions vying for the Chief Muftiship were involved with Islamic charities that supported their claims.

In addition to the "orthodox" charities operating in Bulgaria, the Islamic Development Bank (IsDB) was also active in the country. Although the IsBD was the development bank of the Organization of the Islamic Conference (OIC), its offices were based in Jeddah. Saudi Arabia was by far its largest subscriber, responsible for 27.3 percent of the money contributed, more than double the sum of the second largest donor (Libya, at 11 percent) in 2006.[50] In many countries, the activities of development banks paved the way for the work of Islamic charities. In India, for example, the presence of the IsDB eventually led the way for the establishment in 1999 of an Indian chapter of WAMY, which soon after began setting up new Islamic centers and mosques in the country. Prior to the arrival of WAMY in India, the IsDB had been distributing scholarships in the country for fifteen years and claimed to have helped 2,250 Indian Muslim students in that time.[51]

Similar patterns had emerged in Bulgaria. As early as 1990, the Islamic Development Bank sent missions to the states of the former Soviet Union and Eastern Europe and was providing financial assistance to Bulgaria by 1993.[52] The IsDB scholarship fund also existed in Bulgaria, and was run by none other than Nedim Gendzhev, who was the head of the local IsDB counterpart organization.[53] The program provided interest-free loans for Muslims under the age of twenty-four to study at university in either their own countries or in a handful of countries that were members of the IsDB. When the students repaid their loans, the funds were added to a local charitable trust in the nonmember country and used to promote Islam through community development projects and to provide funds to support future students.[54]

In addition to the scholarship fund, the IsDB donated 800,000 dollars to the Muslim community in Bulgaria in 2000 for the purchase of buildings for Islamic schools and boardinghouses for Muslim students.[55] According to reports in Bulgaria, the chief mufti's office had spent 530,000 dollars of this money by early 2003 on an Islamic institute in Bankya, outside of the capital of Sofia, and on hostels in places such as Momchilgrad, Shumen, and Razgrad.[56] The money, however, was only to be used to finance the construction or purchase of buildings and not for the ongoing expenses of the schools. Those funds would have to come from elsewhere.

Finally, there were many rumors of individual "missionaries" from the Muslim world bringing suitcases full of cash into the Rhodope Mountains to support the instruction of the Pomaks in "orthodox" Islam. In the hearing before the European Court of Human Rights in the case of the expulsion of Dariush Al-Nashif, a Bulgarian woman who was Al-Nashif's second "wife" testified that large amounts of cash were being smuggled into Smolyan to support Qur'an courses.[57] The director of the Religious Denominations Office at the Council of Ministers, Ivan Zhelev, also believed that money from the Muslim world was being brought into the country in cash.[58] More than likely, individuals involved with Islamic NGOs in Bulgaria received funds through the *hawala* system, a mode of transferring money internationally that was common in the Muslim world. An amount of money was given to a *hawala* broker in one country, and then a broker in the receiving country distributed the funds out of his own pocket on the promise that he would be repaid by the first broker at a later time. These *hawala* transactions completely circumvented both the banking system and the state, making it almost impossible to trace the source or the amount of funds transferred.[59]

In addition to the international Islamic organizations and individuals, there were at least twenty foundations and associations officially registered in Bulgaria and engaging in support of the Muslim communities and their spiritual quest to rediscover their religion.[60] Along with their other nonprofit activities, such as supporting local economic development, youth initiatives, or cultural preservation, at least five of these organizations also advocated for more "orthodox" forms of Islamic practice, forms of Islam that challenged local traditions. Some of the money allocated for this work may have been siphoned off to support the political campaigns of the MRF, although there is no solid evidence of this.[61] Interestingly, six of these organizations were based in or near my field sites: four in Madan, one in the neighboring village of Türün, and one in the regional capital of Smolyan, the UIDC (see table 2 in appendix Λ).

These Islamic NGOs were the conduits for channeling foreign aid into local communities in much the same way that local NGOs concerned with women's issues or the environment were subcontracted to carry out work on behalf of international organizations from the West. For the most part, these organizations were involved in valuable social work in Muslim communities. But in a handful of cases, they tailored their efforts toward the conversion of non-Muslims or to introducing "orthodox" Islamic practices into traditional Muslim communities. In all cases, Bulgarian citizens ran these groups, and many sat as "managers" on multiple NGOs at the same time. Some of these groups also had links to commercial enterprises such as trading companies and publishing houses.[62]

Because my research was centered on Madan and, to a lesser extent, neighboring Rudozem, I will focus only on the eastern region of the Smolyan oblast and the activities of three Islamic NGOs: Ikra, Mostove (Bridges) and the Union for Islamic Development and Culture (UIDC, the organization headed by Arif Abdullah and Selvi Shakirov). By the summer of 2006, four key events in or near Madan and Rudozem had drawn national attention to the region as a center of "fundamentalism," leading one local expert to bid "Farewell to Bulgarian Islam."[63]

"Reviving" Islam in the Rhodope

One of the more interesting cultural practices I noticed developing in Rudozem and its surrounding villages was the growing tendency to replace Bulgarian greetings with Arabic ones. I noticed this first while visiting the mosque in Rudozem. I was searching for the imam, and there were some older children in the mosque. I greeted a boy with the standard Bulgarian

"*Dober den*" (good day). Normally, a "*Dober den*" is followed with a reply of "*Dober den*," but he responded with "*As-Salaamu Alaikoum*" (Peace be upon you), very carefully and deliberately pronounced. I thought this odd, and as I left the mosque (the imam was busy teaching classes), I greeted several other children out in the yard in Bulgarian and they also responded in Arabic. Outside of the mosque on the streets of Rudozem, I also noticed some Pomak men meeting, shaking hands, and greeting each other with "*As-Salaamu Alaikoum*," followed by a reply of "*wa Alaikum as-Salaam*." In the village of Chepintsi, about nine kilometers south of Rudozem, the men not only consistently greeted each other in Arabic but also answered their cell phones with "*As-Salaamu Alaikoum*." When I greeted these men in Bulgarian, "*Dober Den*," about half of them responded to me in Bulgarian and about half responded in Arabic.

This practice of greeting in Arabic was quite specific to Rudozem. I had visited many mosques in Bulgaria, as well as the offices of the chief mufti in Sofia and the High Islamic Institute, and nowhere else was this form of greeting common among Bulgarian Muslims. But it was clearly being taught as the appropriate Muslim greeting in some mosques in the Rhodope, and the men and children who used it in their daily conversations were trying to mark themselves as a particular kind of Muslim. I later learned that some of the men had worked or studied in Saudi Arabia and Jordan and therefore spoke Arabic with each other in order to practice their language skills. But these men were a minority; the vast majority of those who used Arabic greetings were Pomaks who otherwise spoke only Bulgarian.

Aside from this growing linguistic habit, the most striking thing that set Madan and Rudozem apart from other Muslim cities in Bulgaria was the size and opulence of their two new mosques. The mosque in Madan was said to be the biggest mosque in the country at the time, even larger than the Ottoman Tombul Mosque in Shumen. Because of its huge mosque, Madan was considered the informal Islamic center of the Smolyan oblast in 2001, even though the regional mufti was headquartered in the city of Smolyan.[64] Both mosques were opened between 2000 and 2001 and received substantial support from outside sponsors (*sponsori*). In 1999, according to local media sources, a new mosque in Smolyan opened, having received about 20,000 dollars (or 35 million leva—a large sum in local currency) from the Saudi foundation Taibah.[65] Another regional newspaper reported that the Madan mosque had been built with "much foreign help from Turkey, Arab countries, and foundations."[66] Still another reported that the Turkish government had donated a 944-square-meter prayer carpet and approximately 9,000 dollars toward the construction costs. A separate donation of another 15,000 dollars reportedly came from the Islamic Development Bank, perhaps channeled through the chief mufti's office under Nedim Gendzhev.[67] The rest of the money came from "anonymous donations."[68] In Rudozem, construction on the mosque started in the early 1990s, but the locals did not have enough money to complete the project. According to the press, when it was finally completed and opened in September 2001, the second largest mosque in the Smolyan oblast had cost around 200,000 dollars, most of which had come from "anonymous donations."[69]

Iordan and Lyubo also believed that foreign states were behind these mosques, acting through *sponsori* (sponsors), *fondatsii* (foundations), and *Arabite* (Arabs). Locals in both cities also remembered seeing what they called *sheikove* (sheiks) in town around the time of the openings, that is, Arab men in long white robes and head coverings. Theories abounded on why "the Arabs" had come, and why they were being so generous. Silvi, the Avon lady, believed that "the Arabs" came to find beautiful Bulgarian wives, and the rumor among the miners was that they would pay good money to have sex with local women. Lyubo claimed to have a colleague whose wife had run off with a "sheik" for a while; the Bulgarian husband was then "compensated" for his troubles. Some of the miners who drank with Lyubo in Sonic believed that the "sheiks" were interested in buying the lead-zinc mines after the liquidation of GORUBSO. The most curious theory I heard was from a Christian teacher at the secondary school. She believed that the foreigners were coming for Bulgaria's water supply, because "water will be more valuable than oil in the future." Hana said that the mosque had been built with local donations and "some help" from foreigners. Of course, young women and men like those who attended Abdullah's "Islam: Pluralism and Dialogue" lecture believed that the "sheiks" were disinterestedly reaching out to help the Pomaks and show them the true path of Islam.

This true path apparently started with the construction of the new mosques, which differed architecturally from the mosques typical of the region. The prayer hall portion of the Madan mosque could accommodate over a thousand people, and the niche (*mihrab*) and pulpit (*minbar*) were significantly more elaborate than those found in most Bulgarian mosques.[70] The mosques in the Smolyan oblast followed the style of the Elhovets mosque, a structure that was hundreds of years old, dating to the Ottoman era. Most mosques were low and rectangular; they looked like typical Bulgarian buildings with the addition of a minaret. The new mosques in Madan and Rudozem were larger than the typical mosque in the region and deviated from the Elhovets style by adding prominent domes and arches. The mosque in Chepintsi, near Rudozem, was even more striking in its divergence from the classic Bulgarian architectural style, and the new mosque in Tŭrŭn had a shiny silver dome and minaret that stood out conspicuously against the green Rhodope

Figure 14 The Elhovets mosque, built during the Ottoman era

mountaintops. Significantly, all the new mosques had separate sections for women.

In addition to their unique architecture, both mosques in Madan and Rudozem were large enough to include sleeping quarters for guests, cafés, and classrooms, and in both cities there were children living permanently in the mosques. In 2001, the local media reported that there were twelve boys living in the Madan mosque,[71] which hosted the special school for the instruction of *hafuzi,* those who can recite the Qur'an from memory.

Figure 15 The new mosque in Tŭrŭn

According to the deputy chief mufti in Sofia in 2006, Madan had the highest concentration of *hafuzi* in all of Bulgaria.[72] The gossips in the local cafés claimed the boys were the abandoned children of Romani women and that the boys were being taught the "new ways." Whenever I saw them in the internet café, they were almost always surfing the www.islam-bg.org website and reading about Islam in other countries. Contact with Muslims around the world was also facilitated by religious tourism, for the mosques in Chepintsi,[73] Rudozem, and Madan attracted visitors. In 2005, both Chepintsi and Madan had hosted the same six visiting Muslims from the United Kingdom who had received a one-month scholarship to travel around Bulgaria. According to the American Peace Corps volunteer who

Figure 16 The new mosque in Rudozem

was briefly asked to translate for them in Madan, the six men were "very weird" and refused her help because she was not wearing a headscarf. The locals in Madan said that the mosque had also received visitors from Kosovo, Bosnia, Saudi Arabia, Jordan, Syria, and Egypt.

Unlike other new mosques built or restored by Islamic charities in Bulgaria and despite their atypically large size, these mosques were full on Fridays. In many other cities and villages, new mosques stood relatively empty, because local Muslims were not interested in "rediscovering" Islam. In Madan and Rudozem, even men from surrounding villages came into town for the religious duty of attending the Friday prayer. While the men prayed and socialized, the women shopped at a special Friday market. I asked Hana if women went to the Friday prayers, and she replied, "It is only required for men." When I asked her if she could go if she wanted to, she said, "Yes, but the Friday prayers are for men."

Thus, it was a mass of male bodies that filled the mosques. In Madan, all of the major businessmen in town (except for the owner of the Regal Complex, who was a Christian) and the mayor and the municipal councilors

Figure 17 The new mosque in Chepintsi

also attended the prayers, lingering afterward to conduct business and discuss local politics. The bulletin board in the entranceway announced everything from job offers in Kuwait to a cow for sale. The men socialized as they reemerged into the city, whose streets were full much in the same way they must have been at the end of a mining shift during the heyday of GORUBSO.

Also, unlike the mosques in other Muslim cities, the Madan and Rudozem mosques had become the new spiritual and cultural, as well as political and economic, centers of their respective communities. They offered free courses for children on the weekends and during the summer months, usually for three hours a day, in which boys and girls studied the Qur'an in addition to English and Arabic. "I know my daughter is safe there," Hana

Figure 18 The mosque in Madan

told me, "and she is learning good things." Foreign-language abilities were highly prized in Bulgaria, and many secular parents sent their children to these lessons as an extra educational opportunity not otherwise available. In a culture that placed a premium on learning, one of the most devastating consequences of the end of communism in these regions was the deteriorating quality of public education and the difficulties faced by impoverished families in sending their children to secondary school or university. Even though the public secondary schools and universities were still free, the costs associated with supporting a young person (who could

Figure 19 Girls leaving a summer Qur'an course

otherwise be working), particularly if he or she was studying in a city
away from home, were too great for most families in this region to bear.
On top of that, there was a widespread practice of hiring private tutors to
prepare students for exams, and these extra lessons were very expensive.
Islamic education provided an affordable alternative.

The courses in the mosques were also a conduit for further religious
education both in Bulgaria and abroad. The mosques regularly advertised
for the Islamic secondary school in Momchilgrad (a city in the eastern
Rhodope) where students were given free room and board. There was also
a fully subsidized course regularly held in Sŭrnitsa for older children and
adult men who wanted to study to become imams. Through these schools,
a young man or woman could go on to attend the High Islamic Institute in
Sofia, fully sponsored by the chief mufti's office. Or a young person might
receive a scholarship or IsDB loan to study abroad in Turkey or one of the
Arab countries, as Abdullah had done for ten years in Jordan. Once students acquired this religious education, they plugged into a vast spiritual
network that as of 2006 was constantly seeking imams for new mosques
and Qur'anic schools. The possibility of guaranteed employment was no
small matter in regions with very high rates of joblessness. Her sons had
been dead set against it, but Donka sometimes wished that they had gone
to the Islamic secondary school in Momchilgrad, where they would have
been given scholarships and fed more than two loaves of white bread each

day. Hana's daughter was still very young, but when the time came, Hana planned to send her to one of the Islamic secondary schools.

The mosques were also a safe place for children; in both Madan and Rudozem there was a ping-pong table for the students to use after lessons, and in Rudozem, I often saw kids kicking a soccer ball around in the courtyard. In fact, both mosques were heavily involved in sponsoring the local youth soccer teams. Muslim leaders helped provide money for uniforms and transportation for away games. In Madan, many of the managers of the Islamic NGO Ikra were also members of the organization called Futbol Club Madan. In Rudozem, the UIDC directly supported the soccer team.

In both cities, the mosques were connected to local Islamic organizations funded by international donors. The foundation known as Mostove (Bridges) was registered in 2006 in Madan, and the association "Ikra"[74] was founded in 2005. The association had its own monthly magazine, the first issue of which was published in January 2005, and its own website. The content of the magazine was a mixture of articles downloaded from the Internet and original texts written by Muslim men and women in the Rhodope. It was sold in the mosque café and in a store that sold headscarves and modest Islamic clothing for women. All of the editors were young men from Madan and its surrounding villages. The magazine specifically targeted the Pomak population and was therefore only published in Bulgarian (unlike the official magazine of the chief mufti in Sofia, which was published in both Bulgarian and Turkish since the majority of Bulgaria's Muslims are Turks). Most of the articles in the magazine promoted a somewhat rigid interpretation of Islam that was at odds with local laxities. The young editor of the magazine also published his own book of "religious conversations," short morality tales to promote the new "orthodox" Islamic values. When I met him on several occasions, he was warm and quite friendly, always eager to give me free copies of *Ikra* and quite excited about a Bulgarian translation of Henry Corbin's *History of Muslim Philosophy* that I gave to Hasan for the mosque café (even though it was a very pro-Shia book).

One striking theme in *Ikra* was its rabid anti-Darwinism. The magazine printed several articles—taken from the website of the Turkish creationist movement, headed by the writer Harun Yahya—that railed against the supposed falsehoods of evolutionary theory.[75] The vast majority of Pomaks, even the fairly religious ones, accepted evolutionary theory, and it was quite rare to find someone who believed in "special creation." Even Lili's father, the hodzha, believed that the story of creation was a metaphor for evolution. The Pomaks had gone through Bulgarian public schools and evolution was a standard part of the curriculum, so these articles exposed many Pomaks to creationist teachings for the first time.

Both Ikra and Mostove were also involved in promoting Islamic lectures and seminars in Madan, Rudozem, and neighboring Smolyan. In August 2006, the foundation Mostove organized a lecture in Smolyan by a Macedonian academic, Petŭr Yapov, who had written a book on the history of the Pomaks. This book was not available in any bookstores; it could only be purchased in the mosques and subsequently disappeared from circulation. It argued that the Pomaks were not Slavs but a separate ethnicity closer to the Arabs, and that Islam had come to Bulgaria directly from Arabia. A similar argument, that the Pomaks were Arabs, had been put forward by Mekhmed Dorsunski, a member of the board of Ikra and a local businessman in Madan. His book, called *The History of the Pomaks*, was also published without a date or place of publication and could not be purchased in bookstores or found in libraries.[76] The newspaper *Demokratzia* (Democracy) claimed that it had been published in Saudi Arabia, where Dorsunski had lived and studied.[77]

In 2006, the newspaper *Rodopi Vesti* published a series of articles pointing out the many historical errors in Dorsunski's book.[78] A few months later, Dorsunski filed a complaint with the antidiscrimination commission alleging that the newspaper was inciting ethnic discrimination by challenging his thesis.[79] Interestingly, those who wanted to embrace "orthodox" Islam had made similar claims in Albania. Isa Blumi has argued that in order to accept the spiritual leadership of the Saudis, Albanians must "buy into the notion that Albanian culture and history is either defunct of value or its best aspects are to be subsumed into a history that is exclusively linked to Arabia."[80] A similar trend seemed to be emerging in the Smoylan oblast, where both Mostove and Ikra supported the establishment of closer links with the Arab World by promoting "scholarship" that reimagined the Pomaks as the descendants of Arab settlers who came to Bulgaria before the Christianization of the Slavs, scholarship that would justify the return to "purer" forms of Islam.

But perhaps the most active organization in the Madan and Rudozem area was Arif Abdullah's Union for Islamic Development and Culture (UIDC), founded in 2004 in Smolyan. The five key leaders of UIDC were all young Pomaks who had been given scholarships to study Islam abroad in the 1990s. As mentioned earlier, Abdullah received his master's degree in Qur'anic interpretation in Jordan. The deputy director, Selvi Shakirov, and Ismet Rashidov, the head secretary of the organization, received their bachelor's degrees in "The Fundamentals of Religion" in the Faculty of Shari'a at the Zarqa Private University, as did the director and deputy director of the UIDC's women's section, Neda Abdullah and Fatme Khairaddin-Rashidova. The Zarqa Private University was established in 1994 with the goal of promoting "a strong belief in the unity and integration of our *Arab* Islamic *Ummah*" (my emphasis) with the explicit stress on "Arab" (as opposed to Turkish or Iranian) Islam.[81] The Faculty of Shari'a was its first department, and these young Bulgarians would have been among the first students to have learned "the basics of true belief in order to defend the Islamic doctrine before false doctrines."[82]

When the young graduates returned to Bulgaria and set up their "Arab" Islamic organization, they threw themselves into the task of reeducating the Pomaks in the Smolyan region, particularly after Shakirov and Abdullah were removed from the regional muftiship. Networked into an international Muslim community, Abdullah and Shakirov attended international conferences in the United Kingdom, Turkey, Jordan, and Saudi Arabia. Within just two short years, their organization had its own office in the center of Smolyan, where it published and distributed Islamic literature in Bulgarian. It also had its own interactive website, held its own Qur'an courses, and toured the region giving Islamic lectures and holding forums and seminars on the "correct" way to practice Islam. A public lecture called "Health and Belief" featured a medical doctor discussing the health hazards of eating pork and drinking even small amounts of alcohol. Afterward, the UIDC bought space[83] on the front page of a local newspaper to recap the major themes of the lecture and proclaim that their organization would bring social equity and true belief to the populations of the Rhodope, with a particular focus on social equality.[84] All of their lectures were recorded on CDs and cassettes, which were distributed from their offices as well as through the mosques.

To support these activities, the UIDC leaders also had links with the World Assembly of Muslim Youth. In a 2006 "News" section of their magazine, the UIDC announced that they had attended the Tenth International Congress of WAMY along with seven hundred other delegates from ninety countries. In this news brief they identified a Bulgarian Muslim named Vezhdi Ahmedov as the chairman of the Bulgarian branch of WAMY who had invited them to the congress.[85] Bulgarian public records, however, did not show that WAMY was officially registered as a charity in the country as of 2007, although the WAMY Malaysia website (home.wamymalaysia .org) did identify a WAMY branch office in the Pomak city of Velingrad.[86] Rather, Ahmedov was the chairman of a foundation called Al-Nedua, which was also registered in Velingrad,[87] and was the local face of WAMY in Bulgaria.

Bulgarian 2007 tax records demonstrated direct links between the UIDC and Al-Nedua as well as between Arif Abdullah and Selvi Shakirov (the leaders of the UIDC) and Vezhdi Ahmedov. Interestingly, Abdullah, Shakirov, and Ahmedov were all partners in a company called Brothers Trading, officially registered in 2006. They each held a 14 percent share in this seemingly all-purpose enterprise, which was involved in real estate, construction, advertising, tourism, and retail sales.[88] Another key leader of the UIDC, Milen Zhurnalov, was also a 14 percent shareholder of Brothers Trading and owned 50 percent of a company that sold imported textiles and other goods from the same building in Smolyan that housed the UIDC office in 2006. Mekhmed Ahmedov, yet another 14 percent shareholder of Brothers Trading, together with the Bulgarian representative of WAMY, owned 100 percent of the publishing house ASKA. This company published all of the magazines and printed materials of the UIDC as well as other "orthodox" Islamic literature. Brothers Trading also linked the UIDC and WAMY/Al-Nedua to the Madan-based Islamic organization Mostove through its chairman, Ismet Rashidov. Thus, money originating in Saudi Arabia could easily circumvent the financial controls on the chief mufti's office by going directly through locally registered foundations and businesses in the Rhodope.

The UIDC's well-developed website (www.oirk.org) and bimonthly glossy color magazine, *Myusyulmansko Obshtestvo* (*Muslim Society*), regularly ran articles that challenged traditional Muslim customs and prescribed the "correct" behavior for Muslims. Most Madanchani erected head- and footstones to mark the graves of their deceased, for example, and preferred to read the Qur'an in Bulgarian rather than Arabic, a practice introduced by reformist Pomaks in the 1930s. Locals rarely prayed five times a day, and men who had jobs did not attend Friday prayers. In the early 1990s, when the mines were still open and there was extra money in the household budget, a trip to Greece or Germany almost always took precedence over making the pilgrimage to Mecca. Instead, Bulgarian Muslims made pilgrimages to the graves of local Muslim saints, such as the grave of Yenihan Baba in Smolyan. Muslim women had long since joined the formal workforce and no longer felt the need to cover themselves but adopted instead the European dress of their Christian comrades. The young people of the UIDC considered many of these practices forbidden innovations[89] and their stated goal was to correct them, "to show the true essence of the Islamic religion." Interestingly, the UIDC also lashed out against materialism and the selfishness and corruption brought to Bulgaria from the West: "orthodox" Islam was superior because it promoted a more just and moral social order.

A close reading of the literature they distributed and the seminars they held in cities throughout the Rhodope shows a particular emphasis on the "true" Islam's commitments to social justice. This was a message that resonated quite well in impoverished cities like Madan and Rudozem, where Pomaks felt excluded from the political process and betrayed by both communism and democracy, particularly after the demise of GORUBSO and the realization that it had intentionally been run into bankruptcy. In a society characterized by ubiquitous criminality and corruption at all levels, the UIDC fashioned itself as a beacon of morality and an advocate for the poor. "They are afraid of us, because we are moral," Arif Abdullah told me in 2007.

Despite their controversial theology, the UIDC practiced what it preached. For instance, in April 2006, Arif Abdullah and the other leaders of the UIDC gathered together businessmen and municipal officials in Smoylan to try to convince them to fund the creation of soup kitchens for the poor in Smolyan, Madan, and Rudozem.[90] Abdullah argued that there were many needy people in these areas that required social assistance and that business leaders and politicians should join together to help those less fortunate than themselves. Interestingly, the kitchens would only operate once a week, on Fridays (the Muslim holy day), although they were to serve people of all religions. The food was to be prepared and served by the poor themselves and presumably would adhere to Muslim dietary restrictions. Abdullah and Khairaddin also emphasized the Islamic duty of *zakat*, or tithing, whereby the wealthy fulfill their religious obligation to assist the poor.

A double-edged critique of capitalism and communism, with an emphasis on social justice, could be found in numerous Islamic publications. For example, one article published in *Ikra*[91] and then reprinted in many of the Islamic publications targeting the Pomaks took aim at both economic systems. The article was called "Materialism: The Dreadful Disease of Humanity," and in it, Hasan Mehmedaliev, the chairman of the organization Mostove in Madan, deconstructs materialism both as a philosophy (i.e., in its Marxist incarnation) and as a current way of life (i.e., as a by-product of global capitalism). Throughout history, according to Mehmedaliev, civilizations have always fallen when they reach the point of becoming too preoccupied with the accumulation of material (rather than spiritual) wealth. "The materialistic striving after goals in our temporal world has caused suffering and destruction to many people . . . [H]istory describes past human and social destinies as tragic because they were mindlessly obsessed by the struggle for material benefits."[92] In an article called "Time Is Money? No, Time Is Life" that appeared in *Myusyulmansko Obshtestvo,* readers are warned that, "sometimes a person gets so obsessed by his desire to possess that he loses his mind."[93] Love of God and one's fellow man should supersede base material interests, readers were admonished—a powerful message in a region already submerged in poverty.

In a published interview with Abdullah in the first issue of *Myusyulmansko Obshtestvo*, he openly claimed that the goals of the UIDC were "reaffirming the moral and spiritual values in society and assisting the poor and those who need help."[94] He couched his ideals in quite universalistic terms, terms that would have a very familiar ring to those who grew up under communism, with its promises of a global workers' fraternity. Abdullah declares, "One of the main goals of Islam is to bring peace, love, and happiness to all people in the human fraternity. To confront everyone who threatens those goals. We are convinced that the righteousness and the stability of Bulgarian society can only be achieved when all of us, the people, hand in hand, work toward this goal."[95] In "The Only Spiritual Force that Can Lead Humankind to Happiness," published in *Ikra* in 2006, another local author from Madan, Ahmed Osmanov, explains that dedicating one's life to Islam is the only true path to personal fulfillment. But this is not an injunction to become lazy and spurn the material world. "Islam does not accept that a man can stop working and turn into a parasite; on the contrary, we should all use our gifts and natural inclinations in order to take advantage of all that God created and to benefit [society] as much as it is possible; after we satisfy our own needs, the extras can go to help the poor."[96] For those living in a country with a strong legacy of Marxist-Leninism, sentiments such as these sound fascinatingly similar to old socialist slogans such as "From each according to his ability, to each according to his need." Thus, although the speeches and articles targeting the Pomaks in Madan and Rudozem are careful to distance themselves from both capitalism and communism, there is an important way in which they are referencing some of Marxism's universal humanism, anti-individualism, and overriding concerns with social justice—something that will be discussed in more detail in the conclusion.

In addition to their publications, lectures, and seminars, the UIDC also began to actively embroil themselves in local conflicts between the growing number of devout Muslims and the surrounding population of secular Muslims and Christians. The UIDC's most controversial action was their defense of two girls from Rudozem banned from wearing headscarves to school. I will discuss this case at length in the next chapter. In addition to the headscarf case, however, they directly instigated three other situations which deepened the rift between traditional and "orthodox" Islam.

The first incident was in Chepintsi, a village south of Rudozem, where the board of governors of the local mosque bought the only disco in the village and closed it down. The closure was justified by the allegedly "naked women" in the disco and its promotion of alcohol use.[97] In a village where there were at least five hundred secondary school students, this was a very unpopular move, even among devout Muslim parents. Not swayed by the moral arguments of the local Muslim leaders, the young people simply drove to Madan or Smolyan for entertainment on the weekends, a very dangerous proposition on poorly lit, winding mountain roads, especially when the young drivers were drunk. The situation put the mayor in a difficult position. Most people in Chepintsi disapproved of the disco closure but were afraid to speak out against the mosque. One local paper suggested that the money to purchase the disco property had come from the UIDC[98] and accused the organization of overstepping its bounds.

A second incident occurred in a village near Smolyan, where a decades-old festival (like the Day of the Miners in Madan) was nearly canceled because, for the first time, the board of governors of the local mosque refused to allow the eating of pork and the drinking of beer on lands owned by the *vakif*. Since summer festivals primarily revolved around eating *kebabcheta* (a grilled specialty of minced pork and beef) and drinking cold *nalivna* (draught) beer, these demands amounted to a cancellation of the celebration for all of the village's inhabitants, whether they were devout Muslims or not. Both stories were covered in the national media,[99] and more attention was focused on the Rhodope as the home to new Islamic practices foreign to Bulgaria.

Two months later, the UIDC was involved in another scandal, this time involving the local boys' soccer team it sponsored in Rudozem. The Bulgarian Football Union filed a complaint with the antidiscrimination commission against the team "Rudozem 2005" because the team wanted to wear green and white uniforms with the UIDC logo on them, a logo that included the crescent moon cradling a map of the world. The UIDC and the boys were branded "Islamists" (*Islyamisti*) in the national press,[100] and eventually they were made to remove the religious symbols from their uniforms.[101] Although seemingly insignificant, these three events were just the tips of the proverbial iceberg. Profound changes were under way in Madan, Rudozem, and its environs. The real trouble began when two young Pomak girls demanded to be able to wear their headscarves to high school and unleashed a heated debate about the new religious mores that were beginning to regulate "appropriate" behavior for Muslim women.

The Miniskirt and the Veil

HIGYAR'S GOLD FRONT TEETH glisten as a ray of late-afternoon sun breaks through the cloud cover and catches her with her mouth open. She wears gold earrings, gold rings, two gold bracelets, and a thick gold chain that hangs low across the front of the dress that modestly hides her ample chest. It is her teeth that somehow seem the most ostentatious aspect of her appearance, especially since I have been programmed by friends in Madan to notice them. So many people have wide gaps in their too infrequent smiles; Higyar's gleaming grin sets her apart from her fellow Madanchani. She is the matriarch of one of the wealthiest families in this now-impoverished city, and gold is the preferred way to demonstrate status. She sits in front of her large store, shelling pistachios at a round white plastic table and waiting for customers. She sells a wide variety of goods: children's toys, bicycles, cosmetics, small electronics, and most importantly, fabric, of which she has the best selection in town. When women in Madan have a little extra income, they often come to Higyar's shop to buy fabric. She is also one of Madan's biggest gossips, a *klyukarka*, trading information and secrets with anyone who will pause to chat at her store on their way up to the city center.

Higyar is a devout Muslim and is well networked in with Madan's older community. She knows when and where almost every *mevlid* (traditional prayer session) is held in Madan, particularly those celebrating the birth of a new child. On the day I visited her, I asked about traditional Pomak fashion and what a typical woman in Madan would wear to such an event. She proudly pops out of her chair and leads me into the store to show me her assortment of cloth and a photo album with pictures of herself in a variety of outfits. Nothing in her store is ready-to-wear; most women sew their own clothes or work with private tailors at one of Madan's many sewing workshops. Sewing is labor, and labor is cheap. Although Higyar is in her early sixties and is a fairly large woman, she models several different styles proudly in the photos.

"The basic dress is called a *fustan*," she explains. "It can be all one piece or a skirt and shirt together of the same fabric. The sleeves are always long, but there are many different styles."

The *fustan* she is wearing now is a two-piece set of brightly colored polyester-blend fabric with red and maroon flowers against a deep blue background. The skirt reaches down to her ankles. Around her waist she wears an embroidered apron called a *mendil*.

"On the head," she continues, "one wears a *kŭrpa*, tied like this." She unfastens the knot below her chin, removes the kerchief from her head, and unfolds the square of cloth on the desk in front of her, watching me to make sure that I am paying careful attention. She then refolds the cloth on the diagonal to make a triangle and drapes that triangle over her head so that there is one point at the back and one point hanging down over her ears on either side of her face. Then she ties the two front corners under her chin in a casual knot. Above her forehead, I can still see the silver roots of her dyed-brown hair, and most of her vertically lined neck is visible beneath the knot of the kerchief. I identify this look with a classic *babushka* (grandmother) look that most Eastern European women, whether Muslim or Christian, tend to adopt as they grow older.

"This is the correct way," Higyar declares. "Our way. Not the other way."

She unties the kerchief once again. This time she takes the triangle and puts it on her head, pulling the long edge across the middle of her forehead and then folding down the sides at her temples. She draws the two loose ends carefully across her cheeks, crossing them beneath her chin, tying them at the back of her neck. Her face is completely framed by the cloth—not a single hair is visible, and her neck is now more hidden. Her face looks more severe. She loses the Eastern European grandmotherly aura in exchange for the look of a devout Muslim woman or a Christian nun.

"But many younger women wear their *kŭrpi* in that way," I comment. "Is this just a different fashion?"

"*Ne*," she exclaims, lifting her chin abruptly in the Bulgarian way of saying "no" while moving her head in a way that looks to a Westerner as if she is nodding "yes." "That is a different style, the Arab style [*arabski stil*] of the girls who are paid to wear the headscarves [*zabradki*] and go to all the seminars and lectures. They say our traditions are wrong. They have different ways. New ways."

She says this with an air of resignation, but I can see that she is agitated. I know from Lili and her hodzha father that Higyar was one of the first people in Madan to reclaim her name after democracy. After the seventies, she had become "Violeta" officially, but she never let anyone call her by that name. When the local communists tried to stop the prayer sessions (*mevlidi*) she organized, she kept doing them anyway, arguing that women needed support after bringing a new baby into the world. There is still something in her eyes that looked like fear; perhaps she was seriously harassed or even spent some time in jail for her devotion to Islam during the communist era. I am not sure how to broach that subject, so I focus on the varieties of *fustan* she is now describing.

She is turning the pages of her photo album of dresses when we both see two young women walking past the store toward the center of town. They are teenagers—maybe fifteen or sixteen—and they are chatting to each other as they walk. They are dressed in long monochrome gowns, and their white headscarves are tied exactly in the "Arab style" Higyar had described. I glance back at the stacks of colorful, patterned fabric that Higyar keeps in her store and recognize that these young women are rejecting the traditional Pomak mode of dress. Maybe they associate the *fustan* with their grandmothers or the old women in the villages. Maybe they think it represents how the Pomaks weakly succumbed to the communist authorities, changing their names and accepting practices forbidden to Muslims. Maybe it merely represents their own rural backgrounds, the dress of peasants working in the tobacco fields and petty-bourgeois traders selling children's toys. Whatever they think it means, these two girls have chosen not to dress like Higyar and the older women in Madan who represent traditional Bulgarian Islam. Many young women do dress in the traditional style, so these two stand out, marking themselves as not only different from, but more devout than, their fellow Madanchanki (female Madan residents).

Higyar sighs. "They will make problems for all of us."

She is referring to the recent case of the two high school girls from Rudozem who wanted to wear their *zabradki* to school in Smolyan—a controversy that was splashed across both the local and national press. For Higyar, who is proud of her traditions and considers herself a good Muslim, the girls from Rudozem represent danger and foreign influences. These young Muslims consider everything she does, the *mevlidi* she organizes and the *muski* (amulets) she carries tucked away in her pockets, un-Islamic innovations that must be stamped out. Higyar struggled her entire life to preserve her own Muslim beliefs and practices during the communist period, only to have them now—at the very moment when there is supposed to be religious freedom in the country—called into question and threatened with extinction by new, "Arab" Islamic practices. For Higyar, people like Hana and Hasan are more of a threat than the communists were. What Higyar considers to be hallowed Muslim traditions are viewed by those who accept the new "Arab Islam" as recently fabricated practices, and what they consider to be the true Islam, she sees as the importation of foreign and new ways.

In 2004, when I first started research for this book in the Rhodope, it was still rather rare to see women dressed in the "Arab style" with headscarves worn in the way that, for Bulgarians, is distinctly nontraditional.

Figure 20 A woman dressed in the traditional style glaring at three girls dressed in the "Arab" style

It is important to point out here that what was called the "Arab style" was not necessarily one distinct style, but anything that was seen as foreign to what Bulgarian Muslims traditionally wore. The adoption of the "Arab" style by the younger generation was an eclectic mix that cobbled together Gulf Arab, South Asian, Indonesian, and, especially, Western styles taken from websites such as www.thehijabshop.com, which gave instructions on how to wear Islamic clothing. Once, in the Internet café in Madan, I saw some young Muslim girls browsing www.alhannah.com, an American website that displays multiple styles of Islamic clothing from throughout the Middle East and South Asia. When the "Arab style" first started appearing more widely in 2005, I saw young women in Rudozem wearing the *niqab* (a face veil that shows only the eyes) as well as three girls dressed head to toe in matching white headscarves and gowns. Other young women took Western clothes and adapted them to make their own style of *hijab*: one woman in Madan wore a long-sleeved denim jacket with a long denim skirt and a bandana-patterned blue headscarf, while a girl in Rudozem wore a long black cardigan-style sweater over a loose dress in the hippie style. Most young women following the "new way" tended to favor the long *jilbab* gowns popular in Britain and France, and I did not see any women wearing the *salwar kameez*, the *chador*, or the *burqa*, although many of the girls knew what they were. "We are European Muslims," a young woman in the Internet café explained to me. "And we must look like Europeans."

Despite the mishmash of styles, in all of the Muslim villages I visited people had a clear sense of what was a Turkish or Bulgarian style of Muslim dress and what was "Arab." Older women always wore their *kŭrpi*, or kerchiefs, with Muslim women tying them beneath their chins and Christian women tying them underneath their hair in the back. In some of the Pomak villages women wore *shalvari* (baggy Turkish trousers), and in others Muslim women wore the *manto*, a long button-down overcoat of light fabric, marking themselves as Muslim women but in a distinctly Turkish/Balkan way. The *jilbab*, *niqab*, and *hijab*, or styles that imitated them, were considered distinctly foreign to Muslim women like Higyar.

In fact, local fashions for women were in general entirely the opposite of the modest garb promoted by "Arab" Islam. In Bulgaria, and perhaps in postsocialist Eastern Europe more broadly, clothing styles for women were quite provocative by American standards. For young women in particular, necklines often plunged over demi-cup push-up bras. The most popular skirt length barely touched the very top of the thigh, and Bulgarian girls had mastered the art of always bending at the knees rather than at the waist when leaning over. If women wore trousers, they were often cut as low as anatomically possible, and after 2003 were combined with a new fashion of visible thong underwear. Exposed abdomens were par for the course in the summer. Other popular looks in the bigger cities were sheer blouses without bras, or white pants or skirts with dark, lacy lingerie visible underneath. One male American friend once joked to me that being in Sofia was like "walking around in a soft porn movie."

All of these provocative fashion options for women were broadcast out of the big cities and into small towns like Madan via the twenty-four-hour Bulgarian pop-folk music channels. On stations such as Vesselina TV and Payner Planeta, silicone-enhanced, bottle-blonde *chalga* (pop-folk) singers crooned and danced their way through five-minute video clips in the skimpiest of outfits, and it was from popular artists like Desislava, Maria, Gergana, and Anelia that most young women, both Christian and Muslim, took their fashion guidance. On the streets of both Madan and Rudozem in the summer, the vast majority of women were not covered, and a good subset of those were dressed in what they considered to be the latest fashion, whether it was bare midriffs or exposed g-strings. In fact, provocative "European" dress with short skirts and high heels was a symbol of urbanity, of those who did not work in agriculture. In a culture where the word "villager" was equated with uncultured backwardness and stupidity for both men (*selyanin*) and women (*selyanka*), many young Pomaks were keen to avoid any association with their rural roots, particularly after the collapse

Figure 21 Two Muslim women in Rudozem in miniskirts in 2005

Figure 22 Muslim women dressed in the new style in 2005

of GORUBSO and the impoverishment of Madan. Perhaps one result of this was that many Pomak women dressed even more provocatively than the already quite liberal style of dress common for Bulgarian Christian women. Thus, in 2004, when I first started doing this research, the majority of women in the Muslim towns of the Rhodope dressed like Bulgarian women in small towns throughout the country, and women's fashion had not yet become the marker of a Muslim town versus a Christian one.

In March 2004, however, the French government passed a national law banning the Islamic headscarf and all other conspicuous religious symbols in public schools.[1] Protests and heated debates ensued, across France and the rest of Europe, about the role of the headscarf in Islam. Was it a symbol of women's oppression, of their subservience to men? Was it merely an expression of piety and religious affiliation? Did it represent the refusal of Europe's Muslim minorities to integrate with the wider society? Would banning it emancipate women or keep them from attending school, thus perpetuating their reliance on men for support? For over a year, the headscarf ban in France galvanized public opinion on either side of the debate, with many feminists and nationalists arguing in favor of the ban and many human rights activists and Muslim groups opposed to it.

Then, in November 2005, the European Court of Human Rights ruled to uphold the Turkish ban on headscarves in all universities, both public and private. The ruling, which was unexpected to many observers, claimed that the headscarf ban upheld the principles of secularism and gender equality embodied in the Turkish constitution. The court argued that in a society where men and women were equal, a ban on headscarves, which were only required of Muslim women, could be justified in order to protect women's rights. The court also acknowledged the political context in Turkey and recognized the presence of "extremist political movements in Turkey which sought to impose on society as a whole their religious symbols and conception of a society founded on religious precepts."[2] Once this decision came down, it was clear that the European Court was likely to uphold the French ban. The Islamic headscarf for women, beyond its religious meaning, took on a newfound political meaning for young Muslims decrying the hypocrisy of so-called pluralist and tolerant Western democracies.

During his lecture in Madan in the summer of 2006, Arif Abdullah had also been critical of the French decision, urging Bulgarians not to follow in the French footsteps. "Why does Bulgaria have to be European? Why can't we be a bridge between East and West? Just because France bans the headscarf, why do we have to do the same thing? Why can't we be better than France? Why can't we be further ahead of the Western European countries in terms of tolerance? [Why can't we] teach them something about tolerance and pluralism?"

It is an interesting coincidence that both *Ikra* and *Myusyulmansko Obshtestvo*, the Islamic magazines published in Madan and Smolyan respectively, as well as the Islamic website run by Ali Khairaddin, www.islam-bg .net, were all started in 2004 or January 2005. In all three cases, a very common and prominent topic of discussion was the *hijab* and whether or not Muslim women were required to wear it. On 30 June 2005, the most popular forum on the islam-bg website was "The Woman in Islam," and the first topic was *hijab*. In this forum, Bulgarians from across the country, and from as far away as Germany and Toronto, debated the proper dress code for Muslim women, and various articles on *hijab* were translated into Bulgarian and posted on the website. In particular, someone with the English user name "submittedtoGod" posted an article on "The Clothes of the Muslim Women in Agreement with the Qur'an and the Sunna," arguing that Bulgarian Muslim women did not understand the Qur'an well enough to dress in the appropriate way—with their heads and bodies completely covered.[3]

This website was very popular among young men and women in Madan. In the Internet café where I checked my e-mail on a daily basis, I often saw boys and girls surfing the pages of the islam-bg website and its URL address was bookmarked on four of the six computers. One young woman in Rudozem told me that before she started attending the seminars at the mosque, everything she had learned about Islam she had learned from the Internet. She spent hours reading the forums and writing in questions. She felt as if she had a virtual community of Bulgarian Muslim friends across the country. Furthermore, the locally produced *Ikra* magazine downloaded a significant portion of its content from the islam-bg website and published it for those who were not technologically savvy enough to access the site from the Internet café. Until the Bulgarian government closed it down in 2007, the website's zealous position regarding the headscarf for women and girls, as well as its defense of polygamy, was reaching the youth audience in the Rhodope.

Combined with these websites and discussion forums targeting women were the local activities of the new Islamic NGOs. In Smolyan, Neda Abdullah, wife of Arif Abdullah, was the chairperson of the women's section of the UIDC, which was very active in promoting the *hijab* among Pomak women in the Smolyan region. The stated activities of the women's section of the UIDC were to "present the true face of the Muslim woman" by issuing literature that supported her intellectual development while preserving her "morality and identity."[4] Through lectures, seminars, and "women's parties," the UIDC promoted Islamic dress codes and more conservative gender roles. Throughout 2005 and 2006, the women's section was active in organizing events on the role of women in Islam. In July 2006, it held a forum in the Culture House in Rudozem entitled "The Islamic Family between the Influence of Society and the Principles of Islam," where the UIDC women argued that Bulgarian culture was often incompatible with true Islamic practices. Other lectures held in Smolyan, such as "The Place of the Woman—Wife and Mother—in Islam," or the women's program at the UIDC national conference held in the ski resort of Pamporovo in November 2005 also promoted modesty and obedience.

In a January 2005 interview with the local Smolyan newspaper, *Otzvuk*, Neda Abdullah explained why Muslim women should wear the headscarf:

[I]t is a religious dogma. When a woman realizes it is an order from God, it is not difficult . . . According to [our] religion, a woman should be covered, so that she is not an object of temptation and seduction

Figure 23 Three young Pomak women in 2005

for the men. She is only for her own husband. He is the only one who
has the right to see her. When she is with an uncovered body outside,
in society, she attracts the eyes of other men, and they are tempted to
have her. She awakens desires, passion in them, which lead to illegal
relationships, and so on. In Islam the woman is appreciated; she is only
for her husband. Usually we give one example, and I don't know how it
will be taken. But the Muslim woman is precious like a piece of jewelry,
and not everyone can touch it. Other women are like vegetables in the
market—everyone can feel them before someone takes them.[5]

This idea that "orthodox" Islam reveres the woman and that devout
Muslim women are more precious than traditional Muslim or Christian

women was a common theme in the articles about appropriate Islamic dress that appeared in local Islamic publications. Most of the articles stressed the moral duty of women to obey God and not provoke the attention of men. But they also emphasized the sinful nature of remaining uncovered and warned that God would punish women who did not comply with the more strict interpretation of Islamic teachings.

This excerpt from an article in the UIDC magazine, *Myusyulmansko Obshtestvo*, demonstrates the kind of language used to convince Pomak women to wear the *hijab*:

Today when young women can be seen in the streets dressed in clothes that barely cover their underwear (and this is taken as normal), when lifestyles lure women to appear as sexually attractive as possible, when girls and women are disappointed if no one turns their head to look at them, women who do not want to behave in this manner are looked down upon as abnormal. This is an offensive case of discrimination. Indeed, there are a great number of girls and women who are modest by nature, who do not want to expose themselves and who do not feel miserable if leering eyes are not fixed upon them. Strange as it may seem, wearing the *hijab* is one of the problems that society has thrust upon girls and women who profess Islam and who want to change the "dress code" and use the headscarf. Ironically, these modest and shy women have to feel uncomfortable for having changed their previous habits of attracting excessive attention. To choose to wear the *hijab* often provokes surprise (especially from people who happen to know you) and questions as to why you feel you are "better" or "holier" than the others, or why you want to have the appearance of an Arab or Pakistani woman . . .

. . . The clothes that a Muslim woman wears are not punishment or ordeal; they give her the chance to look noble and ladylike without any arousal of carnal appetites. The "veiled" women are not necessarily innocent girls. They can be mothers of big families and women who are married and remarried. The *hijab* is not an attribute of fake modesty. It delivers a certain message to people. First, the message is that the woman has decided to submit all aspects of her life to the will of God; and second, that she wants to be judged on the basis of her virtues and deeds and not her beauty, elegance, and sex appeal.[6]

In this passage, there is an explicit judgment about women who only care about their sexual attractiveness in order to arouse the "carnal appetites" of men. Furthermore, the *hijab* serves as a way for women to be valued for their character while at the same time signaling that they have submitted themselves to Islamic standards of modesty and virtue, an act that makes them superior to women who have not.

Similar types of arguments appeared in Madan's own *Ikra* magazine in
a series of articles extolling the benefits of Islam for women while at the
same time warning them that they will face divine punishment if they do
not obey its laws. An article titled "The Veil: An Imperative" lays out a
strict Islamic dress code for Muslim women:

> Guarding virtue is one of the major tasks for both men and women. A
> veiled woman will not attract the eyes and hearts of the men around
> [her], as they [the men] are forbidden to look. Just as one must not do
> forbidden things, so one must not provoke them . . . What parts of the
> body shall be covered? The whole body, except for the hands and the
> face. The hair must be covered completely. The overgarment is ankle-
> long, and its sleeves leave only the hands exposed. It is a two-piece gar-
> ment: the one covers the hair, neck, shoulders and bosom, and the other
> covers the whole body . . . The overgarment averts scandal in this world
> and hellfire in the next. It should be known that when the Almighty
> asks the question, "Why didn't you cover your body in your earthly
> existence?" it will be very difficult for a woman to give an answer.[7]

In a different issue of *Ikra*, "The Code of Conduct for the Muslim
Woman" repeats the same imperatives about clothing, emphasizing that
women who dress appropriately are more precious and valuable than
those who do not and warning that there will be dire consequences for
the latter:

> A Muslim woman must cover her body . . . However, this is not to be
> interpreted as approval to wear tight or see-through clothes! . . . When
> a woman goes out in the street dressed in a garment of which Islam
> approves, she will not provoke lechery because the Islamic dress code
> recommends loose garments that do not suggest the shape of the female
> body. A woman abiding by the Islamic dress code can be compared to
> a sealed letter, the contents of which will be disclosed only to the ad-
> dressee. A woman wearing transparent clothes can be compared to an
> announcement that can be read by anyone. . . . We are eyewitnesses of
> the decadence of society and of the corruption of moral values . . . In
> order to protect the Muslim woman, God commanded that she should
> stay at home soberly and with dignity and that she should not go out
> uncovered like the women in the pre-Islamic time of ignorance and that
> she should not expose her beauty. . . . Hopefully, you understand the situ-
> ation that a woman would face if she shuts her eyes and plugs her ears
> before these words. Let both men and women know that there is a path
> to follow and those who go astray shall be punished accordingly.[8]

These articles, published in Bulgarian and circulated among the Pomaks
in Smolyan, Madan, Rudozem, and surrounding areas, combined with the

lectures and seminars held throughout the region by the UIDC, certainly contributed to the increasing number of young women wearing the *hijab* between 2004 and 2007. For those who promoted it, the *hijab* symbolized a kind of moral superiority over the decadent influence of the West. Another article in *Ikra* argued that, "Regardless of the advances in women's rights, women in Western and Westernized societies are still subjected to and forced to see themselves as commodities to be bought and sold."[9] According to this same article, Islam was the only true path to equality between men and women: "Islam is the final religion and therefore, our last real chance. Its high level of responsibilities encourages humanity to raise itself above unhealthy emotions and underdeveloped instincts. Once we succeed in that challenge, then and only then, will humanity be strong enough to implement equity for all."[10]

Indeed, the desire to resist the hyperobjectification of women in Bulgaria and to distinguish themselves from what were derisively called *silikonki* (silicone girls) was a strong motivation for many women to adopt modest Islamic dress. "There is a lot of pressure on girls to be beautiful in Bulgaria," Hana once told me on the playground while our five- and six-year-old daughters romped around us. "To be tall and thin with breasts out to here," she said, carving two huge half-melons out in front of her chest with her hands. "But everyone knows if you are this thin . . . "—she held up her pinky finger—"then you are flat as a *palachinka* [crepe]. The only way is to fill the chest with silicone. I do not want my daughter cutting herself open to look like a picture of some *kurva* [slut] on television. Better to wear a headscarf and concentrate on her studies than worry about cellulite." Hana herself said that she had felt incredibly liberated when she started wearing the *jilbab*. "My body was mine and my husband's, not a display for public criticism."

But not all women who wore the headscarf were as positive as Hana. One young mother, Emel, from the village of Mitovska in the mountains above Madan confided that it was very hard for her to be a "good" Muslim. As a secondary school graduate, she once had many friends and enjoyed the company of both men and women. "One of my classmates now lives in Plovdiv [Bulgaria's second largest city], and she came back to Madan to visit. She was so elegantly dressed, and I met her on the street. At first, she did not recognize me. She is a Pomak too, but she was very surprised to see me wearing the *kŭrpa* and *fustan*. She told me I had to get out of Madan, but I told her that I was married. She was very upset and did not want to speak with me anymore. We were once very good friends."

Emel explained that she wanted to work, but now her husband felt that it was better for her to stay at home and take care of their child because that is what "good" Muslim women did if their husbands could afford it. Emel, too, believed that it was her duty to stay at home and wear the *hijab*. Although she would have liked to go to university and become a schoolteacher, she felt she would be punished if she disobeyed the will of God. Under communism, successful Pomak masculinity had almost required a wife who worked in the public sphere, but now, in the aftermath of GORUBSO, men who could afford it wanted their wives to stay at home and not leave the house without their permission. For Emel, this was particularly disheartening because she lived with her husband's parents, and her mother-in-law was a very devout Muslim who was always forcing Emel to read the Qur'an.

But other women accepted the roles that the new interpretations of Islam were creating for them. A young woman named Amira from Rudozem told me that women were the moral *vodachi* (leaders) of their families. Their responsibility was to raise their children to be good Muslims. She felt that formal employment was incompatible with her duties as a good Muslim, as she would not be able to pray five times a day if she had a job. Furthermore, she believed that it was a Muslim man's responsibility to look after his family. She was one of a group of newly devout young women in Rudozem that included two girls who had studied Islam in Saudi Arabia and who covered their faces with the *niqab* so that only their eyes were visible in public. When I asked her why these women dressed in a way so foreign to Bulgaria, she replied, "To please God."

Local gender roles were starting to be redefined so that the ideal family had a husband who worked to support a pious, stay-at-home wife whose primary responsibility was the proper Muslim education of her children—a radical departure from the communist past. A good example of this ideal was a woman whose Bulgarian name, given to her at birth, had been Pavlina before she changed it to Aisha. Pavlina had been an excellent student and graduated from the secondary school in Madan with the highest grades. But instead of going on to one of the top national universities as many of her acquaintances expected, she accepted a scholarship to study at the High Islamic Institute in Sofia, where she received a religious education. Those who knew her said that it was during those years that Aisha became a devout Muslim. Upon returning to Madan, she married and had a son. Because her husband did not work in Madan, Aisha kept a small store selling women's and children's clothing. She justified working in the store as part of her *da'wa* (mission) work. Since she could keep her own hours and close when she wanted, she did not see her employment as contradictory with her identity as a pious Muslim. She said all of the required daily prayers and held herself up as an example to other Muslim women in Madan. She also devoted all her efforts to her son's Islamic education. Before he could even read Bulgarian, Aisha was teaching him Arabic and enrolled him in a course at the mosque to memorize the entire Qur'an. As a result of her tireless efforts, the boy officially became a *hafuz* before he had even finished primary school. Although many women looked upon her in her Islamic headscarf and gown as a religious "fanatic," they did admire her dedication and the widely acknowledged genius of her son. This was a great source of pride for Aisha, who believed that her life was guided by the true principles of Islam.

Aisha was always kind to me when I went to visit her in her store, answering my questions and helping me to translate Arabic words that had been transliterated into Bulgarian in *Ikra*. I asked her about the protocol for headscarves, and she said that a woman must cover all of her hair and that the traditional Pomak *kŭrpa* was not appropriate. "We began wearing our *kŭrpi* in that style, because it was the only way the communists would allow. The Qur'an says a woman should not show her hair. But different women interpret the fashion in their own way. I choose to interpret the Qur'an in a literal way, and I know that this is the way of following a religion that brings me peace and happiness."

"But not all Muslim women wear the headscarf?"

"Other women do not care about these things because they have other priorities in life right now. But slowly they will begin to see the right way. Those girls in Rudozem [wearing the *niqab*] want to demonstrate some stronger faith, but the Qur'an does not require it. But it is a matter of personal choice, and they should choose the style that is right for them."

"And when should girls start wearing the headscarf?" I asked.

"When she starts her cycle. But most girls wait until they get married. They think they need their hair to find a husband. But I tell them, do you want your husband to love you for your hair or for your soul?"

Aisha's store was very modest. She got most of her stock from Turkey and sold children's clothes as well as headscarves and a good selection of the long overcoats traditionally worn by Pomak women. Her prices were low for Madan, and she was generous in extending credit to those in need. In addition to the clothing, she also sold phone cards and Islamic literature. She said her husband was very diligent in sending money back to help her, and she had many connections with the mosque. But she did not want to be taken care of and believed that following the true path of Islam required hard work. "One man cries for bread. One man cries for a car. One man cries for a plane. Everyone cries for something, but none of these things will help him find peace. Only true belief brings happiness in life."

Women like Aisha were not passive victims of changing gender roles— indeed, they were actively embracing them. When I asked why women wore the "Arab" style of *hijab* in Madan and Rudozem, I heard a wide variety of explanations. When I asked the women themselves, they replied almost unanimously that the headscarf was mandatory for Muslim women. It was an outward demonstration of their commitment to the "true Islam." *Vyara* (faith) was a very important concept to these women;

Figure 24 A Muslim man and woman in 2005

they felt that their faith made them special and brought them closer to God. Wearing the headscarf was a symbol of this precious relationship.

When I asked more secular Pomaks, like Silvi, or older Muslim women, like Higyar, who wore their *kŭrpi* in the traditional style, I got a wider spectrum of responses. As discussed earlier, the reason that I heard most often was that the women were paid by the imams to wear the *zabradki* (headscarves). So common was this perception among the more secular Pomaks in the region that in every published story or interview about headscarves the question of payment always arose. Of course, the women categorically denied this, but few people I interviewed believed their protestations. It was rumored that some women received as much as 100 dollars a month for wearing the headscarf and attending religious lectures, a very large sum for this region. When the government took down the islam-bg website in February 2007 for containing "fundamentalist" content, the Bulgarian media reported that Ali Khairaddin had paid 200 leva per month (about $150) to women who wore the *hijab*.[11]

Another common reason given to explain the behavior of the younger *"fanatitsi"* (fanatics) was that they were trying to attract *sheikove* (rich Arab men) as husbands. Toward older married women, the locals were more sympathetic. Women explained to me that accepting the new form of Islam could help a woman deal with an unemployed and alcoholic husband. In Columbia, the anthropologist Elizabeth Brusco has argued that women convert to evangelical Protestantism as a way of reining in the macho tendencies of their husbands: alcoholism, womanizing, and domestic violence.[12] Indeed, if a man in Madan or Rudozem embraced "orthodox" Islam and stopped drinking, this was generally looked upon as a good thing for the wife, and the other women in the community understood her decision to wear the headscarf, despite their distaste for the "new ways" (*novi nachini*). Thus, while the individual reasons for accepting stricter gender roles varied, the general climate of gender relations was definitely moving away from the old communist ideals of secular egalitarianism. And it was only a matter of time before these changing gender roles and the practices associated with them in the Rhodope clashed head on with Bulgarian mainstream culture.

Headscarves in Homeroom

The controversy began in 2006, when two Pomak girls from Rudozem were suspended from their secondary school in Smolyan for wearing headscarves in addition to the mandatory school uniform. In fact, the older of the two girls, Michaela, had been wearing her headscarf to school for some time. In the face of a challenge from the school's director, she had written a letter to the Ministry of Education under the NMSS government of Simeon Saxecoburgotski in 2003 and received permission to wear her *zabradka*. The letter, signed by a vice minister, stated, "The wearing of a headscarf as an expression of the Muslim tradition does not violate the orders of the Regulations for Implementing the Law for Public Education; it is not a reason for punishment and is not a basis for humiliating the personal dignity of a student."[13] For over two years, Michaela was the only girl at school who wore the headscarf. She was eventually joined by another young woman who had decided that she also wanted to live her life in accordance with the teachings of the Qur'an and the new Islamic literature in Bulgarian emphasizing the mandatory nature of the headscarf for women.

It was only when the second girl, Fatme, showed up at school that the troubles began. The director of the school feared a trend and immediately moved to ban the headscarves from the classroom by arguing that they were not part of the school's uniform. The question was referred to the regional inspectorate of education, from which it eventually traveled up to the Ministry of Education in Sofia. Following the French precedent, the minister of education argued that Bulgarian public schools were secular and that Islamic headscarves could not be worn to class. At the time, the minister probably thought that his verbal order would be the end of the debate, and it might have been if Arif Abdullah and the UIDC had not decided to get involved in the case.[14]

Instead of allowing the girls or their families to pursue the case on their own, the UIDC filed a complaint with a newly established "Commission for the Protection against Discrimination" (KZD) in Sofia, a national body headed by a Turk from the MRF and charged with protecting the rights of women and ethnic minorities.[15] The UIDC filed this complaint directly against the Ministry of Education, claiming that headscarves were mandatory for Muslim women and that the human rights of the two students were being violated.[16] The minister replied once again that Bulgarian education was secular, and that religious symbols had no place in the classroom.[17] When the KZD agreed to consider the complaint of the UIDC, a national debate ignited. Fatme and Michaela got their fifteen minutes of fame overnight, with their youthful faces displayed across every national newspaper.

The two girls strongly believed that they were on the right side of the issue, that they were defending religious rights in the face of an oppressive state, and that the Turkish-led commission would find in their favor. In a June 2006 interview, Michaela explained her optimism:

> Everyone in my family is Muslim. I have been practicing this religion since I was little. I think that Islam is a way of life. It gives us strength

to fight the hardships of life. In the end we will all join the European Union, and there shouldn't be any discrimination. Everyone's rights should be protected. This is our will. That is how we want to dress, and I don't think we should be facing these problems neither here, nor in Europe . . . I expect a positive response [from the commission]. When I had problems [before], I filed a complaint with the Inspectorate and with the Ministry of Education. I received a response from the Ministry of Education and Sciences, a copy of which was sent to the Inspectorate and the director, that there was no problem for me to go dressed like this to school because according to the constitution of Bulgaria everyone has equal rights.[18]

A month later, during the question-and-answer period following his lecture in the Madan Culture House, Arif Abdullah was similarly confident that they would win the case. Indeed, their complaint to the KZD had propelled the UIDC to national attention, and Abdullah presented his organization as one that promoted tolerance and interreligious dialogue while also restoring an undiluted form of Islam to the Pomaks. Both Arif Abdullah and his deputy, Selvi Shakirov, were featured prominently in the local and national media, arguing the virtues of pluralism in a democratic society. But two unexpected factors complicated their seemingly easy victory.

The first was an all-out assault launched on Bulgaria's Muslims by the nationalist party, Ataka (Attack), and its vitriolic leader, Volen Siderov. In the summer of 2006, some Ataka activists parked a white van on the sidewalk in front of the central mosque in Sofia. The van was draped with the Bulgarian flag, and handwritten cardboard signs announced that they were collecting signatures for two petitions. The first petition was to ban Turkish-language news from the Bulgarian national television station, and the second, the one that ultimately received the most attention and support, was to silence the call to prayer from the megaphone of the mosque.

All day Ataka activists solicited signatures from passersby in one of the busiest areas of Sofia. During the first weeks of their campaign, I went to the park across from the van every other day or so and watched them. In the early days, they seemed to arouse little interest; the far-too-busy urbanites in the capital city rushed past them with mildly amused smiles. But as time passed, the Ataka team's tactics became more clever and aggressive, and in the end they collected tens of thousands of signatures on their petition to silence the call to prayer.

The Ataka activists were able to use the news coverage of the headscarf case from Smolyan to their political advantage. In the beginning of their protest, they focused on their two petitions, shouting the text out to

pedestrians as they walked past the van. But later, they started shouting to
men, "Do you want to see all women in Bulgaria in the *feredzhe* [veil]?"
To women they shouted, "Do you want to wear the *feredzhe*?" Whenever
the call to prayer began playing from the minaret, two loudspeakers from
on top of the Ataka van would blast the Bulgarian national anthem in
response. These antics proved effective and shocked many people into
signing the petitions. Hearing the national anthem played on the street
also got the attention of many soon-to-be signatories, and ethnic/religious
tensions mounted. Siderov submitted the petition to the mayor of Sofia,
Boiko Borissov, who was then forced to intervene, just as Ataka began
organizing similar petitions against the call to prayer throughout Bulgaria.
The media ran stories about the mosque protests and the headscarf case
side by side, fanning the flames of the conflict.[19]

But perhaps even more important than Ataka and its petitions was the
influence of Ahmed Doğan and the MRF. Arif Abdullah and Selvi Shakirov
were both opposed to the MRF's heavy-handed interference with the selection of the chief mufti in 2004 and 2005. Their subsequent removal from
the regional muftiship in Smolyan, despite having been democratically
elected, left a bitter division within the Muslim community—yet another
fracture in addition to the Gendzhev split. When Abdullah and Shakirov
filed the complaint against the Ministry of Education, they may or may not
have expected the support of the chief mufti, but in the end the chief mufti's
office did not throw its weight behind the case. In fact, the headscarf issue
put the secular leadership of the MRF into a dilemma, forcing them to
take a stand on a controversial issue that divided their constituency. The
vast majority of the MRF's supporters were secular Turks, who most likely
agreed with the Turkish government's ban on the headscarves. On the other
hand, the MRF had good networks in the non-Turkish Muslim population
in Bulgaria (both Pomak and Roma), and this issue could serve to drive a
wedge between the MRF and the growing number of devout Muslims in
the country, particularly among the Pomaks in the Smolyan region.

Although these political considerations and inter-Muslim divisions were
lurking in the background, when the day of the hearings arrived, the key
point of contention seemed to revolve around religious rights, the role of
women in Islam, and Bulgaria's commitment to uphold gender equality.
On 17 June 2006, Fatme, Michaela, and Selvi Shakirov appeared before
the antidiscrimination commission in Sofia to give testimony in support
of their complaint. The following is an excerpt from the transcript of the
hearings.[20] Irina Muleshkova was a member of the KZD and the chairperson of the committee hearing the case:

Selvi Shakirov: . . . The headscarf for the woman in Islam is not a religious
    symbol; it is a religious dogma. And when a girl, a woman is convinced

of the essence of the Islamic religion, she makes the decision to put on such clothing with desire and conviction. And this right should not be denied to this individual, whoever she is. This right should exist, and she should be allowed to have it, I am saying again, so that we don't hurt her dignity, feelings, convictions, religion, etcetera.

Irina Muleshkova: I would like to ask you, is there special clothing for men, which is also worn by inner conviction?

Shakirov: No.

Muleshkova: There isn't. A second question: Are men and women equal?

Shakirov: Yes.

Muleshkova: In what sense?

Shakirov: That everyone is "equal in front of the law," as they say.

Muleshkova: Are they only equal in front of the law?

Shakirov: Yes.

Muleshkova: There is no equality in front of God? Is this how I should understand you?

Shakirov: Of course there is. But in Islam, the difference between man and woman—there is a physiological, there is also a psychological difference, and Islam defines norms for both men and women. There is such a norm in clothing, which is subjected to the voluntary choice and conviction of the specific woman or girl—she herself can make a choice. When she is convinced . . . That is it. And I believe that right now we are not somewhere where we can judge the Islamic religion. These are things that are very deep, and those who want to get to know this religion can do it. And I am saying again, it is the personal freedom of the individual to choose for himself, to decide what is good, and when he is convinced [of what is good], to be given this freedom.[21]

In this brief exchange, Shakirov starts by claiming that wearing a headscarf is necessary for Islamic women and that they should have the right to choose to wear it once they have the "conviction" that they should live their lives in accordance with the precepts of the Qur'an. When questioned about whether or not men and women are equal in Islam, he argues that the purpose of the commission is not to judge Islam but to guarantee the individual rights of the girls in question, because religious freedoms are guaranteed under the Bulgarian constitution. Banning headscarves is a violation of religious rights, and Shakirov mobilizes Western, liberal human-rights discourses in order to support his position.[22]

On the other side of the argument, Irina Muleshkova—a law professor who had worked with women's NGOs in Bulgaria for more than a decade—clearly knew the key European precedents regarding headscarves in schools. By asking Shakirov whether Islam recognized the equality of men and women, Muleshkova drew the issue away from the question of individual rights and toward the terrain upon which European courts had found grounds to ban religious symbols in schools. In the case of *Sahin v. Turkey*, the headscarf ban was partially upheld because gender equality was "recognised by the European Court as one of the key principles underlying the [European] Convention [on Human Rights] and a goal to be achieved by member States of the Council of Europe."[23] The European court also invoked the *Dahlab v. Switzerland* case[24] and asserted that the headscarf "appeared to be imposed on women by a precept in the Qur'an that was hard to reconcile with the principle of gender equality."[25]

In the end, the Muleshkova committee found against Shakirov and the girls, and the commission fined all parties in the dispute for their attempt to "incite discrimination," including the UIDC for bringing the complaint forward to the antidiscrimination commission in the first place. Both the school and the regional inspectorate were fined for allowing Fatme and Michaela to wear their headscarves as long as they did. The Turkish chairman of the commission, Kemal Eyun, publicly spoke in favor of the decision, making it clear that the MRF, in accordance with the official policies of the Turkish government, did not support headscarves in schools. The final written decision strategically invoked the gender equality argument. It cited two paragraphs from "Women and Religion in Europe, Resolution 1464 of the Parliamentary Assembly of the Council of Europe (2005)."[26] The first of these paragraphs read:

> It is the duty of the member states of the Council of Europe to protect women against violations of their rights in the name of religion and to promote and fully implement gender equality. States must not accept any religious or cultural relativism of women's human rights. They must not agree to justify discrimination and inequality affecting women on grounds such as physical or biological differentiation based on or attributed to religion. They must fight against religiously motivated stereotypes of female and male roles from an early age, including in schools.[27]

Although there were certainly other political considerations lurking in the background, the reliance on gender equality in the argumentation of the Bulgarian antidiscrimination commission ensured that its decision would be very difficult to challenge since it had the strength of other European and Turkish precedents behind it.

On the day the decision was announced, Mustafa Hadzhi, the chief mufti of all Bulgarian Muslims, happened to be attending Friday prayers in the Madan mosque to celebrate the graduation of a class of new *hafuzi*. The decision and its penalties on all parties was a top news story, and journalists rushed to Madan to get statements from Hadzhi. The

chief mufti made a strong statement against the decision and declared
unequivocally that the headscarf was mandatory for Muslim women.[28]
This was the first time a chief mufti had taken such a firm, public position
on Islamic dress for women in Bulgaria, and against the background of
the mosque protests, it was rather provocatively timed. Finally, the chief
mufti was forced by the furor around the UIDC headscarf case to issue a
public statement from the mosque in Madan calling for ethnic tolerance
in Bulgaria.

Images of Madan, which rarely made the national news after GORUBSO
was privatized, were suddenly beamed into households across Bulgaria.
But this time Madan was represented not by the lead/zinc operation and
miners on strike but by the massive new mosque and the thousand or
more men who attended Friday prayers that day. The image was striking: a large prayer hall packed wall to wall with men of all ages, sitting
together on the floor and wearing white lace prayer caps or black berets.
It was the kind of scene most Bulgarians associated with the Middle East,
not with their own Rhodope. In the minds of many Bulgarians outside of
the region, Smolyan, Rudozem, and Madan became the geographical seat
of the perceived threat of Islamic fundamentalism within the country.

The events that followed the commission's decision did not put the
matter to rest. Thinking to appeal the decision, Abdullah and Shakirov
consulted the Bulgarian Helsinki Committee, but they were told that they
would have had a better case if the girls had filed the complaint on their
own behalf.[29] The UIDC paid their fine and decided not to appeal. About
a month later, a medical university in Plovdiv was faced with a similar
issue when over a hundred tuition-paying nursing students from Turkey
said that they would attend school in Bulgaria only if they were allowed
to wear their headscarves to classes. The students were trying to escape the
Turkish headscarf ban, but the rector of the university decided to forego
the much-needed income and banned headscarves on campus. While this
was happening, the minister of education floated the idea of legislation
that would ban all religious symbols in schools, including small crosses,
in order to prevent a repeat of the headscarf affair. The idea of banning
all religious symbols was met with popular outrage and led the newspaper
Sega to host an Internet forum on the question, "Who would ban wearing
a cross in a Christian country?"[30]

Although no legislation was formally passed, the Ministry of Education wanted some sort of official government policy regarding religious
symbols in schools. The minister of education allegedly gave a verbal
order to the Regional Inspectorate of Education in Smolyan advising all
schools in the Smolyan oblast that headscarves should not be worn to
classes, and that any schools found violating this policy would be subject
to sanctions. This verbal order applied to all schools, even those without

a formal uniform requirement. Any girls wishing to wear headscarves and to continue their education could do so by distance learning; they would study at home and only come to the school for exams. This new policy had immediate impacts in Smolyan, Madan, and Rudozem where a growing number of girls were wearing the headscarf. In 2005 not one girl at the Madan secondary school had worn the headscarf, but after the case in Smolyan, several girls began wearing them to class. Local school directors reluctantly enforced the new requirements.

As a result of the new policy, more complaints were filed with the anti-discrimination commission, this time by the girls and their families. These complaints were made against the advice of the chief mufti and the regional mufti in Smolyan, who feared that the new cases would be struck down too and bring on legislation banning the headscarf altogether. In conversations I had with key Pomak Muslim leaders in March 2007, it was clear that they were growing frustrated with the ongoing controversy. "Bulgaria is not a democracy," Abdullah told me. "There is no tolerance here."

Their arguments revolved around two key points: that headscarves are not merely a symbol but a religious requirement and, alternatively, that they should be treated like a fashion. On the first point, the regional mufti of Smolyan, Hairaddin Hatim, told me, "The headscarf is not a symbol like a cross. A Christian woman chooses to wear the cross, but it is not a sin before God if she does not. It is mandatory for a woman who embraces Islam to wear the headscarf. It is not a symbol; it is religious law." Hatim argued that a headscarf did more than simply allow a woman to display her faith; it was part of her personal relationship with God. Banning the headscarf was thus a fundamental violation of religious rights; it prevented women from freely practicing their religion even though their acts of devotion hurt no one else.

On this point, he was particularly adamant, claiming that the headscarves were just pieces of clothing like any other piece of clothing. "It would be like the government deciding to outlaw Chanel and mandating that all people now have to wear Armani. Would it be fair to the people who prefer the fashion of Chanel to make them wear Armani?" This question of fashion inevitably led to a discussion of miniskirts and the typical Bulgarian woman's preference for provocative dress. "Personally, I do not like women who wear short skirts or when I see a thirteen- or fourteen-year-old girl walking around almost naked. It is offensive to me, but there is nothing I can say about it. How can that be allowed and not a headscarf? Why is a covered woman more offensive than a naked one?"

In a separate conversation, Arif Abdullah also invoked the impropriety of miniskirts in his defense of the headscarf. "You see girls on the streets with skirts up to here," he explained, placing the side of his right hand at the top of his thigh. "Many people find it inappropriate, but there are no regulations banning short skirts in schools. Go to any secondary school without a uniform and see how the girls are dressed. They can choose their own clothes, so why can they not choose to dress in a modest way?" In an earlier conversation, the deputy chief mufti, Vedat Ahmed, had also asked me if headscarves would be banned if popular singers and movie actresses started wearing them. "Girls want to follow the fashion. Why can't the headscarf be seen as another fashion?"

More importantly, both Hatim and Abdullah argued that the Turkish community in Bulgaria was not interested in the headscarf issue because Turkish women did not wear headscarves. Without openly saying it, both men clearly implied to me that the Turks practiced a different form of Islam, one that was not true to the Qur'an but corrupted by the secularization process instigated by Kemal Attaturk in the early part of the twentieth century. As long as the MRF was in control of the Turkish population, Bulgarian Turks could be expected to take their direction from Ankara (the capital of Turkey) rather than the Qur'an, and it was the headscarf issue that definitively seemed to divide the Pomak community from the MRF and the Chief Muftiship.

Due to the headscarf affair, the Eastern Rhodope region started to become the perceived heartland of a more "orthodox" version of Islam in the popular imagination of Bulgarian Christians and Muslims alike. In a conversation with a librarian at the High Islamic Institute in Sofia, I mentioned that I was living in Madan. She smiled, exclaiming, "How wonderful it is there, with mosques in every village and all the women in headscarves!" Abdullah also boasted that unlike mosques in other regions of Bulgaria, those in the Smolyan oblast were always full for Friday prayers, "and not just with old men, but with young people." Indeed, my own experience living in the region and traveling around Bulgaria confirms his claim: nowhere were the mosques as large or full as the mosques in Madan, Rudozem, and their surrounding areas. Nowhere, too, was there a higher concentration of young women wearing headscarves in the "new" style, or as many publications, lectures, and seminars offered to so small a population. So the question remained: Why Madan? And although I posed it to Higyar and others, in different ways and on many different occasions, no one really seemed to have a clear answer. Almost all of them, in fact—Muslim, Christian, or atheist—were asking the same question: Why here? And why now?

Minarets after Marx

SNEZHANA, A WOMAN WHO had been a seamstress in the Austrian-owned garment factory for almost six years, told me the story of the women from Madan and Rudozem who worked there. When the Austrians first bought Rhodope-91 in the late 1990s (the largest garment enterprise in Madan under communism), they had decided to set the piece rate at a level where the average seamstress could earn approximately 300 leva a month. When this fact became public, the mayor of Madan went to the manager and complained that seamstresses could not be allowed to make more than the miners in the town. The wage rate was subsequently cut so that seamstresses would earn between 150–200 leva a month, which was less than the wages of the remaining GORUBSO miners in the town. This story struck me as both ironic and strange since many women who worked in the garment factory had unemployed husbands. Despite the women's outrage at having been cheated out of what the owners were willing to pay them, most people in Madan (both men and women) felt that there was something inherently wrong in paying seamstresses higher wages than miners, even if most of the mines were now closed and women were often the sole supporters of their families.

In this book we have seen how multiple factors have influenced the growing replacement of traditional Islam in the Rhodope with forms of the religion that claim to be cleansed of local innovations and more scripturally sound. In the first place, the Rhodope region was one of the hardest hit economically after the collapse of communism in 1989, with registered unemployment rates reaching as high as 40 percent of the population in the 1990s. Throughout the region there was massive depopulation as people fled local communities for opportunities in the bigger cities or abroad. There was also widespread corruption and a breakdown in public order; whatever public resources these cities had at their disposal in the early 1990s were eventually monopolized by the most aggressive and immoral forces in society. At a time when strong spiritual leaders could have been most useful, the upper echelons of the Muslim denominations were plunged into turmoil in a fight for power and money. Simultaneously, the fragile towns of the Rhodope were inundated with an influx of rich religious workers proffering salvation and charity to those most in need.

Politically, the Pomaks also had no national voice to represent their interests in parliament. The Turkish-led Movement for Rights and Freedom (MRF) was far more concerned with its own ethnic constituency and with monopolizing the Muslim vote without actually defending the religious interests of Muslims. This betrayal by the Turks, whom many Pomaks had regarded as their ethnic kin, may have precipitated an identity crisis among the Pomaks, in part fueled by those who wanted to promote the theory that the Pomaks were neither ethnic Slavs nor Turks but rather Arabs or their own distinct and separate identity. A sense of growing affinity with the Arab world was encouraged in no small measure by generous resources made available through large international Islamic charities, such as the World Assembly of Muslim Youth, working through local Bulgarian associations run by Pomaks who had been sent abroad for education throughout the 1990s. This proclivity to identify with the Arabs and to embrace more "orthodox" forms of Islam was also mapped onto an important intergenerational divide. The local hodzhas, like Lili's father, tended to be older men who charged Muslims directly for their services, whereas the newly educated imams and religious leaders were younger and were net distributors of money and aid to Muslim communities. The latter group claimed spiritual authority because they had studied Islam in the Muslim world, where presumably it had not been corrupted by centuries-long contact with Christianity or undergone a mutation during the communist era when Muslim practices and traditions had been banned and pushed underground.

This potent cauldron of factors informed the redefinition of religious allegiances and the reconfiguration of Muslim faith and practice in the Rhodope, but what is particularly curious is the extent to which these changes were concentrated in a relatively small geographic area. Indeed, Pomaks throughout the Rhodope had had virtually the same experiences after the collapse of communism but it was only in Madan and Rudozem that huge mosques were being built, that women were dressing in the "Arab" style, and that people greeted each other on the street in Arabic rather than Bulgarian. Something interesting was going on in this region at the turn of the millennium, something that required some further explanation.

Snezhana's story, which I was able to confirm with several other Madanchani, led me to believe that the embrace of "orthodox" Islam was also encouraged by the sudden shift in gender roles for both men and women that followed the collapse of the mining enterprise. One of the important things that made Madan and Rudozem relatively unique among Muslim cities in Bulgaria was that both had experienced, after the corrupt privatization of GORUBSO, a sudden and violent upheaval in an existing system of gender relations. For these two towns, the bankruptcy of the mines had not only dire economic consequences but also powerful social ones, particularly with regard to the status and authority of men. After the 1990s, there was a sudden psychosocial loss of the masculine identity that had been intimately tied to men's labor in the mines and the communist valorization of that labor. In a short period, Pomak men lost their economic status as breadwinners and also their social status as proletarian miners, respected and admired by their families and communities. With low levels of education and little valuable work experience outside the mining sector, these men found themselves utterly unprepared to compete in the new market economy. Although other Muslim and Pomak cities and towns were also swept up into the political machinations of the MRF and the dramatic regression in the standard of living, it was mostly in the former mining region where so many men had experienced a sudden drop in power and status, that the "new" Islam found its most fertile soil.

In both cities the performance[1] of masculine identities was inextricably tied to work in the mining enterprise and the high value placed on their labor within the command economy. By Bulgarian communist standards, Pomak men in Madan and Rudozem were the most symbolically powerful in the entire country because of their job descriptions. On account of their symbolic status and high rate of remuneration, their masculinity had not been threatened when women initially began leaving their homes and the tobacco fields in order to get an education and take up formal employment as seamstresses, administrators, teachers, nurses, civil servants, and other types of "service" personnel. Indeed, the state actively encouraged and supported women's participation in the labor force; the ideal communist family had a wife that worked outside the home in a "modern" profession (i.e., not tobacco). Because miners were paid well above the average wage that most women earned, men were still imagined to be the providers for the family even if women's wages and their access to generous state entitlements were sufficient to make them economically independent of men. The previous gender division of labor never disappeared. Although Pomak women in these regions were relatively emancipated, a fundamental asymmetry between the sexes persisted. It is also worth noting that the communist state did not allow many avenues for resistance even if men *had* preferred their wives to remain at home.

Over the course of four decades, however, the traditional gender system in Madan and Rudozem was significantly transformed by the wealth that GORUBSO generated. As the standard of living increased and religion was suppressed, women did experience a measure of real emancipation from male control. Women were expected to be both mothers and workers, and eventually, there were women who became engineers and technical specialists in GORUBSO. Furthermore, sexual freedom for women increased, and women were more active in choosing their future husbands and encountered less parental interference. Some Muslim women in these cities even inter-married with Christian men, something expressly forbidden among Muslims in Bulgaria. Superficially, before 1989, Pomak women in Madan and Rudozem were similar to Bulgarian women everywhere else in the country who were enjoying greater freedom and power than they had before socialism but were not quite achieving the promised full equality with men. But in the nonmining regions of the country these disparities were less pronounced than in Madan and Rudozem, where the divide between men and women was much wider because the majority of men were employed in the mines.

When socialism unexpectedly ended in 1989 and the Bulgarian economy began to falter, the miners were able to maintain their status for a while. The country as a whole still valued their labor and believed that their strike actions would help Bulgaria emerge successfully from communism, as those of the labor movement Solidarity had done in Poland. But in the span of a few short years, the situation was drastically reversed. The GORUBSO enterprise imploded. Although Doğan and the MRF initially seemed to champion the cause of the GORUBSO miners, they soon abandoned what was largely constructed as a Pomak cause. Doğan seemed intent on consolidating his power and influence over the Turks of Bulgaria. When the UDF government turned against the GORUBSO miners, the Madan Pomaks had no one to represent their interests in parliament. Without political representation, and with the Bulgarian unions divided and in disarray, the Pomaks in this region could do nothing to defend their enterprise against the impending liquidation. Once comrades-in-arms and the leaders of strikes that could bring down the government, they were now quite isolated and helpless. The lack of political power and the fracturing of community solidarity exacerbated their marginalization.

Thus the Pomak miners suddenly went from being the embodiment of communist masculinity and the wealthiest workers in their communities to a group of relatively unskilled men lacking the appropriate education to compete in the new national and international labor markets. Initially, the shopkeepers and restaurateurs in Madan and Rudozem were sympathetic to their plight, but as the credit slips added up and it became clear that the mines were not going to reopen, more and more doors were closed to the miners who had lived and worked in these communities their entire lives. Few of them had savings because they had never considered that the mines could close, let alone that communism as an economic and political system would ever collapse.[2] To be a miner became equated with being a debtor and a burden on one's family and friends. Aisha once told me: "It was a horrible time then for the men in Madan. Before they had so much, and then suddenly they had nothing. You could see it in their faces. It was terrible."

Although there were women who worked for GORUBSO, it was largely men who were negatively affected by the privatization and liquidation of the enterprise.[3] More importantly, "successful" femininity during the communist era was defined for women both by their formal employment and by their work in the home, whereas "successful" masculinity was intimately and relatively exclusively tied to work in the mines. The only significant industrial employment available in Madan after the closing of the mines was for seamstresses, an overtly gendered kind of work that few men sought. Although the wages were low, jobs for seamstresses were steadier than most other jobs in the local economy. This created a situation deemed unacceptable in many families: wives, mothers, and daughters were working to support husbands, fathers, and sons, who stayed home and who, because they could no longer provide materially for their families, often felt as if they were somehow less than "real" men.

In Madan and Rudozem, unlike most other parts of Bulgaria, it was men who were most negatively affected by the collapse of communism, both economically and psychologically. In other regions, both Christian and Muslim, it was usually women who bore the economic brunt of privatization and the creation of labor markets.[4] As the state retreated from the market, social supports that once helped women combine work and family disappeared. At the same time, employment discrimination against them became more common. In other places, men and women were equally harmed by the end of the socialist state as whole villages and smaller cities collapsed following the breakup of collective farms or the privatization of the rural industries that created employment.[5] In the few sectors where women were markedly better off than men after 1989 (such as tourism), this was due to certain women's revalued cultural capital. Not all women had this cultural capital, only a select few were lucky enough to have the right education and training.[6] They were being rewarded for their revalued skills relative to the devalued skills of men. It was women's unique skill sets (i.e., foreign-language skills in tourism) that were essential and highly sought after in the few sectors of the old communist economy that were still viable after 1989 and creating new employment opportunities. In Madan and Rudozem, however, women were not better off because they had higher skill levels relative to men who were also employed; they were better off because there were no jobs for men in the formal economy.

The implosion of Bulgaria was surely a cataclysmic event, but it was only a gender cataclysm in cities such as Madan and Rudozem because the entire livelihood of these places depended heavily on one industry, which it-self was structured by sexual difference. It was this nexus of circumstances that made the Rhodope ripe for foreign assistance efforts, which were dominated by Islamic charities because the Rhodope happened to be pre-dominantly Muslim. It was also important that the Pomaks as a whole began to feel increasingly abandoned by the MRF and their Turkish faith-mates, who seemed less concerned with religion and more preoccupied with promoting Turkish-language news on Bulgarian national television and monopolizing resources for their own causes. The Pomaks were look-ing for a way to solidify their own ethnic and religious identity in the face of missionaries, proselytizers, and preachers of so many different denomi-nations. In the midst of all the different factors reshaping local identity, the Madan and Rudozem Pomaks began rearranging gender roles in their communities in a way that would differentiate them both from the Ortho-dox Christian/secular majority and the Turkish Muslim minority. It was perhaps coincidental that "orthodox" forms of Islam, supported by funds derived from international charities, began making their way into the Rhodope at this time. But since Turkish Muslim women in Bulgaria were relatively secular and did not wear the headscarf, the Pomak promotion of "true" Islam gave them a moral and religious high ground from which to critique the "lax" Turks of Bulgaria.

Although in some countries, the embrace of "orthodox" Islam increases women's participation in the public sphere,[7] this was not the case in Bul-garia, where women had been active members of this sphere between 1946 and 1989. The advent of "orthodox" Islam in Bulgaria meant that even if women had to work in the public sphere (in order to support their families), their return to the private sphere became the ideal. Thus, this ideal role for Pomak women began to be reconstructed as one in which women needed to give up their roles as workers, and concentrate on being good mothers and wives in accordance with the new and "proper" interpre-tation of the Qur'an.

These changing gender roles were encouraged by a rebirth of interest in Islam among Pomaks, who truly believed that their traditions were cor-rupted by communism. But the "orthodox" forms of Islam coming into Madan, Smolyan, and Rudozem valorized men's role in the family and com-munity as work in the mines had once valorized their role in the economy. This valorization was based on the spiritual authority of the Qur'an rather than on access to material resources. Thus, some Pomak men who were left unemployed and impoverished by the closure of the mines were attracted to the reimagining of putatively "natural" gender relations endorsed by the new mosques and "orthodox" Muslim NGOs in the region. For many men, the site for the valorization of masculinity in these communities moved from the mines into the mosques exactly at the historical moment when previous material justifications for male authority were eroded. When they attended Friday prayers and mixed with their old friends and neighbors, the former miners could recapture some of the male camaraderie and so-cial respect they used to enjoy when they worked for GORUBSO. More im-portantly, the mosque became the key place for making connections with wealthier and more powerful men, who were able to offer help in times of need. For some men, this also meant policing their wives' bodies more strictly. Ensuring that their women adopted proper Islamic dress and behavior became a marker of this newfound faith and could assuage the shame men felt at having to depend on women financially.

Many women also seemed eager to adopt these new gender roles and religious practices, and certainly many of them did embrace "orthodox" Islam out of their own inner conviction and faith. But faith was not the only influential factor, and it was difficult to understand why women who had been "emancipated" under communism (or their daughters, who had some vicarious memories of it and still enjoyed many of its benefits) would so willingly abandon the ideology of gender equality in favor of a locally negotiated model of gender relations that required women's deference to and economic dependence on men. After all, these Pomak women were not the nonliberal, non-Western subjects of Saba Mahmood's urban women's mosque movement in Cairo, for whom "morality, divinity and virtue"[8] were goals in and of themselves. Rather, most of them were thoroughly modern subjects, encumbered by a complete Marxist social imagination for thinking about resistance to structural (particularly capitalist) oppression, even if Marx's ideas were never fully implemented in practice. This is not to say that "orthodox" Islam is not compatible with gender equality in Bulgaria, but rather that one might expect Bulgarians raised under communism to see the two as incompatible. It may be that the embrace of some other religious faith, or of nationalism, would have precipitated the same rearranging of gender relations and that these new forms of Islam were incidental. But perhaps there was something else going on that could help explain the women's perspective, something about Islam that was resonating with a particularly structural way of viewing the world that Bulgarians had inherited from communism. Perhaps the local conditions were interacting with a global phenomenon in unique and unpredictable ways.

"Globalized Islam" in Eastern Europe

The work of scholars such as Olivier Roy and Gilles Kepel may be useful for understanding these questions in the Bulgarian context.[9] Roy argues that in its most recent incarnations, Islam in Western Europe has become denationalized and deethnicized in a way that is a striking mirror of the internationalist discourses of Marxism or secular humanism. Following Lenin, who recognized that Islam was an alternative internationalism as early as the 1920s,[10] Roy claims that for young immigrants in Western Europe, Islam has become the antiestablishment ideology of choice, replacing Marxism as the favored critique of modern capitalism.

Protest against the established order, which was rather virulent in France during the 1970s, was then carried out beneath the red flag of radical leftist organizations. By the 1990s these movements had disappeared from the suburbs. The only networks of radical protest are Islamic, but they recruit from among the same social categories (outcasts from the educated middle class and dropouts from the working class), carry the same hatred for "bourgeois" values and attitudes, have the same targets (imperialists) and often the same pet guerillas (Palestine), claim to be internationalist (*ummah* instead of the international working class), and are built on the same generation gap.[11]

Gilles Kepel also sees striking similarities between the roles of Marxism and Islam as antibourgeois rallying points for those excluded from the economic and political benefits of liberal democracy and global capitalism. The internal debates between Muslim groups that want to assimilate to the West and those groups that refuse to be thus "co-opted" are similar, he argues, to antagonisms between Western European communist groups of the previous era. "The function of the category 'bourgeoisie' provided contrast, in terms of social identity, with the hated 'other,' just as the category 'unbelievers' provides contrast for Islamist ideology."[12]

This replacement of leftist politics with Islam, however, may have a very different resonance in Eastern Europe than it has in the West. Roy's analysis of "globalized Islam" focuses on Christian countries where Muslims are mostly immigrant minorities or local converts and where liberal-parliamentary democracies coexist with relatively generous, if retreating, welfare states. These immigrants and their children are often economic migrants to Western European countries; they experience xenophobia and exclusion from their host societies but are aware that returning to their mother countries, where their faith would thrive, would entail more dire political and economic consequences. Alternatively, Muslims in the Balkans are remnants of a colonial conquest thrown off by the local population, and Turkish and Albanian Muslims look back at their "mother" countries and see committed secular states. Muslims in Central Asia are now forming their own states and must work out a balance between Islam and Western liberal democracy. In Russia, the background of indigenous Muslim populations varies considerably, with some fighting for independence (Chechnya) while others accept the centralized authority of Putin.[13]

Unlike Russia or countries in the Balkans and Central Asia where democracy is not yet consolidated and states lean in differing degrees toward authoritarianism, Western Europe has a deeply rooted commitment to parliamentary democracy that is relatively fixed. As a result, Kepel believes, Islam is being transformed by its extended contact with Western European values:

In Westminster, the European Parliament, the Bundestag, and in regional and municipal councils throughout Western Europe, the democratic political system that emerged from the European Enlightenment is starting to absorb men and women born in a Muslim tradition, for the first time in history. A promising generation of young Muslims now have opportunities to exercise democratic rights that are forbidden—or so restricted as to be emptied of significance—in countries where Islam represents the majority religion. Their political participation has its roots in local organizations, where many of these entrepreneurs, activists, professionals, and civil servants got their start. Such grassroots political activity requires a separation of mosque and state, as Islam settles into the European milieu.[14]

Although there are more extreme groups, like Hizb ut-Tahrir, which are openly anti-Western and call for the establishment of a supranational Islamic caliphate,[15] many Muslim groups in Western Europe do claim to use the rights afforded to them in a democracy to reshape society so that Islamic beliefs and practices are tolerated. They see Islam as an integral part of Europe, compatible with both modernity and parliamentary democracy.[16]

A brief examination of the rhetoric of groups or intellectuals claiming to represent European Muslims would seem to support Kepel's empirical assessment of the situation, despite the fact that the European press tends to paint Muslims as dangerous radicals. For instance, the Federation of Islamic Organizations in Europe (FIOE), an umbrella organization for groups operating at the national level, is quite explicit in its support for Western-style democracy. "A large proportion of Muslims in many EU countries were born in Europe," says the president of FIOE. "They are increasingly articulating their aspirations in terms of European democratic values, which they perceive as compatible with their basic Islamic values . . . The aspiration of Muslims for a decent and prosperous life under the law, in equity with other fellow citizens of a democratic and pluralist Europe, remains a high priority."[17] Similarly, the first "Muslims in Europe Charter," from the Qatar-based IslamOnline.net website, encourages Muslims to be active citizens by voting and participating in civil society: "Muslims of Europe emphasize their respect for pluralism and the religious and philosophical diversity of the multicultural societies they live in."[18]

The Swiss Muslim intellectual, Tariq Ramadan, also emphasizes that Muslims must take Western European society as they find it. In his "Manifesto for a New 'We,'" Ramadan writes that Muslims "must express confidence in themselves, in their values, in their ability to live and to communicate with full serenity in Western societies . . . They must forcefully insist that Muslims are expected to respect the laws of the countries in which they reside, and to which they must be loyal. Millions of Muslims are, in fact, already proving every day that religious integration is an accomplished fact, that they are indeed at home in the Western countries whose tastes, culture and psychology they have made their own."[19]

Olivier Roy also claims that Islam in Western Europe has been "westernized" in that "religion (a coherent corpus of beliefs and dogmas collectively managed by a body of legitimate holders of knowledge)" has given way to what he calls "religiosity (self-formulation and self-expression of a personal faith)."[20] Thus, Roy argues that in the Western European context the many forms of Islam and Islamism have been individualized; that is, they have come to focus on personal faith and the right to pursue and perform that faith in the public sphere. This call for the recognition of rights extended by the promises of liberal multiculturalism recognizes that democratic pluralism can work in principle but points out that so far it has failed to live up to its own standards. Thus, most Muslims in Western Europe (although there are some significant exceptions) embrace the underlying principles of European parliamentary democracy and multicultural pluralism, but want to see its promises more fully realized. And even those who challenge pluralism and democracy in the name of Islam do so in a way that has been transformed by their contact with the West and reveals the individualization of their beliefs and their desire for religious communities cut free from either national or cultural moorings. Thus, the spiritual and political possibilities of Islam in the West, even in its most radical forms, are fundamentally shaped by their contact with Western democratic values, particularly in the way that Muslims deploy a language of religious rights as being constitutionally guaranteed.

But these democratic values are not entrenched to the same extent in the former communist countries of Eastern Europe. In fact, there is great frustration with "democracy," which has brought a rapid decline in living standards for many former communist citizens. In Bulgaria, for instance, democratically elected leaders, rather than representing their constituents, became the lackeys of unscrupulous foreign investors and local Mafia "entrepreneurs" and sold off viable state-owned enterprises for only a fraction of their value in order to enrich themselves with bribes and kickbacks. Monies that could have been put in the state budget to shore up the social safety net and ease the economic pains of "shock therapy" were squandered, stolen, or used to service Bulgaria's mounting external debts (debts that were themselves incurred by irresponsible politicians who enriched themselves at the expense of the people). Law and order broke down, and newly organized criminal syndicates bullied and racketeered most small private initiatives out of business. Incomes plummeted as crime rates rose. Previously strong social networks broke down under the strains of poverty and competition for increasingly scarce resources. In Madan, this political, economic, and social implosion was felt most acutely in the years following the collapse of GORUBSO.

The chaos of the transition was combined with a general cultural memory of Marxism, its critique of bourgeois democracy and its metanarrative of class struggle giving way to radical social equality.[21] For those excluded from the benefits of transition and disgusted by the lying, cheating, stealing, and violence of Bulgarian capitalism, the old ideals of communist solidarity and struggle against capitalist injustice once again had resonance. Across the former communist world, there were also growing calls for a new kind of "universalism" that could challenge and perhaps replace the political and economic forms of Western hegemony. For example, in 1995, fewer than 30 percent of all Russians expressed favorable views of parliamentary democracy.[22] In 2001, 57 percent of Russians said they wanted to restore the USSR, and 45 percent claimed that communism was better than the current system of democracy.[23] Using the 2001 New Europe Barometer, two Swedish political scientists found across Eastern Europe significant nostalgia for the material security of communism;[24] the majority of postcommunist citizens evaluated the command economic system in positive terms. Moreover, throughout the region the percentage of people who approved of a return to communism increased substantially between 1993 and 2001, and this increase in nostalgia was found among the young as well as the old. The two researchers argue that the desire for a return to the previous system is symptomatic of "dissatisfaction with the present system's ability to deliver the goods—material or non-material."[25] These sentiments seem strongest among religious populations. In 1997, 68 percent of Russians who identified themselves as "traditional believers" felt that the collapse of the USSR was a regrettable mistake made by reformist leaders, and 84 percent agreed that the dissolution of the communist system "could and should have been prevented."[26] Even if some respondents are merely nostalgic for Russia's status as a world superpower, these are striking findings, especially given the communist system's attempts to promote atheism and its forcing of most religions underground.

In fact, it seems that in many places in the former communist world, philosophers and political theorists are being inspired by religion in their search for a new political and economic system that can displace the ideological hegemony of Western liberal democracy and free market capitalism. Nowhere is this trend more consolidated than in Poland (at the University of Warsaw), where a group of Polish intellectuals founded an International Society for Universalism in November 1989. This society, which holds international congresses and has its own journal, *Dialogue and Universalism*, was born out of a local desire to explore the possibility of a "metaphilosophy" that could find the common ground between Catholicism and Marxism, subsuming them both beneath a new "universal universalism," or what Janusz Kuczynski, the leading organizer and first president of the society, has called a "maximal maximalism."[27]

These "metaphilosophical universalists" claim that their "true 'universal universalism'" will replace what they consider to be the "false 'Western Universalism'" of liberal democracy, free markets, and consumerism.[28] The Catholic Poles are scathing in their critiques of Western universalisms and how they have been applied around the world, but particularly in Eastern Europe. Their goal is to expose how these false universalisms justify and support the "Western and American domination of the world."[29] The Polish critique also echoes Islamic critiques of the particularism of the West's supposed universalism.[30]

Similar critique of Western universalisms and their imposition on former communist citizens can also be found in the discourses of Eastern European Muslim populations. The grand mufti of Bosnia-Herzegovina has expressed his own ideals for Muslim unity as a challenge to the liberalism of the West:

> We may recognize the problem of the modern Muslim identity in the debate about the kind of secularization of Muslim history and the method of (re-)Islamization of the Muslim mind. The idea of secularization did not come to Muslims as a result of their own experience. The majority of Muslim *ulama* [scholars], and some Muslim intellectuals as well, have always felt that the idea of secularization of Muslim societies has come from the West by political and sometimes even military pressure. This is one of the reasons why the secularization of Muslim history, except perhaps in Turkey and Tunisia, has failed, and this is why the drive for a kind of re-Islamization of the Muslim mind is taking place. Muslims have refused to give up the idea of a universal community of Islam (the *Ummah*) even if it means, at least for the time being, a utopia.[31]

In Bulgaria, too, some "orthodox" Muslims have mounted a critique of Western democracy/capitalism (which they see as inseparable) because they believe that it has failed, and they view the Islamization of society as the only path forward. In his speech in Madan, Abdullah argued that the material security of communism could be combined with the political freedoms of democracy only in a world governed by Islam, and it is no coincidence that he chose to deliver his message not in the mosque but in the grand hall of the Culture House, which hosted innumerable communist party meetings. Furthermore, as explained in an earlier chapter, some of the Islamic literature that is being translated into Bulgarian explicitly focuses on social justice. One telling example was a brochure from the World Assembly of Muslim Youth that I found in the mosque in Chepintsi; in it there was the following passage about the Islamic obligation of tithing:

Zakah is a means of redistribution of wealth in a way that makes a contribution to social stability, providing a means of survival for those who have not, and reminding those who are wealthy that what they have is a trust from God. By purging the soul of the rich from selfishness, and the soul of the poor from resentment against society, *Zakah* blocks the channels leading to *class hatred* and makes it possible for the springs of *brotherhood* and *solidarity* to gush forth. Such stability is not merely based on the personal generous feelings of the rich: it stands on a firmly based right of the destitute which, if denied by those holding the wealth, would *be exacted by force, if necessary.* [my emphasis][32]

Such language—"class hatred," "solidarity"—may resonate profoundly with postcommunist populations who understand the Marxist critique of capitalism but do not want to return to communism and seek instead an alternative path to social justice. In the Bulgarian context, the UIDC and other Islamic organizations are focusing on social justice; they promote Islam as a way to restore community, morality, and prosperity to their otherwise chaotic societies and challenge the notion of Western democracy and capitalism as fixed norms to which Muslims have to adjust. Thus, the promise of a new Islamic utopia or a new transcendent metaphilosophy is fueled by popular discontent with the material and spiritual realities of the less than ideal implementation of democracy and capitalism in the Bulgarian context. Moreover, these new ideologies are taking root among populations with a recent and collective memory of an actual alternative to these "false universalisms" from the West. This is very different from the situation in Western Europe, where new forms of Islam are faced with deeply rooted and largely immovable political and economic structures.

I have tried to show in this book how the displacement of traditional forms of Islam by new, "orthodox" ones was the result of specific local circumstances, including the historical legacies of communism. The shape of some postsocialist societies is still in flux, despite their accession to the European Union and their seeming embrace of the West. Because of this, Islam in the Eastern European contexts may differ significantly in its political and philosophical possibilities from Islam in the West. Eastern Europe is haunted by the lingering specter of Marxist-Leninism, with its critique of capitalism and bourgeois democracy, and its promise of an ideal end-state of human history that supersedes the present political and economic arrangements. The desire for a new totalizing discourse of social justice may be a key factor that explains why both men and women in Eastern Europe might be open to new ways of organizing gender relations.

All adult Bulgarians living through the decade of the 1990s had first-hand experience of capitalism, and most had either first- or second-hand experience of communism. (If they did not themselves have memories of life under communism, then certainly their parents did.) They were often politically committed to one system or the other due to their own conceptions of how an equitable or efficient society should look, with many Bulgarians initially favoring political freedoms over social and economic security in the period immediately after 1989, when frustration with the communist monopoly on power was high. For the Pomaks in Madan and Rudozem, however, the costs and benefits of communism were more acute than for most of the Bulgarian population: rapid, state-driven economic development raised living standards dramatically in just a few decades but was coupled with severe religious oppression. The postsocialist period has brought religious freedoms but with a decline in living standards and economic possibilities and a degenerating moral climate in which many young people either emigrate or sink into a life of drugs, crime, and/or prostitution; there are few other economic opportunities in a country where employers regularly fail to pay their employees and friendships fall apart over a few unpaid debts. For those trying to promote "orthodox" Islam among the Pomaks, therefore, the claim that religion represents an ideological third way, a system that can provide morality and prosperity, may be appealing, particularly if it is also a conduit for new economic opportunities. For those who have real or vicarious knowledge of communism and now live in a society shaped by a cruel and violent form of capitalism, a kind of universalist Islam could become a way of continuing the social justice project conceived by Marx, but unsuccessfully implemented by either the Russian or Bulgarian communists. This universalist Islam, stripped of its local particularities, is operating in a structurally similar way to the old Marxist discourses that emphasized the inherent problems of capitalism and advocated communal efforts in the interests of a common good.

As different as Islam and Marxism are, there may be some interesting continuities between the ideal versions of communism and the forms of Islam now gaining ground in the Rhodope. Both claim to be able to bring about social justice and are imbued with a self-perception of their own historical inevitability as a global political/spiritual force. Both subsume national and ethnic differences in the dream of transnational community, whether the international proletariat or global *ummah*. Both are overtly prescriptive about how people should live their lives on a daily basis and offer a total ideological package that makes sense of the world, defines clear enemies, codifies "success" within the system, and builds trust and solidarity among "brothers." Perhaps most importantly, both are more communally oriented than free-market capitalism, placing a higher value on social relations and community cooperation than on self-sufficiency and competitiveness. Both provide some form of social safety net for those who are less fortunate and demand that accumulated wealth be redistributed in a more egalitarian manner. Finally, both ideological projects promote the idea that "good people" will be rewarded and "bad people" punished, an appealing prospect in a country where not one corrupt politician or Mafia boss has been put in jail in almost two decades of postcommunism. Of course, there are many important differences, and one is not and cannot be a perfect substitute for the other. My point here is merely that for many of my informants in the Rhodope, many of the characteristics they were attracted to in Islam coincided in interesting ways with the facets of communism that they claimed to miss the most.

Marxism and Islam also seem to share the idea that gender relations between men and women should be organized in such a way as to serve the greater common good and are not just a matter of individual rights. The communists had justified the "emancipation" of Pomak women on the grounds that it provided labor for rapid economic development, modernized the rural Muslim populations, and assimilated the Pomaks into the Bulgarian national fold. Becoming a modern society and building a socialist future required the labor of both men and women, the communists argued. In contrast to Western feminism, women's emancipation under communism was not only about individual autonomy, personal freedom, or agency for women as political and economic subjects, but rather a project which viewed women's increased roles in the public sphere as a necessary step to promote the common good in an inevitable historical process leading to ideal communism. Thus, the radical shift in gender relations during the pre-1989 era was justified because it benefited all members of Bulgarian society and not just the women themselves.

Similarly, Islamic publications and the newly devout women with whom I spoke emphasized that society had been harmed by women's abandonment of the home and that social harmony and God's will could only be done if men and women returned to the roles dictated by the Qur'an; for women, theoretically, this meant a return to the private sphere. Thus, although the ideal gender arrangements of the two systems of thought were at first glance contradictory, the justifications for these arrangements were similar enough to strike a chord with the Pomaks in Madan and Rudozem. Furthermore, the idea of working for the collective good and a growing rejection of materialism and individualistic versions of Western feminism may also help to explain why some Bulgarian Pomaks were embracing "orthodox" Islam: they imagined it as a true alternative to the injustices and spiritual and material poverty of the post-1989 era.

Men and women like Aisha, Hana, and Hasan believe that Islam can provide answers to the immoralities plaguing their societies. This is another specific explanation for the embrace of "orthodox" Islam in this region; the corrupt privatization of GORUBSO gave locals a first-hand taste of the injustices of the market economy. In a world turned upside down, in a social milieu where criminals, liars, cheats, and thugs have been the greatest beneficiaries of the new economic system, Islam provides moral guidance. In a conversation with the regional mufti of Smolyan, I had this point driven home to me as we discussed relative crime rates in Christian versus Muslim areas in Bulgaria. "Why do people equate Islam and terrorism? This is not fair. There is a stronger connection between Christianity and crime, and no one says that all Christians are criminals. But look at our cities in the Rhodope: no theft, no killing, no drugs. Can you say that in the rest of Bulgaria? Our country is full of criminals; it is run by criminals. They did not even want to let us join the European Union because we are such big criminals."[33]

It is very important to note, however, that there is an important difference lurking in the background, and scholars such as David Westbrook,[34] who want to see Islam and Marxism as equally anticapitalist ideological projects, have missed it. In terms of their rhetoric, both ideologies can appear quite similar, and both are attractive to the disenfranchised and disenchanted because they provide powerful metanarratives that challenge the current ideological and material hegemony of the West. Indeed, there are many scholars who promote the equivalency of Marxism and radical Islam (and in some cases Nazism) in order to justify military interventions aimed at "protecting our [Western] way of life."[35] But there is a level at which Islam is closer to capitalism than it is to Marxism. Both Islam and capitalism privilege private property and the particular form of heteronormative, monogamous gender arrangements that it requires, a gender arrangement fundamentally challenged by one of the fathers of scientific socialism in the nineteenth century. For Friedrich Engels, the monogamous, nuclear family was "based on the supremacy of the man, the express purpose being to produce children of undisputed paternity; such paternity is demanded because these children are later to come into their father's property as his natural heirs."[36] Private property and the nuclear family arrangements that facilitate its legitimate transfer from one generation to the next are left unchallenged in both ideological options.

Islam in the West, no matter how radical it becomes, will probably not be able to fundamentally reshape society or redistribute wealth. Although the wealthy are required to pay a tithe and support charitable works, Islam offers no critique of the relations of production. It is relatively silent on the question of exploitation among and between Muslims. On the issue of private property, Western hegemonic ideals and the principles of Islam converge. Even the grand mufti of Bosnia, quoted above as a staunch critic of Western secularism, believes that the right to private property should attain the status of a universal truth. He writes: "The right to have property as a means of decent human life is a value of Europe that should be asserted as a *common human value*. Europe is now a haven for many people who are becoming independent through the European economic prosperity" (my emphasis).[37]

In the immediate postcommunist period in Bulgaria, the reemergence of Islam and the importation of "orthodox" versions of the religion were just two of the many forces reinscribing the importance of private property in communities that had been collectivized or heavily dependent on a state that tempered economic disparity by centrally accumulating and redistributing wealth. On an ideological level, communism had tried to undermine private property by rearranging gender relations and destabilizing the patriarchal, monogamous family. The communists also wanted to undermine the idea of women as the private property of men. Although women's emancipation was an important communist goal in its own right, by requiring women's formal labor force participation and lessening their dependence on men, it also theoretically had the effect of destabilizing the patriarchal, monogamous family as a site where private wealth was accumulated and inherited rather than being shared by society as a whole. In fact, as the anthropologist Katherine Verdery has pointed out, under communism both men and women became equally dependent on the state, which tried to take over the patriarchal role in society as a whole (even while it valorized certain forms of male labor and reinscribed male authority in Madan). It is true that the family never disappeared under communism, and indeed it became a place of resistance to and sanctuary from the totalitarian state,[38] but its primary role as a vehicle for the preservation of wealth from one generation to the next faded relative to its role in capitalist countries.[39] Men and women living in Bulgaria today still know and understand Marx's critique of private property, and for those who have been the victims rather than the beneficiaries of the Bulgarian versions of capitalism and democracy, its lure may still be strong. Therefore, Islam in its current form in postsocialist countries like Bulgaria may be modified to include some kind of critique of private property (particularly if illegally acquired through corrupt privatization) in order to appeal more broadly.

If Islam in Western Europe is being Westernized and increasingly shaped by individualist ideas of religiosity and the assumed compatibility of Islam with a liberal, multicultural society, then it might be reasonable to claim that Islam in Eastern Europe is being "Marx-icized." Islam could be one of many new discourses operating in the postcommunist context that holds out the possibility for a return to collectivist ideals and the vision of a morally and ethically united community striving for common material and spiritual goals. The analogy might be Christian "liberation theology" in Latin America where Marxism was fused with Catholicism and scriptures were reinterpreted as demanding justice for the poor. Pietist discourses might eventually be bent to accommodate a moral critique of private property, and abstinence from conspicuous consumption could become part of pious religious practice. The embrace of a globalized Islam in Madan and Rudozem, or in Bulgaria and Eastern Europe more broadly, was at least partially the result of a latent societal desire for a system that can accommodate all of the positive aspects of communism, capitalism, and personal religious faith but that supersedes all three and aspires to offer some new universal solution to humanity's ills: war, poverty, inequality, etcetera. People that knew, understood, and lived their lives by a totalized metanarrative of history, progress, and humanity united in opposition to capitalist imperialism were predisposed to other narratives that seem to have the same plot. Religious universalisms that enter the postideological space of postcommunism might initially be embraced only to meet this diffuse social longing, even if that is not the intention of their original advocates, just as Islam is being "tamed" by democracy in the West. This does not mean that Islam loses any of its appeal as a religion, as a way to bring oneself closer to God, but only that it could be doing other things as well, promising a path to material as well as spiritual salvation.

That this discontent has financial resources to support it is an interesting part of the equation. The large international Islamic charities, most of which are based in Saudi Arabia and linked at least indirectly with the Saudi state, have proven themselves to be generous supporters of Muslim communities as they rediscover their faith and chart a course away from the perceived injustices and immoralities of the West. While local factors are important, one must also take into account the United States' unilateral global power and the far-reaching fingers of Western cultural imperialism. Muslim communities who want to push back at these geopolitical realities can find support from the Islamic charities, even if it means that more "orthodox" forms of Islam might displace their own traditional forms. Just as the Soviet Union backed a wide array of leftist causes during the Cold War, so too have the Saudi charities supported a wide array of Muslim groups. During the Cold War, those disenchanted with the United States had somewhere to turn for financial and logistical support. But it is important to remember that the reasons that drove countries as different as Cuba, Ethiopia, and Vietnam into the Soviet sphere were diverse, and local historical, political, and economic factors played the largest role. For the Soviets, the enemy of their enemy was always their friend, but the various enemies of their enemy did not have all that much in common, and certainly they adopted Marxist-Leninist ideologies to suit their own local political exigencies. Unlike the USSR, Saudi Arabia does not fund sovereign states but rather groups within states, such as Muslim minorities like the Pomaks. And just as there was a vast array of reasons that led local political elites to seek Russian assistance and adopt a communist ideology, so now there are similarly diverse reasons why Muslim communities might embrace a more "orthodox" form of Islam if it goes along with Saudi financial support. In Europe, Islam may indeed be the oppositional discourse of choice, and its importance will continue to grow as the resources dedicated to spreading "true" Islam increase.

Despite the expansion of the European Union, there are still lingering questions about whether Western and Eastern Europe will be unified under the ideals and values of the West, or whether the former Eastern bloc countries will manage to create Slavoj Žižek's "SECOND way." In its most ideal configuration, this could be a new political/spiritual project to challenge the hegemony of liberal democracy and globalization, particularly as global markets falter. If one can speculate on the future, it might be that the encounter between Islam and Western Europe has been read too optimistically by the likes of Kepel and Roy and that it will prove to be a destructive collision. Excluded and discriminated Muslim minorities may rage against the seemingly immovable legacies of the Enlightenment, struggling to deploy the language of secularism, pluralism, and democracy to their own advantage. But ultimately, they may be relegated to the status of a dangerous internal "other," supposedly incapable of rationality and modernity and thus pushed toward an increasingly violent confrontation. Certainly, these are increasingly polarized debates in Western Europe, and anxieties about the future of Islam there are widespread.

On the other hand, the fluidity and ambiguity of the political and ideological commitment to these Western ideals in Eastern Europe combined with a deeply rooted historical critique of capitalism and private property could mean that Islam on the eastern side of the former Iron Curtain will become something qualitatively different. The contact between Islam and the postsocialist kleptocracy might push these societies into some as-yet-unknown political and economic system that mobilizes both secular and religious collectivist discourses to push past the particular imperialist discourse of the "end of history" that has paralyzed the political and social imagination of intellectuals for the last two decades. Few social scientists predicted the velvet revolutions of 1989, and it may be that some of the former communist countries are still in a state of flux, with populations still capable of imagining alternative political and economic systems.

Of course, it is also possible that these new systems will be built in opposition to both Islam and liberal democracy and will justify their own tenets by pointing to the defects of the other two, or that some Eastern European populations will vote in stronger central governments or even accept revived forms of authoritarianism to rein in the influence of corrupt politicians and free-market bandits. But whatever the future holds, the social embrace of Islam will be informed by the particular ideological histories of the places wherein it takes root. In Bulgaria, receptivity to "orthodox" Islam in Madan and Rudozem may be just the beginning of a wider social phenomenon and the harbinger of some new, big idea yet to come. That new idea might look like an Islamic version of liberation theology. Or it might address the deficiencies of democracy and the market economy in Eastern Europe—inspire a new collectivist political and economic system that would improve the material conditions of people's lives without quashing their spiritual aspirations. Of course, these are just speculations, but it seems fairly obvious that the increasing nostalgia for the communist past, the growing popular frustration with the capitalist present, and the appearance of new transcendent metanarratives of social justice form a powerful brew of social forces, which should not be ignored.

Back down on the ground in Madan and Rudozem and Smolyan, however, these larger social processes go largely unexamined. Silvi goes about her day trying to sell her Avon products, while Iordan works at the construction site in Zlatograd, still wondering whether he should get baptized. Lili secretly changes clothes in the bathroom of the pizzeria. Hana takes her daughter to the playground and finds peace and comfort in her newfound faith, while Higyar organizes her *mevlidi*. Hasan quietly perseveres in his mission to bring the "true" Islam to the city, while Lili's father still makes and sells amulets for those in need of a little magic. Lyubo and the other miners drown their sorrows in *rakiya*, lamenting the loss of their glory days as miners, while hordes of women sew 900-euro ski jackets for 200 dollars a month. Five times a day the muezzin reminds the people in Madan that God is great, and with each prayer more men and women are coming to believe him in their own unique way. What will happen in cities like Madan is occluded in the thick mists of time not yet arrived, but there is no doubt that Islam will play an important role here, even if it is something the majority of the town's residents ultimately reject.

Inevitably, this case study of Madan will be read against similar studies of Muslim communities across Europe or the world, and it will become just one more piece of a larger puzzle perplexing social scientists: why, in an era of unprecedented global integration and technological progress, are individuals and communities finding renewed meaning and purpose in new interpretations of religion? And what happens when people put this new faith at the center of their civic identities and demand accommodation for their religious practices in the public sphere? More importantly, why does this process seem so uneven, with one community embracing an invigorated spirituality while another plods on happily in its traditionally religious or secular ways? Although social scientists must indeed engage with these bigger questions, the specific goal of ethnography is to give faces and names to mass movements, to make sure that human beings are not viewed as mere cogs in the wheel of social change. Each community is unique, and while it may be possible to study many of them and make some larger theoretical claims, it is still crucial to pay attention also to local

Figure 25 A young Pomak girl in 2005

circumstances and the ways in which people themselves make sense of the
processes happening in their lives. For it is in the hands of individuals like
Lili, Silvi, Hana, Lyubo, Iordan, and Higyar that "big ideas" like social
justice, freedom, or faith are received, retooled, and redeployed in ways
that make them relevant to daily life.

Appendix

TABLE 1
Average Annual Wages for Workers in Selected Masculinized and Feminized
Industrial Professions (in Bulgarian leva)

	1985	1989	1990	1991[a]	1992	1993	1994
Male professions							
Electricity and thermal energy production	3,135	3,984	5,540	17,016	43,925	68,393	98,960
Coal industry	3,888	4,740	6,417	17,625	42,338	67,257	93,624
Ferrous metallurgy (incl. mining)	3,435	4,474	5,520	15,154	40,133	61,937	100,465
Nonferrous metallurgy (incl. mining)	**3,704**	**4,737**	**5,741**	**15,185**	**35,840**	**60,101**	**86,808**
Logging and wood product manufacturing	2,635	3,362	3,982	10,888	21,816	31,962	49,003
Production of construction materials	2,841	3,582	4,436	12,362	26,467	41,021	65,867
Female professions							
Textile and knitwear manufacturing	2,456	3,718	3,748	9,293	20,806	28,928	44,439
Apparel manufacturing	2,047	2,680	3,332	8,139	19,399	24,405	39,424
Leather and footwear	2,305	3,124	3,690	9,915	21,211	27,091	43,705

Source: NSI, *Statistical Yearbook* 1993, p. 100; NSI *Statistical Yearbook* 1995, p. 155.
[a] Hyperinflation begins after the resignation of Todor Zhivkov.

TABLE 2
Selected Islamic Foundations and Associations in Bulgaria

Foundation (F) or Association (A)	City of registry	Alleged or known links to
Rosa (F)	Plovdiv	
Mostove (F)	Madan	
Ahmed Dabudoglu (F)	Sofia	Mustafa Hadzhi
Ikra (A)	Madan	
Krŭgozori (F)	Sofia	
Vyara (F)	Sofia	
Al Manar (F)	Sofia	
Utro (A)	Devin	
Taibah (F)	Sofia	Fikri Sali Hasan
Alnedua (F)	Velingrad	WAMY
Blagodenstvie—Region Rodopi (A)	Madan	
Irshad (F)	Sofia	Mustafa Hadzhi
Znanie (F)	Madan	
Svetlina (F)	Tŭrŭn	
Myusyulmanski Duhoven Sŭyuz (A)	Razgrad	Nedim Gendzhev
Branch of Svetovna Islyamska blagotvoritelna organizatsiya (A)	Sofia	Nedim Gendzhev
Uchebno-Obrazovatelen fond na Islyamska banka za razvitie (F)	Sofia	Nedim Gendzhev
Medeniet (F)	Sofia	Nedim Gendzhev
Mezhdunarodna blagotvoritelna Islyamska organizatsia hayatel igasa na kralstvo Sauditska Arabia (F)	Sofia	Nedim Gendzhev
Blagotvoritelna Fondatsia za Razvitie na Kulturata na etnosite v Republika Bŭlgariya (F)	Sofia	Nedim Gendzhev
Obedinenie za Islyamsko Razvitie i Kultura (F)	Smolyan	Arif Abdullah
Sŭyuz na Myusyulmanite v Bŭlgariya (F)	Sofia	Ali Khairaddin

Source: Public records available at www.daxi.bg.

Notes

Introduction
The Changing Face of Islam in Bulgaria

1. All of the names of people in this book, as well as nonessential but identifying details about their lives, have been changed to protect the privacy of my informants. The only exceptions are those who are referenced in media reports or are well-known public figures in Bulgaria. In these cases, I use both their first and last names.

2. The term "Pomak" has a derogatory tinge to some ears, but I chose to employ it in this book because it is the word my informants generally used to describe themselves.

3. Many Bulgarians refer to the period between 1946 and 1996 as the "socialist" period, recognizing that their leaders never achieved the hoped for goal of "communism." The leaders, however, are most commonly referred to as "communists," and so, in everyday parlance, socialism and communism are used interchangeably to refer to the country's past. In this book, I will also use these terms interchangeably, while acknowledging an important difference between real-world socialism and the ideal society many believed possible if countries like Bulgaria had progressed to the more advanced stage of communism.

4. The Beautiful Bulgaria project dispersed funds from the European Union to renovate public spaces throughout the country.

5. Ali Eminov, *Turkish and Other Muslim Minorities in Bulgaria* (New York: Routledge, 1997).

6. Steve Kotkin, "Eurasia: Disease Masquerading as the Cure?" Keynote Address to the 2007 Annual Soyuz Symposium in Princeton, NJ, on 27 April 2007.

7. I initially included a longer literature review on the various terms, but this occupied many pages of an introduction that I was trying to keep succinct and took the reader too long away from Bulgaria, my analytical focus. I have kept some of this material, but I realize that Islamic Studies scholars and social theoreticians will find my discussion here too short, and that the question of terminology alone could have occupied its own chapter.

8. Dale Eickelman and James Piscatori, *Muslim Politics* (Princeton, NJ: Princeton University Press, 1996); Armando Salvatore, "Staging Virtue: The Disembodiment of Self-correctness and the Making of Islam as Public Norm," in Georg Stauth, ed., *Islam: Motor or Challenge of Modernity* (Hamburg: Lit Verlag, 1998), pp. 87–120.

9. Eickelman and Piscatori, *Muslim Politics*, p. 38.

10. Adeeb Khalid, *Islam after Communism: Religion and Politics in Central Asia* (Berkeley: University of California Press, 2007).

11. It is customary among Muslims to follow any mention of the Prophet in text with the acronym PBUH (Peace Be Upon Him). I will not follow this convention,

however, and it is my sincere hope that devout Muslim readers will not take offense at this omission.

12. Khalid, *Islam after Communism*, p. 23.

13. Talal Asad, *Genealogies of Religion: Discipline and Reasons of Power in Christianity and Islam* (Baltimore, MD: Johns Hopkins University Press, 1993); Talal Asad, "The Idea of an Anthropology of Islam," Occasional Papers Series, Center for Contemporary Arab Studies, Georgetown University, 1986.

14. Asad, "The Idea of an Anthropology of Islam," p. 6.

15. Asad, *Genealogies of Religion*, p. 210.

16. Ibid.

17. Eleanor Abdella Doumato, *Getting God's Ear: Women, Islam and Healing in Saudi Arabia and the Gulf* (New York: Columbia University Press, 2000), p. 40.

18. Personal communication with Edward Walker, January 2008.

19. Personal communication with Nikki Keddie, November 2007.

20. Personal communications with Gail Kligman, January and February 2008.

21. Olivier Roy, *Globalized Islam: The Search for a New Ummah* (New York: Columbia University Press, 2004), p. 19.

22. Stephen Schwartz, *The Two Faces of Islam: The House of Sa'ud from Tradition to Terror* (New York: Doubleday, 2002).

23. I owe this term to one of the anonymous readers, a Bulgarian Islamic Studies scholar, to whom Princeton University Press sent the manuscript of this book.

24. Dale Eickelman and James Piscatori, eds., *Muslim Travelers: Pilgrimage, Migration, and the Religious Imagination* (Berkeley: University of California Press, 1990), pp. 4–5.

25. Lara Deeb, *An Enchanted Modern: Gender and Public Piety in Shi'i Lebanon* (Princeton, NJ: Princeton University Press, 2006).

26. I also had some difficulty with Asad's term "traditional," though much less than with his use of "orthodox." The two main alternatives were "heterodox" or "syncretistic." Eleanor Doumato uses the term "heterodox" in opposition to the term "orthodox," and many Bulgarian scholars of Islam use the word "syncretistic" to describe a version of Islam that has been intermixed with Christian practices over the centuries. I did not like the word "heterodox" because it seemed to imply a value judgment on my part, particularly when juxtaposed with the word "orthodox." Furthermore, my colleague Francis Trix, a linguist and scholar of Islam in Albania, convinced me not to use "syncretistic" either, because many of the practices associated with Balkan Islam (saint worship, amulet making, etc.) were also found in Islamic countries where there had been no long contact with Christianity or communism. In the end, I felt that the word "traditional" best reflected the Bulgarian situation, in Asad's sense of an Islam rooted in a particular, culturally defined past.

27. Saba Mahmood, *The Politics of Piety: The Islamic Revival and the Feminist Subject* (Princeton: Princeton University Press, 2004), p. 115.

28. Fatme Ahmedova, "Intervyu s glavniya myuftiya na myusyulmanite v Republika Bŭlgariya G-N Mustafa Hadzhi," *Ikra* 4(2005): 9–11.

29. Fatme Ahmedova, "Intervyu sŭs Sofiiskiya raionen myuftiya G-N Ali Khairaddin," *Ikra* 6(2005): 9–11.

30. The Bulgarian unit of currency is the lev (plural, leva). One lev is made up of 100 stotinki (singular, stotinka).

31. Karl Marx, "Introduction to A Contribution to the Critique of Hegel's Philosophy of Right," (1843), available online at: http://www.marxists.org/archive/marx/works/1843/critique-hpr/intro.htm (accessed 6 December 2006).

32. Kristen Ghodsee, *The Red Riviera: Gender, Tourism and Postsocialism on the Black Sea* (Durham, NC: Duke University Press, 2005).

33. Ken Ham, "After Communism's Collapse: Creation in the Crimea—Ukrainian Geophysicist and Creation Warrior Sergei Golovin," *Creation Ex Nihilo* 22, no. 4 (September 2000): 24–27, available online at http://www.answersingenesis.org/creation/v22/i4/communism.asp (accessed 4 December 2006).

34. P. Yancey, "Praying with the KGB," *Christianity Today* 36, no. 1 (13 January 1992): 16–26.

35. J. Maxwell, "New Kingdoms for the Cults," *Christianity Today* 36, no. 1 (13 January 1992): 37–41.

36. A. Moore, "Fertile Ground for False Teaching," *Christianity Today* 36, no. 1 (13 January 1992): 40–41.

37. For example: Antonina Zhelyazkova, "The East Is Pregnant with the West, and the West Is Pregnant with the East," *Foreign Policy* (Bulgarian edition), August–September 2006, pp. 26–31; Albena Shkodorova, "The End of Bulgarian Islam," *Foreign Policy* (Bulgarian edition), August–September 2006, pp. 32–35; Evgenia Krasteva-Blagoeva, "Identity and Religion: The Case of the Bulgarian Muslims (Pomaks)," lecture given at the Institute for Social and Cultural Anthropology at the University of Oxford, 16 June 2006.

38. Personal communication with Vedat Ahmed, deputy chief mufti, in Sofia, Bulgaria, 23 August 2006.

39. For good overviews of these debates see Omer Turan, "Pomaks, Their Past and Present," *Journal of Muslim Minority Affairs* 19, no. 1 (1999): 69–83; Mary Neuburger, "Pomak Borderlands: Muslims on the Edge of Nations," *Nationalities Papers* 28, no. 1 (March 2000): 181–99; Tsvetana Georgieva, "Pomaks: Muslim Bulgarians," *Islam and Christian-Muslim Relations* 12, no. 3 (July 2001): 303–16.

40. Gerald Creed, *Domesticating Revolution: From Socialist Reform to Ambivalent Transition in a Bulgarian Village* (University Park: Pennsylvania State University Press, 1998); Barbara Cellarius, *In the Land of Orpheus: Rural Livelihoods and Nature Conservation in Postsocialist Bulgaria* (Madison: University of Wisconsin Press, 2004); Venelin I. Ganev, *Preying on the State: The Transformation of Bulgaria after 1989* (Ithaca, NY: Cornell University Press, 2007); Ghodsee, *The Red Riviera*.

41. Janice Broun and Grazyna Sikorska, *Conscience and Captivity* (Washington, DC: Ethics and Public Policy Center, 1990).

42. Wallace L. Daniel, "The Children of Perestroika: Two Sociologists on Religion and Russian Society, 1991–2006," *Religion, State and Society* 35, no. 2 (June 2007): 163–85.

43. Ibid., p. 171.

44. See Alexei Yurchak, *Everything Was Forever Until It Was No More* (Princeton, NJ: Princeton University Press, 2006); Sergei Oushakine, "The Fatal Splitting:

Symbolizing Anxiety in Post-Soviet Russia," *Ethnos: Journal of Anthropology* 66, no. 3 (2001): 291–319.

45. Center for the Study of Democracy, *Organized Crime in Bulgaria: Markets and Trends* (Sofia: CSD, 2008), available online at http://www.csd.bg/artShow .php?id=9120 (accessed 30 November 2008).

46. Phil Zuckerman, *The Cambridge Companion to Atheism* (Cambridge: Cambridge University Press, 2006).

47. Ibid. The problem with these numbers is that they do not differentiate between Muslims and Christians, and in a country like Bulgaria, where religion and ethnicity are intricately linked, it may be that some Bulgarians claim a religious identity even if they do not believe in God or accept the authority of the church.

48. Petar Kanev, "Religion in Bulgaria after 1989: Historical and Sociocultural Aspects," 1/2002 *South-East Europe Review* 1(2002): 75–96.

49. Ibid.

50. Alan Wolfe, "The Coming Religious Peace: And the Winner Is . . . ," *Atlantic Monthly*, March 2008, available online at: www.theatlantic.com/doc/200803/ secularism (accessed 18 June 2008).

51. Duomato, *Getting God's Ear*.

52. The Arabic word *'adl* refers to an Islamic theology of shared or divine justice and can be interpreted as a concept similar to social justice.

53. Khalid, *Islam after Communism*, p. 14.

54. My father was a Persian who emigrated to the United States in the mid-1960s. He claimed to be an atheist for most of his life but grew increasingly religious in his old age. His funeral in 2001 was the first Muslim religious service I attended before beginning fieldwork in Bulgaria.

55. Slavoj Žižek, *NATO as the Left Hand of God?* (Zagreb: Arkzin Press, 1999).

56. I owe this phrase to Michael Watts, "Development II: The Privatization of Everything," *Progress in Human Geography* 18, no. 3 (1994): 371–84.

Chapter One
Names to Be Buried With

1. M. Hakan Yavuz, "Is There a Turkish Islam? The Emergence of Convergence and Consensus," *Journal of Muslim Minority Affairs* 24, no. 2 (October 2004): 213–32.

2. Antonina Zhelyazkova, "Bulgaria in Transition: the Muslim Minorities," *Islam and Christian-Muslim Relations* 12, no. 3 (July 2001): 284–301.

3. Rossitsa Gradeva, ed., *History of Muslim Culture in Bulgarian Lands* (Sofia: International Center for Minority Studies and Intercultural Relations [IMIR], 2001); Maria Kalicin and Krassimira Mutafova, "Historical Accounts of the Halveti Shayk Bali Efendi of Sofia in a Newly Discovered *Vita* Dating from the Nineteenth Century," *Islam and Christian-Muslim Relations* 12, no. 3 (July 2001): 339–53; Stoyan Raichevsky, *The Mohammedan Bulgarians (Pomaks)* (Sofia: Bulgarian Bestseller—National Museum of Bulgarian Books and Polygraphy, 2004).

4. Cemal Kafadar, *Between Two Worlds: The Construction of the Ottoman State* (Berkeley: University of California Press, 1996).

5. The two separate Christian millets reflected two different branches of Orthodox Christianity, the Monophysite and the Duophysite. The Armenian millet ruled over the Monophysite churches, which included the Coptic and Syrian Orthodox churches. The Rum millet oversaw the Duophysite churches.

6. Evgeni Radushev, *Pomatsite, Hristiyanstvo i Islyam v zapadnite Rodopi s dolinata na r. Mesta, XV-30-te godini na XVIII vek* (Sofia: Sts. Kiril and Methodi National Library, Oriental Section, 2005).

7. Hugh Poulton, "Changing Notions of National Identity among Muslims in Thrace and Macedonia: Turks, Pomaks and Roma," in *Muslim Identity and the Balkan State*, ed. Suja Taji-Farouki and Hugh Poulton (New York: New York University Press, 1997), pp. 82–102; Tsvetana Georgieva, "Pomaks: Muslim Bulgarians," in *Communities and Identities in Bulgaria*, ed. Anna Krasteva (Bologna: Longo Editore Ravenna, 1998), pp. 221–38.

8. Omer Turan, "Pomaks, Their Past and Present," *Journal of Muslim Minority Affairs* 19, no. 1 (1999): 69–83.

9. Mario Apostolov, "The Pomaks: A Religious Minority in the Balkans," *Nationalities Papers* 24, no. 4 (1996): 727–42.

10. Georgieva, "Pomaks: Muslim Bulgarians"; Petya Kabakchieva, "From Local to Regional Identity: The Possible Construction of 'Cross-Border' Regional Identity—Case Study of a Border Region, Smolyan," Nexus Research Project paper, synopsis available online at www.ceu.hu/cps/bluebird/rg/see/see_prog_2001jun.pdf (accessed 30 December 2006; Maria Todorova, "Identity (Trans)Formation among the Pomaks in Bulgaria," in *Beyond Borders: Remaking Cultural Identities in the New East and Central Europe*, ed. Lazlo Kurti and Juliet Langman (New York: Westview Press, 1997), pp. 63–82. Interestingly, the Czeck Slavicist P. Shafarik also mentions the theory that the Pomaks are descendants of the Arabs in his 1842 book on Slavic popular history, *Slavianski Narodpis*; see the citation in Raichevsky, *The Mohammedan Bulgarians (Pomaks)*, p. 15.

11. Yulian Konstantinov, "Strategies for Sustaining Vulnerable Identities: The Case of the Bulgarian Pomaks," in *Muslim Identity and the Balkan State*, ed. Suja Taji-Farouki and Hugh Poulton (New York: New York University Press, 1997), pp. 33–53.

12. Todorova, "Identity (Trans)formation," p. 68.

13. Georgieva, "Pomaks: Muslim Bulgarians," p. 299.

14. Ibid., p. 229.

15. Personal communication with Hairaddin Hatim, regional mufti of Smolyan, in Smolyan, March 2007.

16. Mekhmed Dorsunski, "The Term Bulgarian Mohammedans is Assimilationist," *Obektiv: Magazine of the Bulgarian Helsinki Committee* 103 (April–September 2003): 15.

17. For example: Ibrahim Karahasan-Chadar, *Etnicheskite Maltsinstva v Bŭlgariya: Istoria, Kultura, Religiya, Obreden Kalendar* (Sofia: Lik, 2005); Robin Brooks, "Ethnicity and Class in Bulgaria," *Peace Review* 11, no. 2 (1999): 219–23; Georgieva, "Pomaks: Muslim Bulgarians"; Todorova, "Identity (Trans)-formation."

18. For example: Institut za Bŭlgaraska Istoriya, *Iz Minaloto na Bŭlgarite Mo-hamedani v Rodopite* (Sofia: Izdatelstvo na Bŭlgarskata Akademiya na Naukite, 1958); Kiril Vasilev, *Rodopskite Bŭlgari Mohamedani (Istoricheski Ocherk)*, (Plovdiv: Dŭrzhavno Izdatelstvo Hristo G. Danov, 1961); Nikolai Branchev, *Bŭlgari Mohamedani (Pomatsi)* (Sofia: Izdava Bŭlgarsko Narodouchno D-VO, 1948).

19. A very fast way to become unpopular at a Bulgarian dinner party with non-academics is to merely suggest that the Pomaks might not be ethnic Bulgarians.

20. For instance, Margarita Assenova, "Islam in Bulgaria: Historical, Socio-cultural and Political Dimensions," *Briefing Notes on Islam, Society and Politics* (Washington, DC: Center for Strategic and International Studies) 3, no. 1 (June 2000): 4–8.

21. An excellent example is the 1988 film *Time of Violence* (*Vreme na Nasilie*), directed by Ljudmil Staykov, about the attempted mass conversions of Bulgarians during the Ottoman period. The film is based on the 1964 novel *Time of Parting* (*Vreme Razdeleno*), by Anton Donchev.

22. Maria Todorova, "Conversion to Islam as a Trope in Bulgarian Histori-ography, Fiction, and Film," in *Penser la Transition/Rethinking the Transition* ed. Ivaylo Znepolski, Koprinka Tchervenkova, and Alexander Kiossev (Sofia: St. Kliment Ohridski University Press, 2002), pp. 181–205.

23. Evgeni Radushev, *Pomatsite, Hristiyanstvo i Islyam v zapadnite Rodopi s dolinata na r. Mesta, XV-30-te godini na XVIII vek* (Sofia: Sts. Kiril and Methodi National Library, Oriental Section, 2005), p. 426.

24. Ibid., p. 424.

25. Rositsa Gradeva and Svetlana Ivanova, "Researching the Past and Pres-ent of Muslim Culture in Bulgaria: the 'Popular' and 'High' Layers," *Islam and Christian-Muslim Relations* 12, no. 3 (July 2001): 317–37.

26. Raichevsky, *The Mohammedan Bulgarians (Pomaks)*.

27. Ibid., p. 40.

28. Velichko Georgiev i Staiko Trifonov, *Pokrŭstvaneto na Bŭlgarite Moham-edani 1912–1913 Dokumenti* (Sofia: Akademichno Izdatelstvo Prof. Marin Drinov, 1995).

29. Mary Neuberger, *The Orient Within: Muslim Minorities and the Negotia-tion of Nationhood in Modern Bulgaria* (Ithaca, NY: Cornell University Press, 2004); Todorova, "Identity (Trans)formation."

30. Mila Mancheva, "Image and Policy: The Case of Turks and Pomaks in Inter-War Bulgaria, 1918–1944 (with Special Reference to Education)," *Islam and Christian-Muslim Relations* 12, no. 3 (July 2001): 355–74.

31. Evgenija Garbolevsky, *A Church Ossified? Repression and Resurgence of Bulgarian Orthodoxy, 1944–1956* (Sofia: Asconi Izdat, 2005).

32. Janice Broun, *Conscience and Captivity: Religion in Eastern Europe* (Wash-ington, DC: Ethics and Public Policy Center, 1988).

33. Krassimir Kanev, "Law and Politics on Ethnic Religious Minorities in Bul-garia," in *Communities and Identities in Bulgaria*, ed. Anna Krasteva (Bologna: Longo Editore Ravenna, 1998), pp. 55–93.

34. Neuberger, *The Orient Within*, p. 64.

35. Ibid.

36. "Informatsiya za rabota na shkolata za Bŭlgarki Mohamedanki v Gotse Delchev za vremeto ot 16 Noemvri do 29 Dekemvri 1961 godina," State Archive in Blagoevgrad, collection 628, inventory 3, unit 81, sheet 6, 7.

37. Neuberger, *The Orient Within*, p. 76.

38. "Stenografski protokol na sŭveshtanieto na otdel 'Programa i agitatsiya' na TsK na BKP za izpŭlnenie reshenieto na Politbyuro na TsK na BKP za rabota sred Bŭlgaromohamedanite," May, 1959, Central State Archive, collection 1b, inventory 5, sheet 378, pp. 1–86.

39. Ibid.

40. Rosalind Morris, "Theses on the Questions of War: History, Media, Terror," *Social Text* 20, no. 3 (Fall 2002): 149–78; Gregory Massell, *The Surrogate Proletariat: Moslem Women and Revolutionary Strategies in Soviet Central Asia, 1919–1929* (Princeton, NJ: Princeton University Press, 1974).

41. *Constitution of the People's Republic of Bulgaria,* Official Gazette 284 (6 December 1947); English text from Roumen Genov, "Women in Bulgarian Society: History and Recent Changes," available online at http://www.stm.unipi.it/Clioh/tabs/libri/2/06-Genov_83-92.pdf (accessed 30 December 2006).

42. "Uchebna programa na 45-dnevnite kursove za Bŭlgarki Mohamedanki aktivistki na Otechestveniya Front," State Archive Blagoevgrad, collection 628, inventory 3, unit 81, sheet 44–47.

43. The Fatherland Front was originally a coalition of various Bulgarian parties and organizations opposed to the Germans during World War II, but it eventually became a communist mass organization. See John D. Bell, *The Bulgarian Communist Party from Blagoev to Zhivkov* (Washington, DC: Hoover Institution Press, 1985).

44. "Informatsiya za rabota na skolata za Bŭlgarki Mohamedanki."

45. Petŭr Petrov, Asen Spasov, and Donio Donev, eds., *Rodopa: Bŭlgarski Tvŭrdina (Sbŭrnik Veseli) Uchebno Pomagalo* (Sofia: BKP Izdatelstvo, 1960).

46. Ibid., p. 227.

47. Ibid., p. 237.

48. Ignat Penkov, *Novite Gradove v N.R. Bŭlgariya"* (Sofia: Izdatelstvo Narodna Prosveta, 1971), p. 124.

49. Eminov, *Turkish and Other Muslim Minorities in Bulgaria*, p. 58.

50. Ibid., p. 59.

51. Neuberger, *The Orient Within,* p. 69.

52. Klaus Roth, "Socialist Life-Style Rituals in Bulgaria," *Anthropology Today* 6, no. 5 (1990): 8–10.

53. It is important to point out here that Bulgarian Orthodox priests were subjected to similar campaigns if they refused to cooperate with the communists.

54. Again, it is important to note that the authorities also frowned upon Western European names.

55. Although Turks make up the majority of the Muslim population in Bulgaria, this book does not deal with them in detail because as of 2007 they had yet to show any significant interest in the "orthodox" Islam gaining ground among the Pomaks. On the Turks of Bulgaria, see Neuberger, *The Orient Within*; Eminov, *Turkish and Other Muslim Minorities in Bulgaria*; Kemal H. Karpat, ed., *The Turks of Bulgaria: The History, Culture and Political Fate of a Minority* (Istanbul:

Isis Press, 1990); U.S. Helsinki Watch Committee, *Destroying Ethnic Identity: The Turks of Bulgaria* (New York: Helsinki Watch, 1986); Theodore Zang, *Destroying Ethnic Identity: The Expulsion of the Bulgarian Turks* (New York: U.S. Helsinki Watch Committee, 1989).

56. Ulf Brunnbauer, "The Perception of Muslims in Bulgaria and Greece: Between the 'Self' and the 'Other,'" *Journal of Muslim Minority Affairs* 21, no. 1 (2001): 39–61.

57. Eminov, *Turkish and Other Muslim Minorities in Bulgaria.*

58. Mary Neuberger, "Pomak Borderlands: Muslims on the Edge of Nations," *Nationalities Papers* 28, no. 1 (March 2000): 181–99.

59. Neuberger, *The Orient Within.*

60. Indeed, by the middle of the twentieth century, most countries around the world, whether communist, capitalist, or newly liberated from colonial rule, were preoccupied by the question of industrialization and how to spur economic growth.

61. Like the Soviet Union, the communist government of largely peasant Bulgaria hoped that it could skip the capitalist stage of history and move right on through to communism. See John Lampe, *The Bulgarian Economy in the Twentieth Century* (New York and London: Palgrave McMillan, 1986).

62. "Stenografski protokol na sŭveshtanieto na otdel 'Programa i agitatsiya' na TsK," pp. 1–86.

63. Margarita Karamihova, "Emigration from the Rhodope Mountain: A New Phenomenon or a Temporary Response in a Time of Crisis," in *Living There, Dreaming Here: Emigrational Attitudes in the Beginning of the 21ˢᵗ Century* (Sofia: International Center for Minority Studies and Intercultural Relations, 2003).

Chapter Two
Men and Mines

1. *Madan: Kratŭk Spravochnik* (Madan: Organizatsionen Komitet po Chestvuvane 10-Godishninata ot Obyavyavaneto na Madan za Grad, 1963), p. 29.

2. A flotation factory is where lead and zinc ore are refined into lead and zinc concentrates, using xanthates, cyanides, metal sulfates, pine oil, and lime.

3. Lewis Siegelbaum, *Stakhanovism and the Politics of Productivity in the USSR, 1935–1941* (Cambridge: Cambridge University Press, 1990).

4. Tsentralno Statistichesko Upravlenie pri Ministerskiya Sŭvet, *Statisticheski Godishnik na Narodna Republika Bŭlgariya 1967* (Sofia: Tsentralno Statistichesko Upravlenie pri Ministerskiya Sŭvet, 1967), p. 152.

5. *Madan: Kratŭk Spravochnik*, p. 30.

6. Ibid.

7. Ibid.

8. This was the communist trading bloc. The organization promoted socialist economic integration with the other communist nations of Eastern Europe and eventually with Mongolia, Vietnam, and Cuba.

9. Vladimir Kouseff, "Bulgaria," *Mining Journal: Mining Annual Review*, June 1999. All articles from the *Mining Journal* are available online through LexisNexis Academic.

10. M.W. Thompson, "Bulgaria," *Mining Journal: Mining Annual Review*, June 1986.

11. "GORUBSO" is short for "Gorno-rudnoe Bŭlgaro-Sovetskoe Obshtestvo."

12. Bŭlgarska Komunisticheska Partiya Gradski Komitet, *25 Godini Grad Madan* (Madan: Gradski Obshtinski Naroden Sŭvet, 1978), p. 24.

13. *25 Godini Grad Madan*, p. 8.

14. *Madan: Kratŭk Spravochnik*, p. 42.

15. Tsentralno Statistichesko Upravlenie pri Ministerskiya Sŭvet, *Statisticheski Godishnik na Narodna Republika Bŭlgariya 1976* (Sofia: Tsentralno Statistichesko Upravlenie pri Ministerskiya Sŭvet, 1976), p. 102.

16. Tsentralno Statistichesko Upravlenie, *Statisticheski Godishnik na Narodna Republika Bŭlgariya 1989* (Sofia: Tsentralno Statistichesko Upravlenie, 1989), p. 109.

17. *Statisticheski Godishnik na Narodna Republika Bŭlgariya 1967*, p. 332.

18. Tsentralno Statistichesko Upravlenie pri Ministerskiya Sŭvet, *Statisticheski Godishnik na Narodna Republika Bŭlgariya 1986* (Sofia: Tsentralno Statistichesko Upravlenie pri Ministerskiya Sŭvet, 1986), p. 396.

19. Ibid.

20. People's Republic of Bulgaria, "Bulgaria and the World Today" (Sofia: Sofia Press, 1985).

21. Ibid.

22. *Madan: Kratŭk Spravochnik*, p. 44.

23. Ignat Penkov, *Novite Gradove v N. R. Bŭlgariya"* (Sofia: Izdatelstvo Narodna Prosveta, 1971), p. 117.

24. Ibid.

25. *Rudozem: s ukaz na dŭrzhaven sŭvet na Narodna Republika Bŭlgariya No. 38 ot 30 Yanuari 1960 g. Rudozem e obyaven za grad, a na 10 Noemvri 1971 g.—za grad na Bŭlgaro-Sŭvetskata druzhba* (Smolyan, 1985).

26. Rumyana Boyadzhieva, *Grad Rudozem* (Sofia: Fondatsiya "Lyudmila Zhivkova," 1989).

27. Katherine Verdery, *What Was Socialism and What Comes Next?* (Princeton, NJ: Princeton University Press, 1996).

28. Steven Chiodini, "Bulgaria: An East European Revolution in Suspension," *Harvard International Review* 13, no. 2 (Winter 1991).

29. There are still many who claim that Zhivkov's resignation was forced and the change of power was a quiet coup within the internal ranks of the BCP.

30. Peter Law, "Bulgarian Muslims Demand Their Names Back at Landmark Rallies," *Times* (London), 18 December 1989.

31. "Bulgarian Muslims Can Use Own Names," *Toronto Star*, 6 March 1990, p. A14.

32. Ivan Palchev, *Ahmed Doğan and the Bulgarian Ethnic Model* (Sofia: National Museum of Bulgarian Books and Poligraphy, 2002).

33. Nadege Ragaru, "Islam in Post-Communist Bulgaria: An Aborted 'Clash of Civilizations?' " *Nationalities Papers* 29, no. 2 (2001): 293–324.

34. The miners in Romania had also proven themselves to be a formidable political force in the spring and summer of 1990.

35. Tsentralen Stachen Komitet, "Natsionalna Miniorska Stachka: Hlyabŭt, Istinata i Mirŭt," *Sedem Dni Podkrepa*, 15–22 August 1991, p. 1.

36. Asen Michkovski, "Miniorite sreshtu klevetata i pravitelstveniya shant-azh," *Sedem Dni Podkrepa*, 22–29 August 1991, p. 1; "Bulgarian Mine Strike Escalating." *Toronto Star*, 19 August 1991, p. A10.

37. An insert in *Sedem Dni Podkrepa*, 15–22 August 1991.

38. "Doidoh, Vidyah, Pobedih," *Sedem Dni Podkrepa*, 26 September–2 October 1991, p. 3.

39. Barbara Cellarius, *In the Land of Orpheus: Rural Livelihoods and Nature Conservation in Postsocialist Bulgaria* (Madison: University of Wisconsin Press, 2004).

40. S. A. Hiscock, "Lead," *Mining Journal: Mining Annual Review*, June 1987.

41. Stilyan Stoikov, "Miniorite ne iskat da svalyat pravitelstvoto, a da se reshat bolnite problemi," *Podkrepa*, 20 March 1992, p. 1.

42. "Madan—Sŭrtseto na stachkata," *Sedem Dni Podkrepa*, 9–5 April 1992, p. 6.

43. "Madan, Gradŭt na otchayanieto," *Podkrepa*, 1 April 1992, p. 1; Plamen Asenov and Emil Tonev, "I sled pravitelstveniya ultimatum Madan otgovori: Stachkata Prodŭzhava!" *Podkrepa*, 30 March 1992, p. 1.

44. Plamen Asenov and Emil Tonev, "Stachkata zapochna predi polunosht," *Podkrepa*, 27 March 1992, p. 1.

45. Emil Tonev, "Pravitelstvenoto bezsilie predizvika natsionalen protest," *Podkrepa*, 28 March 1992, p. 1.

46. "Madan—Sŭrtseto na stachkata."

47. Emil Antonov, "Miniorite se premestiha v zemetrŭsna zona," *Podkrepa*, 24 March 1992, p. 1.

48. "Government 'Alarmed' by Civil Disobedience Calls; Interior Ministry Warning," Bulgarian Radio, 31 March 1992, in *BBC Summary of World Broadcasts*. All articles from the *BBC Summary of World Broadcasts* are available through LexisNexis Academic.

49. "Stachkata: Vini i Vinovni," *Sedem Dni Podkrepa*, 2–8 April 1992, p. 1.

50. "Madan—Sŭrtseto na stachkata."

51. Palchev, *Ahmed Doğan and the Bulgarian Ethnic Model*.

52. National Statistical Institute, *Statistical Yearbook 1993* (Sofia: NSI, 1994), p. 167.

53. Yuli Tsaneva, "Komisiya shte reshava sŭdbata na uranovite rudnitsi do mesets," *Podkrepa*, 11 December 1993, p. 1; Rumyana Marinova, "Stachka na otchayanieto i na nadezhdata zaliva stranata," *Podkrepa*, 13 December 1993, p. 1.

54. Rumyana Marinova, "Stachkata—Den Pŭrvi," *Podkrepa*, 14 December 1993, p. 1; Rumyana Marinova, "Stachkata—Den Vtori," *Podkrepa*, 15 December 1993, p. 1; Rumyana Marinova, "Stachkata—Den Treti," *Podkrepa*, 16 December 1993, p. 1; Rumyana Marinova, "Miniori ostavat pod zemyata," *Podkrepa*, 17 December 1993, p. 1.

55. "Pollution; Firms to Be Fined for Pollution," Bulgarian Telegraph Agency, 9 March 1996, in *BBC Summary of World Broadcasts*.

56. Ghodsee, *The Red Riviera.*

57. Vladimir Kousseff, "Bulgaria," *Mining Journal: Mining Annual Review,* June 1998.

58. Vladimir Kousseff, "Bulgaria," *Mining Journal: Mining Annual Review,* June 1999, p. 41.

59. "Miner's Strike Spreads," Bulgarian Telegraph Agency, 17 March 1998, in *BBC Summary of World Broadcasts.*

60. Reni Bonkalova, "GORUBSO Restructuring Scheme Has Been Accepted," *Pari Daily,* 23 February 1998. All articles from *Pari Daily* are available online through LexisNexis Academic.

61. Petko Bocharov, "Bulgaria: Miners on Strike Reach Agreement," *Radio Free Europe/Radio Liberty,* 25 February 1998, available online at www.b-info .com/places/Bulgaria/news/98-02/feb25a.rfe (accessed on 16 February 2006).

62. "Bulgarian Miners End Strike: Sign Agreement with Finance Minister," Bulgarian Telegraph Agency, 22 February 1998.

63. Reni Bonkalova, "Subscription against Breaking Up of GORUBSO Launched," *Pari Daily,* 18 May 1998.

64. Rositsa Videlova, "Dismissed GORUBSO Workers to Build Roads," *Pari Daily,* 7 May 1998.

65. "GORUBSO—Zlatograd to Go on Strike," *Pari Daily,* 4 November 1998.

66. "GORUBSO to Be Merged Again," *Pari Daily,* 6 November 1998.

67. "Strike in Zlatograd Mines Postponed," *Pari Daily,* 8 November 1998.

68. "Miners in GORUBSO-Zlatograd Go on Strike," *Pari Daily,* 11 November 1998.

69. "Daily Losses from the Strike in GORUBSO Stand at BGL 45 Million," *Pari Daily,* 12 November 1998.

70. "Bulgaria—Press Review," 13 November 1998, available online at http:// www.b-info.com/places/Bulgaria/news/98-11/nov13d.bta.

71. Reni Bonkalova and Evdokia Dimitrova, "GORUBSO Protesters Seek Support from Parliament," *Pari Daily,* 19 November 1998.

72. "GORUBSO of Zlatograd Faces Liquidation," *Pari Daily,* 22 November 1998.

73. "GORUBSO Mine Closes Following Strike," *Mining Journal,* 27 November 1998, p. 430.

74. Evdokiya Dimitrova, "Premier Refuses to Revoke Liquidation of GORUBSO-Zlatograd," *Pari Daily,* 27 November 1998.

75. "GORUBSO Miners Decide to Go on with Protest," *Pari Daily,* 29 November 1998.

76. "Premier Declares Unemployment Issue in Zlatograd Solved," *Pari Daily,* 30 November 1998.

77. Reni Bonkalova, "Miners in Zlatograd Demand New Agreement with Financial Minister," *Pari Daily,* 3 December 1998.

78. "Debts of GORUBSO Not to Be Cancelled," *Pari Daily,* 6 December 1998.

79. "Next Transformation of GORUBSO Underway," *Pari Daily,* 17 January 1999.

80. "January Expenses of GORUBSO Zlatograd Amount to BGL 700 million," *Pari Daily*, 2 February 1999.

81. Evdokia Dimitrova, "GORUBSO Mines Sold for One Dollar," *Pari Daily*, 7 February 1999.

82. "Bulgaria to Close Lead/Zinc Mines," *Metals Week* 70, no. 6 (8 February 1999): 15; Nadya Christova, "Madan, Rudozem Mines in Zlatograd's Footsteps," *Pari Daily*, 4 February 1999.

83. "Setting Up of Private Mining Company Fails," *Pari Daily*, 8 February 1999.

84. "Ministers Seek Solution for GORUBSO," *Pari Daily*, 27 February 1999.

85. "Bulgarian Lead-Zinc Mines at Risk," *Mining Journal*, 12 February 1999, p. 99. The Kŭrdzhali and Lŭki divisions were successfully sold off. See "Foreign Investors Bid for Bulgarian Ore Mines," Bulgarian Telegraph Agency, 8 May 1999, in *BBC Summary of World Broadcasts*; "Galenit MBO Buys GORUBSO of Kŭrdzhali," *Pari Daily*, 2 June 1999.

86. Nadezhda Semerdzhieva, "The Privatization of GORUBSO Has Entered a Chronicle of Scandals," *Pari Daily*, 28 September 1999.

87. Nadezhda Semerdzhieva, "GORUBSO of Madan Claiming BGN 4.5 Million from Treasury," *Pari Daily*, 13 January 2000.

88. Petar Haradinov, "Rodopa Invest Unable to Pay Back Salaries," *Pari Daily*, 25 July 2001; "Rodopa Invest Failed to Pay Back Salaries," Sofia News Agency, 25 July 2001, from www.novite.com; Petar Haradinov, "Foreign Investor Owing BGN 1.4 Million in Back Salaries," *Pari Daily*, 2 August 2001.

89. Nadya Christova, "Madan Strikers Keep Protest On," *Pari Daily*, 10 August 2001.

90. Tsvetoslav Tsachev, "GORUBSO Pushed to Bankruptcy by Foreign Investor," *Pari Daily*, 16 August 2001.

91. Tsvetoslav Tsachev, "International Company Will Audit GORUBSO," *Pari Daily*, 20 August 2001; "GORUBSO Checked by Expert Auditors," Sofia News Agency, 20 August 2001, available online at www.novinite.com.

92. Nadezhda Semerdzhieva, "Silence Surrounding GORUBSO like Hush before the Storm," *Pari Daily*, 20 August 2001.

93. Ibid.

94. Ibid.

95. "GORUBSO Workers Blockade Again," Sofia News Agency, 30 August 2001, available online at www.novinite.com.

96. "GORUBSO Madan Involved in Insolvency Suit," *Pari Daily*, 3 September 2001; "GORUBSO Bankrupt, Economy Minister Announces," Sofia News Agency, 1 September 2001, available online at www.novinite.com.

97. This was most likely a Mafia enterprise, like so many other "holding companies."

98. National Statistical Institute, *Statistical Yearbook 1994* (Sofia: NSI, 1994), p. 186.

99. World Bank, "Additional Annex 10: Sample Social Assessment of a RIF Micro-project, Social Assessment MP 3730 Madan Municipal Hospital Reconstruction," in *Regional Initiatives Fund*, Project ID: P055156, available online at

http://siteresources.worldbank.org/EXTROMA/Resources/P055156.pdf (accessed 11 January 2007).

Chapter Three
The Have-nots and the Have-nots

1. Petar Mitev, "Relations of Compatibility and Incompatibility in the Everyday Life of Christians and Muslims in Bulgaria (Sociological Studies)," in *Relations of Compatibility and Incompatibility between Christians and Muslims in Bulgaria* (Sofia: International Center for Minority Studies and Intercultural Relations, 1995), p. 195.

2. Dimitrina Mihaylova, "Coping with Marginality: Redefining Christian and Muslim Identification in South-Eastern Bulgaria," *Journal of Mediterranean Studies* 13, no. 2 (2003): 259–80.

3. Center for the Study of Democracy, *The Political Change in Bulgaria: Post-Electoral Attitudes* (Sofia: CSD, 1990), available online at: http.//www.csd.bg/artShow.php?id=12899.

4. Mitev, "Relations of Compatibility and Incompatibility."

5. Margarita Karamihova, "Emigration from the Rhodope Mountain"; Margarita Assenova, "Islam in Bulgaria: Historical, Sociocultural and Political Dimensions," *Briefing Notes on Islam, Society and Politics* (Washington, DC: Center for Strategic and International Studies) 3, no. 1 (June 2000): 4–8.

6. A kind of cross between an omelet and scrambled eggs, filled with a variety of vegetables.

7. It is customary for a church to prepare and give away food to celebrate the day of the saint for which it is named. The church in Madan, named after Saint George, had prepared eight cauldrons of lamb stew and hundreds of loaves of bread to be distributed.

8. Ali Kusat, "The Influence of Minority Feelings on the Formation of Religious Concept and Individual Identity: The Case of the Bulgarian Muslims," *Journal of Muslim Minority Affairs* 21, no. 2 (2001): 363–72.

9. See Janice Broun, "The Bulgarian Orthodox Church: The Continuing Schism and the Religious, Social and Political Environment," *Religion, State and Society* 32, no. 3 (September 2004); Janice Broun, "The Schism in the Bulgarian Orthodox Church, Part 2: Under the Socialist Government, 1993–97," *Religion, State and Society* 28, no. 3 (2000); Janice Broun, "The Schism in the Bulgarian Orthodox Church, Part 3: Under the Second Union of Democratic Forces Government, 1997–2001," *Religion, State and Society* 30, no. 4 (2002).

10. Irena Borowik, "Orthodoxy Confronting the Collapse of Communism in Post-Soviet Countries," *Social Compass* 53, no. 2 (2006): 267–78.

11. Steven Chiodini, "Bulgaria: An East European Revolution in Suspension," *Harvard International Review* 13, no. 2 (Winter 1991).

12. Emil Giatzidis, "Bulgaria on the Road to the European Union," *Southeast European and Black Sea Studies* 4, no. 3 (September 2004): 434–57.

13. Council of Europe, European Court of Human Rights, Case of *Christian Association Jehovah's Witnesses against Bulgaria*, Application No. 28626/95, 1995.

14. "Bulgarian Freedom Books—Bringing the Reformation to Bulgaria," from the website of the Bulgarian Reform Ministries, available online at bulgrefsite .entrewave.com (accessed 30 March 2007).

15. This consisted of starting "pick-up" soccer games on school playgrounds and then using rest times to evangelize unsuspecting Bulgarian youth. See Howard Culbertson, "God's Bulgarian Tapestry," e-book available online at http://home .snu.edu/~hculbert/tape1.htm (accessed 30 March 2007).

16. From the Mission to the World: Bulgaria website at http://www.mtwbg .com/ (accessed 30 March 2007).

17. Ibid.

18. J. Maxwell, "New Kingdom for the Cults," *Christianity Today* 36, no. 1 (13 January 1992): 37–40.

19. A. Moore, "Fertile Ground for False Teaching," *Christianity Today* 36, no. 1 (13 January 1992): 40–41.

20. "Vojvodina; Orthodox Priest Explains His Work among Muslim Slavs," Bulgarian Telegraph Agency, 18 March 1996, in *BBC Summary of World Broadcasts*.

21. Maria Todorova, "Identity (Trans)formation among Pomaks in Bulgaria," in *Beyond Borders: Remaking Cultural Identities in the New East and Central Europe*, ed. Laszlo Kurti and Juliet Langman (New York: Westview Press, 1997).

22. "President Zhelev Warns of Growing Censorship and Communist Restoration," Bulgarian Telegraph Agency, 24 February 1995, in *BBC Summary of World Broadcasts*.

23. Embassy of the Republic of Bulgaria, Washington, DC, "Father Boyan Saruev: There Is a Scheme to Set Up a Muslim Nation," Bulgarian Telegraph Agency, Bulletin of News from Bulgaria, 2 March 1995.

24. Mario Apostolov, "The Pomaks: A Religious Minority in the Balkans," *Nationalities Papers* 24, no. 4 (1996): 727–52.

25. Tsvetana Georgieva, "Pomaks: Muslim Bulgarians," in *Communities and Identities in Bulgaria*, ed. Anna Krasteva (Ravenna: Longo Editore Ravenna, 1998).

26. Marin Delchev, The Battle between the Cross and Crescent Continues to Divide the Rhodopes," *Obektiv* 70 (June/September 2000): 10–11.

27. Although they each owned phones, they rarely made calls. A common practice in Madan was to call someone's mobile phone and hang up after the first ring, sending what was called a "little arrow." The little arrow was often used as a prearranged code between people; since a phone connection was never actually made, no charge was incurred by the sender. Wealthier people in town were often sent little arrows and were expected to call their poorer friends and relations back. In Bulgaria, there is no airtime charge for receiving calls on a mobile phone.

28. "Dead Reckoning," *Economist* 351, no. 8123 (12 June 1999); Michael Specter, "Plunging Life Expectancy Puzzles Russia," *New York Times*, 2 August 1995, available online at http://query.nytimes.com/gst/fullpage.html?sec=h ealth&res=990CE4DD1338F931A3575BC0A963958260 (accessed 12 August 2007).

Chapter Four
Divide and Be Conquered

1. Gaiga Gaigadzhova, "Poslanie na edna Myusyulmanka," *Myusyulmani* 11, no. 2 (134) (2005): 28. Translated with the assistance of Rumyana Delcheva.

2. Kristen Ghodsee, "Right Wing, Left Wing, Everything: Xenophobia, Neo-Totalitarianism and Populist Politics in Contemporary Bulgaria," *Problems of Post-Communism 55*, no. 3 (May–June 2008).

3. The Bulgarian word *veroizpovedanie* translates roughly into "denomination" or "confession" and refers to the institutional organization of a particular faith, such as that of the Catholics, Muslims, Jews, or Eastern Orthodox. It does not have the same meaning as "denomination" in English, where it refers to a particular subdivision of an established religion and not to the religion as a whole.

4. "Ustav na Myusyulmanskoto izpovedanie v Republika Bŭlgariya," 20 March 2005, available online at http://www.genmufti.net/ustav_page.php?chapter=0 (accessed 5 April 2007).

5. These were Aitos, Dobrich, Razgrad, Krumovgrad, Shumen, Haskovo, Pleven, Smolyan, Kŭrdzhali, Delchev, and Plovdiv. There was once a Sofia mufti, but that office was absorbed into the Chief Muftiship.

6. Simeon Evstatiev, "Public Islam on the Balkans in a Wider Europe Context," available online at http://pdc.ceu.hu/archive/00003105/01/simeon_evstatiev_final .pdf (accessed 30 November 2008).

7. Personal communication with Mr. Nikolai Pankov, head of cabinet for Nedim Gendzhev's Supreme Holy Council of the Muslim in the Republic of Bulgaria, in Sofia, July 2005.

8. This subheading is taken from the title of a 2005 article in the Bulgarian news magazine *Tema*. See Ruslan Yordanov, "*Strastite Myuftiiski*" *Tema* 4, no. 27 (143) (12–18 July 2004): 42–44.

9. Personal communication with Mr. Nikolai Pankov in Sofia, July 2005.

10. Personal communication with Dr. Nedim Gendzhev in Sofia, 13 March 2007.

11. Ibid.

12. See, for instance, "IN BRIEF: Chief Mufti says Muslims' Life Returning to Normal," Bulgarian Telegraph Agency, 20 October 1990, in *BBC Summary of World Broadcasts*.

13. "IN BRIEF: Movement for Rights and Freedoms Demands Bulgarian Chief Mufti's Resignation," Bulgarian Telegraph Agency, 22 January 1991, in *BBC Summary of World Broadcasts*.

14. "IN BRIEF: Muslim Clergy in Kurdzhali Demand Chief Mufti's Resignation," Bulgarian Telegraph Agency, 29 January 1992, in *BBC Summary of World Broadcasts*.

15. "Bulgaria: UDF MP's Accuse Chief Mufti of Misuse of Funds," Bulgarian Telegraph Agency, 31 January 1992, in *BBC Summary of World Broadcasts*.

16. "IN BRIEF: Muslim Theological Council Votes Confidence in Chief Mufti," Bulgarian Telegraph Agency, 4 February 1992, in *BBC Summary of World Broadcasts*.

17. For a good background on the disputes relating to the Chief Muftiship, see Council of Europe, European Court of Human Rights, *Case of Supreme Theological Council of the Muslim Community v. Bulgaria*, Application No. 39023/97, Judgment, Strasbourg, 16 December 2004; and Council of Europe, European Court of Human Rights, *Case of Hasan and Chaush v. Bulgaria*, Application No. 30985/96, Judgment, Strasbourg, 26 October 2000.

18. "Police Intervene in Dispute over Chief Mufti's Office in Sofia," Bulgarian Telegraph Agency, 17 June 1993, in *BBC Summary of World Broadcasts*.

19. "Nedim Gendzhev Replaced as Chief Mufti," Bulgarian Telegraph Agency, 13 September 1992, in *BBC Summary of World Broadcasts*.

20. "IN BRIEF: National Muslim Conference Elects New Chief, Mufti Legitimacy Disputed," Bulgarian Telegraph Agency, 19 September 1992, in *BBC Summary of World Broadcasts*.

21. "Internal Affairs: Muslim Clerics Elect New National Leadership," Bulgarian Telegraph Agency, 2 November 1994, in *BBC Summary of World Broadcasts*.

22. ECHR, *Hasan and Chaush v. Bulgaria*.

23. "Rival Islamic Leaders to Hold 'Unifying' Conference," Bulgarian Telegraph Agency, 6 August 1997, in *BBC Summary of World Broadcasts*.

24. ECHR, *Supreme Theological Council of the Muslim Community v. Bulgaria*.

25. "Muslims Want Chief Mufti Replaced over Alleged Link to Bin Laden," Bulgarian Telegraph Agency, 18 April 2000, in *BBC Summary of World Broadcasts*.

26. "Chief Mufti Preaching Radical Islam," *Pari Daily*, 22 August 2000.

27. Ibid.

28. "Muslim Foundation Links Chief Mufti's Office to Radical Islam," Bulgarian National Radio, 21 August 2000, in *BBC Summary of World Broadcasts*.

29. "Turkey to Finance Muslim Schools in Bulgaria," Bulgarian Telegraph Agency, 9 September 1998, in *BBC Summary of World Broadcasts*.

30. Council of Europe, European Court of Human Rights, *Case of Al-Nashif v. Bulgaria*, Application No. 50963/99, Judgment, Strasbourg, 20 June 2002.

31. "Jordanian Organized Muslim Brotherhood Cell in Bulgaria—Security Chief," Bulgarian National Radio, 8 August 2000, in *BBC Summary of World Broadcasts*.

32. David Hendon and Donald Greco, "Notes on Church-State Affairs: Bulgaria," *Journal of Church and State* 42, no. 4 (Autumn 2000).

33. Tolerance Foundation, "Bulgaria: Muslim Expelled from the Country for 'Illegal' Religious Activities," press release, Sofia, 9 August 2000, available online at www.pili.org/lists/piln/archives/msg00646.html (accessed 7 February 2007).

34. "Chief Mufti Denies Allegations of Unlawful Activities," Bulgarian Telegraph Agency, 24 August 2000, in *BBC Summary of World Broadcasts*.

35. "National Conference of Muslims Elects New Chief Mufti," Bulgarian Telegraph Agency, 28 October 2000, in *BBC Summary of World Broadcasts*.

36. "Bulgarian Organization Says 60 Islamic Foundations Linked to Fundamentalism," Bulgarian Telegraph Agency, 24 September 2001, in *BBC Worldwide Monitoring*. All *BBC Worldwide Monitoring* sources are available online at Lexis Nexis Academic.

37. "Bulgarian Moslems Seek Return of Property Seized by Communists," *Deutsche Presse-Agentur*, 31 January 2002.

38. "Chief Mufti: State to Control Foreign Donations for Islam in Bulgaria," Bulgarian Telegraph Agency, 26 November 2002, in *BBC Worldwide Monitoring*.

39. "Bulgarian Muslims Try to 'Avert Influence' of Radicals—Leader," Bulgarian Telegraph Agency, 25 November 2003, in *BBC Worldwide Monitoring*.

40. Polia Alexandrova, "Alerting Bulgaria," *Transitions Online*, 1 December 2003, available online at www.tol.cz (accessed 7 February 2007).

41. Personal communication with Arif Abdullah in Smolyan, Bulgaria, 16 March 2007.

42. Anita Cholakova, "Ot Smolyan trŭgna delo sreshtu glavniya myuftiya," *Otzvuk* 82, no. 928 (21–24 October 2004): 2.

43. Personal communication with Ali Khairaddin in the Chief Mufti's Office in Sofia, Bulgaria, 17 July 2005.

44. "Property Row Mars Registration of New Bulgarian Chief Mufti," Bulgarian Telegraph Agency, 7 January 2004, in *BBC Monitoring International Reports*.

45. Albena Shkodorova and Iva Roudikova, "Bulgaria: Muslim Infighting Fuels Fundamentalist Fears," 7 October 2004, available online at www.iwpr.net (accessed 7 February 2007).

46. See, for instance, Shkodorova and Roudikova, "Bulgaria: Muslim Infighting Fuels Fundamentalist Fears"; Nicholas Wood, "Dispute Splits Bulgaria's Muslims," *International Herald Tribune*, 29 October 2004, available online at www.iht.com (accessed 7 February 2007); Yana Buhrer Tavanier, "Bulgaria: Mysterious Mosques and Schools," *Transitions Online*, 27 January 2005; Yana Buhrer Tavanier, "The Schools That Aren't Schools," *Transitions Online*, 3 February 2005, available online at www.tol.cz (accessed 7 February 2007).

47. Shkodorova and Roudikova, "Bulgaria: Muslim Infighting Fuels Fundamentalist Fears."

48. Ibid.

49. Personal communications with General Atanas Atanassov, in Sofia, Bulgaria, July 2005 and May 2006.

50. Marin Delchev, "The Battle between the Cross and the Crescent Continues to Divide the Rhodopes," *Obektiv: Magazine of the Bulgarian Helsinki Committee* 70 (June/September 2000): 10–11.

51. H. T. Norris, Introduction to *Islam in the Balkans: Religion and Society between Europe and the Arab World* (Columbia: University of South Carolina Press, 1993); Gyorgy Lederer, "Islam in Eastern Europe," *Central Asian Survey* 20, no. 1 (2001): 5–32; Gyorgy Lederer, "Countering Islamist Radicals in Eastern Europe," Crisis States Research Center discussion paper 05/42, September 2005, available online at www.defac.ac.uk/.../csrc/document-listings/special/Special/csrc_mpf.2005-10-17.5799702381/WP-CIST-CEE2.pdf (accessed 14 December 2006); Magnus Ranstorp and Gus Xhudo, "A Threat to Europe? Middle East Ties with the Balkans and Their Impact upon Terrorist Activity throughout the Region," *Terrorism and Political Violence* 6, no. 2 (Summer 1994): 196–223; "Fear of Fundamentalism Makes Bulgaria's Muslims Cautious over Donations," Bulgarian Telegraph Agency, 1 July 2003; Yana Buhrer Tavanier, "Bulgaria: Mysterious

Mosques and Schools," *Transitions Online*, 27 January 2005; Yana Buhrer Tavanier, "The Schools That Aren't Schools," *Transitions Online*, 3 February 2005, available online at www.tol.cz; "Chief Mufti Says State to Control Foreign Donations for Islam In Bulgaria," Bulgarian Telegraph Agency, 26 November 2002, in *BBC Monitoring International Reports*.

52. "European Panel Condemns Bulgaria in Muslim Community Case," *Agence France Presse*, 16 December 2004.

53. "New Bulgarian Chief Mufti Hopes Disputes between Muslims Over," Bulgarian Telegraph Agency, 21 March 2005, in *BBC Monitoring International Reports*.

54. "Bulgarian Muftis Protest against Party's 'Interference' in Muslims' Activity," BGNES web site, 16 March 2005, in *BBC Monitoring International Reports*.

55. "Izbraha ni glaven myuftiya," *Myusyulmansko Obshtestvo* 2 (2005): 5–8.

56. "Ali Khairaddin: Ima i politicheski, i ikonomicheski interesi," *Myusyulmansko Obshtestvo* 2 (2005): 9–10.

57. "Izbraha ni glaven myuftiya," p. 8.

58. "Spravka za delegatite uchastvuvali v natsionalnata myuslyamanska konferentsiya, provedena nezakonno na 20.03.2005 G," document prepared by Nedim Gendzhev and given to the author in March 2007.

59. "Bulgarian National Muslim Conference Elects New Chief Mufti," Bulgarian Telegraph Agency, 20 March 2005, in *BBC Monitoring International Reports*.

60. "Smolyanskiyat myuftiya ochakva da bŭde otstranen ot dlŭzhnost," Big.bg website, 22 March 2005, available online at http://big.bg/article.php?storyid=7684 (accessed 9 April 2007).

61. Personal communication with Krassimir Kanev, chairman of the Bulgarian Helsinki Committee in Sofia, Bulgaria, August 2006.

62. Personal communication with Arif Abdullah in Smolyan, Bulgaria, 16 March 2007.

63. Personal communication with Arif Abdullah in Smolyan, Bulgaria, 16 March 2007; and personal communication with Nedim Gendzhev in Sofia, Bulgaria, 13 March 2007.

64. Anita Cholakova, "Mahat myuftiyata na Smolyan," *Otzvuk* 94 (1041) (24–27 November 2005): 2.

65. Anita Cholakova, "Nov raionen myuftiya poe myusyulmanite v Smolyan," *Otzvuk* 14 (1064) (20–22 February 2005): 3.

66. Anita Cholakova, "Myusyulmanite poiskaha myuftiya na Smolyan da e Selvi Shakirov," *Otzvuk* 8 (1058) (30 January–1 February 2006): 6.

67. Nina Aleksandrova, "Arestuvaha bivshiya myuftiya Nedim Gendzhev," *Darik News*, 15 February 2002, available online at www.darik.bg (accessed 15 September 2006).

68. Milena Slavova, "Nedim Gendzhev arestuvan predi preskonferentsiya," *Vsekiden.com*, 15 February 2006, available online at www.vsekiden.com/news .php?topic=1&id=12211 (accessed 15 September 2006); Valeriya Kasiyan, "DSB iskat komisiya za Myuftiistvoto," *Vsekiden.com*, 16 February 2006, available online at www.vsekiden.com/news.php?topic=1&id=122119 (accessed 15 September 2006).

69. Bogdana Lazarova, "Gendzhev obvini Doğan za aresta si," *Darik News*, 18 February 2006, available online at www.darik.bg (accessed 15 September 2006).

70. Personal communication with Vedat Ahmed, deputy chief mufti of Bulgarian Muslims in Sofia, Bulgaria, 21 August 2006.

71. Ivan Bedrov, "Children of the Rhodope Mountains," *Obektiv* 17, no. 138 (January 2007): 17.

72. Personal communication with Arif Abdullah in Smolyan, Bulgaria, 16 March 2007.

73. Anita Cholakova, "OIRK ne e prestŭpna organizatsiya, tvŭrdi prokuraturata," *Otzvuk* 30 (1182) (14–15 March 2007): 3.

74. "Bulgaria Busts Two Radical Islamic Internet Sites," *Agence France Presse*, 20 February 2007: "4 Arrested for Incitement to Radical Islamism in Bulgaria," *Novinite.com,* 20 February 2007, available online in the www.novinite.com archive (accessed 25 February 2007).

75. Irena Delcheva, "Ex mufti Converts Women to Islam," *Standartnews.com*, 3 February 2007, available online at www.standartnews.com/en/article.php?d= 2007-02-03&article=3448 (accessed 7 February 2007).

76. Personal communication with Mr. Bradley Fredon, councilor for political and economic affairs, U.S. Embassy in Bulgaria, in Sofia, Bulgaria, 14 March 2007.

77. Personal communication with Nedim Gendzhev in Sofia, Bulgaria, 13 March 2007.

78. Personal communication with Deputy Chief Mufti Vedat Ahmed in Sofia, Bulgaria, 21 August 2006.

Chapter Five
Islamic Aid

1. Mahmood, *The Politics of Piety*.

2. Jonathan Benthall and Jerome Bellion-Jourdan, *The Charitable Crescent: The Politics of Aid in the Muslim World* (London and New York: I. B. Tauris, 2003).

3. Many of these organizations referred to themselves as "Arab Aid," and indeed, a website by that name was set up to celebrate their activities (www.arabaid .org).

4. Javid Hassan, "WAMY Calls for Muslim Fighters to Defend Bosnia," *Arab News*, 4 September 1992 in *Moneyclips*. All articles from *Moneyclips* are available online through LexisNexis Academic.

5. Benthall and Bellion-Jourdan, *The Charitable Crescent*, p. 132.

6. J. Burr and Robert Collins, *Alms for Jihad: Charity and Terrorism in the Islamic World* (Cambridge: Cambridge University Press, 2006).

7. Evan Kohlmann, *Al-Qaida's Jihad in Europe: The Afghan-Bosnian Connection* (Oxford and New York: Berg, 2004).

8. Burr and Collins, *Alms for Jihad*.

9. International Crisis Group, "Bin Laden and the Balkans: The Politics of Anti-Terrorism," ICG Balkans Report no. 119, 9 November 2001.

10. With the tacit approval of the U.S., of course.

11. Isa Blumi, "Political Islam among the Albanians: Are the Taliban Coming to the Balkans?" Kosovar Institute for Policy Research and Development, Policy Research Series, no. 2, Prishtina, June 2005.

12. Ibid., p. 11.

13. See Tone Bringa, *Being Muslim the Bosnian Way* (Princeton, NJ: Princeton University Press, 1995).

14. For a comparable case in Saudi Arabia, see Doumato, *Getting God's Ear*.

15. Muhammad Ibrahim, "MWL Urges Shariah Implementation," *Arab News*, 30 January 1992, in *Moneyclips*.

16. See Adeeb Khalid, *Islam after Communism: Religion and Politics in Central Asia* (Berkeley: University of California Press, 2007).

17. Abdulaziz-Al-Nofal, "CEEMY Holds Dawah Campaigns in Albania," *Riyadh Daily*, 19 February 1994, in *Moneyclips*.

18. On the ways in which Islamic charities modeled themselves on Christian ones, see Kristen Ghodsee, "Religious Freedoms versus Gender Equality: Faith-Based Organizations, Muslim Minorities and Islamic Headscarves in Modern Bulgaria," *Social Politics* 14, no. 4 (2007).

19. Benthall and Bellion-Jourdan, *The Charitable Crescent*.

20. See Bringa, *Being Muslim the Bosnian Way*.

21. "Save Kosovo Muslims: MWL," *Riyadh Daily*, 5 June 1998, in *Moneyclips*.

22. Javid Hassan, "WAMY Urges Saudis, Expats to Donate for Kosovo Relief," *Arab News*, 3 July 1999, in *Moneyclips*.

23. Ibid.

24. Michael Sells, "Erasing Culture: Wahhabism, Buddhism, Balkan Mosques," 2 April 2003, available online at http://www.haverford.edu/relg/sells/reports/wahhabismbuddhasbegova.htm (accessed 14 December 2006).

25. Jolyon Naegele, "Yugoslavia: Saudi Wahhabi Aid Workers Bulldoze Balkan Monuments," *Radio Free Europe/Radio Liberty*, 4 August 2000, available online at http://www.rferl.org/specials/yugoslavia/monuments/ (accessed 14 December 2006).

26. "WAMY Plans to Construct 31 Mosques in India This Year," *Arab News*, 7 February 2000, in *Moneyclips*.

27. "Macedonian Muslim Federation Leader visits MWL," *Info-Prod Research (Middle East)*, 26 August 2003, in *Moneyclips*.

28. Isa Blumi, "Indoctrinating Albanians: Dynamics of Islamic Aid," *ISIM Newsletter*, November 2002, available online at http://www.isim.nl/files/newsl_11.pdf.

29. Blumi, "Political Islam among the Albanians," p. 12.

30. Mohammad Ahmad Ali, "Women's Rights Are Islamic Rights," *Journal of Muslim Minority Affairs* 16, no. 2 (July 1996): 301–04.

31. Ghodsee, *The Red Riviera*.

32. P. Mitchell Prothero, "Bosnia's Muslim Aid Hard to Resist," United Press International, 20 May 2002.

33. Here the Bosnian official is erroneously attributing the *burqa* (a specific form of Pashtun Afghan dress) to the Saudi charities, which encouraged women to wear headscarves and not *burqas*.

34. Dada Jovanovic, "Fomenting Fundamentalism? Bosnia: A New Playground for Militant Islamists?" *ABC News*, 18 January 2002.

35. Mustafa Hashim, "WAMY Girds Up to Meet Missionary Challenges in Albania," *Saudi Gazette*, 3 October 1994.

36. Personal communication with Nikolai Pankov, former Cabinet Head of Chief Mufti's Office, in Sofia, July 2005.

37. Personal communication with Vedat Ahmed, deputy chief mufti of Bulgarian Muslims, in Sofia, 21 August 2006.

38. Personal communication with Nikolai Pankov in Sofia, July 2005.

39. See Evstatiev, "Public Islam on the Balkans."

40. "IN BRIEF: Bulgarian Chief Mufti Visits Arab Countries," Bulgarian Telegraph Agency, 19 March 1990, in *BBC Summary of World Broadcasts*.

41. "IN BRIEF: National Muslim Conference Elects New Chief Mufti: Legitimacy Disputed," Bulgarian Telegraph Agency, 19 September 1992, in *BBC Summary of World Broadcasts*.

42. Collins and Burr, *Alms for Jihad*.

43. "The IICO and Charitable Organizations," available online at www.iico .org/home-page-eng/organizations-eng.htm (accessed 29 November 2006).

44. "Bulgarian Muslims' Conference Opens," Bulgarian Telegraph Agency, 7 August 1996, in *BBC Summary of World Broadcasts*.

45. Bulgarian Telegraph Agency, "Muslim World League Delegation in Bulgaria," 16 October 1996.

46. "Nedim Gendzhev: Glavno Myuftiistvo e krepostta na fundamentalizma v Bŭlgariya," *Maritsa Dnes* 256 (3226) (25 September 2001).

47. "Fundamentalistite nastŭpvat v Bŭlgariya?" *Nov Zhivot* 190 (12 October 2001).

48. When I tried to contact the organization, however, the number was out of service, and the office no longer existed. Furthermore, there was no public record of it.

49. By using the Bulgarian public records search engine, Daxy (www.daxy .bg), I was able to find all of the officially registered organizations with which Gendzhev had links.

50. "IDB Member Countries," available online at http://www.isdb.org/english_ docs/idb_home/IDB-M-C.htm (accessed 29 November 2006).

51. M. Ghazanfar Ali Khan, "WAMY Opens Delhi Office to Help Indian Muslims," *Arab News*, 6 July 1999, in *Moneyclips*.

52. Abdul Wahab Bashir, "Islamic Development Bank (IDB) Delegation Returns from Inspection Tour of CIS Projects," *Arab News*, 5 September 1993, in *Moneyclips*.

53. "IDB Scholarship Programme for Muslim Communities in Non-Member Countries," available online at www.isdb.org/english_docs/idb_home/scholarship_ muslimminoritics.htm (accessed 29 November 2006). See also www.isdb.org/ english_docs/idb_home/scholarship_muslimminorities.htm_CPO.htm.

54. See www.isdb.org/english_docs/idb_home/scholarship_muslimminorities_ benefits.htm.

55. "Islamic Development Bank Donates 800,000 Dollars for Bulgaria's Muslims," *Agence France Presse*, 24 August 2000.

56. "Bulgaria Spends over 500,000 Dollars of Islamic Bank Loans on Schools," *Bulgarian Telegraph Agency*, 12 January 2003, in *BBC Monitoring International Reports*.

57. Council of Europe, European Court of Human Rights, *Case of Al-Nashif v. Bulgaria*, Application No. 50963/99, Judgment, Strasbourg, 20 June 2002.

58. Personal communication with Professor Ivan Zhelev, director of the Religious Denominations Directorate, in Sofia, 16 June 2006.

59. Mohammed El Qorchi, Samuel Munzele Maimbo, and John F. Wilson, *Informal Funds Transfer Systems: An Analysis of the Informal Hawala System*, IMF and World Bank Paper, 24 March 2003, available online at http://www .johnfwilson.net/resources/Hawala+Occasional+Paper+_3.24.03_.pdf (accessed 11 January 2007).

60. I found and verified over twenty organizations using public records. There were many other organizations, particularly those associated with "fundamentalism" in the Bulgarian press that I was not able to locate in the public registers, such as Taibah and Al-Manar. The twenty organizations I found were probably just the tip of the iceberg. Because so many of them registered as NGOs with a "noneconomic purpose," there was little information about their activities and they were very difficult to find, particularly those with no official connection to the chief mufti's office.

61. Personal communication with Magdalena Tasheva, journalist for the daily newspaper *Monitor*, in Sofia, 13 March 2007.

62. www.daxy.bg (see note 49).

63. Albena Shkodorova, "Farewell to Bulgarian Islam," *Foreign Policy* (Bulgarian edition), August–September 2006, pp. 32–35.

64. Slavka Radicheva, "Koi chuka ha vratata na dzhamiiskoto shkolo?" *Maritsa Dnes*, no. 3285 (23 November 2001).

65. Anita Cholakova, "Otkriha novata dzhamiya v Smolyan," *Otzvuk* 294 (3 May 1999).

66. Radicheva, "Koi chuka ha vratata na dzhamiiskoto shkolo?"

67. Personal communication with Nedim Gendzhev, in Sofia, 13 March 2007.

68. "Turtsiya dari molitveni kilimi na Madanskata dzhamiya," *Rodopski Pregled*, 135 (27 April 2001): 2.

69. "Otkriha nova dzhamiya v Rudozem," *Rodopski Pregled* 149 (14–21 September 2001): 2.

70. But, interestingly, they were not necessarily as austere as one would expect of Saudi-style mosques.

71. Radicheva, "Koi chuka ha vratata na dzhamiiskoto shkolo?"

72. Personal communication with Vedat Ahmed, deputy chief mufti of Bulgarian Muslims, in Sofia, Bulgaria, 21 August 2006.

73. The Chepintsi mosque contained the second oldest library collection in Bulgaria and was home to a centuries-old Golden Koran.

74. According to the first issue of the magazine, the word "Ikra" refers to the first Arabic word in the Holy Qur'an, and means "read!"

75. The editors of *Ikra* downloaded more than five articles from the Harun Yahya website, http://www.harunyahya.com. All of these articles were already translated into Bulgarian and were opposed to Darwin and evolutionary theory.

76. When I asked the author himself for a copy of the book in August 2006, he said that he had no more to give away. I then asked if I could photocopy his own, but he said that he was hoping to find funding for a second edition soon. I was never able to obtain a copy.

77. Ivana Ikova, "BSP pokaza falshivata istoriya na Pomatsite," *Demokratsia* 302 (11 November 1998), available online at http://www.eunet.bg/media/show_story.html?issue=58096750&media=1523776&class=2407968&story=89213661 (accessed 20 December 2006). I heard that Dorsunski studied for a while in Iran, but I have no independent confirmation of either fact.

78. Nikola Damyanov, "Nedoumnitsi i greshki v enda kniga za Bŭlgarskite Mohamedani," *Rhodopski Vesti* 12 (24 March 2006): 5; "Nedoumnitsi i greshki v enda kniga za Bŭlgarskite Mohamedani," *Rodopski Vesti* 13 (31 March 2006): 5; "Nedoumnitsi i greshki v enda kniga za Bŭlgarskite Mohamedani," *Rodopski Vesti* 14 (7 April 2006): 5.

79. "KZD ne dade hod na prepiskata po zhalba sreshtu diskriminatsiya na etnicheski printsip v publikatsia v presata," *Focus News Agency*, 24 November 2006, available online at http://www.foucs-news.net/?id=n602878 (accessed 20 December 2006).

80. Isa Blumi, "Political Islam among the Albanians: Are the Taliban Coming to the Balkans?" Kosovar Institute for Policy Research and Development, Policy Research Series, no. 2, June 2005, p. 13.

81. From the Zarqa Private University website at http://www.zpu.edu.jo/services/about_usFram.htm (accessed 11 January 2007).

82. From the Zarqa Private University website at http://www.zpu.edu.jo/Academic/academic_fram.htm (accessed 11 January 2007).

83. Some newspapers openly sell editorial space on their front pages, and these are identified as "paid publications."

84. Nikola Ivanov, "Obedinenie za Islyamsko razvitie i kultura ce otvarya kŭm potrebnostite na obshtestvo," *Otzvuk* 14, no. 30 (1080) (17–19 April 2006): 1, 6.

85. "Novini," *Myusyulmansko Obshtestvo* 2, no. 7 (2005): 7.

86. http://home.wamymalaysia.org/index.php?option=com_content&task=view&id=12&Itemid=30 (accessed 22 November 2007).

87. Foundation Alnedua was registered in 2004 in Velingrad under the Bulstat number 112614861.

88. *State Gazette* 43 (1 June 2007). The "Brothers Trading" Bulstat number is 120594480.

89. From the OIRK (UIDC) website at www.oirk.org/aboutus.asp (accessed 11 January 2007).

90. "Myusyulansko sdruzhenie styaga sotsialna kuhniya, kani ot imeto na oblastniya," *Otzvuk* 29 (1079) (13–16 April 2006): 5.

91. Hasan Mehmedaliev, "Materializmŭt: Strashnata bolest za chovechestvoto," *Ikra* 15 (2006): 9–13. Translated with the assistance of Tanya Todorova.

92. Ibid., pp. 9–10.

93. Bozhidar Bashkov, "Vremeto e pari? Ne. Vremeto e zhivot," *Myusyulmansko Obshtestvo* 3 (2005): 34. Translated with the assistance of Tanya Todorova.

94. Zahari Sabev, "Arif Abdullah: Iskame da uverim obshtestvoto, che Islyamŭt e tolerantnost i obich kŭm horata," *Myusyulmansko Obshtestvo* 1 (2005): 4–5. Tanslated with the assistance of Tanya Todorova.

95. Ibid.

96. Ahmed Osmanov, "Edinistvenata duhovna sila, koyato mozhe da otvede chovechestvoto do shtastie," *Ikra* 16 (2006): 23–24.

97. Valentin Hadzhiev, "V Chepintsi spryaha diskoteka, uchela na porotsi," *24 Chasa* 16, no. 183 (5355): 10.

98. Zarko Marinov, "Dzhamiiskoto nastoyatelstvo kupi diskoteka v Chepintsi i ya zatvori," *Otzvuk* 52 (1102) (3–5 July 2006).

99. Hadzhiev, "V Chepintsi spryaha diskoteka, uchela na porotsi."

100. Nadelina Aneva and Dincher Feizov, "Islyamisti iskat da vkarat religiyata vŭv futbola," *Sega*, 18 September 2006, available online at http://www.segabg .com/online/article.asp?issueid=2416&sectionId=2&id=0000389 (accessed 20 December 2006).

101. "Rudozem maha simvolite na Islyama," *Sega*, 10 October 2006, available online at http://www.segabg.com/online/article.asp?issueid=2437&sectionId=12 &id=0002204 (accessed 20 December 2006).

Chapter Six
The Miniskirt and the Veil

1. John Bowen, *Why the French Don't Like Headscarves* (Princeton, NJ: Princeton University Press, 2006); Joan W. Scott, *The Politics of the Veil: Banning Islamic Headscarves in French Public Schools* (Princeton, NJ: Princeton University Press, 2007).

2. Council of Europe, European Court of Human Rights, *Leyla Sahin v. Turkey*, Application No. 44774/98, Judgment, Strasbourg, 29 June 2004.

3. From the islam-bg website, which was taken down by the Bulgarian Interior Ministry in February 2007. I have only a hard copy of the article.

4. www.oirk.org.

5. Anita Cholakova, "Neda Abdullah: Ne sŭm se zabulila za pari," *Otzvuk*: 6 (953) (20–23 January 2005): 7. Translated with the assistance of Tanya Todorova.

6. Asya Raad, "Skromnostta kato osobenost na Islyama," *Mysusyulmansko Obshtestvo* 2, no. 2 (2006): 28–29. Translated with the assistance of Rumyana Delcheva.

7. Fatme Musa Ali, "Pokrivaloto—Edna Kategorichna Zapoved," *Ikra* 2, no. 17 (2006): 31–33. Translated with the assistance of Rumyana Delcheva.

8. Selve Hodzhova, "Nachin na Povedenie na Myusyulmankata," *Ikra* 1, no. 12 (2005): 21–22. Translated with the assistance of Rumyana Delcheva.

9. "Zhenite, koito mogat da se kupyat," *Ikra* 12, no. 16 (2006): 11–13.

10. Ibid. Translated with the assistance of Rumyana Delcheva.

11. Iren Delcheva, "Ex-mufti Converts Women to Islam: Arab Fundamentalists Pay 200 Levs to Muslim Women Who Wear Hijabs," *Standart*, 3 February 2007, available online at www.standartnews.com/en/article.php?d=2007-02-03& article=3448 (accessed 1 August 2007). Of course, the Bulgarian media are no-

torious for being anti-Islamic, and it is doubtful that there is any proof of this claim.

12. Elizabeth Brusco, *The Reformation of Machismo: Evangelical Conversion and Gender in Columbia* (Austin: University of Texas Press, 1995).

13. Anita Cholakova, "Momichetata ot PGI: Nie ne narushavame nichii prava, da ne narushavat nashite," *Otzvuk* 50 (1100) (26–28 June 2008): 6. Translated with the assistance of Tanya Todorova.

14. Tanya Petrova, "Religioznite simvoli s ogranichena upotreba," *Sega* 9, no. 162 (2652) (13 July 2006): 15; "Zabradki sreshtu krŭstcheta," *Politika*, 116 (7–11 July 2006): 48.

15. See: "Law on the Protection against Discrimination," available in English online at http://www.stopvaw.org/sites/3f6d15f4-c12d-4515-8544-26b7a3a5a41e/ uploads/anti-discrimination_law_en.pdf (accessed 7 February 2007). See also "Reshavat dali momicheta ot PGE da nosyat zabradki v uchilishte," *Otzvuk* (Smolyan) 50 (1100) (26–28 June 2006): 6; Cholakova, "Momichetata ot PGE."

16. Zarko Marinov, "OIRK zloupotrebilo s uchenichkite ot PGE," *Otzvuk* (Smolyan) 52 (1102) (3–5 July 2006): 8. Translated with the assistance of Rumyana Delcheva.

17. Valentin Hadzhiev, "Zam.-Ministŭrŭt im razreshil zabradkite prez 2003-a," *24 Chasa* 16, no. 176 (5328) (28 June 2006): 10.

18. Cholakova, "Momichetata ot PGE."

19. Nikolai Tonchev, "V Evropa nyama myasto za zabradki," *Duma* 17, no. 152 (4457) (1 July 2006): 10; Rumiana Buchakova, "Prebrazhdat momicheta c beli shamii," *Plovdiski Trud* 9, no. 127 (2249) (28 June 2006): 1; "Zabranyavat feredzhetata v uchilishte, DPS e protiv," *Ataka* 1, no. 211 (26 June 2006): 6; Kiril Borisov "S shamiya na uchilishte," *168 Chasa* 17, no. 25 (23–29 June 2006): 20; "Novite uchenicheski uniformi v Smolyan," *Ataka* 1, no. 25 (30 June 2006): 2; Valentin Hadzhiev, "Bez feredzheta v uchilishtata," *24 Chasa* 16, no. 174 (5526) (25 June 2006): 5.

20. Obtained by the author from the KZD through the Bulgarian Freedom of Information Act.

21. Commission for Protection against Discrimination, Decision 37, Sofia, 27 July 2006. Translated with the assistance of Tanya Todorova.

22. Kristen Ghodsee, "Religious Freedoms versus Gender Equality: Faith-Based Organizations, Muslim Minorities and Islamic Headscarves in Modern Bulgaria," *Social Politics* 14, no. 4 (2007).

23. ECHR, *Leyla Sahin v. Turkey.*

24. Council of Europe, European Court of Human Rights, "*Case of Dahlab v. Switzerland,* Application No. 42393/98, Judgment, Strasbourg, 15 February 2001.

25. ECHR, *Leyla Sahin v. Turkey.*

26. CPD, Decision 37.

27. "Women and Religion in Europe," Parliamentary Assembly of the Council of Europe, Resolution 1464 (2005), available online at http://assembly.coe .int/Main.asp?link=/Documents/AdoptedText/ta05/ERES1464.htm (accessed 30 January 2007).

28. Aneta Kisiova, "V ikonoma nyama diskrimininatsiya, myuftii iskat zab-

radki," *Rodopi Vest* 7, no. 59 (562) (29 July–1 August 2006): 3; Zarko Marinov, "Myuftiyata da zabuli pŭrvo Emel Etem," *Otzvuk* 60 (1110) (31 July–2 August 2006): 1; Zarko Marinov, "Uchenichkite v Smolyan da Svalyat Zabradkite," *Otzvuk* 60 (1110) (31 July–2 August 2006): 3.

29. Personal communication with Dr. Krassimir Kanev, chairman of the Bulgarian Helsinki Committee, in Sofia, July 2006.

30. "Koi zabranyava noseneto na krŭst v hristiyanska dŭrzhava?" 31 August 2006, available online at www.segabg.com (accessed 19 September 2006).

Conclusion
Minarets after Marx

1. Judith Butler, *Gender Trouble: Feminism and the Subversion of Identity,* Gender Classics, (New York: Routledge, 2006).

2. For an interesting study of the worldview of the last communist generation in Russia, see Alexei Yurchak, *Everything Was Forever until It Was No More* (Princeton, NJ: Princeton University Press, 2005).

3. David Kideckel found a similar type of gender shift had occurred in the Jui Valley mining communities after the closing of several mines. See David Kideckel, "Miners and Wives in Romania's Jiu Valley: Perspectives on Postsocialist Class, Gender, and Social Change," *Identities* 11, no. 1 (2004): 39–63.

4. For example, see Mary Buckley, *Post-Soviet Women: From the Baltic to Central Asia* (Cambridge and New York: Cambridge University Press, 1997); Barbara Einhorn, *Cinderella Goes to Market: Citizenship, Gender, and Women's Movements in East Central Europe* (London and New York: Verso, 1993); Chris Corrin, *Superwomen and the Double Burden: Women's Experience of Change in Central and Eastern Europe and the Former Soviet Union* (Toronto: Second Story Press, 1992); Marilyn Rueschemeyer, *Women and the Politics of Postcommunist Eastern Europe* (Armonk, NY: M. E. Sharpe, 1994).

5. Creed, *Domesticating Revolution.*

6. See Ghodsee, *The Red Riviera.*

7. See Mahmood, *The Politics Piety,* and Deeb, *An Enchanted Modern.*

8. Saba Mahmood, "Feminist Theory, Embodiment and the Docile Agent: Some Reflections on the Egyptian Islamic Revival," *Cultural Anthropology* 16, no. 2 (2001): 209.

9. Its has been pointed out to me on several occasions by Middle Eastern Studies scholars that many researchers working in Islamic Studies question the academic merits of the works of Roy and Kepel. While I understand these objections, the works of both authors have been very useful to me as I tried to contrast Islam in Bulgaria with perceptions of Islam in Western Europe.

10. Vladimir Lenin, cited in Rosalind C. Morris, "Theses on the Questions of War: History, Media, Terror," *Social Text* 20, no. 3 (Fall 2002): 149–78.

11. Olivier Roy, *Globalized Islam: The Search for a New Ummah* (New York: Columbia University Press, 2004), p. 46.

12. Gilles Kepel, *The War for Muslim Minds: Islam and the West* (Cambridge and London: Harvard University Press, 2004), p. 264.

13. "A Benign Growth," *Economist* 383, no. 8523 (7 April 2007): 47–48.

14. Kepel, *The War for Muslim Minds*, pp. 294–95.

15. Emma Tarlo, "Reconsidering Stereotypes: Anthropological Reflections on the *Jilbab* Controversy," *Anthropology Today* 21, no. 6 (December 2005): 16–20.

16. See Deeb, *An Enchanted Modern*, on how Shi'a in Lebanon combine a concept of renewed piety with modernity.

17. Ahmed Al-Rawi, "European Muslims: Towards a More Integrated Future," available online at http://www.eu-islam.com/en/templates/Index_en.asp (accessed 10 May 2007).

18. Muslims in Europe Charter Project, available online at http://www .islamonline.net/English/EuropeanMuslims/PoliticsCitizenship/2006/09/01a .shtml.

19. Tariq Ramadan, "Manifesto for a New 'We,'" available online at http:// www.tariqramadan.com/article.php3?id_article=743&lang=en (accessed 10 May 2007).

20. Roy, *Globalized Islam*, pp. 7–8.

21. Albena Shkodorova, "Bulgarians Join the EU with Marxism on Their Minds," *Balkan Insight*, 21 December 2006, available online at http://www.birn .eu.com/en/64/10/1982/ (accessed 12 August 2007). Marian Adanes, "Social Transitions and Anomie among Post-commnunist Bulgarian Youth," *Young: Nordic Journal of Youth Research* 15, no. 1 (2007): 49–69; Joakim Ekman and Jonas Linde, "Communist Nostalgia and the Consolidation of Democracy in Central and Eastern Europe," *Journal of Communist Studies and Transition Politics* 21, no. 3 (2005): 354–74, Kristen Ghodsee, "Red Nostalgia? Communism, Women's Emancipation, and Economic Transformation in Bulgaria," *L'Homme: Zeitschrift für Feministische Geschichtswissenschaft* (*L'Homme: Journal for Feminist History*) 15, no. 1 (2004): 23–36; Milena Hristova, "Why Are Bulgarian Eyes Nostalgic?" *Novinite.com*, 21 December 2007, available online at http://www.novinite.com/ view_news.php?id=88777 (accessed 30 November 2008). Nancy J. Davis and Robert V. Robinson, "The Egalitarian Face of Islamic Orthodoxy: Support for Islamic Law and Economic Justice in Seven Muslim-Majority Nations," *American Sociological Review* 71, no. 2 (2006): 167–90.

22. Daniel, "The Children of Perestroika," p. 172.

23. Jean-Marie Chauvier, "Russia: Nostalgic for the Soviet Era," *Le Monde Diplomatique*, March 2004, available online at mondediplo.com/2004/03/11russia (accessed 18 June 2007).

24. Joakim Ekman and Jonas Linde, "Communist Nostalgia and the Consolidation of Democracy in Central and Eastern Europe," *Journal of Communist Studies and Transition Politics* 21, no. 3 (September 2005): 354–74.

25. Ibid., pp. 369–70.

26. Daniel, "The Children of Perestroika," p. 170.

27. Janusz Kuczynski, "Metaphilosophy, Science, and Art as Foundation of Wisdom: The Co-Creation of a Rational and Ethical Universal Society," *Dialogue and Universalism* 7–8 (2001): 45–61.

28. Krzystof Gawlikowski, "From False 'Western Universalism' towards True 'Universal Universalism,'" *Dialogue and Universalism* 10–12 (2004): 31–58.

29. Ibid., p. 31.

30. Ali Mazuri, "Pretender to Universalism: Western Culture in a Globolizing Age," *Journal of Muslim Minority Affairs* 21, no. 1 (2001): 11–24; Adam Seligman, "Particularist Universalism: A Response to Abdullahi Ahmed An-Na'im," *Common Knowledge* 11, no. 1 (2005): 81–88.

31. Mustafa Ceric, "Is There an Identity of European Muslims?" available online at http://www.islamonline.net/English/EuropeanMuslims/CommunityCivilSociety/2006/09/03.shtml1 (accessed 17 June 2007).

32. World Assembly of Muslim Youth, "Concept of Worship in Islam," brochure, English text available at http://www.usc.edu/dept/MSA/fundamentals/tawheed/conceptsofworship.html (accessed 30 November 2008).

33. In fact, the European Union suspended some funding to Bulgaria in July 2008 due to several proven cases of high-level embezzlement.

34. David A. Westbrook, "Strategic Consequences of Radical Islamic Neofundamentalism," *Orbis* 51, no. 3 (2007): 461–77.

35. For example, see Westbrook, "Strategic Consequences of Radical Islamic Neofundamentalism"; Hendrik Hansen and Peter Kainz, "Radical Islamism and Totalitarian Ideology: A Comparison of Sayyid Qutb's Islamism with Marxism and National Socialism," *Totalitarian Movements and Political Religions* 8, no. 1 (March 2007): 55–76.

36. Frederick Engels, *Origin of the Family, Private Property and the State* (New York: Pathfinder Press, 1972).

37. Ceric, "Is There an Identity of European Muslims?" (accessed 8 August 2007).

38. Susan Gal and Gail Kligman, *The Politics of Gender after Socialism* (Princeton, NJ: Princeton University Press, 2000).

39. Of course, among the communist elites, privileges continued to be passed down between generations but not so much in the form of private property as in the form of access to power and other state-owned goods and services.

Selected Bibliography

Abu-Lughod, Lila. *Veiled Sentiments: Honor and Poetry in a Bedouin Society.* Berkeley and Los Angeles: University of California Press, 1986.

———. "Zones of Theory in the Anthropology of the Arab World." *Annual Review of Anthropology* 18 (1989): 267–306.

———. "Feminist Longings and Postcolonial Conditions." Introduction to *In Remaking Women: Feminism and Modernity in the Middle East,* ed. Lila Abu-Lughod, pp. 3–31. Princeton, NJ: Princeton University Press, 1998.

———. "Do Muslim Women Really Need Saving? Anthropological Reflections on Cultural Relativism and Its Others." *American Anthropologist* 104, no. 3 (2002): 783–90.

Ahmed, Leila. *Women and Gender in Islam: Historical Roots of a Modern Debate.* New Haven: Yale University Press, 1993.

Ali, Mohammad Ahmad. "Women's Rights Are Islamic Rights." *Journal of Muslim Minority Affairs* 16, no. 2 (July 1996).

Alsanbeigui, Nahid, Steve Pressman, and Gale Summerfield. *Women in the Age of Economic Transformation: Gender Impacts of Reforms in Postsocialist and Developing Countries.* New York: Routledge, 1994.

Apostolov, Mario. "The Pomaks: A Religious Minority in the Balkans." *Nationalities Papers* 24, no. 4 (1996): 727–52.

Asad, Talal. "The Idea of an Anthropology of Islam." Occasional Papers Series, Center for Contemporary Arab Studies, Georgetown University, 1986.

———. *Genealogies of Religion: Discipline and Reasons of Power in Christianity and Islam.* Baltimore: Johns Hopkins University Press, 1993.

Al-Azmeh, Aziz. *Islam and Modernities.* London: Verso, 1993.

Bell, John D. *The Bulgarian Communist Party from Blagoev to Zhivkov.* Washington, DC: Hoover Institution Press, 1985.

Benthall, Jonathan, and Jerome Bellion-Jourdan. *The Charitable Crescent: The Politics of Aid in the Muslim World.* London and New York: I. B. Tauris, 2003.

Blumi, Isa. "Indoctrinating Albanians: Dynamics of Islamic Aid." *ISIM Newsletter,* November 2002.

———. "Political Islam among the Albanians: Are the Taliban Coming to the Balkans?" Kosovar Institute for Policy Research and Development, Policy Research Series, no. 2, Prishtina, June 2005.

Borowik, Irena. "Orthodoxy Confronting the Collapse of Communism in Post-Soviet Countries." *Social Compass* 53, no. 2 (2006).

Bowen, John. *Why the French Don't Like Headscarves.* Princeton, NJ: Princeton University Press, 2006.

Boyadzhieva, Rumyana. *Grad Rudozem.* Sofia: Fondatsiya Lyudmila Zhivkova 1989.

Branchev, Nikolai. *Bŭlgari Mohamedani (Pomatsi).* Sofia: Izdava Bŭlgarsko Narodouchno D-VO, 1948.

Bringa, Tone. *Being Muslim the Bosnian Way*. Princeton, NJ: Princeton University Press, 1995.

Brooks, Robin. "Ethnicity and Class in Bulgaria." *Peace Review* 11, no. 2 (1999).

Broun, Janice. *Conscience and Captivity: Religion in Eastern Europe*. Washington, DC: Ethics and Public Policy Center, 1988.

———. "The Schism in the Bulgarian Orthodox Church, Part 2: Under the Socialist Government, 1993–97." *Religion, State and Society* 28, no. 3 (2000).

———. "The Schism in the Bulgarian Orthodox Church, Part 3: Under the Second Union of Democratic Forces Government, 1997–2001." *Religion, State and Society* 30, no. 4 (2002).

———. "The Bulgarian Orthodox Church: The Continuing Schism and the Religious, Social and Political Environment." *Religion, State and Society* 32, no. 3 (2004).

Broun, Janice, and Grazyna Sikorska. *Conscience and Captivity*. Washington, DC: Ethics and Public Policy Center, 1990.

Brunnbauer, Ulf. "The Perception of Muslims in Bulgaria and Greece: Between the 'Self' and the 'Other.'" *Journal of Muslim Minority Affairs* 21, no. 1 (2001).

Brusco, Elizabeth. *The Reformation of Machismo: Evangelical Conversion and Gender in Columbia*. Austin, TX: University of Texas Press, 1995.

Buckley, Mary. *Post-Soviet Women: From the Baltic to Central Asia*. Cambridge and New York: Cambridge University Press, 1997.

Bŭlgarska Komunisticheska Partiya Gradski Komitet. *25 Godini Grad Madan*. Madan: Gradski Obshtinski Naroden Sŭvet, 1978.

Burr, Millard, and Robert O. Collins. *Alms for Jihad: Charity and Terrorism in the Islamic World*. Cambridge: Cambridge University Press, 2006.

Butler, Judith. *Gender Trouble: Feminism and the Subversion of Identity*. New York: Routledge, 2006.

Cellarius, Barbara. *In the Land of Orpheus: Rural Livelihoods and Nature Conservation in Postsocialist Bulgaria*. Madison: University of Wisconsin Press, 2004.

Center for the Study of Democracy. *The Political Change in Bulgaria: Postelectoral Attitudes*. Sofia: CSD, 1990.

Chiodini, Steven. "Bulgaria: An East European Revolution in Suspension." *Harvard International Review* 13, no. 2 (Winter 1991).

Council of Europe, European Court of Human Rights. *Case of Hasan and Chaush v. Bulgaria*, Application No. 30985/96, Judgment, Strasbourg, 26 October 2000.

———. *Case of Al-Nashif v. Bulgaria*, Application No. 50963/99, Judgment, Strasbourg, 20 June 2002.

———. *Case of Leyla Sahin V. Turkey*, Application No. 44774/98, Judgment, Strasbourg, 29 June 2004.

———. *Case of Supreme Theological Council of the Muslim Community v. Bulgaria*, Application No. 39023/97, Judgment, Strasbourg, 16 December 2004.

Corrin, Chris. *Superwomen and the Double Burden: Women's Experience of Change in Central and Eastern Europe and the Former Soviet Union*. Toronto: Second Story Press, 1992.

Creed, Gerald. *Domesticating Revolution: From Socialist Reform to Ambivalent Transition in a Bulgarian Village*. University Park: Pennsylvania State University Press, 1998.

Daniel, Wallace L. "The Children of Perestroika: Two Sociologists on Religion and Russian Society, 1991–2006." *Religion, State and Society* 35, no. 2 (June 2007).

Deeb, Lara. *An Enchanted Modern: Gender and Public Piety in Shi'i Lebanon*. Princeton, NJ: Princeton University Press, 2006.

Delchev, Marin. "The Battle between the Cross and the Crescent Continues to Divide the Rhodopes." *Obektiv: Magazine of the Bulgarian Helsinki Committee* 70 (June/September 2000).

Eickelman, Dale F. "Islam and the Languages of Modernity." *Daedalus* 129 (2000): 119–35.

———, ed. *Russia's Muslim Frontier*. Bloomington: Indiana University Press, 1993.

Eickelman, Dale, and James Piscatori. *Muslim Politics*. Princeton, NJ: Princeton University Press, 1996.

Einhorn, Barbara. *Cinderella Goes to Market: Citizenship, Gender, and Women's Movements in East Central Europe*. London and New York: Verso, 1993.

Ekman, Joakim, and Jonas Linde. "Communist Nostalgia and the Consolidation of Democracy in Central and Eastern Europe." *Journal of Communist Studies and Transition Politics* 21, no. 3 (September 2005): 354–74.

Eminov, Ali. *Turkish and Other Muslim Minorities in Bulgaria*. New York: Routledge, 1997.

Engels, Frederick. *Origin of the Family, Private Property and the State*. New York: Pathfinder Press, 1972.

Funk, Nanette, and Magda Mueller. *Gender Politics and Post-Communism: Reflections from Eastern Europe and the Former Soviet Union*. New York and London: Routledge, 1993.

Gal, Susan, and Gail Kligman. *The Politics of Gender after Socialism*. Princeton, NJ: Princeton University Press, 2000.

Ganev, Venelin. *Preying on the State: The Transformation of Bulgaria after 1989*. Ithaca, NY: Cornell University Press, 2007.

Garbolevsky, Evgenija. *A Church Ossified? Repression and Resurgence of Bulgarian Orthodoxy, 1944–1956*. Sofia: Asconi Izdat, 2005.

Gawlikowski, Krzysztof. "From False 'Western Universalism' towards True 'Universal Universalism.'" *Dialogue and Universalism* 10–12 (2004): 31–58.

Geertz, Clifford. *Islam Observed: Religious Development in Morocco and Indonesia*. Chicago: University of Chicago Press, 1971.

Georgiev, Velichko, and Staiko Trifonov. *Pokrŭstvaneto na Bŭlgarite Mohamedani 1912–1913 Dokumenti*. Sofia: Akademichno Izdatelstvo Prof. Marin Drinov, 1995.

Georgieva, Tsvetana. "Pomaks: Muslim Bulgarians." *Islam and Christian-Muslim Relations* 12, no. 3 (July 2001): 303–16.

Ghodsee, Kristen. *The Red Riviera: Gender, Tourism and Postsocialism on the Black Sea*. Durham, NC: Duke University Press, 2005.

————. "Men, Mines and Mosques: Gender and Islamic Revivalism on the Edge of Europe." Occasional Papers from the School of Social Science, Institute for Advanced Study, no. 28, January 2007.

————. "Religious Freedoms versus Gender Equality: Faith-Based Organizations, Muslim Minorities and Islamic Headscarves in Modern Bulgaria." *Social Politics* 14, no. 4 (2007).

————. "Right Wing, Left Wing, Everything: Xenophobia, Neo-Totalitarianism and Populist Politics in Contemporary Bulgaria." *Problems of Post-Communism* 55, no. 3 (May–June 2008).

Giatzidis, Emil. "Bulgaria on the Road to the European Union." *Southeast European and Black Sea Studies* 4, no. 3 (September 2004).

Gradeva, Rositsa. *History of Muslim Culture in Bulgarian Lands*. Sofia: International Center for Minority Studies and Intercultural Relations (IMIR), 2001.

Gradeva, Rositsa, and Svetlana Ivanova. "Researching the Past and Present of Muslim Culture in Bulgaria: The 'Popular' and 'High' Layers." *Islam and Christian-Muslim Relations* 12, no. 3 (July 2001).

Haghayeghi, Mehrdad. *Islam and Politics in Central Asia*. New York: St. Martin's Press, 1996.

Ham, Ken. "After Communism's Collapse: Creation in the Crimea—Ukrainian Geophysicist and Creation Warrior Sergei Golovin." *Creation ex Nihilo* 22, no. 4 (September 2000): 24–27.

Hansen, Hendrik, and Peter Kainz. "Radical Islamism and Totalitarian Ideology: A Comparison of Sayyid Qutb's Islamism with Marxism and National Socialism." *Totalitarian Movements and Political Religions* 8, no. 1 (March 2007): 55–76.

Hendon, David, and Donald Greco. "Notes on Church-State Affairs: Bulgaria." *Journal of Church and State* 42, no. 4 (Autumn 2000).

Higonnet, Margaret, Jane Jensen, Sonya Michel, and Margaret Weitz. *Behind the Lines: Gender and the Two World Wars*. New Haven, CT: Yale University Press, 1989.

Hiscock, S. A. "Lead." *Mining Journal: Mining Annual Review*, June 1987.

Humphrey, Caroline. *The Unmaking of Soviet Life: Everyday Economies after Socialism*. Ithaca, NY: Cornell University Press, 2002.

Huntington, Samuel. *The Clash of Civilizations and the Remaking of World Order*. New York: Free Press, 2002.

Inalcik, Halil. "Ottoman Methods of Conquest." *Studia Islamica* 2 (1954): 103–29.

Institut za Bŭlgaraska Istoriya. *Iz Minaloto na Bŭlgarite Mohamedani v Rodopite*. Sofia: Izdatelstvo na Bŭlgarskata Akademiya na Naukite, 1958.

Kafadar, Cemal. *Between Two Worlds: The Construction of the Ottoman State*. Berkeley: University of California Press, 1996.

Kalicin, Maria, and Krassimira Mutafova. "Historical Accounts of the Halveti Shayk Bali Efendi of Sofia in a Newly Discovered *Vita* Dating from the Nineteenth Century." *Islam and Christian-Muslim Relations* 12, no. 3 (July 2001): 339–53.

Kaneff, Deema. *Who Owns the Past? The Politics of Time in a "Model" Bulgarian Village*. New York and Oxford: Berghahm Books, 2004.

Kanev, Krassimir. "Law and Politics on Ethnic Religious Minorities in Bulgaria." In *Communities and Identities in Bulgaria*, ed. Anna Krasteva. Bologna: Longo Editore Ravenna, 1998.

Kanev, Petar. "Religion in Bulgaria after 1989: Historical and Sociocultural Aspects." *South-East Europe Review* 1 (2002): 75–96.

Karahasan-Chadar, Ibrahim. *Etnicheskite Maltsinstva v Bŭlgaria: Istoriya, Kultura, Religiya, Obreden Kalendar*. Sofia: Lik, 2005.

Karamihova, Margarita. "Emigration from the Rhodopi Mountain: A New Phenomenon or a Temporary Response in a Time of Crisis." In: *Living There, Dreaming Here: Emigrational Attitudes in the Beginning of the 21st Century*. Sofia: International Center for Minority Studies and Intercultural Relations, 2003.

Kepel, Gilles. *The War for Muslim Minds: Islam and the West*. Cambridge, MA, and London: Harvard University Press, 2004.

Khalid, Adeeb. *Islam after Communism: Religion and Politics in Central Asia*. Berkeley: University of California Press, 2007.

Kideckel, David. "Miners and Wives in Romania's Jiu Valley: Perspectives on Postsocialist Class, Gender, and Social Change." *Identities* 11, no. 1 (2004): 39–63.

Kohlmann, Evan. *Al-Qaida's Jihad in Europe: The Afghan-Bosnian Connection*. London: Berg, 2004.

Kolarova, Rumyana. "Bulgaria: Could We Regain What We Have Already Lost?" *Social Research* 63, no. 2 (Summer 1996).

Krasteva, Anna. *Communities and Identities in Bulgaria*. Ravenna: Longo, 1998.

Kuczynski, Janusz. "Metaphilosophy, Science, and Art as Foundation of Wisdom: The Co-Creation of a Rational and Ethical Universal Society." *Dialogue and Universalism* 7–8 (2001): 45–61.

Kusat, Alil. "The Influence of Minority Feelings on the Formation of Religious Concept and Individual Identity: The Case of the Bulgarian Muslims." *Journal of Muslim Minority Affairs* 21, no. 2 (2001): 363–72.

Lampe, John. *The Bulgarian Economy in the Twentieth Century*. New York and London: Palgrave McMillan, 1986.

Lederer, Gyorgy. "Islam in Eastern Europe." *Central Asian Survey* 20, no. 1 (2001): 5–32.

Lewis, Bernard. "Communism and Islam." *International Affairs* (Royal Institute of International Affairs) 30, no. 1 (January 1954): 1–12.

Mahmood, Saba. "Feminist Theory, Embodiment and the Docile Agent: Some Reflections on the Egyptian Islamic Revival." *Cultural Anthropology* 16, no. 2 (2002).

———. *Politics of Piety: The Islamic Revival and the Feminist Subject*. Princeton, NJ: Princeton University Press, 2004.

Mancheva, Mila. "Image and Policy: The Case of Turks and Pomaks in Interwar Bulgaria, 1918–1944 (with Special Reference to Education)." *Islam and Christian-Muslim Relations* 12, no. 3 (July 2001).

Massell, Gregory. *The Surrogate Proletariat: Moslem Women and Revolutionary Strategies in Soviet Central Asia, 1919–1929*. Princeton, NJ: Princeton University Press, 1974.

Maxwell, J. "New Kingdoms for the Cults." *Christianity Today* 36, no. 1 (13 January 1992): 37–41.

Mazuri, Ali. "Pretender to Universalism: Western Culture in a Globlizing Age." *Journal of Muslim Minority Affairs* 21, no. 1 (2001): 11–24.

Mihaylova, Dimitrina. "Coping with Marginality: Redefining Christian and Muslim Identification in South-Eastern Bulgaria." *Journal of Mediterranean Studies* 13, no. 2 (2003).

Misiarz, Jan. "Vaclav Havel's Concept of Universalism and Europe." *Dialogue and Universalism* 11, nos. 5–6 (2001): 33–39.

Mitev, Petar. "Relations of Compatibility and Incompatibility in the Everyday Life of Christians and Muslims in Bulgaria (Sociological Studies)." In *Relations of Compatibility and Incompatibility between Christians and Muslims in Bulgaria*. Sofia: International Center for Minority Studies and Intercultural Relations, 1995.

Moore, A. "Fertile Ground for False Teaching." *Christianity Today* 36, no. 1 (13 January 1992): 40–41.

Morris, Rosalind C. "Theses on the Questions of War: History, Media, Terror." *Social Text* 20, no. 3 (Fall 2002).

National Statistical Institute. *Statistical Yearbook 1993*. Sofia: NSI, 1994.

———. *Statistical Yearbook 1994*. Sofia: NSI, 1994.

Neuberger, Mary. "Pomak Borderlands: Muslims on the Edge of Nations." *Nationalities Papers* 28, no. 1 (March 2000).

———. *The Orient Within: Muslim Minorities and the Negotiation of Nationhood in Modern Bulgaria*. Ithaca, NY: Cornell University Press, 2004.

Norris, H. T. Introduction to *Islam in the Balkans: Religion and Society between Europe and the Arab World*. Columbia: University of South Carolina Press, 1993.

Northrop, Douglas. *Veiled Empire: Gender and Power in Stalinist Central Asia*. Ithaca, NY: Cornell University Press, 2004.

Oushakine, Serguei. "The Fatal Splitting: Symbolizing Anxiety in Post-Soviet Russia." *Ethnos: Journal of Anthropology* 66, no. 3 (2001): 291–319.

Palchev, Ivan. *Ahmed Dogan and the Bulgarian Ethnic Model*. Sofia: National Museum of Bulgarian Books and Polygraphy, 2002.

Penkov, Ignat. *Novite Gradove v N.R. Bulgaria*. Sofia: Izdatelstvo Narodna Prosveta, 1971.

People's Republic of Bulgaria. *Bulgaria and the World Today*. Sofia: Sofia Press, 1985.

Petrov, Petŭr, Asen Spasov, and Donio Donev, eds. *Rodopa: Bŭlgarski Tvŭrdina (Sbornik Veseli) Uchebno Pomagalo*. Sofia: BKP Izdatelstvo, 1960.

Prothero, P. Mitchell. "Bosnia's Muslim Aid Hard to Resist." United Press International, 20 May 2002.

Radushev, Evgeni. *Pomatsite, Hristiyanstvo i Islyam v zapadnite Rodopi s dolinata na r. Mesta, XV-30-te godini na XVIII vek*. Sofia: Sts. Kiril and Methodi National Library, Oriental Section, 2005.

Ragaru, Nadege. "Islam in Post-Communist Bulgaria: An Aborted 'Clash of Civilizations?' " *Nationalities Papers* 29, no. 2 (2001).

Raichevsky, Stoyan. *The Mohammedan Bulgarians (Pomaks)*. Sofia: Bulgarian Bestseller—National Museum of Bulgarian Books and Polygraphy, 2004.

Ramadan, Tariq. *Western Muslims and the Future of Islam*. Oxford: Oxford University Press, 2005.

Ranstorp, Magnus, and Gus Xhudo. "A Threat to Europe? Middle East Ties with the Balkans and Their Impact upon Terrorist Activity throughout the Region." *Terrorism and Political Violence* 6, no. 2 (Summer 1994).

Ries, Nancy. *Russian Talk: Culture and Conversation during Perestroika*. Ithaca, NY: Cornell University Press, 1997.

Roberts, Marie Louise. *Civilization without Sexes: Reconstructing Gender in Postwar France, 1917–1927*. Chicago: University of Chicago Press, 1994.

Rosen, Lawrence. *Varieties of Muslim Experience: Encounters with Arab Political and Cultural Life*. Chicago: University of Chicago Press, 2008.

Roth, Klaus. "Socialist Life-Style Rituals in Bulgaria." *Anthropology Today* 6, no. 5 (1990).

Roy, Olivier. *Globalized Islam: The Search for a New Ummah*. New York: Columbia University Press, 2004.

Roy, Olivier, and George Holoch, Jr. *Secularism Confronts Islam*. New York: Columbia University Press, 2007.

Rueschemeyer, Marilyn. *Women and the Politics of Postcommunist Eastern Europe*. Armonk, NY: M. E. Sharpe, 1994.

Salvatore, Armando. *Islam and the Political Discourse of Modernity*. Reading, UK: Ithaca Press, 1997.

———. "Staging Virtue: The Disembodiment of Self-correctness and the Making of Islam as Public Norm." In *Islam, Motor or Challenge of Modernity*, ed. Georg Stauth. Hamburg: Lit Verlag, 1998.

———. "Social Differentiation, Moral Authority and Public Islam in Egypt: The Path of Mustafa Mahmud." *Anthropology Today* 16 (2000): 12–15.

Scott, Joan W. *The Politics of the Veil: Banning Islamic Headscarves in French Public Schools*. Princeton, NJ: Princeton University Press, 2007.

Seligman, Adam. "Particularist Universalism: A Response to Abdullahi Ahmed An-Na'im." *Common Knowledge* 11, no. 1 (2005): 81–88.

Shkodrova, Albena. "The End of Bulgarian Islam." *Foreign Policy* (Bulgarian edition), August–September 2006, pp. 32–35.

Siegelbaum, Lewis. *Stakhanovism and the Politics of Productivity in the USSR, 1935–1941*. Cambridge: Cambridge University Press, 1990.

Taji-Farouki, Suja, and Hugh Poulton. *Muslim Identity and the Balkan State*. New York: New York University Press, 1997.

Tarlo, Emma. "Reconsidering Stereotypes: Anthropological Reflections on the *Jilbab* Controversy." *Anthropology Today* 21, no. 6 (December 2005).

Tavanier, Yana Buhrer. "Bulgaria: Mysterious Mosques and Schools." *Transitions Online*, 27 January 2005.

———. "The Schools That Aren't Schools." *Transitions Online*, 3 February 2005.

Todorova, Maria. "Identity (Trans)Formation among the Pomaks in Bulgaria." In *Beyond Borders: Remaking Cultural Identities in the New East and Central Europe*, ed. Lazlo Kurti and Juliet Langman. New York: Westview Press, 1997.

————. "Conversion to Islam as a Trope in Bulgarian Historiography, Fiction and Film." In *Penser la Transition/Rethinking the Transition,* ed. Ivaylo Znepolski, Koprinka Tchervenkova, and Alexander Kiossev. Sofia: St. Kliment Ohridski University Press, 2002.

Tsentralno Statistichesko Upravlenie pri Ministerskiya Sŭvet. *Statisticheski Godishnik na Narodna Republika Bŭlgariya 1967.* Sofia: TSUMS, 1967.

————. *Statisticheski Godishnik na Narodna Republika Bŭlgariya 1976.* Sofia: TSUMS, 1976.

————. *Statisticheski Godishnik na Narodna Republika Bŭlgariya 1986.* Sofia: TSUMS, 1986.

————. *Statisticheski Godishnik na Narodna Republika Bŭlgariya 1989.* Sofia: TSU, 1989.

Turan, Omer. "Pomaks, Their Past and Present." *Journal of Muslim Minority Affairs* 19, no. 1 (1999).

Vasilev, Kiril. *Rodopskite Bŭlgari Mohamedani (Istoricheski Ocherk).* Plovdiv: Dŭrzhavno Izdatelstvo Hristo G. Danov, 1961.

Verdery, Katherine. *What Was Socialism and What Comes Next?* Princeton, NJ: Princeton University Press, 1996.

————. *The Political Lives of Dead Bodies.* New York: Columbia University Press, 2000.

————. *The Vanishing Hectare: Property and Value in Postsocialist Transylvania.* Ithaca, NY: Cornell University Press, 2003.

Vienna Institute for Comparative Economics. *COMECON Data 1990.* Westport, CT: Greenwood, 1991.

Watts, Michael. "Development II: The Privatization of Everything." *Progress in Human Geography* 18, no. 3 (1994).

Yancey, P. "Praying with the KGB." *Christianity Today* 36, no. 1 (13 January 1992).

Yavuz, M. Hakan. "Is There a Turkish Islam? The Emergence of Convergence and Consensus." *Journal of Muslim Minority Affairs* 24, no. 2 (2004).

Yordanov, Ruslan. "*Strastite Myuftiiski.*" *Tema* 4, no. 27 (143) (12–18 July 2004).

Yurchak, Alexei. *Everything Was Forever Until It Was No More.* Princeton, NJ: Princeton University Press, 2005.

Zhelyazkova, Antonina. "Bulgaria in Transition: The Muslim Minorities." *Islam and Christian-Muslim Relations* 12, no. 3 (July 2001).

————. "The East Is Pregnant with the West, and the West Is Pregnant with the East." *Foreign Policy* (Bulgarian edition), August–September 2006.

Žižek, Slavoj. *NATO as the Left Hand of God?* Zagreb: Arkzin Press, 1999.

Zuckerman, Phil. *The Cambridge Companion to Atheism.* Cambridge: Cambridge University Press, 2006.

Index

Abdullah, Arif, 122, 123–24, 126, 128–29, 143, 153, 154–55, 156; commitment of to "orthodox" Islam, 127; education of, 131; on the goals of the Union for Islamic Development and Culture (UIDC), 156–57; involvement of in the headscarf controversy, 176, 177, 181; lecture of ("Islam: Pluralism and Dialogue"), 31, 130–32, 145; opinion on the French ban on headscarves, 166; opinion on the impropriety of miniskirts, 182–83; removal of from office in the Regional Muftiship of Smolyan, 127, 154

Abdullah, Neda, 153; on wearing the headscarf, 167–68

Adriana, 91, 106

Ahmed, Vedat, 183

Ahmedov, Mekhmed, 155

Ahmedov, Vezhdi, 154–55

Aisha, 13, 172–73, 187, 198

Al Haramain Islamic Foundation (AHIF), 135

Albania, 38, 135, 136, 139, 140, 153; Albanians in Kosovo, 137–38

Albena, 97, 99, 102, 106

alcohol consumption, 154, 157, 158; abuse of, 9, 26, 30, 66, 105, 107, 175; as a pain killer, 98

Alexei, 102–3

Al-Manar, 141, 227n48, 228n60

Al-Nashif, Dariush, 142

Al-Nedua, 154

"Alternative Orthodox Synod," 93

Al-Waqf Al-Islami, 139, 140

Amira, 172

amulets, 136

Ana, 102–3

Andrei, 89–90

Arabka (female Arab), 4

Arabski stil (Arab-style), 4

Armenians, 37

Asad, Talal, 15, 16, 115, 208n26

Ataka (Attack) Party, 111; attempts of to ban the call to prayer from public megaphones, 177–78

Atanassov, Atanas, 124

atheism, 12, 13, 21, 23, 25, 134, 136, 194; in Bulgaria, 24, 49, 88, 89, 92, 117, 140

Baba, Yenihan, 155

Balkan Mines Shareholders Association, 72

Balkans, 30, 94, 134, 135, 140; communism in, 138; diversity of Islam in, 37; introduction of Islam to, 136

"Beautiful Bulgaria" project, 9, 207n4

Bektashis, 14

Bellion-Jourdan, Jerome, 135

Bin Laden, Osama, 120, 121

Blumi, Isa, 153

Borissov, Boiko, 178

Bosnia, 134–35, 136, 139, 140; military support for, 135. *See also* Bosnian War

Bosnian War, 30, 31, 135

Brothers Trading, 154–55

Brusco, Elizabeth, 175

Bulgaria, 4, 5, 30–31, 37, 38, 57, 207n3, 214n61; atheism in, 24, 92, 210n47; capitalism in, 196–97; collapse of the banking system in, 74; crime in, 199, 234n33 (*see also* Bulgarian mafia [*mutri*]); currency of, 209n30; decline in gross domestic product of, 93; economic crisis in (1990–1997), 93; economic development of under communism, 52, 56–58, 214n60; economic exploitation of, 24, 193–94; educational facilities in, 149–51; escalating violence in, 74, 193–94; external debt of, 193; feudalism in, 52; influx of missionaries to, 21, 23, 74, 93–94; Islamic aid to, 139–43; Muslim population of, 12; postcommunist instability in, 92; postcommunist parliamentary elections in, 69; poverty in, 23; relationship of with Turkey, 12–13; resurgence of religious activity in, 24–25; rural tourism in, 28–29; trade unions in, 69, 71–73; unification conference of, 119–20. *See also* Bulgarians; Islam, in Bulgaria; lead-zinc mining industry

Bulgarian Communist Party (BCP), 52, 68

Bulgarian Constitutional Court, 118

Bulgarian Helsinki Committee, 124

Bulgarian mafia (*mutri*), 6, 24, 74, 104,
  218n97
Bulgarian National Assembly, 74, 79
Bulgarian Orthodox Christians, 24, 62, 89,
  93, 111–12, 213n53
Bulgarian Orthodox Church, 93; schism
  in, 93
Bulgarian Socialist Party (BSP ["Reds"]),
  68, 73, 75, 79, 117; failed economic
  policies of, 74; rivalry of with the Union
  of Democratic Forces (UDF), 92
Bulgarian State Security Services, 117, 120
Bulgarian Tolerance Foundation, 121
Bulgarians, 39–40, 41, 50, 89, 91, 132, 161,
  181, 190, 207n3, 212n21; experience
  of with capitalism, 196–97; indifference
  of to religion, 24; integration of into
  Western European Muslim networks,
  12–13; moral relativity among, 23–24;
  Orthodox Christian, 24, 38, 88; religiousness among, 88–89

capitalism, 21, 31–33, 46, 52, 78, 194, 195,
  196, 199, 200; critiques of, 13, 23, 156,
  190–91, 196, 202; experience of in
  Bulgaria, 196–97; global, 32, 156, 191;
  kleptocratic, 27; in postcommunist
  societies, 31–32; violence of Bulgarian
  capitalism, 32, 194, 197
Central Asia, 15, 134, 136, 191
Chechnya, 134
Chepintsi, 141, 144, 147; closing of the
  disco in, 157; mosque of, 145, 147,
  228n73
Chief Muftiship (*Glavno Myuftiistvo*), 115,
  118, 121, 123, 141; benefits of cash flow
  to, 116; struggle for control of, 128–29;
  under communism, 116–17
childcare and childcare facilities, 62–63
children, economic hardship of to a family,
  100
Children of God, 94
Christianity, 25, 35; and crime, 199; Orthodox Christianity, 12, 42, 136, 211n9
Christians, 37, 89
Church of the Nazarene, 93
circumcision, 46; outlawing of under communism, 41, 49
Cold War, 27, 201
communism, 3, 26–27, 43–44, 78, 114,
  116, 136, 139, 187, 196–98, 200, 207n3;

benefits of, 88; criticism of, 87, 104–5;
  demise of, 30–31, 32, 50, 91, 134, 136,
  188; "emancipation" of women under,
  190; idealization of the worker under,
  58; nostalgia for, 194; popularity of,
  97–98; social project of, 25–26, 197. *See
  also* Bulgaria, economic development of
  under communism
communists, 42, 207n3, 234n39; destruction of minarets by, 49; and emancipation program for Pomak women, 64,
  65; emphasis of on modernization, 65;
  modernization programs of, 52; outlawing of "backward" practices of Islam
  by, 49; repression and regulation of
  religious institutions by, 42–43, 46, 49,
  88–89, 116, 138; subversion of religious
  structures by, 43, 138
Confederation of Independent Trade
  Unions in Bulgaria (CITUB), 69, 72, 78,
  81
Council for Mutual Economic Assistance
  (CMEA), 60, 75, 214n8; collapse of,
  70–71
Crystal Hall, 56, 57; purchase of by the
  city of Madan, 82

Dahlab v. Switzerland, 180
democracy, 3, 73, 91, 92, 95, 193, 195,
  196, 200, 201, 202–3; in Eastern
  Europe and Central Asia, 8–9, 12, 191;
  frustration with in Eastern Europe, 88,
  97, 193–94, 195; liberal, 191, 194–95;
  parliamentary, 192, 193, 194
Democrats for a Strong Bulgaria, 126
Demokratzia, 153
Dimitrov, Georgi, 46
Dimitrov, Lyubomir (Lyubo), 65, 66–68,
  71–72, 73, 80, 84, 104, 145, 203; alcoholism of, 107; finances of, 106, 107;
  frustrations of over lack of employment,
  106; support of his extended family by,
  106–7
Dimov, Dimitŭr, 72
Directorate of Religious Denominations,
  119; control of by the Union of Democratic Forces (UDF), 119–20
Doğan, Ahmed, 68–69, 72–73, 116,
  117–18, 127, 128, 140, 187; accusations
  against of receiving American money,
  120; atheism of, 117

Donka, 30, 98, 101, 102, 151
Dorsunski, Mekhmed, 153, 229nn76–77
Duomato, Eleanor Abdella, 15, 26,
  208n26

Eastern Europe, 31; frustration with
  democracy in, 193; "globalized" Islam
  in, 190–204 passim; nostalgia for com-
  munism in, 194
Eastern Orthodox Church. See Bulgarian
  Orthodox Church
Eickelman, Dale, 17
Elena, 99–100, 106
Emel, 171–72
Engels, Friedrich, 199
Europe, 134, 199–200; "old" Europe, 5.
  See also Eastern Europe; Western Europe
European Court of Human Rights, 119,
  142, 166, 180
European Union (EU), 9–10, 104, 234n33
Eyun, Kemal, 180

Fatherland Front, 47, 213n43
Fatme. See headscarves, controversy
  concerning the wearing of in Bulgarian
  public schools
Federation of Islamic Organizations in
  Europe (FIOE), 192
feminism, Western, 198
Foreign Trade Bank, 75
France, 32
Futbol Club Madan, 152

Gadzhev, Valentin, 78
gender relations, 26, 65, 138, 175,
  185–187, 189–90, 196, 198, 200; and
  employment opportunities, 188
gender roles, 25, 65, 167, 172, 173, 175,
  185; rearrangement of in Pomak communities, 189–90
Gendzhev, Nedim, 117, 126–27, 128, 141,
  142, 145; accusations of against Mustafa
  Alish Hadzhi, 120; arrest of for alleged
  embezzlement, 127; attacks of against
  Islamic fundamentalism, 120, 122, 124;
  calls for his removal as chief mufti,
  117, 118; court rulings in favor of,
  124; demotion of the Pomak mufti by,
  117; eviction of as chief mufti, 118; as
  president of the High Muslim Council,
  119; recognition of by the Bulgarian

Socialist Party (BSP), 119; unification of
  Bulgarian Muslim denomination under
  his leadership, 117
Georgiov Den (St. George's Day), 91,
  219n7
Germany, 32; Eastern Germany, 9
globalization, 5, 202
Gori Gori Ogŭnche (Burn, Burn, Little
  Flame), 94
GORUBSO, 7–8, 30, 36, 45, 74, 93, 134,
  185, 187; audit of GORUBSO-Madan,
  82–83; collapse of, 8–9, 26, 66–84
  passim; debt of, 78, 80–81; drop in
  productivity of, 77; economic policies of
  under communism, 75; effect of privatization on, 83–84; financial losses of,
  80–81; fine against for pollution, 73–74;
  liquidation of GORUBSO-Zlatograd, 79;
  main building of, 6, 7; number of apartment houses and residence halls owned
  by, 62; number of workers employed
  at, 59–60; proposed reorganization of,
  78, 79; reasons for collapse of, 75–76;
  refusal of to raise salaries of miners,
  77–78; sale of GORUBSO-Madan,
  81–82; spread of strikes against across
  Bulgaria, 72; strikes against by union
  labor, 69–73, 76, 77–78; subsidization
  of, 60, 71; transfer of its assets into private hands, 103–4; wealth and economic
  growth generated by, 61–63, 186–87;
  yield of concentrated lead produced by
  (1950–1962), 60
GORUBSO Mining Museum, 56; condition
  of, 57; exhibits of, 57, 59–60; purchase
  of by the city of Madan, 82
Gradeva, Rositsa, 40
Greece, 4, 28, 29, 38, 53, 118

hadj. See Mecca, pilgrimage to (hadj)
Hadrales, 18–19
Hadzhi, Mustafa Alish, 18, 120, 121, 123,
  126, 127; reaction to the banning of the
  headscarf in public schools, 180–81
hafuzi, 113, 146–47, 180
Hana, 30, 86–87, 104, 108, 145, 149–50,
  152, 161, 198, 203; on wearing the
  jilbab, 171
Hare Krishnas, 94
Hasan, 10, 11, 109–10, 129, 152, 161,
  198, 203

Hasan, Fikri Sali, 118, 119, 121, 140; election of as chief mufti, 122–23; removal of from office of chief mufti, 124

hatib, 113

Hatim, Hairaddin, 127, 182

hawala financial transactions, 142–43

headscarves (*hijab*; *zabradki*), 31, 49, 139, 157, 158; banning of in French and Turkish public schools, 165–66; wearing of as a means of acquiring money, 102, 175, 230–31n11; wearing of as a demonstration of commitment to "true Islam," 173, 175; wearing of in schools, 127. *See also* headscarves, controversy concerning the wearing of in Bulgarian public schools

headscarves, controversy concerning the wearing of in Bulgarian public schools, 166–67, 169, 170–71, 176–83; involvement of the Movement for Rights and Freedoms (MRF) in, 178, 180; involvement of the Union for Islamic Development and Culture (UIDC) in, 176, 177; order of the Ministry of Education concerning headscarves in school, 181–81; original permission granted to wear headscarves, 176; position of Michaela concerning her right to wear the headscarf, 176–77

"Health and Belief" lecture, 154

High Islamic Institute, 114, 144, 151

High Muslim Council (*Vish Myusyulmanski Süvet*), 115, 118; and court case concerning registration of rival factions, 123–24; rival factions of, 118–19, 123

Higyar, 13, 31, 159–61, 175, 203; as a gossip (*klyukarka*), 159

History of the Pomaks, The (Dorsunski), 39, 153, 229n76

Hizb ut-Tahrir, 192

hodzhas (Muslim preachers), 2, 3, 35, 44, 49, 113, 115–16; divide between hodzhas and foreign-trained imams, 115, 185; as folk preachers, 114; influence of, 46

Hotel Balkan, 103

Ikra (nongovernmental organization), 143, 152; promotion of lectures and seminars by, 152

Ikra (magazine), 110, 128, 152, 156, 166, 228n74; anti-Darwinism of, 152, 228n75;

on the code of conduct for Muslim women, 170; on equality between men and women, 171; on guarding the virtue of women, 170

imams, 49, 113; lack of financial support for, 128; training of, 115, 139

India, 141–42

industrialization, and economic growth, 52, 56–58, 214n60

International Charitable Islamic Organization ("Hayatel Igasa"), 141

International Islamic Charitable Organization, 140

International Islamic Relief Organization (IIRO), 135

International Monetary Fund (IMF), 75, 79, 93

International Society for Universalism, 194–95

"Ioan Predtecha" (John the Precursor) Movement for Christianity and Progress, 94–95

Iordan (Fikret), 13, 30, 51, 96, 106, 145, 203; childhood of, 36; childhood memories of practicing Islam, 42; education of, 44; effect of communism on, 43–44; identity and ancestry issues concerning, 34–35, 36–37; marriage of to Silvi, 53–54; married life of under communism, 54–55; name change of, 52

Iran, 11, 134

Irshad, 139

Islam, 33; as antibourgeois, 190–91; "Arab," 15, 16, 126; attitude of toward ownership of private property, 199–200; Balkan, 136, 208n26; Bosnian, 137; "correcting" of, 16; differing forms of, 5; "globalized," 16–17, 190–204 *passim*; goals of, 156–57; "good," 16; Hanafi Sunnism, 15, 128, 136; "heterodox," 26; influence of in Europe, 5, 136; Islamism, 17; and Marxism, 27, 197–98, 199; objectified, 15, 17–18; "orthodox," 15–16, 18, 19, 124, 126, 128, 153, 155, 189, 190, 195, 196, 201–2, 208n26; "postsocialized," 32; problem of terminology concerning new form of, 14–20, 207n7; "pure," 126, 153; replacement of leftist politics with, 191; Salafism, 16, 17; "Saudi-influenced," 17; and social justice, 26–27, 197; traditional versus orthodox interpretations of, 135–36;

"true," 14–15, 16, 131, 137, 203; "universalist," 17, 32; as "Wahhabism," 15, 16, 17; and Western European values, 191–92. See also Islam, in Bulgaria

Islam, in Bulgaria, 5, 19–20, 37–38, 123, 139, 141, 153, 195–96; Alevis Muslims, 14; appeal and influence of orthodox Islam, 26, 27, 31, 67, 88, 185, 189, 190, 202–3; crisis in Muslim leadership after the collapse of communism, 91–92; differing forms of, 18; financial support for Bulgarian Muslims by "orthodox" Islamic foundations, 133–34, 143, 188–89, 201; Hanafi Sunni Muslims, 14; heterogeneous nature of, 14; "new" Islam, 13; "new" Islam as the "true" Islam, 14–15, 16; post-Marxist Islam, 27; regional muftiships in, 113, 221n5; resurgence of after the fall of communism, 20–22; structure of the Muslim denomination in Bulgaria, 112–16, 221n3; Sufi brotherhoods in, 14; tensions between orthodox and traditional Islam, 18–19; theories explaining the embrace of orthodox Islam in Bulgaria, 20–27, 189, 201–2

"Islam: Pluralism and Dialogue" lecture (A. Abdullah), 31, 130–32, 145

Islamic charitable organizations, 30, 31, 95, 225n3; charitable trust (vakif), 116, 158; Islamic aid in Bulgaria, 139–43; linking of aid with proselytizing, 136–37; Saudi-funded organizations, 136, 201

Islamic Development Bank (IsDB), 141–42, 144

Islamic fundamentalism, 121–22, 143, 181

Islamic Relief Agency, 135

Islamists, anticommunism of, 27

Islamophobia, 5, 32

Ivan Vazov Kulturen Dom (community center), 6, 7, 9–10, 62

Ivanova, Svetlana, 40

Jehovah's Witnesses, 93

Jordan, 122, 128, 134; and aid to Bulgaria, 140–41

Jordanian Muslim Brotherhood, 14

Keddie, Nikki R., 16, 17

Kepel, Gilles, 32, 190, 191, 202, 232n9

Khairaddin, Ali, 19, 121, 123–24, 126, 128–29, 133, 166, 175; arrest of for

promoting Wahhabism, 128; belief that Bulgarian Islam was corrupted by national politics, 123; views of on various religions, 123

Khairaddin-Rashidova, Fatme, 153

Khalid, Adeeb, 14, 27

Kideckel, David, 232n3

Kligman, Gail, 16

Kosovo, 134, 136, 139, 140; Albanians in, 137–38; charitable and relief organizations in, 137

Kostov, Ivan, 72, 126

Krŭstev, Georgi, 124

Kuczynski, Janusz, 195

Kurban Bayram (Feast of the Sacrifice), 11, 18, 49, 98, 113; communist prohibition of, 49

Kŭrdzhali, 57, 117, 218n85

Kuwait, 31, 134

Kuwaiti International Islamic Charitable Organization, 141

Kuwaiti Social Reform Foundation, 121

Kyrgyzstan, 9

Law on Religious Denominations (1949), 42–43

lead: environmental hazards of, 61; price of, 61; use of in industrial components, 60–61

Lead and Zinc Mining Stabilization Program (United States), 61

lead-zinc mining industry, 30, 87–88; and atrocious conditions in the mines, 70; collapse of, 8–9, 25, 26, 30, 84; and decline of lead and zinc production (1985–1992), 73; extensive male labor required for, 56–57; flotation factory of, 57, 214n2; growth of under communism, 44–45; and high wages paid to miners, 59; importance of to Madan, 56–57; labor strikes in, 69–73; and mining as a job for "real men," 59; pollution caused by, 70; problems faced by because of open-market competition, 70–71; restructuring of after the fall of communism, 67; types of ore extracted, 59

liberation theology, 200

Libya, 141

Liliana (Lili), 2–4, 90, 106, 114, 115, 203

London Metals Exchange, 61

Lŭki, 57, 218n85

Macedonia, 38, 136, 137, 139, 140
Madan, 1, 4–5, 24, 33, 38, 47, 52, 57, 76,
126, 130, 143, 158, 183, 193–94, 203;
bartering system used in, 102; Batantsi
neighborhood of, 96; under communism,
45–46; debilitating social effects of unemployment in, 105–106; economic effects
of privatization in, 9; economic growth in
under communism, 53, 61–62; elaborate
credit system of, 101–3; emigration of
workers from after the collapse of
GORUBSO, 95–96; flight of young
people from, 96; gender relations in,
185–86, 188–90; growth of the education
system of under communism, 62; invest-
ments in by the European Union (EU),
9–10; Muslim population of, 10; as the
perceived seat of Islamic fundamentalism,
181; population of, 6; poverty in after the
collapse of GORUBSO, 96–97; proposed
development of tourism in, 28–29; resentment of the mayor in, 104; social assistance provided by the municipality of to
the unemployed, 97; subsistence farming
by citizens of, 99–100; unemployment of
after the collapse of GORUBSO, 84, 105;
vacuum of time in, 105; wealthy businessmen of, 103–4. See also GORUBSO;
lead-zinc mining industry
Madan mosque, 6, 7, 11–12, 59, 146–47,
181; description of, 10–11; funding of,
11, 144–45; prayer hall of, 11; as a spiritual and cultural center, 149–50
Madanchani (residents of Madan), 6, 7
Mahmood, Saba, 17; on "religious sociability," 134
marriage: intermarriage during the communist period, 90–91; mish-mash marriages, 89, 90; of Muslims to Christians,
89, 90; wealth as primary factor in
choosing a husband, 89–90
Marx, Karl, 42
Marxism, 21, 157, 190, 194, 196; commitment of to industrialization, 57–58; and
Islam, 27, 197–98, 199; and liberation
theology, 200
"Materialism: The Dreadful Disease of
Humanity" (Mehmedaliev), 156
Mecca, pilgrimage to (hadj), 129; stipends
given to Muslim families for, 133–34
Mehmedaliev, Hasan, 156

Mekhmed, Selim, 121, 123; calls of for
return of Muslim properties confiscated
under communism, 121–22
"Message from a Muslim Woman," 110–11
Metropolitan Pimen, 93
Michaela. See headscarves, controversy
concerning the wearing of in Bulgarian
public schools
miners, 145, 184, 186, 203, 232n3; under
communism, 66, 68, 69, 71, 78; deaths
of on the job, 80; devastating effects of
unemployment on, 107, 187–88; hunger
strike of the Madan miners, 82, 83; political affiliations of, 79; view of by the
general populace of Bulgaria, 78–79
mobile phones, 101, 220n27
Mormons, 93–94
mosques, 145–52, 185, 228n70; ac-
commodations of for hafuzi, 146–47;
architecture of, 145–46; Friday prayers
for men in, 148–49; funding for, 144–45;
as places for men to connect with each
other, 189–90; religious education in,
151–52; religious tourism to, 147–48; as
a safe place for children, 152; as spiritual
and cultural centers, 149–50. See also
Madan mosque
Mostove (Bridges), 143, 152, 155; promotion of lectures and seminars by, 153
Movement for Rights and Freedoms
(MRF), 68, 69, 70, 73, 75–76, 81, 94,
116, 127–28, 140, 178, 185, 186; atheism among members of, 117; coalition
of with the Union of Democratic Forces
(UDF), 92–93, 117, 118; interference
of in Muslim selection of a chief mufti,
124–26; involvement of in the headscarf
controversy, 178, 180
Muleshkova, Irina, 178, 179–80
multiculturalism, 193
Musa, Ahmad, 120–21
Muslim Brothers, 14, 17, 120, 121, 124,
128
Muslim dress, 41, 139, 159–61, 226n33;
adoption of the "Arab style" of dress
by young women, 161–63; Arab versus
Turkish/Bulgarian style of dress, 163;
button-down overcoat (manto), 163;
dresses (fustan), 159–60; face veil (niqab),
162; fezzes, 41, 49; influence of American
fashion on, 163; jilbab gowns, 162–63,

171; kerchiefs (*kŭrpi*), 160, 163; Turkish
trousers (*shalvari*), 49, 163; vs. wearing
of European-style dress, 163; vs. wearing
of miniskirts, 1, 137, 182–83. *See also*
headscarves (*hijab*; *zabradki*)
Muslim National Conference (2005),
124–26; legitimacy of the delegates attending questioned by Gendzhev, 126
Muslim Women's Society, 137
Muslim World League (MWL), 135, 136,
138, 140
Muslim-Christian relations, 91
Muslims: attraction of to Western-style
democracy, 192–93; Bulgarian, 3, 5,
41–42, 53, 68, 108, 111–12, 116, 155;
Central Asian, 27; educational pathways
into the Muslim clergy, 114; financial aid
to, 133–34; marriages of to Bulgarian
Christians, 89; plea for unity among,
110–11; political conflicts among, 116–
29; portrayal of in the European press,
192; resistance of to name changes,
50–51; Shi'a, 16; Slavic, 42; structure of
the Muslim denomination in Bulgaria,
112–16, 221n3; Sunni, 16; Turkish, 42,
126; unity among, 195
"Muslims in Europe Charter," 192
Myusyulmani, 110, 129
Myusyulmansko Obshtestvo (*Muslim Society*), 110, 125, 155, 156, 166; on Pomak
women wearing the *hijab*, 169

National Association of Bulgarian Muslims, 19
National Electric Company (NEC), 75,
78, 80
neoliberalism, 32
Neuburger, Mary, 43
*New Cities in the People's Republic of
Bulgaria*, 49
nomenklatura (communist elites), 68, 88
nongovernmental organizations (NGOs),
25, 29, 91, 121, 138; "orthodox"
Muslim NGOs, 189; support of for an
Islamic state in Europe, 135

Ofelia, 102
"Only Spiritual Force that Can Lead Hu-
mankind to Happiness" (Osmanov), 157
Organization of the Islamic Conference
(OIC), 135, 141

Osmanov, Ahmed, 157
Ottoman Empire, 37, 136; "blood tax" of,
39; charitable trusts (*vakif*) of, 40, 43;
collapse of, 41
Ottoman Tombul Mosque, 144
Otzvuk, 167

Palestinians, citizenship for in Bulgaria,
139–40
Patriarch Maksim, 93
Pavlina. *See* Aisha
Pentecostal/Charismatic missions, 93
Piscatori, James, 17
pluralism, 131, 177, 193, 202
Podkrepa Miner's Federation (Solidarity),
69–70, 73, 78; Central Strike Committee
of, 71, 72
Poland, 194–95
polygamy, 128, 167
Pomaks, 12, 13, 14, 31, 36, 89, 95, 112,
123, 128, 142, 152, 188–89, 207n2,
212n19; affinity of with the Arab
world, 185; aid to from Jordan and
Saudi Arabia, 140–41; Arabic origin of,
38–39, 211n10; attempted conversion
of back to Orthodoxy, 94; celebration of
Hadrales by, 19; Christianization of, 41,
94–95; under communism, 47, 49; conflict of with Turkish Muslims, 126–27;
conversion of to Islam, 39–40; as descendants of Kuman Turks, 38; as descendants of Thracian Greeks, 38; embrace of
orthodox Islam by, 30, 198–99; ethnicity
of, 38; identity issues of, 22, 34–35, 163,
165, 185, 212n19; indoctrination of
into the communist system, 62; influence
of Muslim missionaries on, 38; loss of
masculine identity among, 186, 187–88;
positive attitudes of toward communism,
88; promotion of Islam among, 197;
spread of atheism among, 89; spread of
to various countries, 38; tenuous sincer-
ity of their conversion to Islam, 40–41;
villages of in the Rhodope, 25
"postmodern eclecticism," 23
Presbyterian Church in America, 93
Prishtina, 138

Qur'an, 109–10, 115, 118, 141, 189, 198;
the Golden Koran, 228n73. See also
hafuzi

Radev, Muravei, 76, 80
Radushev, Evgeni, 40
Raichevsky, Stoyan, 40–41
rakiya (brandy), 9, 26, 42, 70, 73, 84, 98, 99, 102, 203; use of as a pain killer, 97
Ramadan, 11, 49, 91, 109, 113
Ramadan, Tariq, 192–93
Ramazan Bayram, 11, 18, 113; communist prohibition of, 49
Rashidov, Ismet, 153, 155
Regal Complex, 6–7, 90, 104, 148
Regional Muslim Council (Smolyan [2003]), 122–23
religion, and Marxism, 21
Religious Community of the White Brethren, 94
Religious Denominations Act (1949), 116
Rhodope Mountains, 4–5, 37, 40
Rhodope region, 64, 94, 120, 121; construction of new mosques in, 28, 95; effects of the collapse of communism on, 184–85; as the next Chechnya, 128; Pomak villages in, 25; poverty of, 36; religious rivalries in, 95; unemployment in, 184. *See also* Rhodope region, revival of Islam in
Rhodope region, revival of Islam in, 143–58 *passim*; eastern Rhodope as the heartland of "orthodox" Islam, 183; practice of greeting others using Arabic rather than Bulgarian in Rudozem, 143–44
Rodina, 41–42
Rodopa Invest, 81–83; reformation of as Rhodope Holding BG, 83, 218n97
Rodopi Vesti, 153
Roma, 12, 14
Roman Catholicism, 12, 94–95, 136, 200
Roy, Olivier, 16, 32, 190–91, 193, 202, 232n9
Rudozem, 5, 24, 30, 38, 46, 47, 52, 76, 126, 143, 158, 181, 183, 203; Arabic greetings replacing Bulgarian greetings in, 143–44; economic dependency of on lead-zinc mining, 63; gender relations in, 185–86, 188–90; growth of from a village to a city, 63; mosque of, 145, 146, 147; mosque of as a spiritual and cultural center, 149–50; ore-processing plant of, 57
Russia, 9, 23, 107, 191, 194

Sahin v. Turkey, 180
Salafism, 16, 17

Saramov, 6
Saruev, Boyan, 94–95
Saudi Arabia, 5, 11, 14, 16, 31, 118, 128, 134, 201; aid of to Bulgaria, 140–42; pilgrimage to Mecca in, 129
Saudi High Commission for Relief, 135
Saudi Joint Relief Committee for Kosovo (SJRCK), 137
Saxecoburgotski, Simeon, 176
Schwartz, Stephen, 16
secularization, 49, 183, 195
Selyam, 110
Shakirov, Selvi, 122, 123–24, 126, 143, 153, 154–55, 177, 181; commitment of to "orthodox" Islam, 127; removal of from office in the Regional Muftiship of Smolyan, 127, 154; testimony of concerning the wearing of headscarves in public schools, 178–79
Shi'a Muslims, 16
Shivarov, Svetoslav, 141
Siderov, Volen, 177, 178
Silvi, 1–2, 11, 13, 63, 145, 203; atheism of, 89; Avon business of, 20, 101–2; family financial situation of, 100–101; marriage of to Iordan, 53–54; and threats of the new Islam to her business, 20–21
Smolyan, 5, 21, 25, 42, 59, 83, 123, 126, 143; headscarf controversy in, 181–82; soup kitchens for the poor in, 156
Snezhana, 184, 185
soccer, 152, 158, 220n15
social justice, 26–27, 155–56, 196, 197, 210n52
socialism, 5, 47, 59, 187, 207n3; scientific, 12, 47–48, 63, 199
socialist modernism, 50, 52
Sofia, 117
Sofia City Council, 124
Sonic (bar/restaurant), 66, 84, 90, 97, 103, 106, 107, 133, 145
Soviet Union, 10, 14, 57, 60, 71, 201, 214n61; collapse of, 70, 136
Spain, 32
spirituality, and economics, 27, 28
"sports evangelism," 93, 220n15
Stakhanov, Alexei, 58–59
"Stakhanovites," 59
Stoyanov, Petŭr, 80
"Straight Path for Bulgarian Citizens of Turkish Origin, The," 120
Sudan, 134, 135

Sufi mystical orders, 37
Sunni Muslims, 16
Supreme Administrative Court, 119, 120
Supreme Court of Appeal, 124

Taiba, 139, 228n60
Takan, Abdul Rakhman, 120
Taliban, 139
Tanya, 90
Third World Relief Agency (TWRA), 135, 141
"Time Is Money? No, Time Is Life," 156
Time of Violence (1988), 212n21
Todorova, Maria, 38
Trix, Francis, 208n26
Tunisia, 195
Turkey, 12–13, 38, 94, 118, 134, 140, 195; banning of headscarves in public schools in, 166
Turkish Directorate of Religious Affairs (Diyanet), 139
Turkish Movement for Rights and Freedom, 17
Turks (of Bulgaria), 12, 14, 25, 37, 89, 140, 185, 189, 213–14n55; forced emigration of, 118; forced name changes among by the communists, 49–52, 117; and the headscarf controversy, 183
Tǔrǔn, 143; mosque of, 145–46
Two Faces of Islam, The (Schwartz), 16

ummah, 197; financial support of, 134–39
Unification Church of Sun Myung Moon, 94
Union of Bulgarian Muslims, 126, 128
Union of Democratic Forces (UDF ["Blues"]), 68, 69, 70, 71, 73, 76, 79, 95, 118, 187; call of for the dissolution of the National Assembly, 74; coalition of with the Movement for Rights and Freedoms (MRF), 92–93, 117, 118; control of the Directorate of Religious Denominations by, 119–20; economic policies of, 74–75; negotiations of with striking miners, 76–77; rivalry of with the Bulgarian Socialist Party (BSP), 92
Union for Islamic Development and Culture (UIDC), 25, 126, 143, 152, 153–55; and critique of materialism, capitalism, and communism, 155–56; emphasis of on "true" Islamic commitment to social justice, 155–56, 197; goals of, 156–57;

investigations into activities of, 127–28; involvement of in the headscarf controversy, 176, 177, 181; women's section of, 167. *See also* Union for Islamic Development and Culture (UIDC), and the rift between traditional and "orthodox" Islam
Union for Islamic Development and Culture (UIDC), and the rift between traditional and "orthodox" Islam, 157; cancelling of the summer festival near Smolyan, 158; closing of the disco in Chepintsi, 157; uproar over UIDC's soccer team sponsorship, 158
United Kingdom, 32
United Nations Fourth World Conference on Women (1995), 138
United States, importance of lead and zinc production to, 61
universalism, 194–95, 201; "false universalisms," 196; "metaphilosophical universalists," 195; "universalist Islam," 17, 32; "Western universalism," 195

vaiz, 113
Verdery, Katherine, 64, 200
Vesela, 97, 103, 104, 107
Videnov, Zhan, 73

Wahhabism, 15, 16, 17, 121, 124, 128
Walker, Edward, 16
WAMY Series on Islam, 141
Westbrook, David, 199
Western Europe, 31, 202; Islam in, 200
women, 57, 155, 188; abandonment of wives by their husbands, 105–6; agricultural work of, 64; changing gender role of, 172, 173, 175; changing role of under communism, 25–26, 64, 198; communist propaganda lectures concerning, 47–48; constitutionally guaranteed equality of under communism, 46–47; effect of the Wahhabi reforms on, 26; employment of in the garment and cosmetics industries, 63–64; equality of with men, 171, 180; gender expectations of, 31; inclusion of in the labor force, 62, 64; as the moral leaders of the family, 172; and motherhood, 138; orthodox Islam's supposed reverence for, 168–69; pregnancy leave for, 63; "successful" femininity of, 188; as targets of Islamic reform efforts,

women (*cont.*)
138–39; "training" sessions for, 138;
wage discrimination against, 184. *See
also* Muslim dress
"Women and Religion in Europe, Resolution 1464 of the Parliamentary Assembly
of the Council of Europe," 180
World Assembly of Muslim Youth
(WAMY), 135, 137, 138, 141, 154,
195–96; Indian branch of, 142; ties of to
the Saudi royal family, 135
World Bank, 75, 79
www.islam-bg.net website, popularity of,
166–67

Yahya, Harun, 152
Yapov, Petŭr, 153
Yefimovitch, Dimitri, 23

Zakah, 196
Zaman, 110
Zarqa Private University, 153–54
Zhirnalov, Milen, 155
Zhivkov, Todor, 68
zinc: price of, 61; use of in industrial com-
ponents, 61
Žižek, Slavoj, 32, 202
Zlatograd, 7, 34, 57, 76, 80; threatened
hunger strike by miners of, 77–78